Textbook of Taxation

Textbook of Taxation

Nitin Johari

RANDOM

RANDOM PUBLICATIONS

NEW DELHI (INDIA)

Textbook of Taxation

ISBN 978-93-5111-397-3

Published in 2014 in India by

RANDOM PUBLICATIONS

4376-A/4B, Gali Murari Lal, Ansari Road
New Delhi-110 002
Phone : +91-11-43580356, +91-11-23289044
e-mail: randomexports@gmail.com, sales@randompublications.com, info@randompublications.com

Reprinted 2026

Type Setting by : Keystoneprintads, Delhi-110051

Preface

A tax is a financial charge or other levy imposed upon a taxpayer by a state or the functional equivalent of a state such that failure to pay is punishable by law. Taxes are also imposed by many administrative divisions. Taxes consist of direct or indirect taxes and may be paid in money or as its labour equivalent.

Money provided by taxation has been used by states and their functional equivalents throughout history to carry out many functions. Some of these include expenditures on war, the enforcement of law and public order, protection of property, economic infrastructure, public works, social engineering, subsidies, and the operation of government itself. Governments also use taxes to fund welfare and public services. A portion of taxes also go to pay off the state's debt and the interest this debt accumulates. These services can include education systems, health care systems, pensions for the elderly, unemployment benefits, and public transportation. Energy, water and waste management systems are also common public utilities. Colonial and modernizing states have also used cash taxes to draw or force reluctant subsistence producers into cash economies.

Governments use different kinds of taxes and vary the tax rates. This is done to distribute the tax burden among individuals or classes of the population involved in taxable activities, such as business, or to redistribute resources between individuals or classes in the population. Historically, the nobility were supported by taxes on the poor; modern social security systems are intended to support the poor, the disabled, or the retired by taxes on those who are still working. In addition, taxes are applied to fund foreign aid and military ventures, to influence the macroeconomic performance of the economy, or to modify patterns of consumption or employment within an economy, by making some classes of transaction more or less attractive.

A nation's tax system is often a reflection of its communal values and/or the values of those in power. To create a system of taxation, a nation must make choices regarding the distribution of the tax burden-who will pay taxes and how much they will pay-and how the taxes collected will be spent. In democratic nations where the public elects those in charge of establishing the tax system, these choices reflect the type of community that the public wishes to create. In countries where the public does not have a significant amount of influence over the system of taxation, that system may be more of a reflection on the values of those in power.

I thank all members of my team who have helped in the preparation of the book. My special thanks go to "Random Publications" who have published the book.

– Nitin Johari

Contents

1

Tax

INTRODUCTION

To tax is to impose a financial charge or other levy upon a taxpayer by a state or the functional equivalent of a state such that failure to pay is punishable by law. Taxes are also imposed by many subnational entities. Taxes consist of direct tax or indirect tax, and may be paid in money or as its labour equivalent. A tax may be defined as a "pecuniary burden laid upon individuals or property owners to support the government [...] a payment exacted by legislative authority."

A tax "is not a voluntary payment or donation, but an enforced contribution, exacted pursuant to legislative authority" and is "any contribution imposed by government [...] whether under the name of toll, tribute, tallage, gabel, impost, duty, custom, excise, subsidy, aid, supply, or other name."

The legal definition and the economic definition of taxes differ in that economists do not consider many transfers to governments to be taxes. For example, some transfers to the public sector are comparable to prices. Examples include tuition at public universities and fees for utilities provided by local governments. Governments also obtain resources by creating money, through voluntary gifts, by imposing penalties, by borrowing, and by confiscating wealth. From the view of economists, a tax is a non-penal, yet compulsory transfer of resources from the private to the public sector levied on a basis of predetermined criteria and without reference to specific benefit received.

In modern taxation systems, taxes are levied in money, but in-kind and corvée taxation are characteristic of traditional or pre-capitalist states and their functional equivalents. The method of taxation and the government expenditure of taxes raised is often highly debated in politics and economics. Tax collection is performed by a government agency such as Canada Revenue Agency, the Internal Revenue Service in the United States, or Her Majesty's Revenue and Customs in the UK. When taxes are not fully paid, civil penalties or criminal penalties may be imposed on the non-paying entity or individual.

PURPOSES AND EFFECTS OF TAXATION

The funds raised by taxation have customarily been used by different states and their functional equivalents throughout history to carry out the functions such as:

- Upkeep of public property
- Economic infrastructure - roads, legal tender, enforcement of contracts, etc.
- Enforcement of law and public ordero Protection of propertyo Military defenceo Redistribution of wealth
- The operational costs involved in the running of the government itself
- Any work in favour of public interest

So also, most modern day governments also use taxes to fund welfare and public services, such as:

- Pensions for the elderly
- Unemployment benefits
- Education systems
- Health care systems
- Energy, water and waste management systems
- Public transportation

States that were colonies of bigger super power nations which are on the road to modernization have also used cash taxes to draw or force reluctant subsistence producers into cash economies.

Various government bodies use different kinds of taxes and vary the tax rates with the following intentions in mind:

- In order to redistribute resources between individuals or classes within the population. In olden times, the nobility were supported by the taxes paid by the poor, however, in modern social security systems, taxes are intended to support the poor, the disabled or those retired from service, by taxes on those who are still working
- In order to distribute the tax burden between individuals or strata of the population involved in taxable activities, with high turn over of income such as businesses
- In order to modify patterns of consumption or employment within an economy, by making some types of transactions more or less attractive
- In order to influence the macro-economic performance of the economy

The resources taken from the common man through taxation is always more or less greater than the amount that can be used by the government. This difference is called the compliance cost, and includes, for example, the labour cost and other expenses incurred while executing compliance with tax laws and rules. The collection of a tax in order to spend it on a particular purpose, for instance, collection of taxes on alcohol to pay directly to maintain alcoholism rehabilitation centres, is called hypothecation. This practice is seldom liked by finance ministers, since it greatly hampers their freedom of action. Some economic theorists consider this concept to be morally dishonest, since in reality the money is generated by a means that further eats into society. Furthermore, it also often occurs that taxes or excises initially levied to fund a specific government programme are later diverted to the government's general fund. In some cases, such taxes are collected in fundamentally inefficient ways, exemplified by highway tolls.

Some economists, especially neo-classical ones argue that all types of taxation result in distortion of the market and economic inefficiency. They have therefore sought to identify and develop a system of taxation that would minimize this distortion. One of the theories is that the most economically neutral tax is the tax on land. A government's primary duty must be to maintain and defend the title to land, and therefore it must collect most of its revenues in order to provide for this unique service.

Since governments also play a role in resolving commercial disputes, especially in countries where a common law is executed, this doctrine is often used to justify a sales tax or a value added tax. Other libertarians argue that almost all forms of taxes are immoral due to their involuntary and therefore eventually coercive or violent nature. The most extreme anti-tax view is that of anarcho-capitalism, in which the provision of the state interfering with an individual's earnings or demanding a share of it to facilitate salvaging downtrodden classes of society is looked upon with intense scorn.

PROPORTIONAL TAX

A proportional tax could also be called a flat tax rate. It is a system under which the percentage of tax taken from income, or charged to individuals, remains the same no matter how much is made or how much is spent. The US does not have a proportional tax on income, and instead employs a progressive tax system, where higher incomes are taxed at higher amounts than are lower incomes.

The reasoning behind this is that people with less money have a more difficult time paying taxes. A person making just slightly above the poverty rate will pay a much lower percentage of their income in taxes because they need that income in order to survive.The US does have some proportional tax types. Sales tax for instance is a constant where it is applied, though the percentage can vary if cities add additional taxes to sales tax. Person A, who lives in City B will pay the same rate in City B for all items considered taxable. He might pay more or less in another city or in another state if he travels or moves.

Some argue that the proportional taxes on most goods are most difficult to pay for those who are poor. Rich or poor pay the same taxes on a box of detergent, but it hurts the poor man or woman's pocket more when they have little money to spare. These arguments tend to suggest that a proportional tax on sales goods really represents a regressive tax. Poorer people will use more of their income than will rich people to pay for same goods.

A regressive tax in general can be defined as a tax that tends to impact the poorest people the most. Whereas, the wealthiest people tend to pay the least amount of their income under such a situation. There has been some discussion in the US of converting to a flat tax rate or a proportional tax. Yet again, those who argue against such a tax claim it is regressive. Even though the tax rate remains constant, those least able to afford the tax have to pay it, with no exceptions.

Consider a proportional tax of 10% on income. The person who makes $200,000 US Dollars (USD) a year would pay $20,000 USD a year in taxes. That seems like a lot, but it still leaves this consumer with $180,000 USD of income. In contrast, the person making $10,000 USD a year pays $1000 USD in taxes, leaving him or her with $9000 a year to meet all expenses. Those who argue against a flat tax or proportional tax say that an inflexible rate would make it that much harder for the poor to survive. The wealthy might be able to afford to lose $20,000 USD, but can a poor person really afford to lose $1000 USD? It's pretty difficult to attempt to live on $9000 USD a year, especially if sales tax for most items remains in place too.

In order to keep sales taxes from becoming burdensome, many states do not tax items like food. However, many other goods, like toilet paper or dish detergent are taxed. Moreover, proportional taxes exist on many utilities, though the working poor may be able to qualify for reduced rates on certain utilities like telephone and gas and electric service. This helps reduce the overall effect of the proportional tax, making it less regressive in nature.

PROGRESSIVE TAX

A progressive tax is a tax rate applied to either income or profits, or spending, that increases as income/profits, or spending increases. This is the tax system used in the US, and in many other countries. Those who make the least amount of money tend to pay the lowest percentage of their income in taxes. People who make larger amounts of money are taxed at a higher percentage.

Taxation in most countries, including the US, is slightly more difficult to compute. Many misunderstand the progressive tax rate as the following formula: Mr. X who makes $20,000 US Dollars (USD) will pay 10% of his income in taxes. Mr. Y makes $40,000 USD and will pay 15% of his income. Ms. Z makes $60,000 USD and will pay 20% of her income in taxes.

Instead, taxes on amounts made increase progressively. My. Y would pay 10% on the first $20,000 USD he makes, and 15% on the second $20,000. Ms. Z would pay 10% on the first $20,000, 15% on the second, and 20% on the third. There are also a number of things that can reduce taxation percentage. If you are marrying and filing a joint tax return, or if you have a number of dependents to support, progressive tax percentages would diminish because less of your money would be actually considered taxable income. The lowest incomes, especially those below the poverty level would owe very little in actual taxes. Businesses that lose money during a year instead of making profits would probably not owe taxes either.

The progressive tax may be applied to certain types of spending. Any sales tax may remain at a stable amount, but a person who spends more of their income on taxable goods will be proportionately be spending a higher amount of their income on sales tax, even though the sales tax percentage is the same for everyone. Further, some items, like yachts and luxury cars, are subject to luxury taxes, which are much higher percentages of tax for these items.

There are many people who support progressive tax, since they feel it is only fair that those who make more should contribute more to the government. Those who make the least, and can't really afford to lose their income to taxes shouldn't be spending much to fund government programmes. Not all people agree with progressive tax, since it means that people who make more money are "punished" for their success or wealth. Some propose a flat tax rate instead of a progressive tax, or a tax on spending instead of on income.

Others favour a regressive tax, where percentage of taxes decreases when income increases. This would mean people who make the most would pay a much lower percentage in taxes, but since their income is high, they'd still pay quite a bit in taxes. People who make the least would pay the highest percentages, though allowances might still be made for those under the poverty level. This system would purportedly mean everyone would pay about the same amount in taxes each year. Critics of the regressive tax system suggest this would be an unfair burden on those least able to afford taxes.

MEASURING PROGRESSIVITY

Models such as the Suits index, Gini coefficient, Theil index, Atkinson index, and Robin Hood index are sometimes used to factor progressivity through measures of inequality of income distribution or inequality of wealth distribution.

Effective Progression

An effective progression can be computed from inequality measures. *The following example uses the Gini coefficient*:

$$\text{rGini} = \frac{1 - \text{Gnetto}}{1 - \text{Gbrutto}}$$

Inflation and Tax Brackets

Many tax laws are not accurately indexed to inflation. Either they ignore inflation completely, or they are indexed to the Consumer Price Index (CPI), which tends to understate real inflation. In a progressive tax system, failure to index the brackets to inflation will eventually result in effective tax increases, as inflation in wages will increase individual income and move individuals into higher tax brackets with higher percentage rate. One example is the United States Alternative Minimum Tax; since it is not indexed to inflation, an increasing number of upper-middle-income taxpayers have been finding themselves subject to this tax.

Marginal and Effective Tax Rates

The rate of tax can be expressed in two different ways, the marginal rate expressed as the rate on each additional piece of income or expenditure and the effective rate expressed as the total tax paid divided by total income or expenditure. In most progressive tax systems, both rates will rise as amount subject to taxation rises, though there may be ranges where the marginal rate will be constant.

With a system of negative income tax, refundable tax credits, or income-tested welfare benefits, it is possible for marginal rates to fall as amount subject to taxation rises: this can still be seen as progressive providing that the marginal rate is higher than the average rate at any particular level, since the average rate will rise; high marginal rates for those with low means can lead to a poverty trap within a progressive system, even if they face negative average rates.

BASE OF TAXATION

Income

The key concept of progressive income taxation is that income is considered in different steps, where income earned between certain points will be taxed at a certain rate. This is done to avoid creating incentive traps, where earning more might actually decrease your income. The size and severity of the different steps varies a great deal and the differences inside the term "progressive" can be enormous. In this sense, it is not surprising that most economists support progressive taxation to some degree - the primary differences come when looking at the maximum income taxes that the highest earners might have to pay.

Expenditure

While a tax on expenditures can be structured like a pure sales tax, many proposals make adjustments to decrease regressive effects. Using exemptions, graduated rates, deductions, credits or rebates, a consumption tax can be made less regressive or progressive, while allowing savings to accumulate tax-free. A sales tax on luxury goods or the exemption of basic necessities may be described as having progressive effects as it increases a tax burden on high end consumption or decreases a tax burden on low end consumption respectively. Economist Alan J. Auerbach of University of California, Berkeley states that "annual income is not an especially accurate measure of one's ability to pay.

A household's consumption tends to fluctuate less from year to year than its income does, and in some respects offers a better measure of a family's sustainable standard of living. Averaged over periods longer than one year, which smoothes out fluctuations in annual income, consumption taxes look less regressive relative to income than they look on an annual basis." Tax reform proposals that transition from an income tax to a consumption tax would be more equitable because consumption requires a balance between known and complex social costs.

IMPLEMENTATION

There are two ways that a progressive income tax can be implemented:

- *Increasing percentage rates*: When implementing a progressive tax with increasing percentage rates, the percentage of tax of each dollar increases as the total revenue increases. For example, a tax of 15% on all income earned up to $50,000, plus a tax of 25% on each dollar earned between $50,001 and $100,000, plus a tax of 34% of all income earned above $100,000. The United States currently uses increasing percentage rates.
- *Single tax rate*: A progressive tax rate can also be achieved by combining a single flat rate with a threshold. For example, all income up to $100,000 is earned tax free; income above $100,000 is taxed at 35%.

REGRESSIVE TAX

A regressive tax can be defined as a tax that tends to increase the total percentage of income paid on those who must pay the tax. In contrast, those who have a higher income pay less of their total income on items taxed. A tax can also be considered regressive when poorer folks must purchase more of the items taxed than do richer folks.

An example of regressive tax can occur when people who are poorer live, as they tend to do in poorly insulated homes. Due to poor insulation, they may pay more money to heat or cool their homes, and pay a higher tax on the purchase of electricity and gas. Similarly a person with an old car that is a gas-guzzler may have to consume more gas and thus pay a higher proportion of their income on gas taxes, than does a person who is able to afford to purchase an energy efficient car or a hybrid vehicle.

The wealthier person gets something of a tax advantage in these situations, making taxes on energy or fuel regressive in nature. The wealthier person may live in a better insulated home, be able to increase energy efficiency by investing in double-paned windows or newer appliances, and can purchase a hybrid or at least newer vehicle. Thus their energy bills may be less, and the taxes are less. In simpler terms, the person who makes $30,000 US Dollars (USD) per year and drives an old car might need to purchase more gas. Say they need 20 gallons of gas per week, and the tax is $1.00 USD per gallon. In a years time the person pays slightly over $1000 USD on gas taxes alone, about 3% of total income.

Let's say a similar person who makes $60,000 USD has a fuel-efficient car. He purchases 10 gallons of gas a week and pays just over $500 USD a year in total gas taxes. The percentage of income spent on gas tax each year is less than 1%, approximately 0.83%. You can see how this system is regressive tax in nature. The poorer person pays three times the amount of income as the richer person.

Even if a person with greater income chooses to purchase a car with less fuel efficiency, chances are the gas tax will still consume less of his/her income than it does for the poorer person. The person earning $60,000 USD per year does buy 20 gallons of gas a week, he or she is still only paying 1.6% of total income on gas taxes per year, about half of what the poorer person pays.

In order to prevent regressive tax on items purchased, many states make certain types of things non-taxable, especially food. This means the poorer person is not paying taxes when he or she is already consuming a large portion of their income on food expenses. Yet many items considered staples in a home are still taxed, like cleaners or paper products. Another way in which regressive tax can hit people hard is when it comes time to pay things like vehicle registration each year, which can really be difficult for many people to pay. The litmus test then, for defining regressive tax is the percentage of income a person must pay on a tax. Few countries have regressive tax systems in place. However it has been noted that people who make especially high incomes may have access to certain tax shelters unavailable to those with low to moderate incomes. Even though such a system is progressive, tax loopholes can ultimately mean that those who make more pay less of their income in taxes than those who make less, resulting in regressive taxation.

DIFFERENCE BETWEEN PROGRESSIVE AND REGRESSIVE TAX

Progressive taxation refers to a form of taxation where the percentage of income paid by an individual, increases with increasing income. People with higher income pay more total taxes imposed at a higher rate. Thus, a person with an income of $200,000 may pay a tax of $20,000 (at a tax rate of 10%), whereas a person with an income of $50,000 may pay a tax of $4,000 (at a tax rate of 8%). In case of regressive taxation, the proportion of income which is paid in taxes, decreases with an increase in income. This is in direct contrast to progressive tax, where the proportion paid as taxes, rises as the income increases. Sales tax on grocery products is also considered to be a form of regressive taxation because of the fact that a poor individual pays the same amount of tax as a wealthy person. The U.S. Taxation system contains a mixture of both progressive and regressive taxes.

A regressive tax system also includes the taxes imposed on essentials, like, transport, housing and clothing. This is because the income elasticity of the demand for these essentials is less, thus increasing the percentage of a lowly paid individual's budget which is taken as tax. Taxes on alcohol and tobacco are also a form of regressive taxation because both the lowly paid and highly paid individuals consume these products. Taxation on property is also sometimes considered as regressive taxation because the property taxes take up a higher percentage of an individual's budget who has a low income, than it does for an individual with a higher income.

COMMON EXAMPLES

- A value-added tax or other sales tax on food and other essentials such as clothing, transport, and residential rents can be regressive. Since the income elasticity of demand of food is usually less than 1, it tends to take up a higher percentage of the budget of a person or family with a lower income.
- A poll tax is a fixed tax for each person. Since each person pays the same amount of money, it is a lower proportion for people with higher incomes.
- Television licences that are implemented in many countries, especially in Europe, are considered regressive taxes and in most cases consist of a flat annual payment for the use of a television.
- The so called sin taxes are also criticized for being regressive, since the products taxed "are often consumed more by the lower classes".

DIRECT TAXES

A Direct tax is a kind of charge, which is imposed directly on the taxpayer. The examples of direct tax include property tax and income tax. Alternatively, it can be said that a direct tax is one that is taken away from one's salary or wages. When the tax is imposed by the government upon the property, then it is called property tax, which is also a direct tax.

MEANING OF DIRECT TAX: DIFFERENT VIEWS

The term direct tax can be defined from two different perspectives. One is from Colloquial point and the other is from U.S. constitutional law point. Certain taxes may fall under indirect tax categories in the constitutional sense, but fall under direct tax category in the colloquial sense.

DIRECT TAX: COLLOQUIAL SENSE

From the Colloquial point of view, a direct tax is the charge levied directly to the taxpayers by the government. Examples include corporate taxes, income taxes and transfer taxes. The transfer taxes include estate tax and gift tax.

DIRECT TAXATION IN INDIA

Direct taxation in India is taken care by the Central Board of Direct Taxes; it is a division of Department of revenue under Ministry of Finance. CBDT is governed by the revenue act 1963.CBDT is given the authority to create and control direct taxes in India. The most important function of CBDT is to manage direct tax law followed by Income Tax department.

In India the tax structure is divided amongst the central government and state government. The central government levies taxes on income, custom duties, central excise and service tax. While the state government levies tax like state excise, stamp duty, VAT, land revenue and professional tax.

LOCAL CIVIC BODIES LEVY TAX ON PROPERTIES, OCTROI ETC

Capital gains tax, personal income tax, tax on corporate income and tax incentives all come under the purview of direct tax.

Direct taxes are charged on the basis of residential status and not on the basis of citizenship.

The assessee are charged based upon the following factors:

- Resident
- Resident but not ordinary resident.
- Nonresident.

DIRECT TAXES BEFORE REFORM

They had a major impact on economic policies, creation of savings and the trend of investment. There was no proportion in terms of the impact of direct taxes on the economy and there relative share in total tax revenues. The system of direct taxes was very much complex and inefficient because of the combination of high marginal rates of personal income and wealth taxation and high rates of corporate profits. The corporate tax was pretty high. It leads to large scale evasion. Members Of Parliament and Central Government Ministers get comparatively low salaries, but they are given a sitting allowance which is not taxable. Ministers, MP's and other high ranking government officials get government allocated accommodation, where the charges are pretty less in comparison to the prevailing market rate.

GROWTH IN DIRECT TAX COLLECTION DURING THE FINANCIAL YEAR 2008-09

Net direct tax collection during the fiscal 2008-09 stands at ₹.338, 212 crore, up from ₹.312, 202 crore during 2007-08, registering a growth of 8.33 per cent. Growth in Corporate Taxes was 10.84 per cent, while Personal Income Tax grew at 9.09%. Despite economic slow-down and substantial relief to non-corporate taxpayers, direct tax collections exceeded the previous year's collection by about ₹.26, 000 crore.

GROWTH IN DIRECT TAX COLLECTION DURING THE FINANCIAL YEAR 2009-2010

The net direct tax collections grew by 5.77 per cent during the first two months of the current fiscal. It was ₹ 24,158 crore compared to ₹ 22,840 crore at the same time last year. Corporate tax grew at5.56 per cent (₹ 8578 crore against ₹ 8126 crore), while personal income tax (including FBT, STT and BCTT) grew at 5.92 per cent (₹ 15,559 crore as against ₹ 14,690 crore0.Overall refund outgo during the period increased by 26.19 per cent (₹ 11,375 crore as against ₹ 9014 crore)while refunds to non corporate taxpayers grew by 61.7 per cent (₹ 2,149 crore against ₹ 1,329 crore).

INDIRECT TAX

Indirect Tax or the tax that is levied on goods or services rather than on persons or organizations are of different types in India like Excise Duty, Customs Duty, Service Tax, and Securities Transaction Tax. In India, there are a series of Tax laws and regulations in order to control the indirect taxation, which can be either law, made by the central government or even can be state specific laws. As a result these taxes are an important part of the total cost. It is thus essential to make appropriate planning for such costs.

Nearly all of the activities that are subjected to indirect taxation range from manufacturing to those required for final consumption. Activities related to trading, imports, and services are also included in this list. As a result Indirect Tax has an impact on all business lines. At present the Indirect Taxes in India are under a transformation due to the changing fiscal reforms of the Indian government. Many new acts and laws are being introduced replacing the old laws and all related issues, which have become redundant. However, it should be remembered that such new laws while on one hand would create new opportunities, but also at the same time would lead to a certain extent of uncertainty and judicial proceedings.

In general, the Indirect Tax in India is a complex system of interconnecting laws and regulations, which includes specific laws of different states. For this there are many reliable organizations in India, which employs efficient Indirect Tax professionals to help their clients. These tax professionals with their in-depth knowledge and wide-ranging experience offers effective planning methods to their clients in order to help in their cost minimization. The Indirect Taxation regime encompasses various types of taxes like Sales Tax, Service Tax, Custom and Excise Duties, VAT and Anti-Dumping Duties, and the organizations provide services in all these related fields.

In the recent year, the Indian government has undertaken significant reform of indirect taxation system. This includes the initiation of a region-based and state-level VAT on goods. However, it should be noted that as taxes still forms a barrier to inter-state trading in order to attain a secured market for the activities related to services and goods more reform is needed.

Some of the reforms that can be introduced for a better indirect taxation system in India are:

- The serialized set of Indirect Taxes so far activated at the central and state levels should be amalgamated and treated as a single tax.
- The integrated Indirect Tax should be neutral at all levels such that chances of fraudulence would be minimized
- The Central Sales Tax, which obstructs easy trading between different states, is being under the process of termination that would help to abolish the control measures on the inter-state trade

By the year 2010 the Indian government has planned to activate a goods and services tax neutral at all levels in order to fulfill these objectives. The government can undertake either an introduction of a national VAT or a system, which would permit both a state VAT, or a central VAT. Along with this if the government also can incorporate a central VAT that can be rebated, on the trade across the boundary lines, then there would be minimum chances of fraudulence.

INDIRECT TAX SYSTEM INDIA

Indirect Taxes Pre Reforms

The indirect tax structure was extremely irrational between the reforms. The Constitution gives the permission to levy a multitude of indirect taxes. But the most important ones are customs and excise duties charged by the Central government and sales tax excepting inter state sales tax to be charged by the state government. The indirect taxes levied by the centre like customs, excise and central sales tax and the major indirect taxes levied by the states and civic bodies like passenger and goods tax, electricity duty and octroi when taken together did not present a rational system.

Indirect Taxes Post Reforms

- Even post reforms, the indirect tax regime in India is still in the early stages of growth. Both the Central and State governments charge a multitude of indirect taxes. The central government charges tax on goods at the point of import (Customs duty), manufacture (Excise duty), inter state sales (Central sales tax or CST) and on provision of services (Service tax).
- The state governments charge tax on goods sold within the state (Sales tax/Value Added Tax or VAT), and on the goods that enter the state (Entry tax).
- In the present scenario corporate would have to analyse the tax cost

involved in a transaction, have enough backup documentation to support their tax positions and keep looking for ways for tax maximization.

Indirect Taxes

As per the Ministry Of Finance there has been significant development in planning for introducing the goods and services tax (GST) from April 1 2010.As a first step the rate of central sales tax (CST) is under proposal to be decreased to 2 per cent from April1 2008.The general rate of central value added tax (CENVAT) has been decreased from 16 per cent to 14 per cent across all goods.

TAX BURDEN

Tax Burden is also known as Tax Incidence and means the research of the effect of a specific tax on the economic welfare of the people. The Burden of Tax falls on that group of people that has to pay the tax at the end of the day.

Taxes are charged by the state and it is an enforced contribution that the individual or the legal entity has to pay. The various kinds of taxes that have to be paid are income tax, sales tax, property tax, fuel tax, and luxury tax among others. The law of the land states from whom taxes are to be collected but the person who finally pays the Tax Burden is usually decided by the market. It is the market place that decides the person who is going to pay the Burden Tax for the taxes gets embedded with the costs of production.

The Burden of Tax depends on the quantity of product supplied and the demand for it and this is called the elasticities of demand and supply. Depending on it the Tax Burden can be absorbed either by the buyer which it does in the shape of higher prices post- tax or it may be absorbed by the seller in the shape of lower prices pre-tax. In case the supply elasticity is low then more of the Tax Burden is taken by the supplier. On the other hand if demand elasticity is low then more of the Burden Tax is taken by the customer.

Tax Burden in the case the seller is a firm that is competitive flows back to the production factors and this includes the capital investors who have to bear in the shape of loss of money to shareholders, entrepreneurs who have to bear in the shape of less salary of superintendence, landowners who have to bear in the shape of low rents, and workers who have to bear in the shape of lower salary.

The results of Tax Burden are:

- The employer passes on the Burden of Tax on the employee in the shape of lower salary If the employer has to provide his employee with health care facilities according to government regulations then too the Tax Burden will fall on the employee in the shape of lower salary
- Tax Burden puts on added pressure on the person that has to pay

for it for it amounts in him paying more money as tax. And so the government must keep the rate of tax at such a level that everyone is able to bear the Burden of Tax.

TAX INCIDENCE

In economics, tax incidence is the analysis of the effect of a particular tax on the distribution of economic welfare. Tax incidence is said to "fall" upon the group that, at the end of the day, bears the burden of the tax. The key concept is that the tax incidence or tax burden does not depend on where the revenue is collected, but on the price elasticity of demand and price elasticity of supply. For example, a tax on apple farmers might actually be paid by owners of agricultural land or consumers of apples.

The theory of tax incidence has a number of practical results. For example, United States Social Security payroll taxes are paid half by the employee and half by the employer. However, economists think that the worker is bearing almost the entire burden of the tax because the employer passes the tax on in the form of lower wages. The tax incidence is thus said to fall on the employee.

GRAPHICAL ANALYSIS

Inelastic Supply, Elastic Demand

Because the producer is inelastic, he will produce the same quantity no matter what the price. Because the consumer is elastic, the consumer is very sensitive to price. A small increase in price leads to a large drop in the quantity demanded. The imposition of the tax causes the market price to increase from P without tax to P with tax and the quantity demanded to fall from Q without tax to Q with tax. Because the producer is inelastic, the quantity doesn't change much. Because the consumer is elastic and the producer is inelastic, the price doesn't change much. The producer is unable to pass the tax onto the consumer and the tax incidence falls on the producer. In this example, the tax is collected from the producer and the producer bears the tax burden. This is known as back shifting.

Similarly-elastic Supply and Demand

Most markets fall between these two extremes, and ultimately the incidence of tax is shared between producers and consumers in varying proportions. In this example, the consumers pay more than the producers, but not all of the tax. The area paid by consumers is obvious as the change in equilibrium price; the remainder, being the difference between the new price and the cost of production at that quantity, is paid by the producers.

Inelastic Demand, Elastic Supply

Because the consumer is inelastic, he will demand the same quantity no matter what the price. Because the producer is elastic, the producer is very sensitive to price. A small drop in price leads to a large drop in the quantity produced. The imposition of the tax causes the market price to increase from P without tax to P with tax and the quantity demanded to fall from Q without tax to Q with tax. Because the consumer is inelastic, the quantity doesn't change much. Because the consumer is inelastic and the producer is elastic, the price changes dramatically.

The change in price is very large. The producer is able to pass almost the entire value of the tax onto the consumer. Even though the tax is being collected from the producer the consumer is bearing the tax burden. The tax incidence is falling on the consumer, known as forward shifting.

MACROECONOMIC PERSPECTIVE

The supply and demand for a good is deeply intertwined with the markets for the factors of production and for alternate goods and services that might be produced or consumed. Although legislators might be seeking to tax the apple industry, in reality it could turn out to be truck drivers who are hardest hit, if apple companies shift towards shipping by rail in response to their new cost. Or perhaps orange manufacturers will be the group most affected, if consumers decide to forgo oranges to maintain their previous level of apples at the now higher price. Ultimately, the burden of the tax falls on people—the owners, customers, or workers.

However, the true burden of the tax cannot be properly assessed without knowing the use of the tax revenues. If the tax proceeds are employed in a manner that benefits owners more than producers and consumers then the burden of the tax will fall on producers and consumers. If the proceeds of the tax are used in a way that benefits producers and consumers, then owners suffer the tax burden. These are class distinctions concerning the distribution of costs and are not addressed in current tax incidence models. The US military offers major benefit to owners who produce offshore. Yet the tax levy to support this effort falls primarily on American producers and consumers. Corporations simply move out of the tax jurisdiction but still receive the property rights enforcement that is the mainstay of their income.

Other Considerations of Tax Burden

Consider a 5% import tax applied equally to all imports and a direct refund of every penny of collected revenue in the form of a direct egalitarian "Citizen's Dividend" to every person who files Income Tax returns. At the macro level the people as a whole will break even. But the people who consume foreign produced goods will bear more of the burden than the people who consume a mix of goods.

The people who consume no foreign goods will bear none of the burden and actually receive an increase in utility. On the producer side, the tax burden distribution will depend on whether a firm produces its goods within the sovereignty or outside the sovereignty. Firms that produce goods inside the sovereignty will increase their market share and their profits when compared to firms who offshore their production. And if the current mix of firms is tilted towards offshore production then the owners of firms will be burdened more than the consumers while the workers/employees will benefit from greater employment opportunity.

Clarification

The burden from taxation is not just the quantity of tax paid, but the magnitude of the lost consumer surplus or producer surplus. The concepts are related but different. For example, imposing a $1000 per gallon of milk tax will raise no revenue, but this tax will cause substantial economic harm. When examining tax incidence, it is the lost consumer and producer surplus that is important.

OTHER PRACTICAL RESULTS

The theory of tax incidence has a large number of practical results, although economists dispute the magnitude and significance of these results:

- Because businesses are more sensitive to wages than employees, payroll taxes, employer mandates, and other taxes collected from the employer end up being borne by the employee. The tax is passed onto the employee in the form of lower wages.
- If the government requires employers to provide employees with health care, some of the burden will fall on the employee as the employer will pass it on in the form of lower wages. Some of the burden will be borne by employer since both the supply of and demand for labour are highly inelastic and have few perfect substitutes. Employers need employees largely to the extent they can substitute employees for machines, and employees need employers largely to the extent they can become self-employed entrepreneurs. An uneducated population is therefore more susceptible to bearing the burden because they are more easily replaced by machines able to do unskilled work, and because they have less knowledge of how to make money on their own.
- Taxes on easily substitutable goods, such as oranges and tangerines, may be borne mostly by the producer because the demand curve for easily substitutable goods is quite elastic.
- Similarly, taxes on a business that can easily be relocated are likely be borne almost entirely by the residents of the taxing jurisdiction and not the owners of the business.
- The burden of tariffs on imported vehicles might fall largely on the producers of the cars because the demand curve for foreign cars

might be elastic if car consumers may substitute a domestic car purchase for a foreign car purchase.

- If consumers drive the same number of miles regardless of gas prices, then a tax on gasoline will be paid for by consumers and not oil companies. Who actually bears the economic burden of the tax is not affected by whether government collects the tax at the pump or directly from oil companies.

APPRAISAL

Assessing tax incidence is a major economics subfield within the field of public finance. Most public finance economists acknowledge that nominal tax incidence is not necessarily identical to actual economic burden of the tax, but disagree greatly among themselves on the extent to which market forces disturb the nominal tax incidence of various types of taxes in various circumstances. The effects of certain kinds of taxes, for example, the property tax, including their economic incidence, efficiency properties and distributional implications, have been the subject of a long and contentious debate among economists.

The empirical evidence tends support different economic models under different circumstances. For example, empirical evidence on property tax incidents tends to support one economic model, known as the "benefit tax" view in suburban areas, while tending to support another economic model, known as the "capital tax" view in urban and rural areas. There is an inherent conflict in any model between considering many factors, which complicates the model and makes it hard to apply, and using a simple model, which may limit the circumstances in which its predictions are empirically useful.

TAX RATE

In a tax system and in economics, the tax rate describes the burden ratio at which a business or person is taxed. There are several methods used to present a tax rate: statutory, average, marginal, effective, effective average, and effective marginal. These rates can also be presented using different definitions applied to a tax base: inclusive and exclusive.

STATUTORY

A statutory tax rate is the legally imposed rate. An income tax could have multiple statutory rates for different income levels, where a sales tax may have a flat statutory rate.

AVERAGE

A marginal tax rate is the tax rate that applies to the last dollar of the tax base, and is often applied to the change in one's tax obligation as income rises:

To calculate the marginal tax rate on an income tax:

- Let m be the marginal tax rate.

- Let t be the tax liability.
- Let i be the taxable income.

$$m = \frac{\Delta t}{\Delta i}$$

For an individual, it can be determined by increasing or decreasing the income earned or spent and calculating the change in taxes payable. An individual's tax bracket is the range of income for which a given marginal tax rate applies. The marginal tax rate may increase or decrease as income or consumption increases, although in most countries the tax rate is progressive. In such cases, the average tax rate will be lower than the marginal tax rate: an individual may have a marginal tax rate of 45%, but pay average tax of half this amount. In a jurisdiction with a flat tax, everyone pays the same marginal tax rate. Some fixed amount of earnings is typically exempt from the flat tax, which means that not everyone pays the same average tax rate.

In economics, marginal tax rates are important because they are one of the factors that determine incentives to increase income; at higher marginal tax rates, some argue, the individual has less incentive to earn more. This is the foundation of the Laffer curve, which shows taxable income decreasing as a function of marginal tax rate, and therefore tax revenue begins to decrease after a certain point.

Public discussion of "high taxes" may refer to overall tax rates or marginal taxes. Marginal tax rates may be published explicitly, together with the corresponding tax brackets, but they can also be derived from published tax tables showing the tax for each income. It may be calculated noting how tax changes with changes in pre-tax income, rather than with taxable income. Marginal tax rates do not fully describe the impact of taxation. A flat rate poll tax has a marginal rate of zero, while a discontinuity in tax paid can lead to positively or negatively infinite marginal rates at particular points.

EFFECTIVE

An effective tax rate refers to the actual rate, i.e., the rate existing in fact. Both average and marginal tax rates can be expressed as effective tax rates. The effective tax rate is the amount of tax an individual or firm pays when all other government tax offsets or payments are applied, divided by the tax base.

If certain groups have high degrees of tax offsets compared to other groups, their effective tax rate will be different, even where their official tax rates and marginal tax rates will be equal. The effective rate of tax can often be discussed in terms of the effective marginal rate of tax - namely the amount of effective tax paid as a percentage of the last dollar earned or spent.

Effective Average

An effective average tax rate may differ from an average tax rate because some measure of income other than taxable income is used. For example, the

Joint Committee on Taxation typically calculates the effective average tax rate as the ratio of taxes paid to a constructed measure of "economic income".

Effective Marginal

An effective marginal tax rate may differ from a marginal tax rate because the taxpayer may be in an income range in which she/he is subject to a phase-out of some exclusion or deduction. Where social security and other benefits are related to income, the combined tax and benefit effect can also be taken into account giving a result sometimes described as the marginal effective tax rate or the marginal deduction rate.

If the marginal deduction rate exceeds 100%, then an increase in gross income leads to a decrease in disposable income, discouraging attempts to increase income. When this occurs for low income individuals, it is known as the "poverty trap".

INCLUSIVE/EXCLUSIVE

Tax rates can be presented differently due to differing definitions of tax base, which can make comparisons between tax systems confusing. Some tax systems include the taxes owed in the tax base, while other tax systems do not include taxes owed as part of the base. In the United States, sales taxes are quoted exclusively and income taxes are quoted inclusively.

Value added tax countries often display this tax inclusively; however, Goods and Services Tax countries do not. For direct rate comparisons between exclusive and inclusive taxes, one rate must be manipulated to look like the other. When a tax system imposes taxes primarily on income, the tax base is a household's pre-tax income.

The appropriate income tax rate is applied to the tax base to calculate taxes owed. Under this formula, taxes to be paid are included in the base on which the tax rate is imposed. If an individual's gross income is $100 and income tax rate is 20%, taxes owed equals $20. The income tax is taken "off the top", so the individual is left with $80 in after-tax money.

Some tax laws impose taxes on a tax base equal to the pre-tax portion of a good's price. These taxes do not include actual taxes owed as part of the base. A good priced at $80 with a 25% exclusive sales tax rate yields $20 in taxes owed. Since the sales tax is added "on the top", the individual pays $20 of tax on $80 of pre-tax goods for a total cost of $100. In either case, the tax base of $100 can be treated as two parts—$80 of after-tax spending money and $20 of taxes owed. A 25% exclusive tax rate approximates a 20% inclusive tax rate after adjustment. By including taxes owed in the tax base, an exclusive tax rate can be directly compared to an inclusive tax rate.

Inclusive income tax rate comparison to an exclusive sales tax rate:

- Let t be the income tax rate. For a 20% rate, then t = 0.20
- Let a be the rate in terms of a sales tax.
- Let p be the price of the good.

The revenue that would go to the government:

$$t \times p$$

The revenue remaining for the seller of the good:

$$P - t \times p$$

To convert the tax, divide the money going to the government by the money the company nets:

$$a = \frac{t \times p}{p - t \times p} = \frac{t}{1 - t}$$

Therefore, to adjust any inclusive tax rate to that of an exclusive tax rate, divide the given rate by 1 minus that rate.

- 15% inclusive = 18% exclusive
- 20% inclusive = 25% exclusive
- 25% inclusive = 33% exclusive
- 33% inclusive = 50% exclusive
- 50% inclusive = 100% exclusive

TAX RATES IN INDIA

Foreign Investors | Previous Tax rates before 2008 Budget

Table. Individual Income Tax Rates

Taxable Income		Tax Rate
Over	Not Over	
0	₹ 160,000[1]	0
₹ 160,001	₹ 300,000	10%
₹ 300,001	₹ 500,000	20%
₹ 500,001	above	30%[2]

1. ₹ 190,000 for women and ₹ 240,000 for seniors.
2. An education cess of 3% is applicable.
3. (a) Tax exemption on interest in Non-Resident (external) Account and on interest payable by a scheduled bank to Non-Resident Indians (NRI's).
   (b) Tax exemption on the interest payable by a scheduled bank to a non-resident or a person who is not ordinarily resident on deposits in foreign currency where the acceptance of such deposits by the bank is approved by the RBI.

Table. Domestic Corporate and LLP Income Taxes Rates

	Tax Rate	Effective Tax Rate with surcharge and ed. cess
Domestic Corporations/Private Limited Companies	30%	33.99%[1]

Domestic Corporations/Public Limited Companies	30%	33.99%[1]
Limited Liability Partnership (LLP's)	30%	30.9%[2]

1. A surcharge of 10% of the income tax is levied, if the taxable income exceeds ₹ 1 million. Educational cess is also added.
2. An Educational Cess is added to the basic tax rates. Surcharge is not applicable to LLP. Unlike LLP's in the USA where they are pass-through entities for tax purposes, in case of LLP's in India, they are partially pass-through entities for tax paurposes. In India tax an LLP is required to pay income tax on 40% of its income; since an LLP is allowed to pay the balance of 60% as renumerations to it partners. Partners of an LLP are required to pay tax on the amount paid to them. Besides, LLP's are not required to pay dividend distribution tax or Minimum Alternate Tax (MAT).
3. All companies incorporated in India are deemed as domestic Indian companies for tax purposes, even if owned by foreign companies. Contact us for Incorporating in India

Table. Foreign Corporate Income Tax Rates

	Withholding Tax Rate for non-treaty froeign companies India USA Tax Treaty	**Withholding Tax Rates for the USA companies Doing Business in India under the**
Dividends	20%	15%[1]
Interest Income	20%	15%[1]
Royalties	30%	20%[2]
Technical Services	30%	20%[2]
Other income	55%	55%

1. Inter-corporate rates where there is minimum holding. There tax rates are applicable under the India USA Tax Treaty. For other countries the tax rates are different under the tax treaties between India and other countries, including Australia, Austria, Bangladesh, Belgium, Brazil, Belarus, Bulgaria, Canada, China, Cyprus, Czechoslovakia, Denmark, Finland, France, Germany, Greece, Hungary, Indonesia, Israel, Italy, Japan, Jordan, Kazakhstan, Kenya, Libya, Malta, Malaysia, Mauritius, Mongolia, Namibia, Nepal, Netherlands, New Zealand, Norway, Oman, Philippines, Poland, Qatar, Romania, Singapore, South Africa, South Korea, Spain, Sri Lanka, Sweden, Switzerland, Syria, Tanzania, Thailand, Trinidad and Tobago, Turkmenistan, Turkey, U.A.E., U.A.R., U.K., U.S.A., Russian Federation, Uzbekistan, Vietnam and Zambia

2. 10% or 15% in some cases.
3. Withholding tax is charged on estimated income, as approved by the tax authorities.
4. There are other favourable tax rates under various tax treaties between India and other countries..

Wealth Tax

Net Taxable Wealth		Tax Rate
Over	**Not Over**	
0	₹.1,500,000	0
₹.1,500,000	above	1%

Wealth tax is levied on non-productive assets whose value exceeds ₹.1.5 million. Productive assets like shares, debentures, bank deposits and investments in mutual funds are exempt from wealth tax. The non-productive assets include residential houses, jewelry, bullion, motor cars, aircraft, urban land, etc. Foreign nationals are exempt from wealth tax on non-Indian assets. In arriving at the net taxable wealth, any debt incurred in acquiring specified assets is deductible.

Gift Tax

Net Taxable Gift	Tax Rate	
Over	**Not Over**	
0	₹.30,000	0
₹.30,000	above	30%

Gifts to dependent relatives at the time of marriage are exempt upto ₹.100,000. Foreign nationals are exempt from gift tax on non-Indian assets. *Tax on cash withdrawal from banks*: Withdrawn in the 2008 Budget. [0.1% tax used to be levied on cash withdrawals of over ₹ 25,000 from banks on a day. (Yes, this is true)]

ECONOMICS OF TAXATION

Taxation is any compulsory levy from individuals, households and firms to central or local government. The British economy imposes a wide range of taxes on people.

The breakdown of this revenue is shown in the chart below:

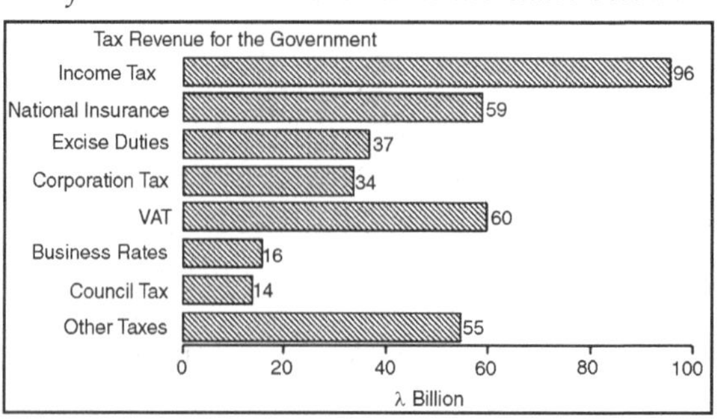

The system is always evolving as the government seeks to develop and maintain a tax system that meets objectives and targets. In the financial year 2000-01, the British government received £377 billion in tax revenue.

WHY DO WE NEED TO PAY TAXES

Taxation is levied for a number of reasons. To raise revenue to finance spending on goods and service by central and local government The government when managing the level of AD output and prices uses taxation. When demand is perceived as being too strong the government can increase direct taxation, to reduce the level of real disposable income and household spending. A progressive system of taxation can be utilised to achieve great equality in income and wealth between individuals and households Taxes can correct for externalities and other forms of market failure (such as monopoly) Import taxes may control imports and therefore help the country's international balance of payments and protect industries from overseas competition.

OBJECTIVES FOR THE TAX SYSTEM

- The Labour Government has identified six main objectives for its tax system - these are summarised below
- To keep the overall tax burden as low as possible
- To reduce tax rates on income to sharpen incentives to work and create wealth in the economy
- To maintain a broad tax base - having a range of taxes helps to keep each separate tax rate low
- To shift the balance of taxation away from taxes on income towards taxes on spending
- To ensure taxes are applied equally and fairly to everyone
- To use taxes to make markets work better

PROGRESSIVE REGRESSIVE AND PROPORTIONAL TAXES

Generally, indirect taxes are seen as regressive; the proportion of income paid in tax decreases as income rises. Direct taxes are progressive because the proportion of income paid in tax increases as income rises. With a progressive tax, the marginal rate of tax exceeds the average rate of tax.

As a result, progressive taxes act to reduce inequalities in the distribution of income. The post-tax distribution of income will be less dispersed than the pre-tax distribution.

With a proportional tax, the proportion of income paid in tax remains constant as income changes. In this situation, the marginal rate of tax will be equal to the average rate of tax. Any tax that does not vary with income is called a lump sum tax.

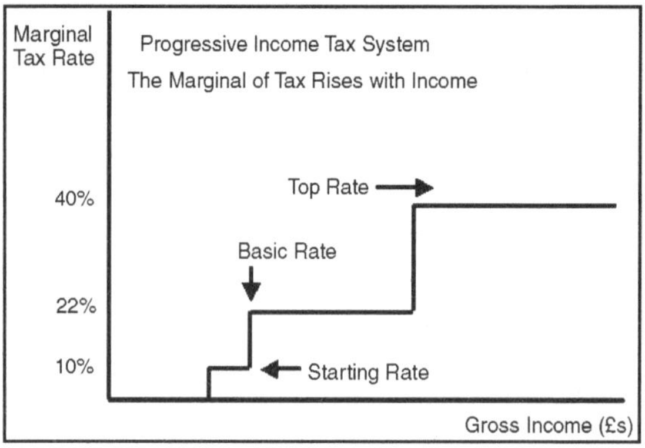

TYPES OF TAXES

The Organisation for Economic Co-operation and Development (OECD) publishes perhaps the most comprehensive analysis of worldwide tax systems. In order to do this it has created a comprehensive categorisation of all taxes in all regimes which it covers:

AD VALOREM

An ad valorem tax is a type of tax which is levied on property according to its value. Under an ad valorem tax, people who own certain types of property are required to pay periodic taxes which represent a percentage of the assessed value of the property. One of the most widespread forms of this tax is the property tax which people are required to pay on real estate. The Latin phrase "ad valorem" means "according to value."

Depending on how regional laws concerning taxation are laid out, an ad valorem tax may be assessed when property is purchased, in the form of a sales tax or value added tax (VAT), or it may be levied later on a set basis, such as once a year or once a quarter. Ad valorem taxes can also be assessed on estates, imports, and in other circumstances where property of value changes hands.

The funds raised by such taxes are used to support the workings of government. Many provincial governments have an ad valorem tax code, and municipalities have their own ad valorem taxes, such as additional property taxes for people within city limits. The rate of taxation may be determined by the legislature, or by popular vote; the citizens of a town, for example, could vote for an extra quarter per cent of sales tax to support a civic initiative. This is why sales taxes can vary significantly from city to city, as retailers must collect the state or provincial government's share, and the share demanded by the municipality. In the case of an ad valorem tax assessed on real estate, cars, and other personal property, it is possible to appeal the assessed value in the event that people think it is unfair. As a general rule, property is not reassessed until it changes hands, which sometimes works to the advantage of the owner, as when the value of real estate increases but he or she pays property taxes based on the sales price of 10 years ago, but this can also be a problem when the value of property declines. Tax assessors do not charge a fee to re-evaluate a property.

Legislatures occasionally battle over ad valorem taxation. Some people feel that such taxation is a very efficient and effective way to quickly raise money to fund various government enterprises, while others argue that these types of taxes penalize people for buying or maintaining property of value. Conservatives tend to favour a reduction in ad valorem taxes, while liberals often push for a maintenance or increase, under the argument that these funds are needed to support the smooth operation of the government.

BANK TAX

A bank tax ("bank levy") is a proposed tax on banks. One of the earliest modern uses of the term "bank tax" occurred in the context of the Financial crisis of 2007–2010. On April 16, 2010, the International Monetary Fund (IMF) proposed the idea of a "financial stability contribution" (FSC), which many media have referred to as a "bank tax." It was proposed as one of three possible options to deal with the crisis.

These options were presented in response to an earlier request of the G-20 leaders, at the September 2009 Pittsburgh summit, for a investigative report on all possible options to deal with the crisis. Both before and after that IMF report, there was considerable debate amongst national leaders as to whether such a "bank tax" should be "global," "semi-global," or whether it should be applied only in certain nations.

CAPITAL GAIN TAX

As per Indian Income Tax laws, a capital gain tax is a voluntary tax payable on the sale of assets, investments, capital accumulation, and productivity.

A Capital Gain can be defined as an any income generated by selling a capital investment. A capital investment can be anything from business stocks, paintings, and houses to family businesses and farmhouses. The 'gain' here, refers essentially to the difference between the price originally paid for the investment and money received upon selling it.

A capital gain can be categorized under the following heads, depending on how long the investment has been under your possession:

- *The Registrars of Companies in different states chiefly manage*:
  - *Short-term*: If you sell an investment within three years from the date of its purchase, it will be defined as a short-term capital gain. But if the investment is in the form of mutual funds/ company shares, the allowed time duration is one year.
  - *Long-term*: If you sell an investment after three years from the date of its purchase, it will be defined as a long-term capital

gain. However, selling mutual funds and company shares after one year will also constitute a long-term capital gain.

- In case of a short-term capital gain related to sale of property, the gained amount needs to be added to your total annual income. Then you'll be need to pay capital gain tax, depending on the total taxable amount.
- In case of a long-term capital gain related to sale of property, factors such as inflation are usually taken into consideration. The seller of the property needs to pay a tax not just on the real capital gain, but also on the projected gain as a result of inflation.
- You need to pay a capital gain tax on all your capital gains, though the government will allow you only a partial tax deduction in case you suffer a loss as a result of selling your investment.

Capital Gain Tax Rates

For short-term capital gains, you will be taxed depending on the tax slab relevant to you after you have added the capital gain to your annual income. But if the transaction was levied with Securities Transaction Tax (STT), your gain will be taxed 10%. For long term capital gains, you will be taxed 20%. But if the transaction was levied with STT, you need not pay any tax on your gain. In case of long term capital gains, you can either calculate your capital gain using an indexed acquisition cost, or you can choose not to opt for indexing.

CONSUMPTION TAX

Consumption Tax is applicable on the consumption of any type of good or service. This particular tax is based on consumption and not on income or labour. The Consumption Tax can be regarded as a sales tax, as this tax is also regressive in nature like the other pure sales taxes. However, there are some remedies by which the Consumption Tax can be made progressive in nature. Some of the methods for reducing the regressive trait of this tax include use of exemptions, deductions, graduated rates, or rebates. This will in other terms allow accumulation of savings exempting the tax burdens.

History of the Consumption Tax

The Consumption Tax is more of a western concept than gaining grounds in the eastern countries. In the United States for consumption of goods and services, this tax was levied. The Consumption Tax was very popular out in the American countries as they are difficult to bring up at the levels of confiscation compared to that of the income tax.

Features of the Consumption Tax

The consumption Tax are a lot similar to those of the present income tax systems.

Some of the main characteristics of the tax on consumption are:

- All those who are paying this tax would be subjected to certain exemptions and a standard deduction such that those categorized, as the poor do not have to pay any tax
- All those who are liable to pay the Consumption Tax, will not enjoy any other deductions as this would not be allowed since their all savings are already subjected to deduction
- In order to estimate the total liability of the Consumption Tax there might be withholding of the system, however this poses problems for the taxpayers. This creates trouble, as they had to pay no tax throughout the year to receive a huge tax receipt at the termination of the assessed year
- All those paying the Consumption Tax enjoys the exemption of being taxed on all incomes placed in some investment projects, this is because this tax is only concerned with consumption
- In order to transform the regressive nature of the Consumption Tax and to make it a progressive tax, all the taxpayers should expend more on consumption such that they are liable to pay more taxes on consumption.

Generally, Consumption Taxes are more favoured than the income taxes, as these taxes do not depend on the investment rates. For the taxpayer, in order to buy one investment when he sells another investment, there is no extra tax imposed on the profit.

This implies that the Consumption Tax in general favours investment policies and in turn this would increase the capital stock, productivity, and the size of the economy as a whole.

CORPORATE TAX

A company has been defined as a juristic person having an independent and separate legal entity from its shareholders. Income of the company is computed and assessed separately in the hands of the company. However the income of the company which is distributed to its shareholders as dividend is assessed in their individual hands. Such distribution of income is not treated as expenditure in the hands of company, the income so distributed is an appropriation of the profits of the company.

TAXABLE CORPORATE INCOME

The tax levied on a company's income is based on its legal residence. Companies of Indian origin are levied tax in India, while International companies are levied tax on earnings from their Indian operations. For International companies' royalty, interest, gains from sale of capital assets within India, dividends from Indian companies and fees for technical services are all treated as income arising in India.

TAX ON DISTRIBUTED PROFITS

Till 1997, a company was not required to pay any income tax on the amount of dividends declared, distributed or paid by such company. But such dividend was included in the income of the shareholders under the head "income from other sources". The finance act 1997 brought about changes to the rule.

- Tax On Distributed Profits Of The Domestic Company: The domestic company would be required to pay additional income tax on any amount declared, distributed or paid by such company by way of dividend on or after 1-06-1997,be it from current or accumulated profits. Such additional income tax shall be payable @ 10 per cent of the amount so distributed. Even if no income tax is payable by the company on it total income, the additional tax would have to be paid.
- Exemption Of Dividend In The Hands Of Shareholders: Such additional tax will have to be paid by the principal officer of the domestic company within 14 days from the date of:
  - Declaration of any dividend.
  - Distribution of any dividend.
  - Payment of any dividend, whichever is earlier.

CORPORATE TAX IN INDIA

Corporate tax rate in India is at par with the tax rates of other nations of the world. The corporate tax rate in India is based on the origin of the company. If the company is domicile to India, then the tax rate is flat at 30%. But for a foreign company, then the tax rate depends on several other factors and considerations. For companies that are domicile to India, tax is charged on the global income whereas for the foreign companies present in India, tax is charged on their income within Indian Territory. Incomes that are taxable for foreign companies include income from the capital assets in India, interest gained, income from sale of equity shares of the company, royalties, dividends earned, etc.

Domestic Corporate Income Taxes Rates

Incase of Domestic Corporations the effective tax rate as well the tax rate with surcharge as is 30%. It should be noted that if the taxable income is greater than ₹ 1 million then a surcharge of 10% of the tax on income is also levied. It is important to note the fact that all the companies formed in India are considered as Indian domestic companies, even for ancillary units with mother companies in foreign countries

Foreign Companies income tax rates:

- *For dividends*: 20% for non-treaty foreign companies and 15% incase of companies under the treaty based in the United States

- *For interest gains*: 20% for non-treaty foreign companies and 15% for companies under the treaty based in the United States
- *For royalties*: 30% for non-treaty foreign companies and 20% for companies under the treaty based in the United States
- For the technology based services in case of non-treaty foreign companies and 20% for companies under the treaty based in the United States
- *For all other kinds of income and gains*: 55% in case of non-treaty foreign companies and 55% for the companies under the treaty based in the United States
- Attention should be given on levying inter corporate rates in case holding is minimum
- Attention should be given on the fact that sanctions of the tax authorities on tax withholding
- Attention should be given on several of the tax treaties that India signed with other countries and also on the various encouraging tax rates

Some of the tax rebates under corporate tax rate in India:

- Gains pertaining to long term capital are subject to low tax incidence
- Venture capital funds and venture capital companies have special tax provisions
- Specula tax provisions are applicable for non resident Indians involved in activities in India
- Under the Finance Bill 1996, the minimum alternative tax (MAT) is levied on the corporate sector

ENVIRONMENTAL TAX

This includes natural resources consumption tax, Greenhouse gas tax, "sulfuric tax", and others. The stated purpose is to reduce the environmental impact by repricing.

EXCISES

Unlike an ad valorem, an excise is not a function of the value of the product being taxed. Excise taxes are based on the quantity, not the value, of product purchased. For example, in the United States, the Federal government imposes an excise tax of 18.4 cents per U.S. gallon of gasoline, while state governments levy an additional 8 to 28 cents per U.S. gallon. Excises on particular commodities are frequently hypothecated. For example, a fuel excise (use tax) is often used to pay for public transportation, especially roads and bridges and for the protection of the environment.

A special form of hypothecation arises where an excise is used to compensate a party to a transaction for alleged uncontrollable abuse; for example, a blank media tax is a tax on recordable media such as CD-₹, whose proceeds are typically allocated to copyright holders. Critics charge that such taxes blindly tax those who make legitimate and illegitimate usages of the products; for instance, a person or corporation using CD-R's for data archival should not have to subsidize the producers of popular music.

Excises are also used to modify consumption patterns. For example, a high excise is used to discourage alcohol consumption, relative to other goods. This may be combined with hypothecation if the proceeds are then used to pay for the costs of treating illness caused by alcohol abuse.

Similar taxes may exist on tobacco, pornography, etc., and they may be collectively referred to as "sin taxes". A carbon tax is a tax on the consumption of carbon-based non-renewable fuels, such as petrol, diesel-fuel, jet fuels, and natural gas. The object is to reduce the release of carbon into the atmosphere. In the United Kingdom, vehicle excise duty is an annual tax on vehicle ownership.

EXPATRIATION TAX

An Expatriation Tax is a tax on some who renounce their citizenship of some governments. The most significant Expatriation Tax is one found in the USA.

The American Jobs Creation Act of 2004, passed by the Republican-controlled government, amended section 877 of the Internal Revenue Code of the USA. Under the new law, any individual who has a net worth of $2 million or an average income-tax liability of $127,000 who renounces his or her citizenship and leaves the country is automatically assumed to have done so for tax avoidance reasons and is victim to severe tax laws.

FINANCIAL ACTIVITIES TAX

As a regulatory response and proposal to the financial crisis of 2007-2010, on April 16, 2010, the IMF proposed three types of global taxes on banks: First, the "Financial Stability Contribution" is a straight tax on a bank's gross profits—before deducting compensation. It would initially be at a flat rate, this would eventually be refined so that riskier businesses paid more. Second, the "Financial Activities Tax" aims directly at excess bank profit and pay. The third, which was not endorsed by the IMF, but not ruled out as administratively difficult, is a financial transaction tax.

FINANCIAL TRANSACTION TAX

A financial transaction tax is a tax placed on a specific type of financial transaction for a specific purpose. This term has been most commonly associated with the financial sector, as opposed to consumption taxes paid by consumers. There are several types of financial transaction taxes. Each has its own purpose. Some have already been implemented, and some remain unimplemented concepts. Concepts are found in various organizations and regions around the world. Some are domestic and meant to be used within one nation; whereas some are multinational.

INCOME TAX

An income tax is a tax levied on the financial income of persons, corporations, or other legal entities. Various income tax systems exist, with varying degrees of tax incidence. Income taxation can be progressive, proportional, or regressive. When the tax is levied on the income of companies, it is often called a corporate tax, corporate income tax, or corporation tax. Individual income taxes often tax the total income of the individual, while corporate income taxes often tax net income.

The "tax net" refers to the types of payment that are taxed, which included personal earnings, capital gains, and business income. The rates for different types of income may vary and some may not be taxed at all.

Capital gains may be taxed when realised or when incurred. Business income may only be taxed if it is significant or based on the manner in which it is paid. Some types of income, such as interest on bank savings, may be considered as personal earnings or as a realised property gain. In some tax systems, personal earnings may be strictly defined where labour, skill, or investment is required; in others, they may be defined broadly to include windfalls.

Personal income tax is often collected on a pay-as-you-earn basis, with small corrections made soon after the end of the tax year. These corrections take one of two forms: payments to the government, for taxpayers who have not paid enough during the tax year; and tax refunds from the government for those who have overpaid. Income tax systems will often have deductions available that lessen the total tax liability by reducing total taxable income. They may allow losses from one type of income to be counted against another. For example, a loss on the stock market may be deducted against taxes paid on wages. Other tax systems may isolate the loss, such that business losses can only be deducted against business tax by carrying forward the loss to later tax years.

INFLATION TAX

An inflation tax is the economic disadvantage suffered by holders of cash and cash equivalents in one denomination of currency due to the effects of Expansionary monetary policy, which acts as a hidden tax that subtracts value from those assets. Many economists hold that the inflation tax affects the lower and middle classes more than the rich, as they hold a larger fraction of their income in cash, they are much less likely to receive the newly created monies before the market has adjusted with inflated prices, and more often have fixed incomes, wages or pensions. Some argue that inflation is a regressive consumption tax.

There are systemic effects of an expansionary monetary policy, which are also definitively taxing, imposing a financial charge on some as a result of the policy. Because the effects of monetary expansion or counterfeiting are never uniform over an entire economy, the policy influences capital transfers in the market, creating economic bubbles where the new monies are first introduced. Economic bubbles increase market instability, and therefore increase investment risk, creating the conditions common to a recession. This particular tax can be understood to be levied on future generations that would have benefited from economic growth, and it has a 100% transfer cost. One example of a strong supporter of this tax was the former Federal Reserve chair Beardsley Ruml.

INHERITANCE TAX

Inheritance tax, estate tax, and death tax or duty are the names given to various taxes which arise on the death of an individual. In United States tax law, there is a distinction between an estate tax and an inheritance tax: the former taxes the personal representatives of the deceased, while the latter taxes the beneficiaries of the estate. However, this distinction does not apply in other jurisdictions; for example, if using this terminology UK inheritance tax would be an estate tax.

POLL TAX

A poll tax, also called a per capita tax, or capitation tax, is a tax that levies a set amount per individual. It is an example of the concept of fixed tax. One of the earliest taxes mentioned in the Bible of a half-shekel per annum from each adult Jew was a form of poll tax. Poll taxes are administratively cheap because they are easy to compute and collect and difficult to cheat. Economists have considered poll taxes economically efficient because people are presumed to be in fixed supply.

However, poll taxes are very unpopular because poorer people pay a higher proportion of their income than richer people. In addition, the supply of people is in fact not fixed over time: on average, couples will choose to have fewer children if a poll tax is imposed. The introduction of a poll tax in medieval England was the primary cause of the 1381 Peasants' Revolt. Scotland was the first to be used to test the new poll tax in 1989 with England and Wales in 1990. The change from a progressive local taxation based on property values to a single-rate form of taxation regardless of ability to pay, led to widespread refusal to pay and to incidents of civil unrest, known colloquially as the 'Poll Tax riots'.

PROPERTY TAX

A property tax is a tax put on property by reason of its ownership. Property tax can be defined as "generally, tax imposed by municipalities upon owners of property within their jurisdiction based on the value of such property." There are three species of property: land, improvements to land and personal property. Real estate or realty is the combination of land and improvements to land.

Property taxes are usually charged on a recurrent basis. A common type of property tax is an annual charge on the ownership of real estate, where the tax base is the estimated value of the property. For a period of over 150 years from 1695 a window tax was levied in England, with the result that one can still see listed buildings with windows bricked up in order to save their owners money. A similar tax on hearths existed in France and elsewhere, with similar results. The two most common type of event driven property taxes are stamp duty, charged upon change of ownership, and inheritance tax, which is imposed in many countries on the estates of the deceased.

In contrast with a tax on real estate, a land value tax is levied only on the unimproved value of the land. Proponents of land value tax argue that it is economically justified, as it will not deter production, distort market mechanisms or otherwise create deadweight losses the way other taxes do. When real estate is held by a higher government unit or some other entity not subject to taxation by the local government, the taxing authority may receive a payment in lieu of taxes to compensate it for some or all of the foregone tax revenue.

In many jurisdictions, there is a general tax levied periodically on residents who own personal property within the jurisdiction. Vehicle and boat registration fees are subsets of this kind of tax. The tax is often designed with blanket coverage and large exceptions for things like food and clothing. Household goods are often exempt when kept or used within the household. Any otherwise non-exempt object can lose its exemption if regularly kept outside the household. Thus, tax collectors often monitor newspaper articles for stories about wealthy people who have lent art to museums for public display, because the artworks have then become subject to personal property tax. If an artwork had to be sent to another state for some touch-ups, it may have become subject to personal property tax in that state as well.

SOCIAL SECURITY TAX

Some countries with social security systems, which provide income to retired workers, fund those systems with specific dedicated taxes. These often differ from comprehensive income taxes in that they are levied only on specific sources of income, generally wages and salary. A further difference is that the total amount of the taxes paid by or on behalf of a worker is typically considered in the calculation of the retirement benefits to which that worker is entitled. Examples of retirement taxes include the FICA tax, a payroll tax that is collected from employers and employees in the United States to fund the country's Social Security system; and the National Insurance Contributions collected from employers and employees in the United Kingdom to fund the country's national insurance system. These taxes are sometimes regressive in their immediate effect. For example, in the United States, each worker, whatever his or her income, pays at the same rate up to a specified cap, but income over the cap is not taxed. A further regressive feature is that such taxes often exclude investment earnings and other forms of income that are more likely to be received by the wealthy. The regressive effect is somewhat offset, however, by the eventual benefit payments, which typically replace a higher percentage of a lower-paid worker's pre-retirement income.

SALES TAX

Sales taxes are levied when a commodity is sold to its final consumer. Retail organizations contend that such taxes discourage retail sales. The question of whether they are generally progressive or regressive is a subject of much current debate. People with higher incomes spend a lower proportion of them, so a flat-rate sales tax will tend to be regressive. It is therefore common to exempt food, utilities and other necessities from sales taxes, since poor people spend a higher proportion of their incomes on these commodities, so such exemptions would make the tax more progressive. This is the classic "You pay for what you spend" tax, as only those who spend money on non-exempt items pay the tax.

A small number of U.S. states rely entirely on sales taxes for state revenue, as those states do not levy a state income tax. Such states tend to have a moderate to large amount of tourism or inter-state travel that occurs within their borders, allowing the state to benefit from taxes from people the state would otherwise not tax. In this way, the state is able to reduce the tax burden on its citizens. The U.S. states that do not levy a state income tax are Alaska, Tennessee, Florida, Nevada, South Dakota, Texas, Washington state, and Wyoming. Additionally, New Hampshire and Tennessee levy state income taxes only on dividends and interest income. Only Alaska and New Hampshire do not levy a state sales tax. Additional information can be obtained at the Federation of Tax Administrators website.

In the United States, there is a growing movement for the replacement of all federal payroll and income taxes with a national retail sales tax and monthly tax rebate to households of citizens and legal resident aliens. The tax proposal is named FairTax. In Canada, the federal sales tax is called the Goods and Services tax and now stands at 5%. The provinces of British Columbia, Saskatchewan, Manitoba, Ontario and Prince Edward Island also have a provincial sales tax [PST]. The provinces of Nova Scotia, New Brunswick, and Newfoundland and Labrador have harmonized their provincial sales taxes with the GST - Harmonized Sales Tax [HST], and thus is a full VAT. The province of Quebec collects the Quebec Sales Tax [QST] which is based on the GST with certain differences. Most businesses can claim back the GST, HST and QST they pay, and so effectively it is the final consumer who pays the tax.

TARIFFS

An import or export tariff is a charge for the movement of goods through a political border. Tariffs discourage trade, and they may be used by governments to protect domestic industries. A proportion of tariff revenues is often hypothecated to pay government to maintain a navy or border police. The classic ways of cheating a tariff are smuggling or declaring a false value of goods. Tax, tariff and trade rules in modern times are usually set together because of their common impact on industrial policy, investment policy, and agricultural policy. A trade bloc is a group of allied countries agreeing to minimize or eliminate tariffs against trade with each other, and possibly to impose protective tariffs on imports from outside the bloc. A customs union has a common external tariff, and, according to an agreed formula, the participating countries share the revenues from tariffs on goods entering the customs union.

TOLL

A toll is a taxor fee charged to travel via a road, bridge, tunnel, canal, waterway or other transportation facilities. Historically tolls have been used to pay for public bridge, road and tunnel projects. They have also been used in privately constructed transport links. The toll is likely to be a fixed charge, possibly graduated for vehicle type, or for distance on long routes. Shunpiking is the practice of finding another route to avoid payment of tolls. In some situations where tolls were increased or felt to be unreasonably high, informal shunpiking by individuals escalated into a form of boycott by regular users, with the goal of applying the financial stress of lost toll revenue to the authority determining the levy.

TRANSFER TAX

Historically, in many countries, a contract needed to have a stamp affixed to make it valid. The charge for the stamp was either a fixed amount or a percentage of the value of the transaction. In most countries the stamp has been abolished but stamp duty remains. Stamp duty is levied in the UK on the purchase of shares and securities, the issue of bearer instruments, and certain partnership transactions. Its modern derivatives, stamp duty reserve tax and stamp duty land tax, are respectively charged on transactions involving securities and land. Stamp duty has the effect of discouraging speculative purchases of assets by decreasing liquidity. In the United States transfer tax is often charged by the state or local government and can be tied to the recording of the deed or other transfer documents.

VALUE ADDED TAX/GOODS AND SERVICES TAX

A value added tax, also known as 'Goods and Services Tax', Single

Business Tax, or Turnover Tax in some countries, applies the equivalent of a sales tax to every operation that creates value. To give an example, sheet steel is imported by a machine manufacturer. That manufacturer will pay the VAT on the purchase price, remitting that amount to the government. The manufacturer will then transform the steel into a machine, selling the machine for a higher price to a wholesale distributor.

The manufacturer will collect the VAT on the higher price, but will remit to the government only the excess related to the "value added". The wholesale distributor will then continue the process, charging the retail distributor the VAT on the entire price to the retailer, but remitting only the amount related to the distribution mark-up to the government. The last VAT amount is paid by the eventual retail customer who cannot recover any of the previously paid VAT. For a VAT and sales tax of identical rates, the total tax paid is the same, but it is paid at differing points in the process.

VAT is usually administrated by requiring the company to complete a VAT return, giving details of VAT it has been charged and VAT it has charged to others. The difference between output tax and input tax is payable to the Local Tax Authority. If input tax is greater than output tax the company can claim back money from the Local Tax Authority.

WEALTH TAX

Some countries' governments will require declaration of the tax payers' balance sheet, and from that exact a tax on net worth, as a percentage of the net worth, or a percentage of the net worth exceeding a certain level. The tax may be levied on "natural" or legal "persons".

ETHICS OF TAXATION

ETHICAL BASIS OF TAXATION

According to most political philosophies, taxes are justified as they fund activities that are necessary and beneficial to society. Additionally, progressive taxation can be used to reduce economic inequality in a society. According to this view, taxation in modern nation-states benefit the majority of the population and social development. A common presentation of this view, paraphrasing various statements by Oliver Wendell Holmes, Jr. is "Taxes are the price of civilization".

It can also be argued that in a democracy, because the government is the party performing the act of imposing taxes, society as a whole decides how the tax system should be organized. The American Revolution's "No taxation without representation" slogan implied this view. For traditional conservatives, the payment of taxation is justified as part of the general obligations of citizens to obey the law and support established institutions. The conservative position is encapsulated in perhaps the most famous adage of public finance, "An old tax is a good tax". Conservatives advocate the "fundamental conservative premise that no one should be excused from paying for government, lest they come to believe that government is costless to them with the certain consequence that they will demand more government 'services'." Social democrats generally favour higher levels of taxation to fund public provision of a wide range of services such as universal health care and education, as well as the provision of a range of welfare benefits.

As argued by Tony Crosland and others, the capacity to tax income from capital is a central element of the social democratic case for a mixed economy as against Marxist arguments for comprehensive public ownership of capital. Many libertarians recommend a minimal level of taxation in order to maximize the protection of liberty.

Compulsory taxation of individuals, such as income tax, is often justified on grounds including territorial sovereignty, and the social contract. Defenders of business taxation argue that it is an efficient method of taxing income that ultimately flows to individuals, or that separate taxation of business is justified on the grounds that commercial activity necessarily involves use of publicly established and maintained economic infrastructure, and that businesses are in effect charged for this use. Georgist economists argue that all of the economic rent collected from natural resources is unearned income, and belongs to the community rather than any individual. They advocate a high tax on land and other natural resources to return this unearned income to the state, but no other taxes.

OPTIMAL TAXATION THEORY

Most governments need revenue which exceeds that which can be provided by non-distortionary taxes or through taxes which give a double dividend. Optimal taxation theory is the branch of economics that considers how taxes can be structured to give the least deadweight costs, or to give the best outcomes in terms of social welfare.

Ramsey problem deals with minimizing deadweight costs. Because deadweight costs are related to the elasticity of supply and demand for a good, it follows that putting the highest tax rates on the goods for which there is most inelastic supply and demand will result in the least overall deadweight costs.

Some economists sought to integrate optimal tax theory with the social welfare function, which is the economic expression of the idea that equality is valuable to a greater or lesser extent. If individuals experience diminishing returns from income, then the optimum distribution of income for society involves a progressive income tax. Mirrlees optimal income tax is a detailed theoretical model of the optimum progressive income tax along these lines.

Over the last years the validity of the theory of optimal taxation was discussed by many political economists. Canegrati demonstrated that if we move from the assumption that governments do not maximise the welfare of society but the probability of winning elections, the tax rates in equilibrium are lower for the most powerful groups of society, instead of being the lowest for the poorest as in the optimal theory of direct taxation developed by Atkinson and Joseph Stiglitz.

VIEWS OPPOSED TO TAXATION

Because payment of tax is compulsory and enforced by the legal system, some political philosophies view taxation as theft, or tyranny, accusing the government of levying taxes via force and coercive means. Voluntaryists, Individualist anarchists, objectivists, anarcho-capitalists, and libertarians see taxation as government aggression. The view that democracy legitimizes taxation is rejected by those who argue that all forms of government, including laws chosen by democratic means, are fundamentally oppressive. According to Ludwig von Mises, "society as a whole" should not make such decisions, due to methodological individualism. Libertarian opponents of taxation claim that governmental protection, such as police and defence forces might be replaced by market alternatives such as private defence agencies, arbitration agencies or voluntary contributions. Walter E. Williams, professor of economics at George Mason University, stated "Government income redistribution programmes produce the same result as theft. In fact, that's what a thief does; he redistributes income. The difference between government and thievery is mostly a matter of legality."

Discourse surrounding taxation generally places an emphasis on the intended benefits; healthcare, schools and so on, but rarely points to the harm caused by forced removal of possessions.

Taxation has also been opposed by communists and socialists. Karl Marx assumed that taxation would be unnecessary after the advent of communism and looked forward to the "withering away of the state". In socialist economies such as that of China, taxation played a minor role, since most government income was derived from the ownership of enterprises, and it was argued by some that taxation was not necessary. While the morality of taxation is sometimes questioned, most arguments about taxation revolve around the degree and method of taxation and associated government spending, not taxation itself.

EFFECTS OF INCOME TAXATION ON DIVISION OF LABOUR

If a tax is paid on outsourced services that is not also charged on services performed for oneself, then it may be cheaper to perform the services oneself than to pay someone else — even considering losses in economic efficiency.

For example, suppose jobs A and B are both valued at $1 on the market. And suppose that because of your unique abilities, you can do job A twice over in the same effort as it would take you to do job B. But job B is the one that you need done right now. Under perfect division of labour, you would do job A and somebody else would do job B. Your unique abilities would always be rewarded.

Income taxation has the worst effect on division of labour in the form of barter. Suppose that the person doing job B is actually interested in having job A done for him. Now suppose you could amazingly do job A four times over, selling half your work on the market for cash just to pay your tax bill. The other half of the work you do for somebody who does job B twice over but he has to sell off half to pay his tax bill. You're left with one unit of job B, but only if you were 400% as productive doing job A! In this case of 50% tax on barter income, anything less than 400% productivity will cause the division of labour to fail.

In summary, depending on the situation a 50% tax rate can cause the division of labour to fail even where productivity gains of up to 300% would have resulted. Even a mere 30% tax rate can negate the advantage of a 100% productivity gain.

NON-TAX REVENUE

Non-tax revenue or non-tax receipts are government revenue not generated from taxes.

Examples include:

- Aid from another level of government —for example, in the United States, federal grants may be considered non-tax revenue to the receiving states
- Aid from abroad
- Tribute or indemnities paid by a weaker state to a stronger one, often as a condition of peace after suffering military defeat. The war reparations paid by the defeated Central Powers after the First World War offer a well-known example.
- Revenue from state-owned enterprises
- Revenue from investment funds, sovereign wealth funds, or endowments
- Revenues from sales of state assets
- Rents, concessions, and royalties collected by the state when it contracts out the right to profit from some good or service to a private corporation. An example are contracts for resource extraction collected privately under license from state-owned lands
- Fines collected and assets forfeitured as a penalty. Examples include parking fines, court costs levied on criminal offenders
- Fees for the granting or issuance of permits or licenses. Examples include vehicle registration plate permits, vehicle registration fees, watercraft registration fees, building fees, driver's licenses, hunting and fishing licenses, fees for professional licensing, fees for visas or

passports, fees for demolition, rezoning, and land grading, and sometimes for increasing stormwater run-off, destroying native vegetation, and cutting-down healthy trees.

- User fees collected in exchange for the use of many public services and facilities. Tolls charged for the use of toll roads are an example
- Donations and voluntary contributions to the state

2

Indian Tax System

STRUCTURE OF INDIA TAXATION

India is a federal republic with an area of 3,287,590 sq. km and the population in 2002 stood at about one billion and 52 million persons and the population density was 320. At the turn of the century, GDP totals about US$ 440 billion. This aggregate figure stays at the world's fourth place, but its per capita counterpart is less than US$ 450. Poverty remains an enormous problem: according to World Bank, India has some 433 million people living on less than US$ 1 a day, 36 percent of the total number of poor in the world. Also non-income poverty represents a huge problem and many social indicators are going bad.

This notwithstanding, India's economic performance has been impressive over the last two decades. Total GDP grew yearly at about 6 percent, per capita GDP at about 4 percent. During the 1990s the average gross fiscal deficit level was 7.2 percent of GDP, while during latest years gross fiscal deficit went up to the 9-10 percent of GDP range. The general government debt fell from 72.5 percent of GDP in 1990-91 to 65.1 percent at the middle of 1990s, but then rose to 79.8 percent in 2001-2002. At the late 1990s Indian general government public expenditure totaled near 25 percent of GDP. This figure is not low with respect to the Indian per capita income. However the joint share of education and health is poor and that of social security is still poorer. Around the turn of the century, about 80 percent of public expenditure is financed by means of taxes, whose total pressure stays around 15 percent of GDP. Central government collects more than half of tax revenue, but about a quarter is transferred to the states.

Taxes on goods and services are definitively the dominant item. Direct taxes' revenue is far lower and barely reaches 20 percent of total taxes. On the contrary, import duties are still a not negligible share of total taxation's yield. Finally, social contributions are wholly lacking. Beginning with the early 1990s Indian tax system entered a way of reforms. Until now the accomplishments were of some relevance but neither radical nor fast coming. They largely are still under way or planned for the incoming years. Obviously one must be aware that the economic structure as well as administrative difficulties severely constrains tax system's features in developing countries. Anyway in India the change over to the typical "modern" system has not been accomplished yet and it is still expected to be take place and being completed in the near future. India has a tax structure with a three-tier federal structure.

The main taxes/duties that the union government is empowered to levy are: income tax, customs duties, excise duties, sales tax and service tax. It is worthwhile to notice some peculiar features of this tax bundle. Income tax is a single tax that is levied on a comprehensive basis both on persons and companies. The structure of custom duties is particularly intricate and the burden hits almost entirely the import side of international trade. Also internal indirect taxes are a complicated matter: they are separately levied on goods, services and intra-states' sales. During the time excise duties and service tax had benefited of a credit system compensating paid tax on inputs and capital goods that has grown to avoid cascading effects and to approximate a VAT-type structure. The main taxes levied by the state governments are sales tax, stamp duty, state excise, land revenue, duty on entertainment and tax on professions & callings.

The local bodies are empowered to levy tax on properties, octroi, tax on markets and tax/user charges for utilities. Indian tax system is still too largely made up of a big, complex and obsolete bundle of excises and sales taxes. The room of the direct taxation, both on individuals and companies, is very smaller. Consequently a number of issues arise. The share of the personal income tax is more limited than in countries where the value of the per capita income is not far from the Indian one. This may be aimed to preserve poverty income from taxation, but unavoidably the poor are then hit by regressive consumption taxes. Furthermore, the argument that the collection costs are higher for the direct than for the indirect taxes does not seem well demonstrated.

Finally, some traditional argument of economic theory - i.e. that the income tax is not adequately saving preserving and might induce supply disincentives - is not consistent with the situation of Indian economy. Relative to the companies' taxation, its basis should be broadened through the reduction of a large number of multifaceted incentives. To conclude on this point, a great deal of rationalization is still mandatory to avoid cascading effects - between national excises and states' sales tax -, random 'all in' rates charged on final goods, and high costs of collection. Since few years the long-term strategy moves towards a double VAT system, leaving to survive just some excises on specific goods.

As we have already noticed, India is a federal republic with a complex structure of local authorities. The assignment of tax powers is based on the principle of tax separation and the consequence is a vertical fiscal imbalance.

The inadequacy of the states to meet expenditure from their own resources is recognized by the Constitution, which provides for grant-in-aid both purposed-based and need-based. Since the last two decades impressive catching-growth is going on in the Indian economy. In 2003-04 real GDP at factor cost has been estimated to have grown by 8.2 percent and was accompanied by a relative stability of prices. The fiscal deficit of the central government, in GDP terms, after declining from 6.6 percent in 1990-91 to 4.1 percent in 1996-97, started rising to 5.3 percent in 2002-03. The combined fiscal deficit of the centre and the states increased from a level of 9.4 percent of GDP in 1990-91 to a level of 10.1 percent of GDP in the revised estimates for 2002-03.

In 1991, in reaction to a severe macroeconomic crisis involving high fiscal deficits, India carried out a series of economic reforms, among which a tax reform. The main proposals comprised: a) the reduction in the rates of the most important taxes; b) the enlargement of all taxes' bases; c) the transformation of the taxes on domestic production into something similar to a value added tax; d) the simplification of laws and administrative procedures. Most of the recommendations have been implemented over the years, at least at the central level. In the case of the states the reforms of their tax systems did not proceed. In September 2002 the Government set up a new Task Force on tax reforms headed by V. Kelkar. The Kelkar committees suggested sweeping reforms including: a) raising the limits of income tax exemption and two-tier brackets; b) cut in corporate tax rate; c) three-rate basic customs duty structure; d) service tax levied in a comprehensive manner; e) repeal of wealth tax; f) removal of tax exemptions, rationalization of incentives for savings and simplification of procedures; g) gradual moving over the destination based, consumption type value added taxes at the state level. The introduction of VAT was repeatedly postponed, mainly because of the lack of administrative preparation and of disagreements between union government and some states.

In July 2004 a Task Force on Implementation of Fiscal Responsibility and Budget Act, also headed by V. Kelkar, has come up with a proposal for an integrated VAT on goods and services to be levied by the central government and the states in parallel, removing all cascading taxes. Of course dismantling and deeply reforming about 60 percent of taxation will be an operation neither easy nor without the risk of loosing yield.

SOME QUANTITATIVE AND INSTITUTIONAL FEATURES OF MAIN TAXES

India has a tax structure with a three-tier federal structure. The power to levy taxes and duties is distributed between the union government and the state governments in accordance with the provisions of the Indian Constitution. The state government may delegate any of its fiscal powers to local authorities that do not have any constitutionally reserved powers of taxation. The main taxes/duties that the union government is empowered to levy are: income tax customs duties, excise duties, sales tax and service tax. The principal taxes levied by the state governments are sales tax, stamp duty, state excise, land revenue, duty on entertainment and tax on professions & callings. The local bodies are empowered to levy tax on properties, octroi, tax on markets and tax/user charges for utilities like water supply, drainage, etc.

DIRECT TAXES

INCOME TAX

Income tax is charged under the Indian Income Tax Act, 1961. It is an annual tax on income of both individuals and companies levied by the union government. Every person, whose total income exceeds the maximum exemption limit, is chargeable to the income tax at the rates prescribed in the Finance Act passed each year by the parliament. The income tax is paid on the total income of an individual, determined on the basis of her/his residential status in India.

The tax is charged in respect of the income of the previous year - that is the financial year, beginning on 1st April and ending on 31st March -and the same is chargeable in the assessment year - that is the next financial year. In the taxable income are included the following heads: salaries; income from house property; profits and gains of business or profession; capital gains; income from other sources. The basis of taxation is the gross receipts after deducting the related expenses incurred in connection with earning such receipts. Such deductions, determined according to rules varying from head to head of income, are allowed from the aggregate of income and are in the nature of incentive provisions of different kinds. The main deductions are the following:

- Standard deduction – available to certain taxpayers receiving salary or pension;
- Entertainment allowance – provided to government employees that may claim a deduction up to 20 percent of their salaries or 5,000 rupees, whichever is lower, for certain entertainment allowances granted by the employer;
- Tax – for any sum paid by an employee on account of state or municipal tax on employment;
- Annuity and insurance payment – up to 10,000 rupees per annum for payments made in respect of an annuity contract in order to receive a pension;
- Repayment of loan – deduction of up to 40,000 rupees per annum for the repayment, including interest, of loans used to finance higher education; deduction of up to 150,000 rupees in respect of interest

on capital borrowed to purchase or construct owner-occupied residential property;

- Donation – to charities approved for tax purposes up to the limit prescribed by the tax authorities,
- Investment income – up to 9,000 rupees per annum in respect of interest received from certain specified investment, including dividends from cooperative societies and interest on bank deposits; up to 3,000 per annum for interest received from government securities;
- Permanent physical disability – up to 40,000 rupees for a permanent physical disability certified by a competent person.

Other deductions are granted as tax incentives: for example, new export-oriented undertakings are entitled to an exemption from income tax; new industrial undertakings that fulfill certain conditions are entitled to a deduction of the profits for a period of 10 consecutive assessment years; a deduction of 50 percent of profits is available to hotels in hilly/rural areas and pilgrimage centers and so forth. After reducing the gross total income by the amount of deductions, what is left is the total income that is the basis for taxation. If the total income is below the basic exemption limit, no tax is chargeable. All receipts having the character of income are taxable unless they are specifically exempt from taxation. For tax purposes spouses are treated separately and generally their income is not clubbed. On the contrary, income of all minors, except handicapped ones, is clubbed with the income of their parents, unless the income is derived from manual work or an activity involving skill, specialized knowledge and experience. Different types of assessments are provided:

- Self-assessment;
- Regular assessment;
- Best judgment assessment.

WEALTH TAX

Wealth tax is charged under the Indian Wealth Tax Act, 1957 and the union government levies it. The tax is charged on individuals, Hindu Undivided Families and companies in respect of the net wealth held by them during the assessment year. Indian citizens, resident companies and HUF are charged in respect of their worldwide assets, whereas non-resident is charged in respect of assets located in India. Net wealth is the aggregate of the assets owned by the taxpayer, less the debts owned by her/him relative to the taxable assets. From the computation of net wealth some assets are excluded. Among the assets subject to wealth tax there are, for example: buildings, or land belonging with them, used for residential or commercial purposes or as a guest house or farm house, within 25 km of the local limits or cantonment board; motor cars; jewels or precious metals; yachts, boats and aircraft; urban land;

cash in hand in excess of ₹ 50,000. Among the entities that are exempt from the wealth tax there are: any social club; any political party; any cooperative society; any company whose object is the promotion of art, science, religion, charity, commerce, etc... The rate is 1 percent on net wealth exceeding ₹ 1.5 million. It is provided a self-assessment scheme.

OTHER TAXES ON CAPITAL AND PROPERTY

Other taxes on capital and property are levied by the states and the local authorities. The states impose: - a land tax on the value of land; - a tax on motor vehicles, whose yield is used for the development and the maintenance of state roads. The local authorities impose: - land cesses in the form of a surcharge on land revenue; - a tax on land and buildings, generally based on the annual rental value; - betterment taxes, based on increases of land value caused by town planning and town improvement; - taxes on the transfer of immovable property, based on the value of the property and in addition to state stamp duty.

EXPENDITURE TAX

The expenditure tax is charged under the Indian Expenditure-tax Act, 1987 and it is imposed by the union government. The tax is charged at the rate of 10 percent on any chargeable expenditure incurred in a hotel wherein the room charges for any unit of residential accommodation are three thousand rupees or more per day. The expenditure tax is collected by the person who carries on the business of such hotel. The tax collected during any calendar month is paid to the credit of the union government by the 10th of the month immediately following the said calendar month. Any person responsible for collecting the expenditure tax who fails to collect it shall pay, in addition to paying the tax, a sum equal to the amount of tax that s/he failed to collect. From the 1st October, 1991 to the 31st May, 1992 a tax at the rate of 15 percent of the chargeable expenditure incurred in a restaurant was levied.

INDIRECT TAXES

CUSTOMS DUTIES

The Constitution has given to the union the right to legislate and collect duties on goods imported into or exported from India. The Customs Act, 1962 is the basic Statute, effective from 1st February 1963. The categories of items and the rates of duties which are leviable have been specified in two schedules to the Customs Tariff Act, 1975. The first schedule specifies the various categories of import items, in accordance with an international scheme of classification of internationally traded goods. All goods are classified into categories, called "headings" and "subheadings"; for each sub-heading, a specific rate of duty is prescribed. The duties are levied both on specific and ad-valorem basis, while there are few cases where at times specific-cum-ad valorem duties are also collected on imported items. Where advalorem duties are collected, the value of the goods has to be determined for customs duty purposes according to WTO Valuation Agreement. Under the Custom Tariff Act, 1975 and other laws, there are the following types of duties that are leviable:

- Basic Customs Duty - that is duty specified against each heading or sub-heading in the first schedule. There are different rates of duty for different commodities and there are preferential rates for goods imported from certain countries in accordance with bilateral agreements with such countries. The duty may be ad valorem or specific.
- Surcharge - that is levied at the rate of 10% of the Basic Customs Duty on imported goods, unless exempted by a notification.
- Additional duty of customs - equivalent to the excise duty leviable on goods produced or manufactured in India. Generally it is on ad valorem basis, though specific rates are prescribed for some items. For imported goods to be used as inputs for manufacture of other goods, it is generally eligible for a credit equal to the additional duty of customs paid on the imported goods. This credit can be used for paying central excise duties.
- Special additional duty – whose amount is computed by applying the specified rate on the total of the assessable value, the basic customs duty and the additional duty of customs described above.

There are also additional levies on particular items and other levies which are specific to the country of origin. Among the later there are anti-dumping duty, on specified goods imported from specified countries to protect indigenous industry, and safeguard duty, applicable on certain goods for specified periods in order to check their excessive imports which may damage the Indian industry. The rates vary and are based on official notification. The custom duty on exports is levied on items listed in the second schedule to Customs Tariff Act, 1975. Currently, the rates vary from 10 to 60 percent and they are either ad valorem, specific or a combination of both. Very few items are subject to customs duties on their export. In order to make the exports more competitive, it is provided a duty exemption scheme for registered exporters so that they may import the inputs required for export production at international prices and free from duty. Imported items that are exempt from customs duty are raw materials, components and consumables.

CENTRAL EXCISE DUTIES

Central excise duties are charged under the Central Excise Act, 1944 at the rates specified in the schedules to the Central Excise Tariff Act, 1985. They are an indirect tax levied on goods produced or manufactured in India, excluding those produced or manufactured in special economic zones. There are several types of duties which become payable at the time of clearance of such goods. These duties are:

- Basic excise duty actually called the "Central Value Added Tax.
- Special excise duty.
- Additional duties of excise.
- Cess.

The duty is payable by the manufacturer at the time of removal of goods from the factory premises or warehouse; the taxable base is the wholesale price of the goods manufactured. However, to achieve particular objectives - for example, to promote exports, to avoid multiple taxation, to promote educational and research activities, or to encourage the use of specified raw material - it is in the power of the central government to exempt certain excisable goods from the whole or any part of the duty leviable on such goods. The general rate of the basic excise duty in 2002/2003 is 16 percent, but there are a number of items that are subject to either a "nil" or ad valorem rate. In the same fiscal year the special excise duty is levied at a rate of 16 percent, although there are a number of items subject to a rate of 8 percent; additional duties of excise are imposed at rates ranging from 5 percent to 18 percent, or at ad valorem rates.

Cess is applied at varying rates. Unless the assessee is a cigarette manufacturer, a self-assessment procedure is provided.

SERVICE TAX

Service tax was introduced in India for the first time in 1994. It extends to whole of India except the state of Jammu and Kashmir. It is levied, collected and appropriated by the union government. Service tax is levied on specified taxable services and the responsibility of payment of the tax is cast on the service provider. The Finance Act 2001 introduced selfassessment for service tax returns, which are expected to be filled half yearly and by the 25th of the month following the half-year.

This is in replacement of the monthly/quarterly returns prescribed earlier. Initially the service tax was imposed on the following services: telephone, stockbroker, general insurance. Over the years it was extended to other services, as advertising agencies and courier agencies. At present the total number of services on which service tax is levied has gone up to 58, despite withdrawal of certain services from the tax net or grant of exemptions. In the budget 2003-04 more services have been added to the tax net and the levy of service tax on these services is effective from July 1st, 2003. Service tax is levied on the gross or aggregate amount charged by the service provider on the receiver; only in particular cases the tax is permitted to be paid on the value received. Since the 14th May 2003 it is collected at a rate of 8 percent, while the previous rate was 5 percent. To reduce the cascading impact of tax on tax and to help restoring competitiveness of service sector, a credit of the service tax paid on the input-service is allowed since 2002. At present the assessee can avail of input credit in respect of any of the categories of the services and utilize the said service tax credit for payment of service tax on any of the output services.

SALES TAX

Sales tax is charged under the Central Sales Tax Act, 1956. It is levied on the sale or purchase of goods. There are two kinds of sales tax:

- Central sales tax, imposed by the union government;
- Sales tax, imposed by each state. Central sales tax is generally payable on the sale of all goods by a dealer in the course of inter-state trade and commerce and it is levied in the state where the movement of goods commences.

Although the tax is imposed by the central government, the revenue is administered by the state in which it is levied. The taxable base is determined by applying the appropriate rate, depending on the type of transaction, to the dealer's turnover. Sales tax on intra-state sale or purchase of goods may only be imposed by the state in which the sale or purchase takes place. Nearly all the states impose sales taxes at rates that range from 4 to 15 percent.

SOME CRITICAL ISSUES OF THE INDIAN TAX SYSTEM

THE LARGE PREVALENCE OF A COMPLEX SYSTEM OF INDIRECT TAXES

We have already noticed that the Indian tax system is still largely made up of a big, complex and entangled bundle of excises and sales taxes. The room of direct taxation, both on individuals and companies, is very smaller. Formal rates are not particularly low, especially for corporations but the wideness of the bases is just so. Such a system -we have already reminded- is not just a consequence of free tax policy choices, but mainly draws its model from the severe constraints - economic, social and administrative in nature - , which limit the room of manoeuvre to build the tax system of developing countries. The large prevalence of a complex system of indirect taxes however raises a number of critical issues that require some discussion.

The limited share of direct taxes on individuals

The per capita income is not the only explaining factor of the total fiscal pressure, as well as of the level of a particular tax. Anyway, it is a key factor and a starting point to compare different countries' tax levels, not to be disregarded. Put the issue in that way, the current level of personal income tax in India stays about one third below the figure computed by the prevailing literature with reference to the bracket that encompasses the Indian per capita income. Why not a bigger amount of PIT? Why just 32 million of taxpayers file income's tax return, over a population of more than 1 billion and sixty five million people? A first argument to limit the room of income tax could be the need to preserve poverty incomes from taxation. Otherwise avoiding any taxation of the poor' consumption is virtually impossible. It is also commonly recognized that consumption taxes tend to be regressive, especially in developing countries, if they are not coupled with commanding and administratively costly measures of prices' subsides, in kind rations and transfers. Furthermore the rates should be scheduled according to a steeply -revenue reducing- increasing tax rates' profile. Might well be that a proper behaved structure of larger income taxation could cooperate to do a better redistributive job. Of course also agriculture incomes should be taxed at a non-negligible level, but without burdening poor peasant households. Land tax may be a good solution in terms of both efficiency and equity. It also is often assumed that the costs of administration and compliance are higher for direct than for indirect taxes, especially inside the informal setting of developing countries' economies. Here the true difficulty is more specific but common to the two kinds of taxation: the need to improve the capabilities of both the tax administration and of the taxpayers.

In this connection, it has been demonstrated that simple reforms of personnel policy inside the Indian income tax administration can imply significant enforcement and compliance gains so that to reduce the cost of collection per unit of yield. Furthermore, when one looks at the complexity system of the Indian indirect taxes, the unavoidable suspicion arises of not having to cope with an inexpensive system of tax collection. Finally, according to standard economic theory, consumption taxes would be more saving preserving and income taxes could induce supply disincentives, especially as steeper is their rates' schedule. Notice however that these arguments mainly apply to countries where the per capita income is already higher than it is today in India. On the contrary, we may infer that the taxation has little to do with the savings in a still so poor country and with the labor supply in a country where the employed workers are not more than 24 percent of the total population.

Broadening companies' tax base

The native literature unambiguously recognizes that the corporate backward effective rates are far lower than the legal ones. This is mainly due to tax holidays for new small undertakings and venture capitals, to incentives to exports, to a lot of allowances for FDI, to deductions for particular sectors. This happens when it is well recognized by a general authoritative opinion that playing the field and reducing the standard rate is more incentives inducing than the sector allowances, in transition and developing economies too.

Rationalizing indirect taxes

We have already noticed that the present large system of indirect taxes is quite complicated and confused. A state sales tax is added to the national excise duties. The national excises hit goods at the production stage, while the services are subject to a different separate tax. Furthermore, the national excises are organized in a multiclasses structure, according to various types of goods. In its turn, the sales tax is set by the central government for the inter-states trade and by the states themselves for the intra-states trade. This system unavoidably raises cascading effects and may result in random 'all in' rates charged on final goods and services.

Many recent government's reports underline the need to deeply rationalize the structure of the indirect taxation and to improve the tax administration and the tax-payers compliance, also to reduce the costs of collection. Since some years the long-term strategy is in the direction of a double Vat system. Just some excise duties on particular goods should survive. Unambiguously the literature favors this move whose current steps are reported below. Anyway, the setting of rates will not be easy: the unavoidable trade-off between equity and efficiency clearly emerged in a seminal paper devoted just to India. Finally a deep reform of what accounts for about 60 percent of total taxation will not be easy neither without risk of an, at least temporary, revenue's losses. All this would make unsustainable the Indian budget position, already suffering a high level deficit.

INTERGOVERNMENTAL FISCAL RELATIONS

As already noted, India is a federal republic and its government consists of a central government, 28 state governments and 7 union territories. Many states have autonomous regions with regional councils and in different states there are three tiers of local bodies. There also are 602 districts administered by their respective state/UT government. The Indian federal system is quite centralized. Indian Constitution makers divided the government functions in three lists: federal, state and concurrent. Under the Seventh Schedule of the Indian Constitution, the central government has exclusive powers on foreign policy, defence, communications, currency, taxation on corporations and non-agricultural income, and railroads; while state governments have the exclusive power to legislate on such subjects as law and order, public health and sanitation, local government, betting and gambling, and taxation on agricultural income, entertainment, and alcoholic beverages. On some issues both the central government and state governments may legislate, though a union law generally takes precedence.

Among these areas are criminal law, marriage and divorce, contracts, economic and social planning, population control and family planning, trade unions, social security, and education. All residuary issues lie within the exclusive domain of the central government. An exceedingly important power of the central government is that of creating new states, combining states, changing state boundaries, and terminating a state's existence. The central government may also create and dissolve any of the union territories, which have more limited powers than those of the states. Although the states exercise either exclusive or joint control over a substantial range of issues, the Constitution establishes a more dominant role for the union government. The assignment of tax powers is based on the principle of separation; most broad based taxes are assigned to the centre, whereas in practice the states have a narrower tax base and the consequence is a vertical fiscal imbalance. In 2002-03 the states on average raised about 38 percent of central revenues, but incurred about 58 percent of expenditures.

The capacity of the states to finance their current expenditures from their own sources of revenues has declined from 69 percent in 1955-56 to 52 percent in 2002-03. Transfers from the centre made up the balance. The inadequacy of the states to meet expenditures from their own resources is recognized by the Constitution of India at Articles 275 and 282. Grants-in-aid under Article 275 are need-based, on the recommendations of the Finance Commission, while grants under Article 282 are purpose-based, in the sense that the central government has the power to make discretionary grants to the states. The Finance Commission is appointed by the President of India every five years or earlier if needed and it is the mechanism provided by the Constitution to regulate the flow of transfers from the central government to the states and their allocation among different states. Generally, the Finance Commission makes recommendations on the following matters:

- The distribution between the union and the states of the net proceeds of taxes which are to be divided between them under Chapter I Part XII of the Constitution and the allocation among the states of the respective shares of such proceeds;
- The principles which should govern the grants-in-aid of the revenues of the states out of the consolidated Fund of India and the sums to be paid to the states which are in need of assistance by way of grants-in-aid of their revenues under article 275 of the Constitution;
- The measures needed to augment the consolidated Fund of a state to supplement the resources of the panchayats and municipalities in the state on the basis of the recommendations made by the Finance Commission of the state.

Moreover, the Commission reviews the financial situation of the union and the states and suggests a plan by which the governments, collectively and severally, may bring about a restructuring of the public finances restoring budgetary balance, achieving macro-economic stability and debt reduction along with equitable growth. Over the last fifty years the Finance Commissions have elaborated a sophisticated methodology to deal with horizontal and vertical fiscal imbalances. To distribute horizontally the two major taxes that are shared between the centre and the states the Finance Commissions used a large number of criteria, among which: population, tax effort, collection assessment, income distance, income adjusted total population, indices of social and economic backwardness, territorial area, post-devolution deficits, poverty, revenue equalization, etc.. The Eleventh Finance Commission set a new benchmark in the centre-state fiscal relations: it reduced weight of population from 20-30 percent in the recent past to 10 percent, maintained weight of income distance criterion at 62.5 percent and chose to allocate 27.5 percent of states' share of pooled proceeds according to area, infrastructure, tax effort and fiscal discipline.

The central government also distributes substantial grants to the states through its development plans as elaborated by the Planning Commission. While the Finance Commission decides on tax shares and makes grants-in-aid, the Planning Commission makes grants and loans to implement development plans. It is worth to notice the problem of coordination between the two independent commissions that arises. The loan-grant composition of the assistance given to special category states is 10:90 while that to other states is 70:30. Before 1969, plan transfers were project-based; since then, the distribution has been done on the basis of a formula that takes into account population, per capita income, fiscal performance and special problems. Plan revenue grants make about 7-8 percent of the total revenue receipts of the union.

TAX REFORMS

A QUICK GLANCE AT MACRO ECONOMIC AND BUDGET OUTLOOK

Over the last two decades the Indian economy made significant improvements at an annual average growth rate rising from 2.9 percent in the 1970s to 5.8 percent in the 1990s. Notwithstanding this improvement, the per capita income remains very low in comparison with other East Asian countries, particularly China, which had the same level of per capita income as India in the 1970s. The progress in growth was accompanied by structural changes quite different from those experienced in other developing countries, where a decline in the share of agriculture in GDP was coupled by a remarkable expansion of industry. In India between the 1970s and 2003-04, the share of agriculture and allied sectors in GDP declined from an average of 42.8 percent to 22.1 percent, while that of services rose from an average of 34.5 percent to 51.0 percent.

The share of industry showed a little increase from an average of 22.8 percent to 26.9 percent. In 2002-03 the GDP growth decelerated from 5.8 percent of the previous year to 4.0 percent, mainly because of a heavy decline of 5.2 percent in the agriculture and allied sectors, due to a severe drought. In

2003-04 real GDP at factor cost has been estimated to have grown by 8.2 percent, sustained by a growth of 9.1 percent in agriculture and allied sectors, 6.7 percent in industry sector and 8.7 percent in the services sector. The growth recovery in 2003-04 was accompanied by a relative stability of prices; inflation, as measured by the wholesale price index was 5.5 percent on average, while retail price inflation, as measured by the consumer price index for industrial workers, declined from 5.1 percent in April 2003 to 2.2 percent in April 2004. Higher growth rates are needed for the rapid elimination of poverty, in spite of the fact that there already was a significant decline in the poverty ratio from 36 percent in 1993-94 to 25 percent in 2001-02.

In recent years domestic demand was the main driver of growth; during the period 1998-99 to 2002-03, on average, the contributions of private final consumption expenditure and investment to growth of GDP at current market prices were 64.2 percent and 21.0 percent respectively. Since 2001-02 the current account of India's balance of payments recorded a surplus, indicating that the rest of the world has contributed to support aggregate demand; moreover, a strong balance of payments position in recent years resulted in a steady accumulation of foreign exchange reserves. Public finances, which have been under pressure since 1997-98 on account of the pay revision of government employees and the economic slowdown, showed a further deterioration. The fiscal deficit of the central government, in GDP terms, after declining from 6.6 percent in 1990-91 to 4.1 percent in 1996-97, started rising to 5.3 percent in 2002-03.

The deterioration in revenue deficit was sharper: in 1990-91 it reached 3.3 percent of GDP, then declined to 2.4 percent in 1996-97 and started rising to 4.4 percent in 2002-03. The main factors that have contributed to this deterioration have been rising expenditure on salaries, interest payments unfounded pensions, improperly targeted subsidies and stagnation in the tax-GDP ratio that continue to remain at a lower level even as compared with the pre-reform year of 1990-91. The tax-GDP ratio for the central government declined from 10.1 percent in 1990-91 to 8.8 percent in 2002-03 and the decline was entirely due to the sharp decrease in the ratio of indirect taxes to GDP. That decrease was mainly imputable to the reduction of customs duty provided by the tax reforms to improve both resource allocation and efficiency and to make Indian manufacturing competitive.

The total expenditure-GDP ratio of the central government, after declining from 17.3 percent in 1990-91 to 13.9 percent in 1996-97, started rising from 14.2 percent in 1997-98 to 16.2 percent in 2002-03. The fiscal situation improved in 2003-04: in the revised estimate, the fiscal deficit and the revenue deficit came down, respectively, to 4.8 and 3.6 percent of GDP. The deterioration in the fiscal situation of the states was even sharper. The fiscal deficit increased from 3.3 percent of GDP in 1990-91 to 4.7 percent in the revised estimates for 2002-03. In the same period the revenue deficit deteriorated from 0.9 percent to 2.5 percent of GDP on account of the growing burden of interest payments, pension liabilities and administrative expenditure. Losses of state owned public enterprises, inappropriate user charges and deceleration in central transfers finished the job of deteriorating revenue deficit. The combined fiscal deficit of the center and the states increased from a level of 9.4 percent of GDP in 1990-91 to a level of 10.1 percent of GDP in the revised estimates for 2002- 03, whereas the combined revenue deficit as a proportion of GDP was 4.2 percent and 6.7 percent in the same years.

TAX REFORMS OF LAST YEARS, UNDER WAY AND PLANNED

In 1991, in reaction to a severe macroeconomic crisis involving high fiscal deficits, India carried out a series of economic reforms, among which a tax reform. Tax reform strategy was largely based on the Raja Chelliah Committee Report. The main proposals put forth by the Committee comprised: a) the reduction in the rates of the most important taxes - namely individual and corporate income taxes, excises, customs – still maintaining the progressivity of the system but not such as to induce evasion; b) the enlargement of the tax base of all taxes by reducing exemptions and concessions; c) the transformation of the taxes on domestic production into a value added tax; d) the simplification of laws and procedures to make the administration and enforcement of the tax system more effective. Most of the Committee's recommendations have been implemented over the years, at least at the central level. Relative to personal income tax, to try to decrease tax evasion there have been a strong reduction of tax rates, both in the number and in the value, the tax threshold was raised from ₹ 40,000 to ₹ 50,000, and the number of brackets was reduced from seven to three. Also the rates of corporate income tax were reduced but there was not a wide broadening of the corporation tax's base, mainly due to tax holidays and rapid depreciation given to investments in many activities.

Notwithstanding the reduction in the marginal tax rates, the revenues from personal and corporate income taxes increased after the reforms and therefore the share of revenue from direct taxes as a proportion of GDP showed a significant increase. A not-unimportant share of that increase was due to the voluntary disclosure scheme that was introduced in 1997-98 to provide an opportunity for individuals, companies and non-resident Indians to declare their concealed income and assets by paying 30 percent tax. There also were reductions in the wealth tax rate and in the basic exemption of the gift tax. As regards the tariffs, both the average and peak tariff rates were drastically reduced, whereas in terms of rate differentiation the number of tax rates remained high and in more recent years has even increased.

In the case of union excise duties there was an important simplification and rationalization: the number of rates was reduced and, in respect of the majority of commodities, the tax was progressively transformed from a specific into ad valorem levy. Exemptions and the lowest rate were removed thus broadening the tax base. A tax on specific services was introduced in 1994-95 and successively that tax was extended to a large number of services. The reforms' effect on revenue was to reduce it: the improvement in direct tax revenue only partly compensated the decline in indirect tax revenue, mainly due to the reduction in import duty rates and in excise duty rates for items of mass consumption.

While the reform of the central government's tax system has been implemented during the 1990', although not completely, in the case of the states the reforms of their tax systems did not proceed, notwithstanding the recommendations of the study group appointed by the Government of India to rationalize and harmonize the states tax systems themselves. In September 2002 the Government set up a new Task Force on tax reforms and successively a Task Force on Implementation of Fiscal Responsibility and Budget Act, 2003 both headed by Vijay Kelkar. The Kelkar committees had suggested sweeping reforms including:

- Raising income tax exemption limit to ₹ 100,000 and two-tier rate structure;
- Cut in corporate tax rate from 35.875 percent to 30 percent for domestic companies - to remove the gap between the peak rate for personal income tax and the corporate tax rate - and cut in depreciation rate for plant and machinery to 15 percent from 25 percent;
- Three-rate basic customs duty structure (raw materials 5 percent, intermediate goods 8 percent and finished goods 10 percent);
- Service tax levied in a comprehensive manner, leaving out only few services (public utilities and social services) to be included in a negative list;
- Abolition of wealth tax;
- Merging of tax on expenditure in hotels with service tax;
- Abolition of the concessional treatment of long-term capital gains through a reduced scheduler tax rate;
- Removal of tax exemptions, rationalization of incentives for savings and simplification of procedures;
- Gradual moving over the destination based, consumption type value added taxes at the state level.

The decision to introduce VAT was discussed first at a conference of state chief ministers and finance ministers in 1999 and the deadline of April 2002 was decided to bring in the tax. However the introduction of VAT was postponed to April 2003 and successively to April 2005, mainly because of the lack of administrative preparation of some states. Moreover, there was not an agreement between the central government and the states on the system of compensating the states that incur revenue loss on account of VAT's implementation. Only on 2 November 2004 that agreement has been reached after all states, except three, declared they were ready with the necessary legislation. Therefore, sales taxes of the states are going to be replaced with a harmonized VAT from April 2005, based on a blueprint finalized by the empowered committee of state finance ministers. Meanwhile in July 2004 the above quoted Task Force on Implementation of the FRBM Act has come up with a proposal for an integrated VAT on goods and services to be levied by the central government and the states in parallel, removing all cascading taxes, such as, for example, octroi, central sales tax, state level sales taxes etc.. The Task Force proposed a "grand bargain" whereby the states would have the power to tax all services currently with the center, and therefore both central and state government would exercise concurrent but independent jurisdiction over common tax bases extending over all goods and services.

The new goods and services tax (GST) would have three ad valorem rates, in addition to the zero rate. The proposed rate structure considers a floor rate, equal to 6 percent for the centre and 4 percent for the states, a standard rate, equal to 12 percent for the center (to replace the CENVAT of 16 percent) and 8 percent for the states, and a higher rate, equal to 20 percent for the centre and 14 percent for the states. Under this proposal, the total tax burden on most goods and services would work out to 20 percent, comparable with the standard VAT rates in OECD countries. Moreover, the treatment of imports and exports should be fully integrated with the dual-GST system. In particular, for imports a two-part levy should replace the countervailing duty (CVD) proposed with the first part reflecting the central GST and the second reflecting state-level GST. All imports should be charged to the central and state GST at the same rate applicable to domestic goods.

According to this proposal, the states would obtain revenues from taxation of services and from access to GST on imports, but, in our opinion, their fiscal autonomy should be undermined owing to the uniform rates across the states. According to the Task Force, the reforms proposed would have great positive implications for India's outlook and would make the most of tax system, as part of efforts to cancel revenue deficit and lower fiscal deficit to less than 3.0 percent of GDP by 2009. Moreover, the implementation of the proposed fiscal reforms should reduce both tax evasion and costs of compliance, and should eliminate most of the distorted behavior coming from tax avoidance.

INDIAN TAX REFORMS SINCE 1991

There have been major changes in tax systems of countries with a wide variety of economic systems and levels of development during the last two decades. The motivation for these reforms has varied from one country to another and the thrust of reforms has differed from time to time depending on the development strategy and philosophy of the times. In many developing countries, the immediate reason for tax reforms, has been the need to enhance revenues to meet impending fiscal crises. As Bird states, "...fiscal crisis has been proven to be the mother of tax reform". Such reforms, however, are often ad hoc and are done to meet immediate exigencies of revenue. In most cases, such reforms are not in the nature of systemic improvements to enhance the long run productivity of the tax system. One of the most important reasons for recent tax reforms in many developing and transitional economies has been to evolve a tax system to meet the requirements of international competition.

The transition from a predominantly centrally planned development strategy to market based resource allocation has changed the perspective of the role of the state in development. The transition from a public sector based, heavy industry dominated, import substituting industrialization strategy to one of allocating resources according to market signals has necessitated systemic changes in the tax system. In an export-led open economy, the tax system should not only raise the necessary revenues to provide the social and physical infrastructure but also minimize distortions. Thus, the tax system has to adjust to the requirements of a market economy to ensure international competitiveness. As in other countries, the systemic reforms in the tax system in India in the 1990s were the product of crisis but the reforms were calibrated on the basis of detailed analysis.

The objective of this paper is to analyse the evolution of the India tax system with special reference to the systemic reforms in the design and implementation of the structure and operation of the taxes in Indian federal polity. In section I, the evolution of tax system reforms, alternative paradigms employed in reform exercises in different countries and the best practice approaches to reform are described to provide a framework for analysing the Indian tax reform experience. Section II describes the Indian tax system and the reform initiatives undertaken until the comprehensive tax reform exercise was taken up in 1991. The salient features of comprehensive tax reform since 1991 and its impact on revenues are analysed in section III. The last section brings out the major shortcomings still persisting in the tax system and lists the challenges faced by the government in developing a co-ordinated tax system in the Indian federal polity.

PARADIGMS OF TAX REFORM

The philosophy of tax reform has undergone significant changes over the years in keeping with the changing perception of the role of the state. With the change in the development strategy in favour of market determined resource allocation, the traditional approach of raising revenues to finance a large public sector without much regard to economic effects has been given up. The recent approaches to reform lay emphasis on minimizing distortions in tax policy to keep the economy competitive. Minimizing distortions implies reducing the marginal rates of both direct and indirect taxes. This also calls for reducing differentiation in tax rates to reduce unintended distortions in relative prices. To achieve this, the approach suggests broadening of the tax bases. Thus, over the years, emphasis has shifted from vertical equity in which both direct and indirect taxes are subject to high marginal rates with minute differentiation in rates, to horizontal equity in which, the taxes are broad-based, simple and transparent, and subject to low and less differentiated rates. Equity in general, is taken to mean improving the living conditions of the poor.

This has to be achieved mainly through expenditure policy and human resource development rather than reducing the incomes of the rich as was envisaged in the 1950s and 1960s. Conventional wisdom on tax reforms provides us with at least three different model of tax reform. The optimal tax (OT) model is satisfactory in terms of its theoretical soundness, but has been found to be impractical in its applications. Besides the trade-off between efficiency and equity in tax policy, the information and administrative costs of designing an optimal tax model have been found to be prohibitive and, therefore, as a practical guide to tax policy this has not been useful. The Harberger tax model (HT) like the OT model is well grounded in theory. It, however, draws much more on practical experience. According to this, while efficiency is clearly desirable in the design of tax policy, administrative capability is equally, if not more, important.

The principal concern, according to this approach, is not to design a system that will be optimal, but emphasise the system that will minimize tax-induced distortions and at the same time be administratively feasible and politically acceptable. In fact, Harberger suggests that tax reformers should pay less attention to the economic methodology and more to best practice experiences.

The basic HT reform package for developing countries that are price takers in the international market consists of, inter alia, a uniform tariff and a broad-based VAT. The third is the supply-side tax model (SST). This model emphasises the need to reduce the role of the state. Reduction in the volume of public expenditures has to be achieved by cutting the tax rates, particularly the direct tax rates to minimize disincentives on work, saving and investment.

The proponents of this model emphasise the need to broaden the base with minimal exemptions and preferences and to have low marginal tax rates. Again emphasis is on minimizing distortions in relative prices and, therefore, the approach emphasises less rate differentiation. The recent reform approaches combine elements of all three models sketched above. This incorporates both theory and past reform experiences and takes into account administrative, political and information constraints in designing and implementing reforms. The thrust of this approach is to enhance the revenue productivity of the tax system while minimizing relative price distortions. The best practice approach has attempted to make the tax systems comprehensive, simple and transparent. As mentioned earlier, the general pattern of these reforms has been to broaden the base of taxes, reduce the tax rates and lower the rate differentiation both in direct and indirect taxes. A broader base requires lower rates to be levied to generate a given amount of revenues.

Lower marginal rates not only reduce disincentives to work, save and invest, but also help to improve tax compliance. More importantly, broadening the tax base helps to ensure horizontal equity, is desirable from the political economy point of view as it reduces the influence of special interest groups on tax policy, and reduces administrative costs. In the case of indirect taxation, the reform agenda includes the levy of a broad-based VAT with minimal exemptions and supplemented by a few luxury excises. As regards import duties, quantitative restrictions should be replaced by tariffs, export taxes eliminated, and dispersion in tariffs should be minimized. Personal income tax too is to be levied on all but a small number of persons with income levels less than twice the per capita income of the country.

Much of the direct taxes should be collected by withholding, but for the "hard-to-tax" groups, presumptive taxation is to be applied. Emphasis on horizontal equity also implies emphasis on strengthening administration and enforcement of the tax and the development of proper information systems and automation.

INDIA'S TAX SYSTEM PRIOR TO COMPREHENSIVE REFORMS 1991

The trends in tax revenues presented in table present three distinct phases.

Table. Level and Compostition of taxes in india (%)

Tax	*1970-71*	*1980-81*	*1990-91*	*1995-96*	*1996-97*	*1997-98*
Direct taxes of which:	21.3	16.4	14.0	20.4	20.5	23.6
Corporation tax	7.8	6.6	6.1	9.4	9.3	9.4
Personal Income tax	10.0	7.6	6.1	8.9	9.1	12.6
Agricultural taxes	2.8	1.0	0.9	0.8	0.6	0.6
Others	0.7	1.2	0.9	1.3	1.5	1.0
Indirect taxes of which:	78.7	83.6	86.0	79.6	79.5	76.4
Customs	11.0	17.2	23.5	20.4	21.4	18.0
Union excise duties	37.0	32.8	27.9	22.9	22.5	20.9
Sales tax	16.6	20.3	20.8	20.4	21.1	21.2
State excise duties	4.1	4.2	5.7	4.9	4.5	5.0
Others	10.0	9.1	8.1	10.9	10.0	11.3
Total tax revenue	100.0	100.0	100.0	100.0	100.0	100.0
Tax-GDP percentage	11.0	14.6	16.4	14.4	14.2	14.6

In the first, right from the 1970s to mid-1980s, there has been a steady increase in the tax-GDP ratio in keeping with the buoyant economic conditions and acceleration in the growth rate of the economy. The tax ratio, which was about 11 per cent in 1970-71, increased steadily to 14.6 per cent in 1980-81. The ratio continued to increase steadily during the early 1980s.

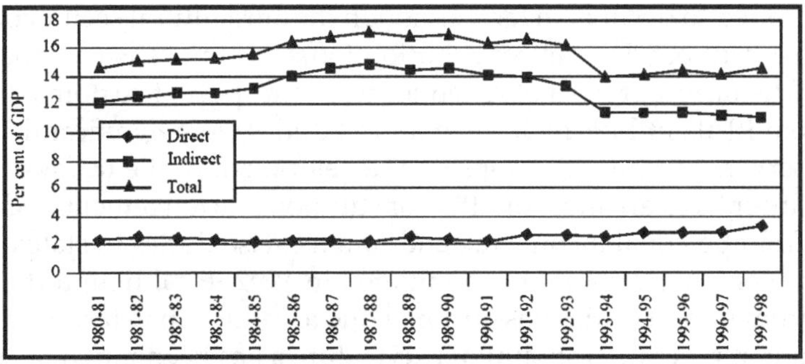

Fig. Chart trends in direct and indirect taxes

In addition to the economy attaining a higher growth path, the buoyancy in tax revenues was fuelled by the progressive substitution of quantitative restrictions with tariffs following initial attempts at economic liberalization in the 1980s.

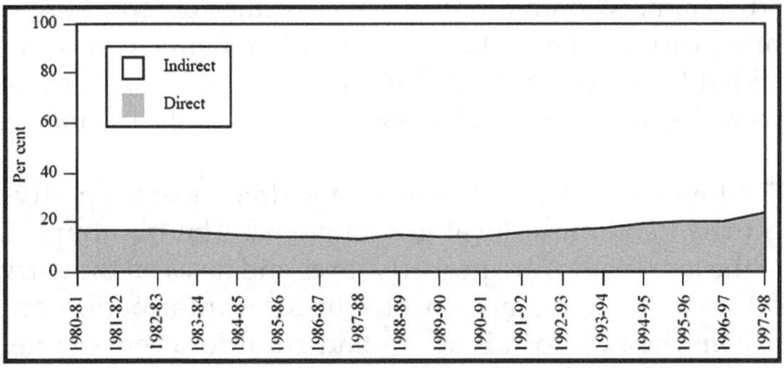

Fig. Chart the Shares of direct and indirect taxes

The economic recession following the severe drought of 1987 resulted in stagnation in revenues in the second phase until 1992-93. Following the economic crisis of 1991 and the subsequent reforms in the tax system, particularly reduction in tariffs, actually caused a decline in the tax ratio. Overall, it is seen that the tax ratio which reached the peak of about 17 per cent in 1987-88, declined thereafter to 13.9 per cent in 1993-94 and gradually recovered to 14.6 per cent in 1997-98. Overall, the level of tax revenues, although reasonable as compared to the average tax level in developing countries, is clearly inadequate from the viewpoint of resource requirements of the economy. In terms of composition of tax revenue, there has been a steady decline in the share of direct taxes from 21 per cent in 1970-71 to about 14 per cent in 1990-91.

After the introduction of tax reforms in 1992, the revenue from direct taxes has grown faster than revenue from other taxes as well as GDP and consequently, the share of direct taxes increased by almost ten percentage points to 24 per cent on 1997-98. An increase was seen in both corporate income and individual income taxes though, taxes on agricultural land and incomes have continued to decline. In fact, although the agricultural sector contributes over 30 per cent of GDP, its contribution to tax revenues is just about half a per cent. The fastest growth of revenues was in respect of customs during the period from 1970 until 1992-93, when import duties were significantly reduced. Some observers attribute this lopsided development of the tax system to the perverse incentives arising from the constitutional arrangement of devolving revenue from personal income tax and union excise duties to states. It is also seen that even after reforms were initiated in 1992-93, although the share of revenue from import duties has declined due to reduction in tariffs, the decline in the share of revenue from union excise duties has been much faster. In the Indian federal polity, both central and state governments exercise revenue powers and the latter raise about 37 per cent of total revenues.

The Seventh Schedule to the Constitution specifies revenue sources of the centre and the states respectively in the union and state lists. The major tax powers of the central government consist of taxes on non-agricultural income and wealth, corporate profits, excise duties except those on alcohol and customs duties. The states, on the other hand, can levy taxes on agricultural land, incomes and wealth, excises on alcohol, sales taxes, taxes on motor vehicles and goods and passengers, stamp duties and registration fees.

The 72nd and 73rd Constitutional amendments also specify some tax sources to urban and rural local governments. The two important taxes assigned to the local bodies are property taxes and taxes on the entry of goods into a local area for consumption, use or sale. Information on local tax collections consolidated for all urban and rural local governments is not available. However, available information shows that local governments have very little revenue raising powers and much of the expenditures of the local governments are met from devolution of revenues from the state governments. Analysis shows that, revenue trends of both the centre and the states follow a similar pattern.

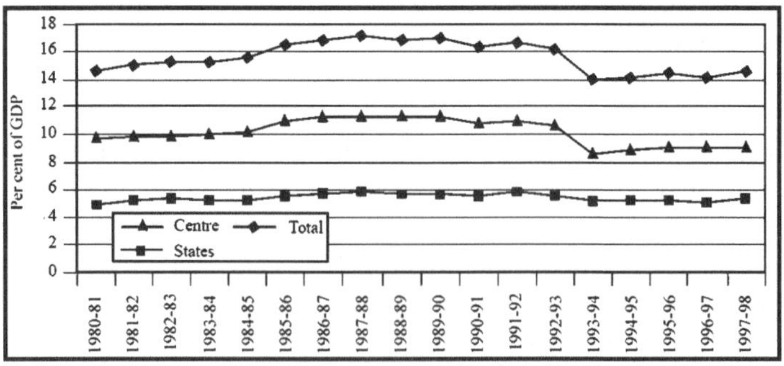

Fig. Chart Trends in tax revenue – centre and states

However, decline in the ratio of tax revenue to GDP in the case of the central government has been much faster than that of the states. This is understandable, as the central government had to reduce tariffs as a part of the structural adjustment programme. On the other hand, there have been hardly any worthwhile reforms at the state level and yet, the tax ratio has shown a decline, albeit marginal.

Tax reform attempts until 1990

There have been a number of attempts at improving the tax system since independence. The principal objective of these attempts has been to enhance revenue productivity to finance large development plans. Although the various tax reform committees considered economic efficiency as one of the objectives, the recommendations do not bear much testimony to this aspect. The recommendations were in keeping with the philosophy of the times. Further, even when the committees did recommend certain measures on efficiency considerations, this was not acted upon if it involved loss of revenues.

The first comprehensive attempt at reforming the tax system was by the Tax Reform Committee in 1953. This provided the backdrop for the generation of resources for the Second Five Year Plan and was required to fulfil a variety of objectives such as raising the level of savings and investment, effecting resource transfer from the private to the public sector and achieving a desired state of redistribution. Since then, there have been a number of attempts, most of them partial, to remedy various aspects of the tax system. The expenditure tax levied on the recommendation of the Kaldor Committee in 1957-58 had to be withdrawn after three years as it did not generate the expected revenues. The attempt to achieve the desired state of redistribution caused the policy makers to design the income tax system with confiscatory marginal rates. The consequent moral hazard problems led the Direct Taxes Enquiry Committee in 1971 to recommend a significant reduction in marginal tax rates. On the indirect taxes side, a major simplification exercise was attempted by the Indirect Taxes Enquiry Committee in 1972.

At the state and local level, there were a number of tax reform committees in different states that went into the issue of rationalization and simplification of the tax system. The motivation for almost all these committees was to raise more revenues to finance ever-increasing public consumption and investment requirements. As mentioned earlier, although the effect of the rationalization has been to reduce the marginal tax rates, the prevailing philosophy still dictated keeping the rates very high.

It may be noted that in the early 1970s the marginal tax rate including the surcharge was as high as 93.5 per cent. Combined with the highest marginal wealth tax rate of 8 per cent tax on wealth, the tax system produced enormous incentives for evasion and avoidance of the tax. On the recommendation of the Direct Taxes Enquiry Committee, the marginal tax rate was brought down to 77 per cent in 1974-75 and further to 66 per cent in

1976. Similarly, the highest wealth tax rate was reduced to 2.5 per cent. On the indirect taxes front, the most important reform before 1991 was the conversion of the union excise duties into a modified value added tax in 1986. The MODVAT was introduced in a limited manner on a few commodities and the coverage was gradually extended over the years. It was an income type VAT applicable only to a few manufactured goods. Also, there was an attempt to substitute ad valorem taxes to specific levies though quite a few commodities are subject to specific tax even today. There were attempts to simplify and rationalize the structures, but these cannot be considered comprehensive.

IMPACT OF TAX REFORMS SINCE 1991

Report of the Tax Reform Committee

Tax reform since 1991 was initiated as a part of the structural reform process, following the economic crisis of 1991. In keeping with the best practice approaches, the TRC adopted an approach of combining economic principles with conventional wisdom in recommending comprehensive tax system reforms. There are three parts in the report. In the first interim report, the Committee set out the guiding principles of tax reform and applied them to important taxes namely, taxes on income and wealth, tariffs and taxes on domestic consumption. The first part of the final report was concerned mainly with the much-neglected aspect of reforms in administration and enforcement of both direct and indirect taxes. The second part of the report dealt with restructuring the tariff structure. In keeping with the structural adjustment of the economy, the basic principles taken in the recommendations were to broaden the base, lower marginal tax rates, reduce rate differentiation, and undertake measures to make the administration and enforcement of the tax system more effective. The reforms were to be calibrated to bring about revenue neutrality in the short term and to enhance revenue productivity of the tax system in the medium and long term. The overall thrust of the TRC was to:

- Decrease the share of trade taxes in total tax revenue;
- Increase the share of domestic consumption taxes by transforming the domestic excises into VAT and
- Increase the relative contribution of direct taxes.

The important proposals put forward by the TRC included reduction in the rates of all major taxes, viz. customs, individual and corporate income taxes and excises to reasonable levels, maintain progressivity but not such as to induce evasion. The TRC recommended a number of measures to broaden the base of all taxes by minimizing exemptions and concessions, drastic simplification of laws and procedures, building a proper information system and computerization of tax returns, and a thorough revamping and modernization of the administrative and enforcement machinery. It also recommended that the taxes on domestic production should be fully converted into a value added tax, and this should be extended to the wholesale level in agreement with the states, with additional revenues beyond the post-manufacturing stage passed on to the state governments. In the case of customs, the TRC recommendations were the weakest.

The TRC recommended tariff rates of 5, 10, 15, 20, 25, 30 and 50 to be achieved by 1997-98. The tariff rate was to vary directly with the stage of processing of commodities, and among final consumer goods, with the income elasticity of demand. Excessive rate differentiation and according varying degrees of protection depending on the stage of processing has been severely criticized by Joshi and Little when they state, "....this is a totally unprincipled principle, for it has no foundation in economic principles". In addition to continued complexity, the proposed tariff structure creates very high differences in effective rates and provides a higher degree of protection to inessential commodities. The TRC recommendation also falls much short of developing a co-ordinated domestic trade tax system in the country.

This, in a sense, is understandable, as it had no mandate to go into the state level taxes. However, the Committee was aware of the serious problems of avoidance and evasion in respect of sales taxes levied by the states predominantly at the manufacturing stage. Therefore, it did recommend the extension of the central VAT to the wholesale stage with the revenues from the extended levy assigned to the states.

Implementation of reforms since 1991

The government accepted the recommendations of the TRC and has implemented them in phases. Although it did not entirely follow the recommendations and is yet to implement many of the measures to strengthen the administration and enforcement machinery, most of the recommendations have been implemented. It must also be noted that the pace and content of reforms have not been exactly true to TRC recommendations. As regards the personal income taxes, the most drastic and visible changes have been seen in the reduction in personal and corporate income tax rates. In the case of personal income taxes, besides exemption, the number of tax rates have been reduced to three and the tax rates were drastically reduced to 10, 20 and 30 per cent.

At the same time, the exemption limit was raised in stages to ₹ 50,000. Combined with the standard deduction, a salaried taxpayer up to an income of ₹ 75,000 need not pay any tax. In addition, saving incentives were given by exempting investment in small savings and provident funds up to a specified limit. Attempts have also been made to bring in the self-employed income earners into the tax net. Every individual living in large cities covered under any of the specified conditions is necessarily required to file a tax return.

Empirical evidence shows that this drastic reduction in the marginal tax rates has improved the compliance index significantly. Thus, revenues from personal and corporate income taxes have shown appreciable increases after the reforms were initiated in spite of the fact that the rates of tax have been reduced significantly. Voluntary disclosure scheme to allow a one time amnesty to tax defaulters by paying the necessary tax was introduced in 1997-98. In the case of corporate income taxes, the rates were progressively reduced on both domestic and foreign companies to 35 per cent and 48 per cent respectively. The dividend tax at the individual income tax level has been abolished.

However, very little has been done in terms of broadening the base of corporation tax. In fact, besides depreciation allowances and exemptions for exporters, generous tax holidays and preferences are given for investment in various activities. Consequently, the tax base has not grown in proportion to the growth of corporate profits. As many corporate entities took generous advantage of all these tax preferences, there were a number of "zero-tax" companies. To ensure minimum tax payments by them, a Minimum Alternative Tax was introduced in 1997-98. In the case of tariffs, there has been a drastic reduction in both the average and peak tariff rates. In 1990-91, the unweighted average nominal tariff was 125 per cent and peak rate was 355 per cent.

These were progressively reduced over the years. The peak rate of import duty in 1997-98 was 40 per cent and the average rate of tariff is just about 25 per cent. It is proposed to reduce the tariffs further to the levels prevailing in the South-East Asian countries in the next five years. In terms of rate differentiation, the number of tax rates continues to remain high. While in the initial years, there was an attempt to reduce the rate differentiation, in more recent years, the variations have, in fact, increased. Again, the pattern of tariffs with the rates varying with the stage of processing has resulted in very high incentives given to the assembly of consumer durables and luxury items of consumption.

There has been a considerable simplification and rationalization of union excise duties as well. Besides reduction in the number of rates, the tax has been progressively converted from a specific into ad valorem levy in respect of the majority of commodities. The facility of providing credit on input taxes under the MODVAT too has been progressively extended to a larger number of commodities. As of now almost 80 per cent of the goods covered under excise duties are provided with the MODVAT facility. The base of the tax was broadened by removing the exemptions and levying excise duty at the lowest rate (8 per cent). There has also been a simplification of the tax on the small-scale sector. As the government realized that there was considerable misuse, availability of MODVAT credit was reduced to 95 per cent instead of 100 per cent. Another important change that has been brought about since

1991 is the introduction of a selective tax on services. The constitution does not assign this tax base specifically either to the centre or the states. However, the central government by invoking residuary powers has introduced a tax on services since 1994-95. Beginning with three services (telephones, non-life insurance and stock brokerage), the base of the tax has been broadened to cover a large number of services such as transporters, car rentals, air travel agents, architects, interior designers, management consultants, chartered accountants, cost accountants, company secretaries, credit rating agencies, market research agencies, underwriters, private security/detectives, real estate agencies and mechanized slaughter houses. There have been significant attempts to improve the administration and enforcement of the tax as well, though progress in actual implementation has not been commensurate.

Besides amnesties given from time to time, efforts have been made to reduce arrears by introducing simplified assessment procedures. A large number of pending cases in courts have been decided through out of court settlements. There have also been attempts to establish special tax courts to deal exclusively with tax disputes. With the assistance of the Canadian International Development Agency (CIDA), the government has started an ambitious programme of computerising tax returns and building a management information system.

State tax systems

While a good deal of progress has been made in the tax system reform of the central government, progress in the case of state tax systems has not been commensurate. The sales taxes, which account for over 60 per cent of states' revenues, have, over the years, become stagnant. The states prefer to levy the tax at the first point of sale, and this makes the tax base narrow. With as many as 16-20 rate categories introduced to fulfil a variety of objectives, the tax has become complicated. This has given rise to a large number of classification disputes as well. Taxation of inputs and capital goods, in addition, has contributed to cascading. In an imperfect market characterized by mark up pricing, the taxes on inputs and capital goods results in the phenomenon tax-on-tax, and mark up on the tax with consumers paying much more than the revenues collected by the government.

In addition, there is a tax on inter-state sales, which not only causes severe distortions but also results in inter-state tax exportation in favour of richer states. All these have combined to make the sales tax system complicated, opaque and distorting. Above all, with independent and overlapping commodity tax systems at the central and state levels, co-ordinated and harmonized development of domestic trade taxes has become difficult. The Government of India appointed a study group to recommend measures to harmonise and rationalize the domestic trade tax system in the country. The study group made a thorough analysis of the distortions of the prevailing system of taxation and has recommended the gradual moving over to destination based, consumption type value added taxes at the state level. At the central level, the study group recommended complete switching over to the manufacturing stage VAT.

At the state level, the existing sales taxes were to be transformed into retail stage destination type VAT. In order to persuade the states to rationalise their tax systems on the lines recommended by the study group the Government of India appointed a state Finance Ministers' Committee. The Committee has made recommendations to switch over to the VAT in a given time frame through stages. Unfortunately, in spite of the consensus on the need for reforms in the sales tax systems at the state level, there has been very little action in terms of actual rationalization.

Revenue implications of reforms

The economic crisis of 1991 resulted in a significant decline in revenues. Although the tax reforms were intended to be a revenue neutral exercise, the natural consequence of a significant decline in tax rates was to reduce revenues. As there was no commensurate increase in the tax base, the revenue naturally showed a declining trend. Thus, the tax-GDP ratio, which was over 16 per cent in 1990-91, declined sharply to less than 14 per cent in 1993-94. Although thereafter there has been some improvement, it still remains less than 15 per cent and this remains a matter for concern. Thus, the reforms in the Indian context have in fact, caused an immediate loss of revenues, though in the next few years, they are likely to reach pre-reform levels. Interestingly, in spite of significant reductions in the rates of both individual and corporate income taxes, the revenues have shown a significant increase. The share of revenue from direct taxes showed a significant increase as a proportion of GDP as well as total tax revenue.

The contribution of revenue from direct taxes, which was less than 14 per cent in 1990-91, increased sharply to 24 per cent in 1997-98. However, it is not clear to what extent the increase in revenue productivity is due to increase in public sector wages following the implementation of pay commission recommendations, how much of this is attributable to better compliance arising from lower marginal tax rates and how much due to administrative measures. The decline in the tax-GDP ratio since the reforms were initiated has to be attributed to lower yield of indirect taxes. Naturally, some reduction in customs revenue was only to be expected as the prevailing tariffs were extremely high and had to be drastically reduced. For the same reason, the reforms in excise duties were to be calibrated to compensate revenue loss from import duties.

This, however, did not happen and in fact, the revenue from union excise duties showed a drastic decline. Analysis shows that the revenue from import duties as a ratio of GDP declined by 1.3 percentage points from 3.9 per cent in 1990-91 to 2.6 per cent in 1997-98. However, decline in the revenue from excise duties was faster, by 1.5 percentage points from 4.6 per cent to 3.1 per cent during the same period. Consequently, the share of excise duties in total revenue declined by about 7 percentage points (from 28 to 21 per cent) as compared to a 6 percentage point decline in the share of customs (from 24 to 18 per cent). Significant improvements in the tax ratio, therefore, have to come from improvement in the revenue productivity of domestic indirect taxes. The continued heavy reliance on import duties as a source of revenue rather than as an instrument of protection is an issue that merits some discussion.

It has been pointed out that the central government does not have the incentive to raise revenues from the taxes that are shared with the states. According to the existing intergovernmental fiscal arrangement, the central government should share 87.5 per cent of the net collections from personal income tax and 47.5 per cent of gross revenues from union excise duties with the states. This is alleged to have created a moral hazard problem and it is stated that the central government concentrates on those taxes which are not shared. Consequently, while the share of revenues from the taxes that are shared with the states have declined, the revenues from the sources that are not shared have shown a steady increase.

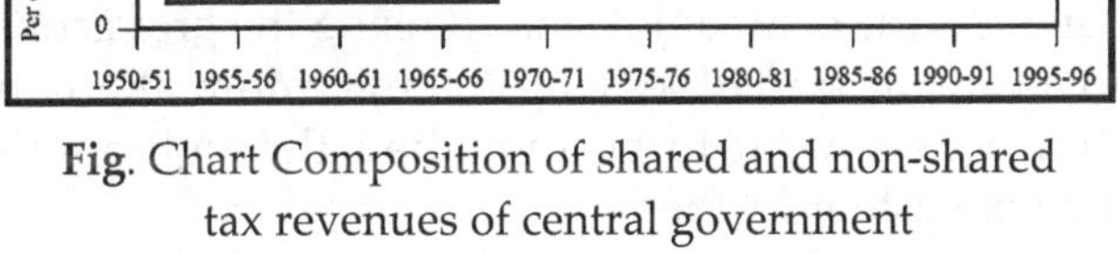

Fig. Chart Composition of shared and non-shared tax revenues of central government

Therefore, Joshi and Little state, "...there is no doubt that this cockeyed growth of the tax system has harmed the development of the whole economy."

SHORTCOMINGS AND CHALLENGES

After eight years of tax reform, as already mentioned, a number of disquieting features in the tax system still remain. Improving the productivity of the tax system continues to be a major challenge in India. The tax ratio is yet to reach the pre-reform levels. Although the coverage under income tax has shown significant improvement, much remains to be done to reach the hard-to-tax groups. The ratio of domestic trade taxes in particular has continued to decline and this has posed a major constraint in reducing tariffs which is necessary to achieve allocative efficiency. Designing of tariffs itself needs to be re-examined to ensure lower tariffs a well as a low level of dispersion to ensure that effective rates of protection are as intended. Reforms in excise duties have not reached the stage of achieving a simple and transparent manufacturing stage VAT. Much remains to be done to simplify and rationalize the state and local consumption taxes. Concerted efforts are necessary to create a proper management information system and automating tax returns.

Above all, tax reforms should become systemic, a continuous process to keep the economy competitive instead of being sporadic and crisis-driven. In the case of direct taxes, as already mentioned, the revenue ratio has shown an upward trend. Marked decline in tax rates seems to have improved tax compliance, though much of the increase seems to have come about due to increases in public sector wages. Yet, the revenues realized are nowhere near the potential and much remains to be done to improve the horizontal equity of the tax system by extending the tax net to hard-to-tax groups. The criteria stipulated for filing tax returns has increased the number of tax returns from less than half a per cent of population to more than 2 per cent. But this has not brought about a corresponding increase in revenues. Inability to bring in the hard-to-tax groups into the net has continued to exert pressure to increase the standard exemption limit deductions.

There is also scope for rationalizing savings incentives. Perquisites continue to receive favourable tax treatment and the coverage of tax deduction at source needs to be expanded before long. In the case of corporate income taxes, too, it is necessary to broaden the tax base by minimizing tax concessions and preferences. Rather than minimizing them, the recent coalition governments have gone about proliferating tax incentives to complicate the tax system and to create a wide wedge between the nominal and effective corporate tax rates. As the companies started using the provisions, for revenue reasons, the government started levying the minimum alternative tax. Thus one imperfection was sought to be remedied through another. This has complicated the tax system further.

As already mentioned, complete rethinking is necessary in designing tariffs. The TRC recommendation of having seven tax rate categories, the rates varying according to the stage of production, would create large dispersal in the effective rate of protection. Levying lower rates on necessities and higher rates on consumer durable and luxury items of consumption enormously increases protection to these products. It is essential that the highest tariff rate should be brought down to 15-20 per cent and there should be no more than three rate categories. Unless this is done, it would not be possible for Indian manufacturing to achieve international competitiveness in the medium term.

The most important challenge in restructuring the tax system in the country is to evolve a co-ordinated consumption tax system. Although tax assignment between different levels of government follows the principle of separation, as these separate taxes levied by the centre (excise duties), states (sales taxes, state excise duties, taxes on motor vehicles, goods and passengers), and local governments (octroi) fall on the same tax base, we end up in a chaotic situation with tax on tax and mark up on the tax. Besides cascading and relative price distortions, this results in a totally non-transparent tax system. Development of dual VAT – a manufacturing stage VAT by the centre and a consumption type destination based retailed stage VAT by the states is a solution, which needs to be progressively applied. However, neither the centre nor the states have made appreciable progress in this regard. To achieve this, in the case of the centre, the excise duties should be levied entirely as ad valorem levies.

The rates should be rationalised into a maximum of two and tax credit should be provided on a systematic basis. For this, developing a proper information system is imperative. At the state level, transforming the state taxes into VAT has to be calibrated even more carefully. Rate rationalization, systematic provision of tax credit on inputs and those paid on previous stages, removal of competing tax incentives and concessions, zero rating the tax on inter-state sales – all these have to be done in phases. A major difficulty in evolving a destination based retail stage VAT at the state level arises from the fact that the states do not have the power to levy tax on services. As mentioned earlier, the states can levy sales taxation of only goods. Taxation of services is not assigned to either the centre or the state, but the former levies taxes on selected services based on power to levy taxes on residual items. Proper levy of goods and services tax would, therefore, require an amendment of the Constitution.

The central government can use this as a leverage to persuade the states to reduce and eventually eliminate the taxation on inter-state sales so that a levy of destination based VAT becomes a reality.

3

Transfer Pricing and Taxation

AN OVERVIEW

A small operation managed by a few individuals was the typical beginning of a large corporation with a hundred operating affiliates dispersed around the world. Decision making was highly centralized and lines of communication were short.

As the company grew, the founding management team found it more difficult to keep matters under control. This problem was greatly exacerbated when operations within the company became physically separated. Centres of activity in different locations called for a different style of management. Funneling of all decisions from diverse locations through a small group of individuals, who no longer possess the necessary intimate awareness of the circumstances surrounding each decision, is a surefire prescription for stifling growth.

Growth is the name of the game for modern corporations. Growth entails individual operating affiliates taking appropriate action to enhance productivity, market share, and the scope of a company's product line. It has been found that operating affiliates physically separated from the parent organization can best achieve these objectives under a decentralized style of management.

Responsibility now falls on the shoulders of the manager of an operating affiliate to make the necessary decisions that will lead to improved financial results, the universal measure of performance. The parent organization takes on a new role as coordinator and monitor of activities now that responsibility for operations has been transferred to the operating units. Far from playing a passive role, the parent organization focuses its attention on optimizing the performance of its semiautonomous operating affiliates. To do this, the parent organization must establish, and articulate, a set of strategic goals and allocate limited corporate resources to the various operating affiliates to best achieve these goals. It must ensure that the short-term action plans of the operating affiliates are in accord with its long-term plans.

Top management positions in the operating affiliates must be filled with individuals capable of leading their affiliates in the right direction and an incentive system must be set up to induce managers to orient their thinking to the goals of the company. Finally, the parent organization must set up a financial reporting and control system to monitor its global operations, to provide necessary information for the making of decisions and to evaluate the performance of the affiliate managers.

Although operating affiliates appear to be semiautono-mous units in that they are given a wide spectrum of decision-making responsibility in managing their local operations, they are not independent centres of corporate activity. They are often united in manufacturing and marketing a common product line, in the course of which they routinely buy and sell finished goods, components, or raw materials from one another. These intra company exchanges of goods, components, and raw materials require a transfer price. The parent organization sets the transfer price after considering various factors with an eye on optimizing corporate perfor-mance as a whole.

Transfer prices are often not negotiated and agreed on by the actual buyers and sellers of the goods and components being shipped between operating affiliates. Yet transfer prices directly affect the revenue and cost of goods sold, and therefore, the profitability of the operating affiliates. Because the affiliate managers are monitored by a financial reporting and control system that scrutinizes their financial results, one can expect that affiliate managers have an entirely different perspective on transfer pricing than the executives of the parent organization. Transfer pricing can easily embroil executives of the parent organization and the managers of operating affiliates in endless disputes. Some firms have even established an administrative panel for reviewing transfer prices to resolve sharp differences of opinion between those responsible for managing operating affiliates and those responsible for setting transfer prices.

TRANSFER PRICES AND TAXES

A global company with operations in many nations must deal with a new dimension of complexity in establishing transfer prices, which is not present when a company operates solely within the confines of a single nation. A company whose operations are within a single nation pays the same taxes on profits regardless of the transfer pricing policy. The consolidation process, whether for financial or tax accounting purposes, eliminates intra company transactions to arrive at either a book profit or a before-tax profit. When a company transacts business through affiliate companies in different nations, however, transfer pricing provides a mechanism for shifting taxable profits between tax jurisdictions.

Tax authorities in various nations are concerned with the notion that transfer pricing, often set by parent organizations outside their jurisdiction, is based on minimizing taxes paid in their jurisdictions. There certainly is an element of truth in this contention, but there are other considerations in administering transfer prices than minimizing taxes. The setting of transfer prices provides a way of moving funds internationally for a variety of purposes, of circumventing currency exchange controls that threaten to choke the operations of a company, of minimizing the deleterious impact of other artificial barriers to trade such as duties and tariffs, and of reducing currency risk exposure.

A transfer pricing policy attempts to satisfy a multiple set of objectives. Some of these objectives call for high transfer prices, whereas others require low transfer prices. A company must select what it considers to be an optimal transfer price, which is a compromise price for best achieving divergent objectives. This optimal transfer price may not be the one that minimizes taxes on profits. The selected transfer price may not be satisfactory both to the local tax authority and to the manager of an affiliate if it reduces the reported profitability of the affiliate. However, setting the transfer price is critical to optimizing the financial performance of the corporation as a whole, given the conditions that prevail at a point in time.

MINIMIZING TAXES

Tax authorities of most countries have guidelines or controls that are expected to be complied with in setting transfer prices. Management is not free to arbitrarily select transfer prices without having to substantiate their transfer price decisions. Nevertheless, there is still an element of choice where a selected transfer price may reduce the tax burden of a company. Suppose that a company consists of a parent organization and two operating affiliates—one in nation A, where the tax rate on profits is 30 per cent, and one in nation B, where the tax rate on profits is 40 per cent. The tax is applied to each affiliate's gross margin for illustrative purposes. The affiliate in nation A makes a product that is entirely sold through the affiliate in nation B. Two cases are considered—a low and a high transfer price.

Table. Case I-Low Transfer Price

	Nation A	Nation B	Consolidated
	Tax 30%	Tax 40%	
Sales	$2000	$3200	$3200
Cost of Goods Sold	1500	2000	1500
Gross Margin	500	1200	1700
Tax	150	480	630
Net Income	$350	$720	$1070

Everything made in a factory in nation A is sold through a marketing organization in nation B. Therefore, total sales in nation A, calculated on the basis of an administered transfer price, is also the cost of goods sold in nation B. Sales in nation B of $3,200 is the net consolidated sales for the company, because all goods produced in nation A are sold in nation B. The actual cost of manufacturing the goods in nation A is $1,500. Because nation B does not add value to the goods, the consolidated cost of goods sold for the company is also $1,500. The consolidated tax is the sum of the $150 and the $480 paid to the tax authorities of nations A and B, respectively. The consolidated net income is $1,070, the sum of the net incomes of the two affiliates.

Suppose that the transfer price is increased from $2,000 to $2,500 for goods shipped between the two affiliates. Consolidated sales, cost of goods sold, and gross margin are unaffected by the change in the transfer price, because it is netted out in the consolidation process. Taxes paid in each nation are no longer the same because of the change in the transfer price. In case II, the increase in the transfer price shifts the profit to Nation A, which has the lower tax rate. The affiliate in nation A earns more taxable income and pays more in taxes than in case I. The affiliate in nation B earns less taxable income and pays less in taxes in case II than in case I. The net effect, as seen by comparing case II with case I, is that the company as a whole is paying less in taxes, which increases its consolidated net income.

It is true that had the two nations the same tax rate, the total taxes paid by the company, and the consolidated net income, would not be affected by changes in the transfer price. Even so, transfer prices determine what portion of total taxes are to be paid to the tax authority in nation A and to the tax authority in Nation B. Although the parent organization may be relatively insensitive concerning to whom it pays taxes, needless to say, the tax authorities are very much concerned as to which is collecting taxes. The problem is compounded, from the point of view of a tax authority, because the transfer price is probably set by a parent organization not under its jurisdiction. The importance of transfer pricing to both managers and tax authorities can be appreciated when it is realised that between 40 per cent and 60 per cent of international trade involves goods moving between affiliates of the same company. Corporate decisions on transfer prices do have a meaningful impact on what a tax jurisdiction collects.

There are nations, islands, and localities where tax authorities exhibit little interest in transfer prices. Ireland, Puerto Rico, and other nations or areas designated as free trade zones or having special tax privileges may not tax corporate profits, or have a very low tax rate. These nations or locales are interested in companies building plants on their soil for the social benefits that accrue from employment of individuals who might otherwise be unemployed. Companies operating in such nations or locales can substantially decrease their overall tax rate. The effective reduction in tax rates depends on the transfer prices of imported components and semifinished goods and the transfer prices of exported finished goods. Granting tax concessions is one way for a nation to attract companies. At this time, eastern European nations offer tax incentives but do not have a prescribed accounting methodology to calculate profits, which makes it impossible to quantify the tax benefit. More than one company has set up an operation in eastern Europe to later discover that the government had a much different version in mind of the nature of the tax benefits than the investors anticipated. Such shortsightedness by government officials has a deleterious impact on attracting other companies.

Many nations are discovering that viewing business solely as a way to fill the public coffers may not be in their long-term best interests. Within the United States, states with high corporate tax rates have experienced companies moving to states with low corporate tax rates.

The higher they raise their corporate tax rates, the less they collect in taxes. As once companies moved from one state to another, now they move from one nation to another. In selecting a potential site, a businessman considers many factors, of which taxes are but one. Some of these are social and political stability; a system of commercial law to resolve disputes; a set of acceptable accounting practices (both to assess tax liabilities and evaluate tax incentives); a labour force with the requisite skills and will to work; and an infrastructure of transportation, communication, and utility and social (education, medical care) services.

There are more locations that offer good potential sites for factories than before. Managers no longer feel that their factories must be anchored to one nation and have learned to manage far-flung operations.

Nations must now compete for factories. Tax authorities in developed nations are beginning to realise that they may end up collecting less tax revenue in their eagerness to collect more tax revenue by raising tax rates. The United States was forced to repeal a luxury tax on pleasure boats because pleasure boat construction virtually ceased with the passage of the new tax. New Jersey was forced to repeal a sales tax on trucks when truck selling companies moved their operations to nearby Pennsylvania. In both cases, tax revenues fell when tax rates were raised, and the tax authorities were forced to rescind tax increases. In a global economy, companies are mobile and will relocate to avoid especially burdensome taxes.

INTERNATIONAL FUNDING

Businesses operating in hard currency nations have the advantage of being able to transfer and convert currencies as necessary. Many nations, however, have currencies that lack convertibility, the so-called soft currencies. Transfer pricing provides a means of moving funds from one country to another, when direct currency convertibility is not possible.

If a nation has an affiliate that completes the manufacturing process and sells its output within that nation, funds can be moved out of that nation by increasing the transfer price for goods imported by the affiliate. The same objective can be accomplished by increasing the charges for services rendered by the parent organization to the affiliate, such as selling and administrative (SandA) fees, research and development (RandD) expenses, financial charges on transferred assets, and royalties for rights to patents and dividends. Sometimes currency exchange controls focus on the amount of dividends that can be paid by an affiliate to its parent. A quasi-dividend can be paid by raising the transfer price of goods moving into the nation or by increasing corporate fees, financial charges, and royalty payments.

Some nations with severe restrictions on dividend outflows will permit increases in transfer prices and service fees. These quasi-dividend payments are allowed because the local government recognizes that few companies can afford the luxury of investing in a nation that prohibits the company from earning a return on its investment. However, actions such as these that drain funds out of a soft currency nation eventually result in some sort of currency exchange restriction. This often results in affiliate profits accumulating in a currency that may not be particularly desirable. Sometimes currency exchange restrictions can be bypassed by the affiliate making an investment, or lending funds, to an affiliate in another nation.

CONTROLLING REPORTED PROFITS

Shifts in transfer prices, corporate administrative fees, and other parent company charges to an affiliate are means of managing the affiliate's reported profitability. It may be in the interest of a parent organization to lower the reported profitability of an affiliate for reasons other than tax minimization.

These include deflecting union demands for higher wages, reducing political pressure to nationalize or expropriate a profitable affiliate, and dissuading potential competitors from entering the market. Lowering profitability is also a way to counter price controls that limit profitability. If a government has set price controls based on the cost of production plus a limited markup for profits, increases in the transfer price of goods sent to the affiliate lowers the profit margin of goods sold in that nation. This may permit goods to be sold at government decreed profit margins with the company as a whole still able to earn its normal profits.

A few nations have tax rates that are linked to profitability. The greater the profitability, the higher the tax rate. The logic behind this taxation policy is that there is a level of profits on investment that seems"excessive" to the government. Such excessive profitability should be punished by the government, and there is no greater punishment than taking away the excess profits through a higher tax rate. By increasing the transfer price of goods being imported into the nation, the degree of profitability is decreased, lowering the tax rate and, presumably, restoring respectability in the eyes of the government.

Alternatively, it may be in the interests of the parent organization to enhance the profitability of an affiliate. This may be done by lowering the transfer price of imported goods. One reason for enhancing the profitability of an affiliate is to provide sufficient financial resources to the affiliate for it to withstand price cutting by competitive companies. Improving an affiliate's profitability, even at the cost of paying more in taxes, may allow the affiliate to borrow needed funds for operation from local banks and other financial institutions, to improve its credit rating to qualify for lower interest loans and to fund capital outlays from its own resources.

CIRCUMVENTING EXCHANGE CONTROLS

Governments with soft currencies often limit the amount of their currency that companies operating in their nations can exchange for other currencies. Their motivation is to discourage the selling of the domestic soft currency and the buying of a hard currency, which would exert downward pressure on the value of the local currency. In other words, exchange controls are set up to keep a soft currency from becoming softer.

From the point of view of a parent organization, restricting hard currency outflows inhibits an affiliate's ability to pay for imported components or other items necessary for its operations. Transfer prices for the needed components can be kept artificially low to expand the volume of goods that are being imported into a soft currency nation. This sustains an affiliate's manufacturing operation without exceeding government decreed restrictions on converting soft currency to hard currency. But there is an adverse consequence because such a course of action results in a parent corporation accumulating even larger amounts of soft currency. These holdings of soft currency are constantly losing purchasing power through inflation.

The soft currency cannot be converted to a more desirable currency because of currency exchange restrictions and the soft currency, which has little value within the nation, has no value outside the nation. One of the knottiest problems associated with an operating affiliate in a soft currency nation is funding of hard currency imports necessary for its operation and obtaining a hard currency return on a hard currency investment.

Some companies will not set up an operation in a soft currency nation unless there is a prearranged means to earn hard currency to pay for hard currency imports and to provide a hard currency return on a hard currency investment.

Pepsi Cola struck a barter deal for producing its soft drink in the former Soviet Union. Its soft ruble revenue, net of soft ruble expenses, is exchanged for Russian built tankers, which are then sold for hard currencies. Oil companies will not set up operations in the Commonwealth of Independent States, and other soft currency nations, unless they receive a share of the output, which is shipped out of the nation and sold for hard currency.

The easiest way for a company to earn hard currency in a soft currency nation would be to export a portion of its output to hard currency nations. However, most soft currency nations do not permit the hard currency revenue to remain with the company. The hard currency revenue is exchanged for an equivalent amount of soft currency, which is then credited to the exporter's bank account. In essence, the national government receives the hard currency revenue from exports and pays soft currency to the exporter. Sometimes international banks are at fault for imposing this condition on a nation as a means to guarantee repayment of international debt. Regardless of whether the nation or the international banks impose this condition, it is self-defeating because the economic development of a developing nation is held back by the inability of companies to earn sufficient hard currency to justify their investments.

MINIMIZING DUTIES AND TARIFFS

Duties and tariffs imposed on goods imported into a nation can be reduced by lowering the transfer price. This is the exact opposite of reducing taxes on profits by increasing the transfer price. Because the tariff rate is usually less than the tax rate on profits, lowering transfer prices to reduce import tariffs often results in a higher tax on profits.

In some nations, however, tariffs on certain imported goods and commodities are not set by a corporate-determined transfer price but by an internationally posted price. This can be done only for generic goods (steel) or commodities (oil), where there is an active market with published and verifiable prices. Sometimes tax authorities will reference costs not to a "transfer price" cost but to an internationally agreed standard. One example of this is tanker rates in the oil business. An oil company can manage the profitability, and therefore, the tax liability, of a refinery by the transfer price associated with international tanker transportation for moving oil to and from a refinery.

The tax authorities of many nations and the oil companies have agreed to a panel of experts determining a fair and representative tanker rate that is used for the computation of taxes independent of the transfer price, or internal cost, that oil companies charge for shipping oil among their affiliates. This eliminates arguments between tax authorities and oil companies concerning the appropriate shipping charge.

Determining the optimal transfer-pricing policy is further complicated when a nation in which an affiliate operates has an export subsidy programme or provides a tax credit on the value of exports. It may be advantageous to lower transfer prices to an affiliate whose output is exported to third parties or other affiliates in other nations to take advantage of these tax incentives.

The optimal transfer price depends on the nature of the export subsidy or tax credit, the volume of the affiliate's output that is exported from the nation, the relationship between taxes on profits and the generation of tax credits and on the capacity of the affiliate to utilize the tax credit or export subsidy.

The nature of the taxes paid in a nation in the form of income taxes, duties and tariffs on imported goods, and export subsidies or tax credits on exported goods influence the setting of transfer prices.

There is no hard and fast rule on whether a high or a low transfer-pricing policy is best for a company. The particular circumstances of a company's operations in a nation and the nature of taxes and subsidies determine the best transfer-pricing policy. A transferpricing system integrated into a financial reporting and control system should be capable of analyzing "what" if scenarios to evaluate the effect of different transfer-pricing policies.

REDUCING CURRENCY EXCHANGE RISK

Changes in currency exchange rates result in transaction and translation gains and losses. More importantly, they affect the competitive position of an affiliate. If an affiliate manufactures and markets its goods in a nation, and imports components from another nation, a revaluation of the currency where the finished goods are being sold relative to the currency of its purchased components reduces manufacturing costs.

This makes the affiliate more competitive and profitable. A devaluation, on the other hand, increases the cost of imported components, making the affiliate less competitive and less profitable.

Reality is much more complex than this simple example because affiliates may export and import components and finished goods to and from a variety of nations. Changes in exchange rates benefit some affiliates and hurt others, and it may not be obvious because of the nature of buying and selling of goods and services. It is possible that a change in currency exchange rates that is adverse to a particular affiliate may be beneficial to the company as a whole because of the nature of the net exposure of the company to the affected currencies. Adjustments to transfer prices may affect currency holdings before an anticipated change in exchange rates takes place and may be able to restore a company's competitive position after the change has taken place.

Therefore, a financial reporting and control system should have the capacity to assess changes to both transfer prices and currency exchange rates to enable the parent organization to respond both to anticipated changes in currency exchange rates and to subsequent shifts in its competitive position.

TRANSFER PRICING AND JOINT VENTURES

A joint venture partner, a local partner owning a portion of an affiliate, and a minority shareholder are going to be as interested in transfer pricing as the local tax authority. Less often, a partnership is structured on the basis of a claim, or royalty, on revenue. More often, it is a claim on profits.

If one party to a venture or partnership can influence revenue, costs, and profitability through transfer pricing, then the other party or partner, or a minority shareholder, will be deservedly concerned. One way to manage transfer pricing with regard to having partners or minority shareholders is to formalize the setting of transfer prices in some verifiable manner such as a set markup above costs, another is to reference transfer prices to an observable market transaction. Either way minimizes the opportunity for one party to a partnership or joint venture to manipulate transfer prices to its advantage. If the partners, participants, and minority shareholders feel that their interests are vulnerable by virtue of the other party to a business venture controlling transfer prices, then they may not contribute to the venture that which was expected of them.

Avoiding these problems can be more easily said than done. Some years ago, Ford Motor Company purchased the minority shares of its partially owned subsidiaries because the company felt that it could not administer transfer pricing in a way that was fair to all concerned.

Some managements have made the strategic decision not to enter into joint ventures, or have local partners or minority shareholdings in corporate affiliates, where they can manage the profitability of the venture through transfer prices. Sometimes, the solution for a problem is to avoid the problem.

TRANSFER PRICING AND MANAGERIAL PERFORMANCE EVALUATION

It may be in the interest of the corporation as a whole to transfer in components that are more highly priced than those an affiliate can purchase from other sources. It may be in the interest of the corporation as a whole to transfer goods made in one affiliate to another affiliate for less than what the affiliate can sell them for to third parties. Although the corporation may gain by such a set of transfer prices for goods moving among affiliates, it does not serve the interests of the affiliate managers if they are subsequently judged on profitability. This dichotomy of purpose in establishing a transfer-pricing policy for the good of the whole company, yet holding managers of affiliates accountable for profits that are contaminated, so to speak, by transfer prices has not been successfully addressed when transfer prices are different from market prices.

In fact, this is one potent argument in favour of companies having transfer pricing policies based on the market price for comparable goods. If transfer prices are set at the price for goods exchanged between unrelated parties, then there is no dichotomy of purpose in setting transfer prices and measuring performance. Managers of affiliates can be judged in an unbiased fashion on the profitability of their operations because they are buying and selling at market prices—the same prices that would prevail if they were independent companies.

The disadvantage of letting the market set transfer prices is that the parent corporation can no longer utilize transfer pricing as a means to pursue the overall optimization of the financial performance of the corporation. One possible approach to the dysfunctional aspects of setting transfer prices at other than market prices and measuring management performance of affiliates is to isolate and separately state the amount of inter company "profit" or "loss" that each affiliate is experiencing in its transactions with other affiliates. This approach provides the parent organization with information on whether an affiliate is suffering from unwarranted decreased profitability or enjoying unwarranted increased profitability because of transfer pricing.

SETTING TRANSFER PRICES BY COST OF PRODUCTION

There are two general approaches for setting transfer prices: the cost of production and market prices associated with third party, or unrelated, transactions. The cost-of-production approach bases the price of goods to be transferred between affiliates on the variable cost of production, an allowance for fixed costs that are general in nature and are apportioned over the entire product line, and an allowance for fixed costs that can be apportioned among the individual products.

This latter category usually includes research and development costs and selling and administrative costs. The remaining components may include financial fees and royalties associated with tangible and intangible assets to be apportioned to individual products and the selection of an appropriate profit margin. The variable cost of production includes labour, material, and other direct costs that are consumed in the production of an item. If the policy of the company is to hire and fire (lay off) factory workers as production rises and falls, then labour is a variable cost. If a company is reluctant to let go of their workers when sales decline, then factory labour should be considered part of fixed costs. Factory labour costs are usually part variable and part fixed. Other variable costs can be the unit financing and utility costs associated with machinery and processes used in the manufacture of a particular product and unit shipping costs. These costs can also be treated as fixed costs depending on how the company's cost accounting system is set up.

Fixed costs are all costs not included in variable costs. Fixed costs are the financing or depreciation costs of the factory; the overhead costs of marketing, accounting, and supervision; the cost of inventories, warehouses, insurance, utilities, communication, property taxes, and other non-variable cost items.

Fixed costs may not be entirely fixed in that there is some variation as production levels change. For instance, bonuses, which would be considered part of the fixed costs of having an executive suite, rise and fall with profits, which are related to production levels. The number of staff personnel in marketing, accounting, engineering, and other overhead functions can vary with the production level.

Some elements of fixed costs are allocated in the transfer price setting mechanism in a way that fairly apportions the fixed cost burden among the various products. Other elements of fixed costs can be apportioned more on the basis of the benefit derived by an individual product. One of these is research and development, where the allocation can be made over a product line in proportion to the degree of RandD expenditures associated with the development of an individual product. Although there is general agreement that this is a fair way to apportion RandD expenses of successful undertakings, there is lack of agreement on how to apportion RandD expenses for failed projects.

Some maintain that the allocation of expenses associated with failed RandD projects should be apportioned to all products on the basis that every product should bear the risk of failed RandD efforts. Others object on the grounds that had the RandD effort succeeded, a particular product might not have benefited. Therefore, it makes no sense for the transfer price to contain the cost of a failed RandD effort, which, had it succeeded, would not be part of the transfer price of the product. The question as to the proper treatment of failed RandD projects is not an internal accounting matter. Tax authorities are interested in who takes the write off of a failed RandD project. In the United States, the Internal Revenue Service (IRS) is concerned whether a transfer price contains a provision for failed RandD expenditures.

If a transfer price contains only that portion of RandD expenditures that were successful with regard to a particular product, then failed RandD projects of a U.S. corporation are being written off solely against U.S. income. A portion of the tax loss write-off is passed on to the tax authority of another nation by including an element of failed RandD expenditures in the transfer price. Another fixed cost element that can be separated and apportioned in a different manner than general fixed costs are services provided to an individual product. These may be coordination and control expenses associated with a product; costs for enhancing the efficiency of operations for manufacturing the product or expanding the scope of its market; and the costs of recruiting and training of management and operations personnel associated with manufacturing, marketing, and repairing or servicing the product. The allocation of these service costs to individual products provides another element in deriving their transfer prices.

The derivation of the transfer price also includes elements for tangibles and intangibles associated with a product. Tangibles are the plant, equipment, and other physical assets dedicated to the manufacture of the product. Part of the transfer price provides a financial return for tangibles based on their value. Intangibles represent the technical knowledge and expertise and applicable patents that can be allocated to a particular product. The transfer price also contains an element that provides a company with a return on intangibles. Intangible costs within a transfer price cannot be capriciously determined by management because intangible costs affect taxable profits. For this reason, the IRS has established guidelines for determining the intangible cost element in a transfer price.

An intangible cost element must be present if there are intangible costs associated with the manufacture or marketing of a product and must be so identified. Intangible costs can be proportioned in relation to the income attributable to the intangibles by units of production, sales, net or gross profits, or other reasonable methods. The fee for intangible property incorporated in a transfer price must be similar to what would have been arranged with an independent third party.

The last part of the cost approach in setting transfer prices is determining the proper profit margin on the goods made by one affiliate and shipped to another. This may be the average profit margin for the company as a whole or a profit margin associated with a specific product line. Regardless, the stipulated profit margin must be reconciled in some manner with the profitability of the company or a product line to satisfy the tax authorities.

The need for reconciliation of the profit and the various cost elements of the transfer price with the tax authorities sometimes results in the tax group within the finance department of a company being responsible for administering transfer prices. However, this choice may hinder general management from using transfer prices as a means to achieve corporate objectives. The chief advantage of the cost of production approach for setting transfer prices is that the costs are available and are subject to quantification. For this reason, the production cost approach has been more common in the past than the market price approach.

The chief disadvantage is that there is no real incentive for an affiliate to improve its manufacturing process, to enhance its efficiency, or to take steps to lower costs. Mistakes, errors, inefficiencies in manning or machinery, management inattention to detail, worker carelessness, and excessive remuneration of white and blue collar workers alike may all be incorporated in the determination of costs and passed on to the affiliates in the transfer price. Another disadvantage is that both the tax authority and the affiliates may object to the nature of the apportionment of RandD, SandA, tangibles, and intangibles among the various products and the assigned profit margin.

SETTING TRANSFER PRICES BY MARKET PRICES

The disadvantages associated with the cost-of-production method of setting transfer prices can be mostly avoided by referencing transfer prices to third party transactions for identical, or nearly identical, products.

If an affiliate can obtain the item being purchased from a third party for a certain price, then that price can be the basis for setting the transfer price. The proponents of market-oriented transfer prices maintain that letting the market set the transfer price is inherently more fair than a production-cost-based system because one affiliate is not supporting the inefficiencies of another. If an affiliate receives only the global competitive price for its products, then there is an incentive for it to take whatever actions are needed to correct the inefficiencies in its operations that are resulting in higher costs.

In a truly decentralized operation, managers are expected to make their decisions on an independent basis, and unrelated companies are permitted to compete for the business of an affiliate, along with other affiliates. The parent organization does not set transfer prices and has little or no influence over the decisions made by the managers of the affiliates. No favour or special consideration is shown to fellow affiliates in the competitive process of selecting suppliers for components and goods. The hope, of course, is that everyone is kept on his or her competitive toes to produce salable goods at the lowest possible cost. This managerial philosophy, where each affiliate is treated as an independent company, is sometimes referred to as the small business unit (SBU) management philosophy. The disadvantage is that, although each affiliate is focused on optimizing its operations, the end result may be suboptimal performance of the corporation as a whole.

Suppose that affiliate X produces all of a component (part X) for a number of widget manufacturing affiliates. Total demand for part X is 2 million per year. Affiliate X has $10 million in fixed annual costs, which include a profit margin on the investment in manufacturing facilities plus a return on the RandD investment for the development of part X. The variable costs for manufacturing part X is $5. The transfer price based on the fixed and variable costs of affiliate X supplying all other affiliates with part X is $10.

Table. Volume Of Sales: 2,000,000

Fixed Costs	$10,000,000
Variable Costs at $5 per Unit	10,000,000
Total Costs	$20,000,000
Transfer Price Based on Cost of Making 2,000,000	$10.00

Affiliate A is free to cut its best deal and obtains a quote of $9.50 from another company. Affiliate A does what is best for maximizing its profits and purchases 200,000 part X's from a third party for $9.50 rather than pay $10 to affiliate X. Affiliate X has lost a contract for 200,000 part X's and now operates on a basis of a sales volume of 1,800,000 per year.

Table. Volume Of Sales: 1,800,000

Fixed Costs	$10,000,000
Variable Costs at $5 per Unit	9,000,000
Total Costs	$19,000,000
Transfer Price Based on Cost of Making 1,800,000	$10.56

The remaining affiliates must pay a higher price because there is less sales volume to cover the fixed costs of affiliate X. The increase in transfer price to cover the fixed and variable costs is essentially equivalent to treating fixed costs as a component of variable costs, which it is not. Nevertheless, affiliate X must cover all its costs. When affiliate X announces the increase in price, affiliate B concludes a deal with a third party at $9.75 causing another loss of 200,000 for affiliate X.

Table. Volume Of Sales: 1,600.000

Fixed Costs	$10,000,000
Variable Costs at $5 per Unit	8,000,000
Total Costs	$18,000,000
Transfer Price Based on cost of Making 1,600,000	$11.25

Now it's time for affiliate C to say goodbye to affiliate X, as it maximizes its profit by reducing the cost of part X by paying $10.50 to another outside source. This is higher than the $10 price that applied when all the affiliates received part X from affiliate X. It is clear from the continuation of this exercise that, as each affiliate maximizes its profits by cutting costs, the corporation as a whole is being sub optimized. Even if the various affiliates do not pay more than an average price of $10 per unit for part X in purchasing all part X's from outside sources, the global company is stuck with an affiliate with no sales and a fixed annual cost of $10 million that represents, in large measure, financing costs on plant and equipment.

It is highly likely that the fixed costs in affiliate X contain an allowance for RandD expenses and product development that have to be recouped in the operation of a company, but do not have to be recouped by another company if it is essentially manufacturing a copy of part X. Copying is fairly common in global commerce because patent protection is limited to the nation issuing the patent. Global companies often obtain patents in a number of nations, but this may not be possible for all nations.

A company may manufacture a copy of a product in one of these nations. Although it is true that affiliate X is free to pursue patent infringement action against sales in a particular nation where it has patent protection, the time involved in enforcement proceedings and the legal expenses may make such protection prohibitively expensive. Furthermore, there is no internationally recognized legal structure to handle patent infringements.

In addition to RandD expenses, the fixed costs of affiliate X may also contain a service element for the benefit of the affiliates purchasing its output that may not be provided by third parties. By each affiliate "doing its own thing," the RandD and service costs cannot be covered. One principal problem associated with using market reference points for transfer pricing is that the affiliates may be shipping components and parts that are not readily available from other firms.

Most components and parts are specifically designed for a company's product line and are not available from third parties unless contracted for by an affiliate. Market prices for similarly designed components that cannot be actually used in the company's product line may not be relevant. Moreover, the quality inherent in third-party quotes for similar parts may not be up to the standards imposed on products made within a global corporate family.

There is no easy answer as to which approach for determining transfer prices should be followed. Both have their adherents and detractors. Either approach restricts transfer prices to something related to third-party, or market, transactions or to the cost of manufacture. Surveys have shown that nations seem to exhibit cultural preferences as to which approach to follow and as to what motivates companies in setting transfer prices.

Companies in some countries favour costbased transfer prices, whereas companies in other nations favour market-based transfer prices. U.S. based corporations have historically preferred setting transfer prices by the cost approach because the necessary data is available, whereas the necessary data for setting transfer prices on the basis of market transactions may not be available. Oftentimes, market quotes for uniquely designed parts and components may have to be derived rather than observed because there are no market transactions for the precise item.

Should General Motors set its transfer price on carburetors being shipped to Europe based on its cost of production or on what Toyota charges its U.S. transplants? The two carburetors are not the same and do not have the same cost of production. Furthermore, there may not be a data base available for prices for carburetors sold between related and unrelated parties from which to derive a market price. Preferences change with time. Surveys done in the 1970s indicated that the preponderance of U.S. companies were motivated by tax minimization in setting transfer prices. More recent surveys indicate that companies are more interested in setting transfer prices on the basis of measuring the performance of affiliate managers and of providing reliable and unbiased information for the making of decisions.

This change in attitude in U.S. companies may be the result of the United States becoming a relative tax haven compared to other nations. Its corporate tax rate of 34 per cent, plus state taxes, is less than in many other industrialized nations, where tax rates range between 40 per cent and 55 per cent. A U.S. company's total tax bill may, in fact, be reduced by allocating more profits to the United States. Regardless of changes in attitudes as to what is important in setting transfer prices, the essential point is that there is no unanimity on which approach to use and on what motivates companies in setting transfer prices. Up to this point, an important assumption has been that the parent company has real control over transfer prices to manage corporate cash flows and the profits reported by affiliates and to overcome artificial barriers to trade in the form of custom duties, currency exchange, and price controls. Some recent surveys suggest that competitive forces and market conditions within a nation seem to be more important in setting transfer prices than decisions made by a parent organization. If transfer prices are being set by exogenous commercial forces, then the presumption that a parent organization is able to achieve optimal financial performance of a global family of affiliates through the careful orchestration of transfer pricing is being challenged.

TAX CONSIDERATIONS

Taxation and transfer pricing are intimately entwined, because transfer pricing of goods, parts, and components moving in and out of a nation has a direct impact on taxes on profits and on the amount of duties and tariffs paid to the tax authority. The discussion on transfer pricing based on the cost-of-production approach shows an intimate involvement with the tax authority in the methodology for calculating various elements of the transfer price. There is little uniformity on taxation among nations. Taxes range from taxation of a corporation's activities to the "water's edge" or on its global earnings, the so-called "unitary tax." The state of California invented the unitary tax in the 1930s when movie companies in California began moving out of the state to avoid state taxes. A unitary tax was applied against the global earnings of a company and the tax was determined by the proportion of a company's sales, property, and payroll within the state to its global sales, property, and payroll. The resulting tax had no relation to the degree of profitability of a company's operation in California. A company could operate at a loss in California and still pay a tax based on its global profits.

Needless to say, both foreign governments and multinational companies have vigourously fought the unitary tax. A number of court decisions confirmed or restricted unitary taxation over the years. Ultimately, opposition to the unitary tax succeeded. In November 1991, Alaska was the last state to abandon having a company's state tax liability based on the global earnings of the company. The unitary tax still exists in a truncated form, where earnings are restricted to the "water's edge." The state tax is calculated on the portion of a company's activities within a state as compared to its activities within the United States.

Although most other countries limit their assessment on what is to be taxed to the operations of a company within their jurisdiction, there is no universal agreement as to what constitutes revenue and expenses in the calculation of taxable income and no uniformity on tax rates. Every nation decides what is subject to taxation and the applicable tax rates. The complexity of tax regulations, in general, and the diversity of tax laws among nations are such that it is necessary for an affiliate to retain the technical expertise necessary to understand and comply with local tax regulations. The parent organization must retain the technical knowledge for its own tax jurisdiction and have sufficient knowledge of tax matters elsewhere to coordinate tax planning among the various affiliates.

The vigour with which tax payments are enforced varies among nations. Some countries with seemingly high tax rates permit an underground economy to flourish without much in the way of enforcing tax payments. The other side of the coin is the willingness of companies to adhere to tax laws. In some nations, a businessman who scrupulously follows the tax laws and pays what is owed to the tax authority will find himself at a competitive disadvantage.

NATURE OF TAXES

Taxes can be direct or indirect. The United States relies more on direct taxation, which is applied to each taxable entity. A U.S. corporation is taxed at 34 per cent on its profits. If a corporation pays a dividend to its shareholders, then the next taxable entity, the individual, pays a tax, which may be 28 per cent or more. This is double taxation. Some nations, such as Germany, have two corporate tax rates on profits—one for retained profits and the other for distributed profits in the form of dividends. A lesser tax rate applies to profits that are distributed to shareholders to reduce the degree of double taxation.

Europe relies more on indirect taxes—particularly, the value added tax (VAT). The VAT is basically a tax applied to each stage of the production process and is not directly associated with the degree of profitability. Indeed, only a small portion of a VAT is associated with profits. Suppose that a company's manufacturing operations has the following financial results.

Wages, rents, interest, profit	$400,000
Outside purchases of goods and services for which VAT has already been paid	600,000
Total sales	$1,000,000

The additive method is to apply the VAT rate, say 10 per cent, to all costs associated with the production of goods, including profit and excluding purchases of goods and services from third parties for which the VAT has already been paid. In this case, $400,000 of a company's activities falls into this category resulting in a VAT of $40,000. A simpler method of calculation is to take the gross sales of the company ($1,000,000), subtract all purchases of goods and services for which VAT has already been paid ($600,000), and apply the VAT rate to the balance ($400,000). Either method yields the same result. The VAT is essentially equivalent to a national sales tax, because every company associated with the production and marketing of goods and providing services pays a tax on whatever value it adds to the goods or services. The value added tax, like a sales tax, is a tax on consumption, whereas U.S. taxes are on income and profits.

Value added tax rates vary widely from country to country and according to the nature of the business. Certain European countries have low VAT rates (5 per cent) for business transactions associated with food and high VAT rates (40 per cent) for luxury products. Others attempt to have one rate that applies to most forms of commerce. Because the VAT is not paid on items that have already been exposed to a value added tax, and with the European economy becoming more integrated, there is a powerful incentive for the European Community to harmonize VAT rates and coordinate the handling of VAT payments for products or components shipped between members of the European Community.

The amounts of value added by a company are frequently disclosed in European financial statements. In the excerpt from the British company, the company had gross revenues of 3,213 million pounds in 1987 of which 919.1 million pounds represents added value by the company. Of the total of 919.1 million pounds of added value, 496.8 million pounds was paid to the company's employees, 157.1 million pounds was paid in taxes to government tax authorities, and the remainder was paid to the internal and external providers of capital.

U.S. TAXATION OF GLOBAL COMPANIES

Nations have different ways of taxing global companies domiciled within their jurisdiction. If a parent corporation is domiciled in the United States, it does not pay taxes in the United States on profits earned by incorporated affiliates in other nations, unless the nation is considered a tax haven. This, in the United States, is known as Subpart F income, which will be discussed later under rein voicing centres. Unlike an incorporated affiliate, a branch of a U.S. company located in a foreign nation is taxed directly on its earnings regardless of whether the earnings are remitted to the home office or not. The taxes paid on remitted and unremitted earnings are not the same, in that unremitted earnings have to be translated to U.S. dollars before a tax liability can be assessed, and therefore, are influenced by changes in currency exchange rates. Taxes can also be calculated on the basis of the increase in the net worth of the branch, which can also be affected by changes in currency exchange rates. Sometimes a U.S. company will first open a branch operation in another country to permit startup losses to flow back to the parent organization. When the branch becomes profitable, it may be reorganized as a wholly owned subsidiary, reducing the company's overall tax liability.

U.S. based companies usually operate in the global market through operating affiliates whose stock is owned by the parent corporation. The parent corporation pays U.S. taxes only on the profits generated from dividends, royalties, and other service payments and fees paid by a non-U.S. domiciled affiliate to the parent organization. Taxes paid on profits by affiliates in their nations of domicile can be treated either as a tax credit or a tax deduction by the parent organization in the calculation of its U.S. taxes. To the degree that a tax paid on profits to a foreign government is treated as a tax credit, the net effect of a company paying taxes on its profits in a foreign country is that these taxes are essentially paid for by the U.S. government foregoing an equivalent amount of U.S. source based tax revenue.

Obviously, taxes paid to foreign governments must pass certain criteria set forth by the Internal Revenue Service to be considered for a tax credit. Foreign tax credits apply to taxes paid on foreign source profits calculated in a conventional way as U.S. source profits. Tax credits are also available for foreign government withholding taxes on dividends, interest payments, and royalties paid by a foreign-based affiliate to a U.S. parent company. There is a maximum permissible limit on tax credits linked to the ratio of foreign source income to total worldwide income multiplied by the tax liability of U.S. operations. This effectively limits the foreign tax credit to the U.S., not the foreign, tax rate. A company doing business in a nation with a higher tax rate on profits than in the United States does not receive a tax credit equal to the taxes paid to the foreign government. The tax credit is based on the U.S. tax rate. With U.S. tax rates being lower than in most other industrialized nations, U.S. based global companies are not being fully compensated by tax credits on foreign income taxes. This may provide an incentive to shift taxable income back to the United States through changes in transfer prices.

The U.S. tax authorities permit a credit for taxes paid on profits to other nations under the notion of tax equity and tax neutrality. The principle of tax equity implies that a U.S. taxpaying entity with an operation in another nation should not pay more in taxes than having the operation domiciled in the United States. Were the equity principle absolutely true, a U.S. taxpaying entity would be indifferent, or neutral, to whether the operation was located in another nation or in the United States. Some maintain that the U.S. tax code does not adhere to the tax neutrality principle because a company doing business in New York City does not obtain a tax credit on its federal taxes for taxes paid to the state and city of New York on profits made in their jurisdiction. A company with an affiliate in another nation not only receives a tax credit, which neutralizes its foreign and U.S. income taxes, but does not have to pay U.S. taxes on its foreign source earnings until those earnings are remitted to the parent in the form of a dividend, a royalty payment, or an equivalent thereof.

As long as foreign source profits remain in the coffers of the affiliate, no taxes are due to the U.S. government, even though, under special circumstances, the affiliate may lend these funds to the parent company. Deferral of dividend payments is essentially an interest-free loan made by the U.S. government to the foreign affiliate of a U.S. parent company on the amount of U.S. taxes due if, and when, these funds are repatriated to the U.S. parent. The principles of equity and neutrality built into the U.S. tax code were designed to provide an incentive for U.S. firms to invest overseas as part of the national policy of rebuilding war-torn nations. U.S. companies would be better off confining their activities within the United States, and would not invest in foreign affiliates, if the profits of these foreign affiliates were exposed to double taxation.

Qualified foreign taxes, which cannot be utilized as tax credits, may be used as a tax deduction. A tax deduction is not as valuable as a tax credit. Tax deductions apply when there is not sufficient U.S. taxes to be shielded by tax credits, or where the overall limitation on tax credits has been exceeded. Tax deductions can be carried back or carried forward, whichever is more useful.

REIN VOICING CENTRES

Some companies have set up rein voicing centres to manage all intra company trading of products. A rein voicing centre is at a single location, buying the output of the manufacturing affiliates and selling it to the marketing affiliates. Each affiliate receives or pays in its own currency, thus concentrating all intra company transaction currency exposure at the rein voicing centre. The centre possesses the necessary data to assess the net currency exposure of intra company transactions and can enter into appropriate currency hedges. The centre may also receive better quotes from currency exchange dealers because all intra company currency exchange transactions are done at one location.

The rein voicing centre can mark up the price of all products flowing through the centre to cover its administrative expenses. If there is little or no profitability associated with the operations of a rein voicing centre, it does not matter where the rein voicing centre is located from a tax viewpoint. However, it is possible to increase the markup to the point where corporate profit can be diverted from the nations where the goods are manufactured and marketed to the nation where the rein voicing centre is located. Now the location of the rein voicing centre is critical from a tax viewpoint.

In the 1960s, the U.S. government became concerned with the accumulation of profits in rein voicing centres located in tax havens. Tax havens were characterized as nations imposing no, or a very low, tax on profits, having a high degree of bank secrecy, and little or no currency controls. These nations consider financial activities of importance to their economy, provide modern communication facilities, and promote themselves as offshore financial centres. Bahamas, Bermuda, Cayman Islands, Liberia, Panama, and Vanuatu have been identified as tax havens.

It is possible to "run" a rein voicing centre through these nations without a physical presence of personnel or products. Profits can be easily diverted to tax havens by increasing the markup on selling prices, thus reducing tax liabilities to the nations where the products are manufactured and marketed. If the criteria for determining a tax haven is satisfied, then the income earned by a rein voicing centre, or any corporate entity in the declared tax haven, is deemed Subpart F income. This income flows directly to the U.S. parent corporation and is taxed as though the income was earned in the United States.

TAXATION IMPACT ON TRANSFER PRICING

Companies operating in the United States are guided by Section 482 of the Internal Revenue Code when setting transfer prices. Specifically, the IRS, through the Secretary of the Treasury, has the right to "distribute, apportion, or allocate gross income, deductions, credits, or allowances... between or among... businesses, if he determines that such distribution, apportionment, or allocation is necessary in order to prevent evasion of taxes. The IRS has been granted wide latitude to do whatever it wants if the IRS deems that dealings between a U.S. parent and its affiliates do not meet its standards. For instance, the IRS can reallocate income and deductions if loans have been made between a parent corporation and an affiliate at an unrealistic interest rate.

Unrealistic interest rates are those that would not occur for similar transactions between unrelated third parties. This also applies to charging for services and use of property, and transfers of tangible and intangible property including lease payments and royalties. A reference to IRS guidelines has already been made in discussing RandD and intangible costs in setting transfer prices by the production cost approach. Basing transfer pricing on published data rather than corporate derived prices is another example of the close working relationship, voluntary or not, between tax authorities and managers responsible for transfer prices.

In general, the IRS standard for determining transfer pricing, and other dealings between a parent and its affiliates, is whether it is an "arm's-length" transaction—one that would occur between a company and a third party having no affiliation other than the commercial transaction under consideration. This is independent of whether the transfer price is based on the cost of production or on market prices. If the transfer price between affiliates is seemingly out of line with a price that would have been charged to an unrelated party, then the IRS has the right to reallocate income or deductions according to what it feels to be the appropriate transfer price.

The IRS specifies various methods for establishing an appropriate transfer price. The preferred one is the comparable uncontrolled price method where prices are the same for goods sold to affiliated and to nonaffiliated companies. The price for goods sold to an unrelated third party establishes the transfer price for goods transferred to an affiliate.

This method does not work when goods are not sold to third parties, but are totally transferred between affiliates. Under these circumstances, the second method for setting the transfer price is the resale price method. This is the price for which the company would sell the item to an unspecified third party. The third party would add the same comparable value as the affiliate and sell the completed product with an appropriate markup. By netting the market price of the appropriate markup and the value added to the product by an affiliate, one can "back into" an appropriate transfer price from the point of view of the tax authority. The third method is the "cost plus" method, where the IRS permits three different ways of allocating costs (full absorption, direct cost, and incremental cost). All these methods leave some margin of discretion as to what is the appropriate transfer price.

If all these fail, as they frequently do for high-technology products, customised components, or subassemblies, then so-called fourth methods are permitted, such as determining transfer pricing on the basis of a predetermined profit for the foreign firm's operations and, through a netting process of accounting for applicable costs, establishing an appropriate transfer price.

Regardless of the methodology, the burden of proof in supporting a transfer price is with the taxpayer, not the IRS. To confuse matters more, there have been occasions when the tax courts have rejected the notion of arm's-length transfer pricing in settling tax disputes between corporations and the IRS.

OTHER NATIONS' POLICIES CONCERNING TRANSFER PRICING

The tax authority in Canada views transfer pricing of goods similar to the way the United States does. Transfer pricing for services differs in that it is based on a pro rata sharing of actual incurred costs between the parent corporation and its affiliate, and not necessarily at an arm's-length price.

Tax authorities in Japan follow a system comparable to that of the United States. German tax code provisions permit the reallocation of domestic source income if revenue or income has been shifted to another nation through a transaction that is different from those that would have been entered into by unrelated parties. In other words,

transfer pricing should be arm's-length, although the code is not specific in defining arm's-length pricing. The United Kingdom is similar to Germany in not specifically defining arm's-length pricing. The Inland Revenue may adjust taxable income based on fairness and arm's-length criteria. Disputes between corporations and Inland Revenue agents are frequently settled by negotiation, resulting in some sort of compromise between the two parties. This is unlike in Germany, where the adjustments made by the tax authorities are considered final, and unlike in the United States, where adjustments are litigated in tax courts. Tax authorities in many nations are currently taking a much closer look at transfer pricing practices. Recently, the U.K. Inland Revenue recast the accounts of one non-British company operating in the United Kingdom and assessed back taxes of nearly 2 billion pounds. In the United States, there is growing political pressure for the IRS to take more vigourous action against foreign-owned companies operating through U.S. based affiliates.

This pressure stems from the realization that the aggregate expenses for foreign-owned businesses operating in the United States exceed aggregate revenues. This means that, in the aggregate, foreign-owned subsidiaries are claiming to operate at a loss, although individual foreign-owned subsidiaries may be paying taxes on profits. Some foreign-owned affiliates operating in the United States have a twenty-year string of consecutive losses. This is not considered a realistic appraisal of performance because there are few profit-motivated foreign-based parent companies that would support twenty years of successive losses were they real. Poor or nonexistent profits for foreign-based affiliates operating in the United States are blamed on transfer pricing.

Transfer price manipulation is felt to have resulted in tax underpayments of between $12 and $50 billion. Legislation was passed in 1989 to require foreign-owned businesses in the United States to keep records, in English, of transactions with foreign related parties. Much of this legislation has to do with substantiating transfer pricing on either a cost or arm'slength transaction with an unrelated third party. A growing risk associated with manipulating transfer prices for the purpose of tax minimization.

The risk is that the tax authorities will recast the company's statements with their own version of the proper transfer price, thus exposing a company to the risk of double taxation. Most nations have entered into tax treaties with various other nations with regard to taxing of affiliates of parent organizations domiciled in the treaty nations. These treaties determine withholding taxes on dividends, interest, and royalties; relief from double taxation; and the types of taxes and organizations covered by the treaty. Overall exposure to taxation can be reduced by judicious structuring of the legal corporate entities of a parent company and its affiliates in accordance with the provisions of these treaties.

Some of these treaties contain formal agreements for the mutual examination of the tax returns of affiliates of a parent company. The tax returns of affiliates and parent organizations are exchanged and examined by the tax authorities to determine correct tax liabilities, detect tax avoidance maneuvers, scrutinize trans- fer pricing practices, and exchange information useful to the tax authorities. These treaties also provide a forum for one tax authority to complain about the actions taken by another, when these actions are deemed detrimental to its interests.

Recent developments in international cooperation of tax authorities include the establishment of a formal agreement on transfer prices. The mutual agreement of various nations to reference a published source for tanker rates in determining oil company tax liabilities is an example of this. Australia and the United States are attempting to grant "advance determinations" of the proper transfer price for Australian companies dealings with their U.S. affiliates. A recent survey has shown that about half of IRS tax examinations of multinational companies involve transfer prices. If a mutually agreeable methodology could be arranged between a company and the IRS, many of these tax examinations could be eliminated.

The IRS is attempting to develop a procedure whereby a company and the IRS would mutually agree to a transfer-pricing agreement covering the distribution of finished goods, sales of raw materials and components, general and administrative expenses, and managerial and technical services. If the taxpayer develops an acceptable transfer-pricing methodology, then the taxpayer and the IRS would enter into an advance-pricing agreement. The IRS would limit its examinations to an audit to ensure that the taxpayer has complied with the agreement. However, the taxpayer is obliged to submit pricing data of independent transactions, or an adequate substitute, to show that the transfer price possesses the necessary attributes of an arm's-length transaction. The taxpayer is also responsible to show that the agreed transfer-pricing methodology is generating acceptable transfer prices from an arm's-length perspective.

The preference of tax authorities in many nations for arm's-length transfer pricing may act as an inducement to switch from the cost-of-production to the market price approach in setting transfer prices because, presumably, they are one and the same. The financial and taxation departments of multinational, or global, companies must deal daily with what are considered to be the most pressing issues in international accounting today. Those involved with transfer pricing must measure the consequences of their transfer-pricing decisions both on corporate profits and on current and potential tax liabilities. Potential tax liabilities, stemming from tax authorities rejecting management's transfer price decisions, and substituting their own, are enormous. This must weigh heavily on the shoulders of those responsible for setting transfer prices.

4

Recording of Transfer Pricing and Taxation

INTRODUCTION

A small operation managed by a few individuals was the typical beginning of a large corporation with a hundred operating affiliates dispersed around the world. Decision making was highly centralized and lines of communication were short. As the company grew, the founding management team found it more difficult to keep matters under control.

This problem was greatly exacerbated when operations within the company became physically separated. Centers of activity in different locations called for a different style of management. Funneling of all decisions from diverse locations through a small group of individuals, who no longer possess the necessary intimate awareness of the circumstances surrounding each decision, is a surefire prescription for stifling growth.

Growth is the name of the game for modern corporations. Growth entails individual operating affiliates taking appropriate action to enhance productivity, market share, and the scope of a company's product line. It has been found that operating affiliates physically separated from the parent organization can best achieve these objectives under a decentralized style of management. Responsibility now falls on the shoulders of the manager of an operating affiliate to make the necessary decisions that will lead to improved financial results, the universal measure of performance. The parent organization takes on a new role as coordinator and monitor of activities now that responsibility for operations has been transferred to the operating units.

Far from playing a passive role, the parent organization focuses its attention on optimizing the performance of its semiautonomous operating affiliates. To do this, the parent organization must establish, and articulate, a set of strategic goals and allocate limited corporate resources to the various operating affiliates to best achieve these goals. It must ensure that the short-term action plans of the operating affiliates are in accord with its long-term plans.

Top management positions in the operating affiliates must be filled with individuals capable of leading their affiliates in the right direction and an incentive system must be set up to induce managers to orient their thinking to the goals of the company. Finally, the parent organization must set up a financial reporting and control system to monitor its global operations, to provide necessary information for the making of decisions and to evaluate the performance of the affiliate managers.

Although operating affiliates appear to be semiauton-omous units in that they are given a wide spectrum of decision–making responsibility in managing their local operations, they are not independent centers of corporate activity. They are often united in manufacturing and marketing a common product line, in the course of which they routinely buy and sell finished goods, components, or raw materials from one another.

These intra company exchanges of goods, components, and raw materials require a transfer price. The parent organization sets the transfer price after considering various factors with an eye on optimizing corporate performance as a whole. Transfer prices are often not negotiated and agreed on by the actual buyers and sellers of the goods and components being shipped between operating affiliates. Yet transfer prices directly affect the revenue and cost of goods sold, and therefore, the profitability of the operating affiliates. Because the affiliate managers are monitored by a financial reporting and control system that scrutinizes their financial results, one can expect that affiliate managers have an entirely different perspective on transfer pricing than the executives of the parent organization. Transfer pricing can easily embroil executives of the parent organization and the managers of operating affiliates in endless disputes. Some firms have even established an administrative panel for reviewing transfer prices to resolve sharp differences of opinion between those responsible for managing operating affiliates and those responsible for setting transfer prices.

TRANSFER PRICES AND TAXES

A global company with operations in many nations must deal with a new dimension of complexity in establishing transfer prices, which is not present when a company operates solely within the confines of a single nation. A company whose operations are within a single nation pays the same taxes on profits regardless of the transfer pricing policy.

The consolidation process, whether for financial or tax accounting purposes, eliminates intra company transactions to arrive at either a book profit or a before-tax profit. When a company transacts business through affiliate companies in different nations, however, transfer pricing provides a mechanism for shifting taxable profits between tax jurisdictions.

Tax authorities in various nations are concerned with the notion that transfer pricing, often set by parent organizations outside their jurisdiction, is based on minimizing taxes paid in their jurisdictions. There certainly is an element of truth in this contention, but there are other considerations in administering transfer prices than minimizing taxes. The setting of transfer prices provides a way of moving funds internationally for a variety of purposes, of circumventing currency exchange controls that threaten to choke the operations of a company, of minimizing the deleterious impact of other artificial barriers to trade such as duties and tariffs, and of reducing currency risk exposure. A transfer pricing policy attempts to satisfy a multiple set of objectives. Some of these objectives call for high transfer prices, whereas others require low transfer prices. A company must select what it considers to be an optimal transfer price, which is a compromise price for best achieving divergent objectives.

This optimal transfer price may not be the one that minimizes taxes on profits. The selected transfer price may not be satisfactory both to the local tax authority and to the manager of an affiliate if it reduces the reported profitability of the affiliate. However, setting the transfer price is critical to optimizing the financial performance of the corporation as a whole, given the conditions that prevail at a point in time.

MINIMIZING TAXES

Tax authorities of most countries have guidelines or controls that are expected to be complied with in setting transfer prices. Management is not free to arbitrarily select transfer prices without having to substantiate their transfer price decisions. Nevertheless, there is still an element of choice where a selected transfer price may reduce the tax burden of a company. Suppose that a company consists of a parent organization and two operating affiliates—one in nation A, where the tax rate on profits is 30 per cent, and one in nation B, where the tax rate on profits is 40 per cent. The tax is applied to each affiliate's gross margin for illustrative purposes. The affiliate in nation A makes a product that is entirely sold through the affiliate in nation B. Two cases are considered—a low and a high transfer price.

Table. Case I-Low Transfer Price

	Nation A Tax 30%	Nation B Tax 40%	Consolidated
Sales	$2000	$3200	$3200
Cost of Goods Sold	1500	2000	1500
Gross Margin	500	1200	1700
Tax	150	480	630
Net Income	$350	$720	$1070

Everything made in a factory in nation A is sold through a marketing organization in nation B. Therefore, total sales in nation A, calculated on the basis of an administered transfer price, is also the cost of goods sold in nation B. Sales in nation B of $3,200 is the net consolidated sales for the company, because all goods produced in nation A are sold in nation B.

The actual cost of manufacturing the goods in nation A is $1,500. Because nation B does not add value to the goods, the consolidated cost of goods sold for the company is also $1,500. The consolidated tax is the sum of the $150 and the $480 paid to the tax authorities of nations A and B, respectively.

The consolidated net income is $1,070, the sum of the net incomes of the two affiliates. Suppose that the transfer price is increased from $2,000 to $2,500 for goods shipped between the two affiliates. Consolidated sales, cost of goods sold, and gross margin are unaffected by the change in the transfer price, because it is netted out in the consolidation process. Taxes paid in each nation are no longer the same because of the change in the transfer price.

In case II, the increase in the transfer price shifts the profit to Nation A, which has the lower tax rate. The affiliate in nation A earns more taxable income and pays more in taxes than in case I. The affiliate in nation B earns less taxable income and pays less in taxes in case II than in case I. The net effect, as seen by comparing case II with case I, is that the company as a whole is paying less in taxes, which increases its consolidated net income.

It is true that had the two nations the same tax rate, the total taxes paid by the company, and the consolidated net income, would not be affected by changes in the transfer price. Even so, transfer prices determine what portion of total taxes are to be paid to the tax authority in nation A and to the tax authority in Nation B. Although the parent organization may be relatively insensitive concerning to whom it pays taxes, needless to say, the tax authorities are very much concerned as to which is collecting taxes.

The problem is compounded, from the point of view of a tax authority, because the transfer price is probably set by a parent organization not under its jurisdiction. The importance of transfer pricing to both managers and tax authorities can be appreciated when it is realized that between 40 per cent and 60 per cent of international trade involves goods moving between affiliates of the same company. Corporate decisions on transfer prices do have a meaningful impact on what a tax jurisdiction collects. There are nations, islands, and localities where tax authorities exhibit little interest in transfer prices. Ireland, Puerto Rico, and other nations or areas designated as free trade zones or having special tax privileges may not tax corporate profits, or have a very low tax rate.

These nations or locales are interested in companies building plants on their soil for the social benefits that accrue from employment of individuals who might otherwise be unemployed. Companies operating in such nations or locales can substantially decrease their overall tax rate. The effective reduction in tax rates depends on the transfer prices of imported components and semi finished goods and the transfer prices of exported finished goods.

Granting tax concessions is one way for a nation to attract companies. At this time, eastern European nations offer tax incentives but do not have a prescribed accounting methodology to calculate profits, which makes it impossible to quantify the tax benefit. More than one company has set up an operation in eastern Europe to later discover that the government had a much different version in mind of the nature of the tax benefits than the investors anticipated.

Such shortsightedness by government officials has a deleterious impact on attracting other companies. Many nations are discovering that viewing business solely as a way to fill the public coffers may not be in their long-term best interests. Within the United States, states with high corporate tax rates have experienced companies moving to states with low corporate tax rates. The higher they raise their corporate tax rates, the less they collect in taxes. As once companies moved from one state to another, now they move from one nation to another. In selecting a potential site, a businessman considers many factors, of which taxes are but one.

Some of these are social and political stability; a system of commercial law to resolve disputes; a set of acceptable accounting practices (both to assess tax liabilities and evaluate tax incentives); a labour force with the requisite skills and will to work; and an infrastructure of transportation, communication, and utility and social (education, medical care) services.

There are more locations that offer good potential sites for factories than before. Managers no longer feel that their factories must be anchored to one nation and have learned to manage far–flung operations. Nations must now compete for factories. Tax authorities in developed nations are beginning to realise that they may end up collecting less tax revenue in their eagerness to collect more tax revenue by raising tax rates. The United States was forced to repeal a luxury tax on pleasure boats because pleasure boat construction virtually ceased with the passage of the new tax. New Jersey was forced to repeal a sales tax on trucks when truck selling companies moved their operations to nearby Pennsylvania. In both cases, tax revenues fell when tax rates were raised, and the tax authorities were forced to rescind tax increases. In a global economy, companies are mobile and will relocate to avoid especially burdensome taxes.

INTERNATIONAL FUNDING

Businesses operating in hard currency nations have the advantage of being able to transfer and convert currencies as necessary. Many nations, however, have currencies that lack convertibility, the so-called soft currencies. Transfer pricing provides a means of moving funds from one country to another, when direct currency convertibility is not possible.

If a nation has an affiliate that completes the manufacturing process and sells its output within that nation, funds can be moved out of that nation by increasing the transfer price for goods imported by the affiliate. The same objective can be accomplished by increasing the charges for services rendered by the parent organization to the affiliate, such as selling and administrative

(S&A) fees, research and development (R&D) expenses, financial charges on transferred assets, and royalties for rights to patents and dividends.

Sometimes currency exchange controls focus on the amount of dividends that can be paid by an affiliate to its parent. A quasi–dividend can be paid by raising the transfer price of goods moving into the nation or by increasing corporate fees, financial charges, and royalty payments. Some nations with severe restrictions on dividend outflows will permit increases in transfer prices and service fees. These quasi–dividend payments are allowed because the local government recognizes that few companies can afford the luxury of investing in a nation that prohibits the company from earning a return on its investment.

However, actions such as these that drain funds out of a soft currency nation eventually result in some sort of currency exchange restriction. This often results in affiliate profits accumulating in a currency that may not be particularly desirable. Sometimes currency exchange restrictions can be bypassed by the affiliate making an investment, or lending funds, to an affiliate in another nation.

CONTROLLING REPORTED PROFITS

Shifts in transfer prices, corporate administrative fees, and other parent company charges to an affiliate are means of managing the affiliate's reported profitability. It may be in the interest of a parent organization to lower the reported profitability of an affiliate for reasons other than tax minimization. These include deflecting union demands for higher wages, reducing political pressure to nationalize or expropriate a profitable affiliate, and dissuading potential competitors from entering the market.

Lowering profitability is also a way to counter price controls that limit profitability. If a government has set price controls based on the cost of production plus a limited markup for profits, increases in the transfer price of goods sent to the affiliate lowers the profit margin of goods sold in that nation. This may permit goods to be sold at government decreed profit margins with the company as a whole still able to earn its normal profits.

A few nations have tax rates that are linked to profitability. The greater the profitability, the higher the tax rate. The logic behind this taxation policy is that there is a level of profits on investment that seems "excessive" to the government. Such excessive profitability should be punished by the government, and there is no greater punishment than taking away the excess profits through a higher tax rate.

By increasing the transfer price of goods being imported into the nation, the degree of profitability is decreased, lowering the tax rate and, presumably, restoring respectability in the eyes of the government. Alternatively, it may be in the interests of the parent organization to enhance the profitability of an affiliate. This may be done by lowering the transfer price of imported goods. One reason for enhancing the profitability of an affiliate is to provide sufficient financial resources to the affiliate for it to withstand price cutting by competitive companies. Improving an affiliate's profitability, even at the cost of paying more in taxes, may allow the affiliate to borrow needed funds for operation from local banks and other financial institutions, to improve its credit rating to qualify for lower interest loans and to fund capital outlays from its own resources.

CIRCUMVENTING EXCHANGE CONTROLS

Governments with soft currencies often limit the amount of their currency that companies operating in their nations can exchange for other currencies. Their motivation is to discourage the selling of the domestic soft currency and the buying of a hard currency, which would exert downward pressure on the value of the local currency. In other words, exchange controls are set up to keep a soft currency from becoming softer.

From the point of view of a parent organization, restricting hard currency outflows inhibits an affiliate's ability to pay for imported components or other items necessary for its operations. Transfer prices for the needed components can be kept artificially low to expand the volume of goods that are being imported into a soft currency nation.

This sustains an affiliate's manufacturing operation without exceeding government decreed restrictions on converting soft currency to hard currency. But there is an adverse consequence because such a course of action results in a parent corporation accumulating even larger amounts of soft currency. These holdings of soft currency are constantly losing purchasing power through inflation. The soft currency cannot be converted to a more desirable currency because of currency exchange restrictions and the soft currency, which has little value within the nation, has no value outside the nation. One of the knottiest problems associated with an operating affiliate in a soft currency nation is funding of hard currency imports necessary for its operation and obtaining a hard currency return on a hard currency investment.

Some companies will not set up an operation in a soft currency nation unless there is a prearranged means to earn hard currency to pay for hard currency imports and to provide a hard currency return on a hard currency investment. Pepsi Cola struck a barter deal for producing its soft drink in the former Soviet Union. Its soft ruble revenue, net of soft ruble expenses, is exchanged for Russian built tankers, which are then sold for hard currencies.

Oil companies will not set up operations in the Commonwealth of Independent States, and other soft currency nations, unless they receive a share of the output, which is shipped out of the nation and sold for hard currency. The easiest way for a company to earn hard currency in a soft currency nation would be to export a portion of its output to hard currency nations. However, most soft currency nations do not permit the hard currency revenue to remain with the company.

The hard currency revenue is exchanged for an equivalent amount of soft currency, which is then credited to the exporter's bank account. In essence, the national government receives the hard currency revenue from exports and pays soft currency to the exporter. Sometimes international banks are at fault for imposing this condition on a nation as a means to guarantee repayment of international debt. Regardless of whether the nation or the international banks impose this condition, it is self-defeating because the economic development of a developing nation is held back by the inability of companies to earn sufficient hard currency to justify their investments.

MINIMIZING DUTIES AND TARIFFS

Duties and tariffs imposed on goods imported into a nation can be reduced by lowering the transfer price. This is the exact opposite of reducing taxes on profits by increasing the transfer price. Because the tariff rate is usually less than the tax rate on profits, lowering transfer prices to reduce import tariffs often results in a higher tax on profits. In some nations, however, tariffs on certain imported goods and commodities are not set by a corporate-determined transfer price but by an internationally posted price.

This can be done only for generic goods (steel) or commodities (oil), where there is an active market with published and verifiable prices. Sometimes tax authorities will reference costs not to a "transfer price" cost but to an internationally agreed standard. One example of this is tanker rates in the oil business. An oil company can manage the profitability, and therefore, the tax liability, of a refinery by the transfer price associated with international tanker transportation for moving oil to and from a refinery.

The tax authorities of many nations and the oil companies have agreed to a panel of experts determining a fair and representative tanker rate that is used for the computation of taxes independent of the transfer price, or internal cost, that oil companies charge for shipping oil among their affiliates. This eliminates arguments between tax authorities and oil companies concerning the appropriate shipping charge.

Determining the optimal transfer-pricing policy is further complicated when a nation in which an affiliate operates has an export subsidy programme or provides a tax credit on the value of exports. It may be advantageous to lower transfer prices to an affiliate whose output is exported to third parties or other affiliates in other nations to take advantage of these tax incentives.

The optimal transfer price depends on the nature of the export subsidy or tax credit, the volume of the affiliate's output that is exported from the nation, the relationship between taxes on profits and the generation of tax credits and on the capacity of the affiliate to utilize the tax credit or export subsidy. The nature of the taxes paid in a nation in the form of income taxes, duties and tariffs on imported goods, and export subsidies or tax credits on exported goods influence the setting of transfer prices.

There is no hard and fast rule on whether a high or a low transfer-pricing policy is best for a company. The particular circumstances of a company's operations in a nation and the nature of taxes and subsidies determine the best transfer-pricing policy. A transferpricing system integrated into a financial reporting and control system should be capable of analyzing "what" if scenarios to evaluate the effect of different transfer-pricing policies.

REDUCING CURRENCY EXCHANGE RISK

Changes in currency exchange rates result in transaction and translation gains and losses. More importantly, they affect the competitive position of an affiliate. If an affiliate manufactures and markets its goods in a nation, and imports components from another nation, a revaluation of the currency where the finished goods are being sold relative to the currency of its purchased components reduces manufacturing costs.

This makes the affiliate more competitive and profitable. A devaluation, on the other hand, increases the cost of imported components, making the affiliate less competitive and less profitable. Reality is much more complex than this simple example because affiliates may export and import components and finished goods to and from a variety of nations.

Changes in exchange rates benefit some affiliates and hurt others, and it may not be obvious because of the nature of buying and selling of goods and services. It is possible that a change in currency exchange rates that is adverse to a particular affiliate may be beneficial to the company as a whole because of the nature of the net exposure of the company to the affected currencies. Adjustments to transfer prices may affect currency holdings before an anticipated change in exchange rates takes place and may be able to restore a company's competitive position after the change has taken place.

Therefore, a financial reporting and control system should have the capacity to assess changes to both transfer prices and currency exchange rates to enable the parent organization to respond both to anticipated changes in currency exchange rates and to subsequent shifts in its competitive position.

TRANSFER PRICING AND JOINT VENTURES

A joint venture partner, a local partner owning a portion of an affiliate, and a minority shareholder are going to be as interested in transfer pricing as the local tax authority. Less often, a partnership is structured on the basis of a claim, or royalty, on revenue. More often, it is a claim on profits. If one party to a venture or partnership can influence revenue, costs, and profitability through transfer pricing, then the other party or partner, or a minority shareholder, will be deservedly concerned.

One way to manage transfer pricing with regard to having partners or minority shareholders is to formalize the setting of transfer prices in some verifiable manner such as a set markup above costs, another is to reference transfer prices to an observable market transaction. Either way minimizes the opportunity for one party to a partnership or joint venture to manipulate transfer prices to its advantage.

If the partners, participants, and minority shareholders feel that their interests are vulnerable by virtue of the other party to a business venture controlling transfer prices, then they may not contribute to the venture that which was expected of them. Avoiding these problems can be more easily said than done. Some years ago, Ford Motor Company purchased the minority shares of its partially owned subsidiaries because the company felt that it could not administer transfer pricing in a way that was fair to all concerned.

Some managements have made the strategic decision not to enter into joint ventures, or have local partners or minority shareholdings in corporate affiliates, where they can manage the profitability of the venture through transfer prices. Sometimes, the solution for a problem is to avoid the problem.

TRANSFER PRICING AND MANAGERIAL PERFORMANCE EVALUATION

It may be in the interest of the corporation as a whole to transfer in components that are more highly priced than those an affiliate can purchase from other sources. It may be in the interest of the corporation as a whole to transfer goods made in one affiliate to another affiliate for less than what the affiliate can sell them for to third parties. Although the corporation may gain by such a set of transfer prices for goods moving among affiliates, it does not serve the interests of the affiliate managers if they are subsequently judged on profitability.

This dichotomy of purpose in establishing a transfer-pricing policy for the good of the whole company, yet holding managers of affiliates accountable for profits that are contaminated, so to speak, by transfer prices has not been successfully addressed when transfer prices are different from market prices. In fact, this is one potent argument in favour of companies having transfer pricing policies based on the market price for comparable goods.

If transfer prices are set at the price for goods exchanged between unrelated parties, then there is no dichotomy of purpose in setting transfer prices and measuring performance. Managers of affiliates can be judged in an unbiased fashion on the profitability of their operations because they are buying and selling at market prices—the same prices that would prevail if they were independent companies.

The disadvantage of letting the market set transfer prices is that the parent corporation can no longer utilize transfer pricing as a means to pursue the overall optimization of the financial performance of the corporation. One possible approach to the dysfunctional aspects of setting transfer prices at other than market prices and measuring management performance of affiliates is to isolate and separately state the amount of inter company "profit" or "loss" that each affiliate is experiencing in its transactions with other affiliates. This approach provides the parent organization with information on whether an affiliate is suffering from unwarranted decreased profitability or enjoying unwarranted increased profitability because of transfer pricing.

SETTING TRANSFER PRICES BY COST OF PRODUCTION

There are two general approaches for setting transfer prices: the cost of production and market prices associated with third party, or unrelated, transactions. The cost-of-production approach bases the price of goods to be transferred between affiliates on the variable cost of production, an allowance for fixed costs that are general in nature and are apportioned over the entire product line, and an allowance for fixed costs that can be apportioned among the individual products.

This latter category usually includes research and development costs and selling and administrative costs. The remaining components may include financial fees and royalties associated with tangible and intangible assets to be apportioned to individual products and the selection of an appropriate profit margin. The variable cost of production includes labour, material, and other direct costs that are consumed in the production of an item.

If the policy of the company is to hire and fire (lay off) factory workers as production rises and falls, then labour is a variable cost. If a company is reluctant to let go of their workers when sales decline, then factory labour should be considered part of fixed costs. Factory labour costs are usually part variable and part fixed. Other variable costs can be the unit financing and utility costs associated with machinery and processes used in the manufacture of a particular product and unit shipping costs. These costs can also be treated as fixed costs depending on how the company's cost accounting system is set up. Fixed costs are all costs not included in variable costs. Fixed costs are the financing or depreciation costs of the factory; the overhead costs of marketing, accounting, and supervision; the cost of inventories, warehouses, insurance, utilities, communication, property taxes, and other non-variable cost items.

Fixed costs may not be entirely fixed in that there is some variation as production levels change. For instance, bonuses, which would be considered part of the fixed costs of having an executive suite, rise and fall with profits, which are related to production levels. The number of staff personnel in marketing, accounting, engineering, and other overhead functions can vary with the production level.

Some elements of fixed costs are allocated in the transfer price setting mechanism in a way that fairly apportions the fixed cost burden among the various products. Other elements of fixed costs can be apportioned more on the basis of the benefit derived by an individual product. One of these is research and development, where the allocation can be made over a product line in proportion to the degree of R&D expenditures associated with the development of an individual product. Although there is general agreement that this is a fair way to apportion R&D expenses of successful undertakings, there is lack of agreement on how to apportion R&D expenses for failed projects. Some maintain that the allocation of expenses associated with failed R&D projects should be apportioned to all products on the basis that every product should bear the risk of failed R&D efforts.

Others object on the grounds that had the R&D effort succeeded, a particular product might not have benefited. Therefore, it makes no sense for the transfer price to contain the cost of a failed R&D effort, which, had it succeeded, would not be part of the transfer price of the product. The question as to the proper treatment of failed R&D projects is not an internal accounting matter. Tax authorities are interested in who takes the write off of a failed R&D project. In the United States, the Internal Revenue Service (IRS) is concerned whether a transfer price contains a provision for failed R&D expenditures. If a transfer price contains only that portion of R&D expenditures that were successful with regard to a particular product, then failed R&D projects of a U.S. corporation are being written off solely against U.S. income. A portion of the tax loss write-off is passed on to the tax authority of another nation by including an element of failed R&D expenditures in the transfer price. Another fixed cost element that can be separated and apportioned in a different manner than general fixed costs are services provided to an individual product.

These may be coordination and control expenses associated with a product; costs for enhancing the efficiency of operations for manufacturing the product or expanding the scope of its market; and the costs of recruiting and training of management and operations personnel associated with manufacturing, marketing, and repairing or servicing the product. The allocation of these service costs to individual products provides another element in deriving their transfer prices.

The derivation of the transfer price also includes elements for tangibles and intangibles associated with a product. Tangibles are the plant, equipment, and other physical assets dedicated to the manufacture of the product. Part of the transfer price provides a financial return for tangibles based on their value. Intangibles represent the technical knowledge and expertise and applicable patents that can be allocated to a particular product.

The transfer price also contains an element that provides a company with a return on intangibles. Intangible costs within a transfer price cannot be capriciously determined by management because intangible costs affect taxable profits. For this reason, the IRS has established guidelines for determining the intangible cost element in a transfer price.

An intangible cost element must be present if there are intangible costs associated with the manufacture or marketing of a product and must be so identified. Intangible costs can be proportioned in relation to the income attributable to the intangibles by units of production, sales, net or gross profits, or other reasonable methods. The fee for intangible property incorporated in a transfer price must be similar to what would have been arranged with an independent third party.

The last part of the cost approach in setting transfer prices is determining the proper profit margin on the goods made by one affiliate and shipped to another. This may be the average profit margin for the company as a whole or a profit margin associated with a specific product line. Regardless, the stipulated profit margin must be reconciled in some manner with the profitability of the company or a product line to satisfy the tax authorities.

The need for reconciliation of the profit and the various cost elements of the transfer price with the tax authorities sometimes results in the tax group within the finance department of a company being responsible for administering transfer prices. However, this choice may hinder general management from using transfer prices as a means to achieve corporate objectives.

The chief advantage of the cost of production approach for setting transfer prices is that the costs are available and are subject to quantification. For this reason, the production cost approach has been more common in the past than the market price approach. The chief disadvantage is that there is no real incentive for an affiliate to improve its manufacturing process, to enhance its efficiency, or to take steps to lower costs.

Mistakes, errors, inefficiencies in manning or machinery, management inattention to detail, worker carelessness, and excessive remuneration of white and blue collar workers alike may all be incorporated in the determination of costs and passed on to the affiliates in the transfer price. Another disadvantage is that both the tax authority and the affiliates may object to the nature of the apportionment of R&D, S&A, tangibles, and intangibles among the various products and the assigned profit margin.

SETTING TRANSFER PRICES BY MARKET PRICES

The disadvantages associated with the cost-of-production method of setting transfer prices can be mostly avoided by referencing transfer prices to third party transactions for identical, or nearly identical, products. If an affiliate can obtain the item being purchased from a third party for a certain price, then that price can be the basis for setting the transfer price.

The proponents of market-oriented transfer prices maintain that letting the market set the transfer price is inherently more fair than a production-cost-based system because one affiliate is not supporting the inefficiencies of another. If an affiliate receives only the global competitive price for its products, then there is an incentive for it to take whatever actions are needed to correct the inefficiencies in its operations that are resulting in higher costs. In a truly decentralized operation, managers are expected to make their decisions on an independent basis, and unrelated companies are permitted to compete for the business of an affiliate, along with other affiliates. The parent organization does not set transfer prices and has little or no influence over the decisions made by the managers of the affiliates. No favour or special consideration is shown to fellow affiliates in the competitive process of selecting suppliers for components and goods. The hope, of course, is that everyone is kept on his or her competitive toes to produce salable goods at the lowest possible cost. This managerial philosophy, where each affiliate is treated as an independent company, is sometimes referred to as the small business unit (SBU) management philosophy. The disadvantage is that, although each affiliate is focused on optimizing its operations, the end result may be suboptimal performance of the corporation as a whole. Suppose that affiliate X produces all of a component (part X) for a number of widget manufacturing affiliates. Total demand for part X is 2 million per year. Affiliate X has $10 million in fixed annual costs, which include a profit margin on the investment in manufacturing facilities plus a return on the R&D investment for the development of part X. The variable costs for manufacturing part X is $5. The transfer price based on the fixed and variable costs of affiliate X supplying all other affiliates with part X is $10.

Table. Volume of Sales: 2,000,000

Fixed Costs	$10,000,000
Variable Costs at $5 per Unit	10,000,000
Total Costs	$20,000,000
Transfer Price Based on Cost of Making 2,000,000	$10.00

Affiliate A is free to cut its best deal and obtains a quote of $9.50 from another company. Affiliate A does what is best for maximizing its profits and purchases 200,000 part X's from a third party for $9.50 rather than pay $10 to affiliate X. Affiliate X has lost a contract for 200,000 part X's and now operates on a basis of a sales volume of 1,800,000 per year.

Table. Volume of Sales: 1,800,000

Fixed Costs	$10,000,000
Variable Costs at $5 per Unit	9,000,000
Total Costs	$19,000,000
Transfer Price Based on Cost of Making 1,800,000	$10.56

The remaining affiliates must pay a higher price because there is less sales volume to cover the fixed costs of affiliate X. The increase in transfer price to cover the fixed and variable costs is essentially equivalent to treating fixed costs as a component of variable costs, which it is not. Nevertheless, affiliate X must cover all its costs. When affiliate X announces the increase in price, affiliate B concludes a deal with a third party at $9.75 causing another loss of 200,000 for affiliate X.

Table. Volume of Sales: 1,600.000

Fixed Costs	$10,000,000
Variable Costs at $5 per Unit	8,000,000
Total Costs	$18,000,000
Transfer Price Based on cost of Making 1,600,000	$11.25

Now it's time for affiliate C to say goodbye to affiliate X, as it maximizes its profit by reducing the cost of part X by paying $10.50 to another outside source. This is higher than the $10 price that applied when all the affiliates received part X from affiliate X. It is clear from the continuation of this exercise that, as each affiliate maximizes its profits by cutting costs, the corporation as a whole is being sub optimized.

Even if the various affiliates do not pay more than an average price of $10 per unit for part X in purchasing all part X's from outside sources, the global company is stuck with an affiliate with no sales and a fixed annual cost of $10 million that represents, in large measure, financing costs on plant and equipment. It is highly likely that the fixed costs in affiliate X contain an allowance for R&D expenses and product development that have to be recouped in the operation of a company, but do not have to be recouped by another company if it is essentially manufacturing a copy of part X.

Copying is fairly common in global commerce because patent protection is limited to the nation issuing the patent. Global companies often obtain patents in a number of nations, but this may not be possible for all nations. A company may manufacture a copy of a product in one of these nations. Although it is true that affiliate X is free to pursue patent infringement action against sales in a particular nation where it has patent protection, the time involved in enforcement proceedings and the legal expenses may make such protection prohibitively expensive.

Furthermore, there is no internationally recognized legal structure to handle patent infringements. In addition to R&D expenses, the fixed costs of affiliate X may also contain a service element for the benefit of the affiliates purchasing its output that may not be provided by third parties. By each affiliate "doing its own thing," the R&D and service costs cannot be covered.

One principal problem associated with using market reference points for transfer pricing is that the affiliates may be shipping components and parts that are not readily available from other firms. Most components and parts are specifically designed for a company's product line and are not available from third parties unless contracted for by an affiliate. Market prices for similarly designed components that cannot be actually used in the company's product line may not be relevant.

Moreover, the quality inherent in third-party quotes for similar parts may not be up to the standards imposed on products made within a global corporate family. There is no easy answer as to which approach for determining transfer prices should be followed. Both have their adherents and detractors. Either approach restricts transfer prices to something related to third-party, or market, transactions or to the cost of manufacture.

Surveys have shown that nations seem to exhibit cultural preferences as to which approach to follow and as to what motivates companies in setting transfer prices. Companies in some countries favour costbased transfer prices, whereas companies in other nations favour market-based transfer prices. U.S. based corporations have historically preferred setting transfer prices by the cost approach because the necessary data is available, whereas the necessary data for setting transfer prices on the basis of market transactions may not be available.

Oftentimes, market quotes for uniquely designed parts and components may have to be derived rather than observed because there are no market transactions for the precise item. Should General Motors set its transfer price on carburetors being shipped to Europe based on its cost of production or on what Toyota charges its U.S. transplants? The two carburetors are not the same and do not have the same cost of production. Furthermore, there may not be a data base available for prices for carburetors sold between related and unrelated parties from which to derive a market price. Preferences change with time. Surveys done in the 1970s indicated that the preponderance of U.S. companies were motivated by tax minimization in setting transfer prices. More recent surveys indicate that companies are more interested in setting transfer prices on the basis of measuring the performance of affiliate managers and of providing reliable and unbiased information for the making of decisions. This change in attitude in U.S. companies may be the result of the United States becoming a relative tax haven compared to other nations.

Its corporate tax rate of 34 per cent, plus state taxes, is less than in many other industrialized nations, where tax rates range between 40 per cent and 55 per cent. A U.S. company's total tax bill may, in fact, be reduced by allocating more profits to the United States. Regardless of changes in attitudes as to what is important in setting transfer prices, the essential point is that there is no unanimity on which approach to use and on what motivates companies in setting transfer prices. Up to this point, an important assumption has been that the parent company has real control over transfer prices to manage corporate cash flows and the profits reported by affiliates and to overcome artificial barriers to trade in the form of custom duties, currency exchange, and price controls. Some recent surveys suggest that competitive forces and market conditions within a nation seem to be more important in setting transfer prices than decisions made by a parent organization.

If transfer prices are being set by exogenous commercial forces, then the presumption that a parent organization is able to achieve optimal financial performance of a global family of affiliates through the careful orchestration of transfer pricing is being challenged.

TAX CONSIDERATIONS

Taxation and transfer pricing are intimately entwined, because transfer pricing of goods, parts, and components moving in and out of a nation has a direct impact on taxes on profits and on the amount of duties and tariffs paid to the tax authority. The discussion on transfer pricing based on the cost-of-production approach shows an intimate involvement with the tax authority in the methodology for calculating various elements of the transfer price. There is little uniformity on taxation among nations. Taxes range from taxation of a corporation's activities to the "water's edge" or on its global earnings, the so-called "unitary tax." The state of California invented the unitary tax in the 1930s when movie companies in California began moving out of the state to avoid state taxes. A unitary tax was applied against the global earnings of a company and the tax was determined by the proportion of a company's sales, property, and payroll within the state to its global sales, property, and payroll. The resulting tax had no relation to the degree of profitability of a company's operation in California. A company could operate at a loss in California and still pay a tax based on its global profits.

Needless to say, both foreign governments and multinational companies have vigorously fought the unitary tax. A number of court decisions confirmed or restricted unitary taxation over the years. Ultimately, opposition to the unitary tax succeeded. In November 1991, Alaska was the last state to abandon having a company's state tax liability based on the global earnings of the company. The unitary tax still exists in a truncated form, where earnings are restricted to the "water's edge." The state tax is calculated on the portion of a company's activities within a state as compared to its activities within the United States. Although most other countries limit their assessment on what is to be taxed to the operations of a company within their jurisdiction, there is no universal agreement as to what constitutes revenue and expenses in the calculation of taxable income and no uniformity on tax rates.

Every nation decides what is subject to taxation and the applicable tax rates. The complexity of tax regulations, in general, and the diversity of tax laws among nations are such that it is necessary for an affiliate to retain the technical expertise necessary to understand and comply with local tax regulations. The parent organization must retain the technical knowledge for its own tax jurisdiction and have sufficient knowledge of tax matters elsewhere to coordinate tax planning among the various affiliates. The vigour with which tax payments are enforced varies among nations.

Some countries with seemingly high tax rates permit an underground economy to flourish without much in the way of enforcing tax payments. The other side of the coin is the willingness of companies to adhere to tax laws. In some nations, a businessman who scrupulously follows the tax laws and pays what is owed to the tax authority will find himself at a competitive disadvantage.

NATURE OF TAXES

Taxes can be direct or indirect. The United States relies more on direct taxation, which is applied to each taxable entity. A U.S. corporation is taxed at 34 per cent on its profits. If a corporation pays a dividend to its shareholders, then the next taxable entity, the individual, pays a tax, which may be 28 per cent or more. This is double taxation.

Some nations, such as Germany, have two corporate tax rates on profits—one for retained profits and the other for distributed profits in the form of dividends. A lesser tax rate applies to profits that are distributed to shareholders to reduce the degree of double taxation.

Europe relies more on indirect taxes—particularly, the value added tax (VAT). The VAT is basically a tax applied to each stage of the production process and is not directly associated with the degree of profitability. Indeed, only a small portion of a VAT is associated with profits. Suppose that a company's manufacturing operations has the following financial results.

Wages, rents, interest, profit	\$400,000
Outside purchases of goods and services for which VAT has already been paid	600,000
Total sales	\$1,000,000

The additive method is to apply the VAT rate, say 10 per cent, to all costs associated with the production of goods, including profit and excluding purchases of goods and services from third parties for which the VAT has already been paid. In this case, \$400,000 of a company's activities falls into this category resulting in a VAT of \$40,000. A simpler method of calculation is to take the gross sales of the company (\$1,000,000), subtract all purchases of goods and services for which VAT has already been paid (\$600,000), and apply the VAT rate to the balance (\$400,000).

Either method yields the same result. The VAT is essentially equivalent to a national sales tax, because every company associated with the production and marketing of goods and providing services pays a tax on whatever value it adds to the goods or services. The value added tax, like a sales tax, is a tax on consumption, whereas U.S. taxes are on income and profits.

Value added tax rates vary widely from country to country and according to the nature of the business. Certain European countries have low VAT rates (5 per cent) for business transactions associated with food and high VAT rates (40 per cent) for luxury products. Others attempt to have one rate that applies to most forms of commerce.

Because the VAT is not paid on items that have already been exposed to a value added tax, and with the European economy becoming more integrated, there is a powerful incentive for the European Community to harmonize VAT rates and coordinate the handling of VAT payments for products or components shipped between members of the European Community. The amounts of value added by a company are frequently disclosed in European financial statements. In the excerpt from the British company, the company had gross revenues of 3,213 million pounds in 1987 of which 919.1 million pounds represents added value by the company. Of the total of 919.1 million pounds of added value, 496.8 million pounds was paid to the company's employees, 157.1 million pounds was paid in taxes to government tax authorities, and the remainder was paid to the internal and external providers of capital.

U.S. TAXATION OF GLOBAL COMPANIES

Nations have different ways of taxing global companies domiciled within their jurisdiction. If a parent corporation is domiciled in the United States, it does not pay taxes in the United States on profits earned by incorporated affiliates in other nations, unless the nation is considered a tax haven. This, in the United States, is known as Subpart F income, which will be discussed later under rein voicing centers.

Unlike an incorporated affiliate, a branch of a U.S. company located in a foreign nation is taxed directly on its earnings regardless of whether the earnings are remitted to the home office or not. The taxes paid on remitted and unremitted earnings are not the same, in that unremitted earnings have to be translated to U.S. dollars before a tax liability can be assessed, and therefore, are influenced by changes in currency exchange rates.

Taxes can also be calculated on the basis of the increase in the net worth of the branch, which can also be affected by changes in currency exchange rates. Sometimes a U.S. company will first open a branch operation in another country to permit startup losses to flow back to the parent organization.

When the branch becomes profitable, it may be reorganized as a wholly owned subsidiary, reducing the company's overall tax liability. U.S. based companies usually operate in the global market through operating affiliates whose stock is owned by the parent corporation. The parent corporation pays U.S. taxes only on the profits generated from dividends, royalties, and other service payments and fees paid by a non-U.S. domiciled affiliate to the parent organization. Taxes paid on profits by affiliates in their nations of domicile can be treated either as a tax credit or a tax deduction by the parent organization in the calculation of its U.S. taxes. To the degree that a tax paid on profits to a foreign government is treated as a tax credit, the net effect of a company paying taxes on its profits in a foreign country is that these taxes are essentially paid for by the U.S. government foregoing an equivalent amount of U.S. source based tax revenue.

Obviously, taxes paid to foreign governments must pass certain criteria set forth by the Internal Revenue Service to be considered for a tax credit. Foreign tax credits apply to taxes paid on foreign source profits calculated in a conventional way as U.S. source profits. Tax credits are also available for foreign government withholding taxes on dividends, interest payments, and royalties paid by a foreign-based affiliate to a U.S. parent company.

There is a maximum permissible limit on tax credits linked to the ratio of foreign source income to total worldwide income multiplied by the tax liability of U.S. operations. This effectively limits the foreign tax credit to the U.S., not the foreign, tax rate. A company doing business in a nation with a higher tax rate on profits than in the United States does not receive a tax credit equal to the taxes paid to the foreign government.

The tax credit is based on the U.S. tax rate. With U.S. tax rates being lower than in most other industrialized nations, U.S. based global companies are not being fully compensated by tax credits on foreign income taxes. This may provide an incentive to shift taxable income back to the United States through changes in transfer prices. The U.S. tax authorities permit a credit for taxes paid on profits to other nations under the notion of tax equity and tax neutrality. The principle of tax equity implies that a U.S. taxpaying entity with an operation in another nation should not pay more in taxes than having the operation domiciled in the United States. Were the equity principle absolutely true, a U.S. taxpaying entity would be indifferent, or neutral, to whether the operation was located in another nation or in the United States. Some maintain that the U.S. tax code does not adhere to the tax neutrality principle because a company doing business in New York City does not obtain a tax credit on its federal taxes for taxes paid to the state and city of New York on profits made in their jurisdiction.

A company with an affiliate in another nation not only receives a tax credit, which neutralizes its foreign and U.S. income taxes, but does not have to pay U.S. taxes on its foreign source earnings until those earnings are remitted to the parent in the form of a dividend, a royalty payment, or an equivalent thereof. As long as foreign source profits remain in the coffers of the affiliate, no taxes are due to the U.S. government, even though, under special circumstances, the affiliate may lend these funds to the parent company.

Deferral of dividend payments is essentially an interest-free loan made by the U.S. government to the foreign affiliate of a U.S. parent company on the amount of U.S. taxes due if, and when, these funds are repatriated to the U.S. parent. The principles of equity and neutrality built into the U.S. tax code were designed to provide an incentive for U.S. firms to invest overseas as part of the national policy of rebuilding war-torn nations. U.S. companies would be better off confining their activities within the United States, and would not invest in foreign affiliates, if the profits of these foreign affiliates were exposed to double taxation. Qualified foreign taxes, which cannot be utilized as tax credits, may be used as a tax deduction. A tax deduction is not as valuable as a tax credit. Tax deductions apply when there are not sufficient

U.S. taxes to be shielded by tax credits, or where the overall limitation on tax credits has been exceeded. Tax deductions can be carried back or carried forward, whichever is more useful.

REIN VOICING CENTERS

Some companies have set up rein voicing centers to manage all intra company trading of products. A rein voicing centre is at a single location, buying the output of the manufacturing affiliates and selling it to the marketing affiliates. Each affiliate receives or pays in its own currency, thus concentrating all intra company transaction currency exposure at the rein voicing centre.

The centre possesses the necessary data to assess the net currency exposure of intra company transactions and can enter into appropriate currency hedges. The centre may also receive better quotes from currency exchange dealers because all intra company currency exchange transactions are done at one location. The rein voicing centre can mark up the price of all products flowing through the centre to cover its administrative expenses. If there is little or no profitability associated with the operations of a rein voicing centre, it does not matter where the rein voicing centre is located from a tax viewpoint. However, it is possible to increase the markup to the point where corporate profit can be diverted from the nations where the goods are manufactured and marketed to the nation where the rein voicing centre is located. Now the location of the rein voicing centre is critical from a tax viewpoint. In the 1960s, the U.S. government became concerned with the accumulation of profits in rein voicing centers located in tax havens. Tax havens were characterized as nations imposing no, or a very low, tax on profits, having a high degree of bank secrecy, and little or no currency controls. These nations consider financial activities of importance to their economy, provide modern communication facilities, and promote themselves as offshore financial centers.

Bahamas, Bermuda, Cayman Islands, Liberia, Panama, and Vanuatu have been identified as tax havens. It is possible to "run" a rein voicing centre through these nations without a physical presence of personnel or products. Profits can be easily diverted to tax havens by increasing the markup on selling prices, thus reducing tax liabilities to the nations where the products are manufactured and marketed. If the criterion for determining a tax haven is satisfied, then the income earned by a rein voicing centre, or any corporate entity in the declared tax haven, is deemed Subpart F income. This income flows directly to the U.S. parent corporation and is taxed as though the income was earned in the United States.

TAXATION IMPACT ON TRANSFER PRICING

Companies operating in the United States are guided by Section 482 of the Internal Revenue Code when setting transfer prices. Specifically, the IRS, through the Secretary of the Treasury, has the right to "distribute, apportion, or allocate gross income, deductions, credits, or allowances... between or among... businesses, if he determines that such distribution, apportionment, or allocation is necessary in order to prevent evasion of taxes. The IRS has been granted wide latitude to do whatever it wants if the IRS deems that dealings between a U.S. parent and its affiliates do not meet its standards. For instance, the IRS can reallocate income and deductions if loans have been made between a parent corporation and an affiliate at an unrealistic interest rate. Unrealistic interest rates are those that would not occur for similar transactions between unrelated third parties.

This also applies to charging for services and use of property, and transfers of tangible and intangible property including lease payments and royalties. A reference to IRS guidelines has already been made in discussing R&D and intangible costs in setting transfer prices by the production cost approach. Basing transfer pricing on published data rather than corporate derived prices is another example of the close working relationship, voluntary or not, between tax authorities and managers responsible for transfer prices.

In general, the IRS standard for determining transfer pricing, and other dealings between a parent and its affiliates, is whether it is an "arm's-length" transaction—one that would occur between a company and a third party having no affiliation other than the commercial transaction under consideration. This is independent of whether the transfer price is based on the cost of production or on market prices. If the transfer price between affiliates is seemingly out of line with a price that would have been charged to an unrelated party, then the IRS has the right to reallocate income or deductions according to what it feels to be the appropriate transfer price.

The IRS specifies various methods for establishing an appropriate transfer price. The preferred one is the comparable uncontrolled price method where prices are the same for goods sold to affiliate and to nonaffiliated companies. The price for goods sold to an unrelated third party establishes the transfer price for goods transferred to an affiliate.

This method does not work when goods are not sold to third parties, but are totally transferred between affiliates. Under these circumstances, the second method for setting the transfer price is the resale price method. This is the price for which the company would sell the item to an unspecified third party. The third party would add the same comparable value as the affiliate and sell the completed product with an appropriate markup.

By netting the market price of the appropriate markup and the value added to the product by an affiliate, one can "back into" an appropriate transfer price from the point of view of the tax authority. The third method is the "cost plus" method, where the IRS permits three different ways of allocating costs (full absorption, direct cost, and incremental cost).

All these methods leave some margin of discretion as to what is the appropriate transfer price. If all these fail, as they frequently do for high-technology products, customised components, or subassemblies, then so-called fourth methods are permitted, such as determining transfer pricing on the basis of a predetermined profit for the foreign firm's operations and, through a netting process of accounting for applicable costs, establishing an appropriate transfer price. Regardless of the methodology, the burden of proof in supporting a transfer price is with the taxpayer, not the IRS.

To confuse matters more, there have been occasions when the tax courts have rejected the notion of arm's-length transfer pricing in settling tax disputes between corporations and the IRS.

OTHER NATIONS' POLICIES CONCERNING TRANSFER PRICING

The tax authority in Canada views transfer pricing of goods similar to the way the United States does. Transfer pricing for services differs in that it is based on a pro rata sharing of actual incurred costs between the parent corporation and its affiliate, and not necessarily at an arm's-length price. Tax authorities in Japan follow a system comparable to that of the United States.

German tax code provisions permit the reallocation of domestic source income if revenue or income has been shifted to another nation through a transaction that is different from those that would have been entered into by unrelated parties. In other words, transfer pricing should be arm's-length, although the code is not specific in defining arm's-length pricing.

The United Kingdom is similar to Germany in not specifically defining arm's-length pricing. The Inland Revenue may adjust taxable income based on fairness and arm's-length criteria. Disputes between corporations and Inland Revenue agents are frequently settled by negotiation, resulting in some sort of compromise between the two parties. This is unlike in Germany, where the adjustments made by the tax authorities are considered final, and unlike in the United States, where adjustments are litigated in tax courts.

Tax authorities in many nations are currently taking a much closer look at transfer pricing practices. Recently, the U.K. Inland Revenue recast the accounts of one non-British company operating in the United Kingdom and assessed back taxes of nearly 2 billion pounds. In the United States, there is growing political pressure for the IRS to take more vigorous action against foreign-owned companies operating through U.S. based affiliates.

This pressure stems from the realization that the aggregate expenses for foreign-owned businesses operating in the United States exceed aggregate revenues. This means that, in the aggregate, foreign-owned subsidiaries are claiming to operate at a loss, although individual foreign-owned subsidiaries may be paying taxes on profits. Some foreign-owned affiliates operating in the United States have a twenty-year string of consecutive losses. This is not considered a realistic appraisal of performance because there are few profit-motivated foreign-based parent companies that would support twenty years of successive losses were they real. Poor or nonexistent profits for foreign-based affiliates operating in the United States are blamed on transfer pricing.

Transfer price manipulation is felt to have resulted in tax underpayments of between $12 and $50 billion. Legislation was passed in 1989 to require foreign-owned businesses in the United States to keep records, in English, of transactions with foreign related parties. Much of this legislation has to do with substantiating transfer pricing on either a cost or arm's length transaction with an unrelated third party.

A growing risk associated with manipulating transfer prices for the purpose of tax minimization. The risk is that the tax authorities will recast the company's statements with their own version of the proper transfer price, thus exposing a company to the risk of double taxation. Most nations have entered into tax treaties with various other nations with regard to taxing of affiliates of parent organizations domiciled in the treaty nations.

These treaties determine withholding taxes on dividends, interest, and royalties; relief from double taxation; and the types of taxes and organizations covered by the treaty. Overall exposure to taxation can be reduced by judicious structuring of the legal corporate entities of a parent company and its affiliates in accordance with the provisions of these treaties.

Some of these treaties contain formal agreements for the mutual examination of the tax returns of affiliates of a parent company. The tax returns of affiliates and parent organizations are exchanged and examined by the tax authorities to determine correct tax liabilities, detect tax avoidance maneuvers, scrutinize transfer pricing practices, and exchange information useful to the tax authorities. These treaties also provide a forum for one tax authority to complain about the actions taken by another, when these actions are deemed detrimental to its interests. Recent developments in international cooperation of tax authorities include the establishment of a formal agreement on transfer prices. The mutual agreement of various nations to reference a published source for tanker rates in determining oil company tax liabilities is an example of this. Australia and the United States are attempting to grant "advance determinations" of the proper transfer price for Australian companies' dealings with their U.S. affiliates.

A recent survey has shown that about half of IRS tax examinations of multinational companies involve transfer prices. If a mutually agreeable methodology could be arranged between a company and the IRS, many of these tax examinations could be eliminated. The IRS is attempting to develop a procedure whereby a company and the IRS would mutually agree to a transfer-pricing agreement covering the distribution of finished goods, sales of raw materials and components, general and administrative expenses, and managerial and technical services.

If the taxpayer develops an acceptable transfer-pricing methodology, then the taxpayer and the IRS would enter into an advance-pricing agreement. The IRS would limit its examinations to an audit to ensure that the taxpayer has complied with the agreement. However, the taxpayer is obliged to submit pricing data of independent transactions, or an adequate substitute, to show that the transfer price possesses the necessary attributes of an arm's-length transaction. The taxpayer is also responsible to show that the agreed transfer-pricing methodology is generating acceptable transfer prices from an arm's-length perspective. The preference of tax authorities in many nations for arm's-length transfer pricing may act as an inducement to switch from the cost-of-production to the market price approach in setting transfer prices because, presumably, they are one and the same.

The financial and taxation departments of multinational, or global, companies must deal daily with what are considered to be the most pressing issues in international accounting today. Those involved with transfer pricing must measure the consequences of their transfer-pricing decisions both on corporate profits and on current and potential tax liabilities. Potential tax liabilities, stemming from tax authorities rejecting management's transfer price decisions, and substituting their own, are enormous. This must weigh heavily on the shoulders of those responsible for setting transfer prices.

5

Taxation Policies

GOVERNMENT REVENUE

Government re venue is revenue received by a government. It is an important tool of the fiscal policy of the government and is the opposite factor of government spending. Revenues earned by the government are received from sources such as taxes levied on the incomes and wealth accumulation of individuals and corporations and on the goods and services produced, exported and imported from the country, non-taxable sources such as government-owned corporations' incomes, central bank revenue and capital receipts in the form of external loans and debts from international financial institutions.

TAX REVENUE

Tax revenue is the income that is gained by governments through taxation.

Just as there are different types of tax, the form in which tax revenue is collected also differs; furthermore, the agency that collects the tax may not be part of central government, but may be an alternative third-party licenced to collect tax which they themselves will use. For example:

In the UK, the DVLA collects vehicle excise duty, which is then passed onto the treasury.

Tax revenues on purchases can come from two forms: 'tax' itself is a *percentage* of the price added to the purchase (such as sales tax in US states, or VAT in the UK), while 'duty' is a *fixed amount* added to the purchase price (such as is commonly found on cigarettes). In order to calculate the total tax raised from these sales, we must work out the effective tax rate multiplied by the quantity supplied.

CHANGES IN TAXATION LEVEL

The effect of a change in taxation level on total tax revenue depends on the good being investigated, and in particular on its price elasticity of demand. Where goods have a low elasticity of demand (they are price inelastic), an increase in tax or duty will lead to a small decrease in demand—not enough to offset the higher tax raised from each unit. Overall tax revenue will therefore rise. Conversely, for goods which are price elastic, an increase in tax rate or duty would lead to a fall in tax revenue.

Laffer curve

The Laffer curve theorises that, even for price inelastic goods (such as addictive necessary items), there will be a tax revenue maximising point, beyond which total tax revenue will fall as taxes increase. This may be due to a number of causes:

- A cost limit on what can actually be afforded
- The existence of expensive substitutes (which become less expensive)
- An increase in tax evasion (through the black market or similar)
- The shrinking of business caused by increased taxes

The laffer curve however is not necessarily widely accepted as economic reality with promient economists such as Paul Krugman referring to it as "Junk economics". Former white house economic adviser Austan Goolsbee was even more dismissive stating [The]"Moon landing was real. Evolution exists. Tax cuts lose revenue. The research has shown this a thousand times. Enough already.", during a panel where of 40 economists surveyed, none believed tax cuts could increase government revenue.

REVENUE ADMINISTRATION

Public sector

A limiting factor in determining the size of a budget in the public sector is the capacity to tax. Per capita personal income(PCI) is the most often used measure of relative fiscal capacity. But this measure fails to base tax capacity computation on other important tax bases like the sales and property tax and corporate income taxes. A representative tax system should assess the level of personal income, the value of retail sales and the value of property to compute fiscal capacity. To do so the average tax rate for each base is computed by dividing the total revenue derived by the total value of the base. Thus, as an example, income taxes collected would be divided by total income to yield a rate of taxation.

Personal Income Tax	Sales Tax	Property Tax	Corporate Tax
total revenue	total revenue	total revenue	total revenue

The averages of each tax base can be used in comparison to other states or communities, that is, the average of other states or communities, to determine whether or not a government compares favorably regionally or nationally. A state or community's standing on these various bases may affect its ability to attract new industry. The resulting rates, high or low in comparison, can become targets for change. The mission of revenue administration is to provide prudent and innovative revenue, investment and risk management and to regulate the use of government capital.

There are four core responsibilities for the revenue administrator: 1. Manage and invest financial assets prudently. 2. Administer tax and revenue programs fairly and efficiently. 3. Manage risk associated with loss of public assets. 4. Regulate capital expenditures. Example of Balance: The Conflict of Economic Development and the Tax Base

New real estate development may not only enhance the economic base of a state or community, and it may also expand the tax base. It is not always the case, however, that new developments, especially if not properly planned, can in the aggregate, have a negative impact on the tax base. Economic development traditionally focuses on such things as job generation, the provision of affordable housing, and the creation of retail centers. Tax base expansion focuses primarily on maintaining and enhancing real estate values within the municipality. Municipalities tend to pursue economic development with almost a religious fervor, and often do not think strategically about the overall real estate impacts of their economic development initiatives. Yet the existing tax base in almost every municipality throughout the United States is an important source of revenue for funding municipal and school expenditures.

For public sector officials it is important to recognize the potential for a conflict between these two distinct, yet overlapping areas of public policy, and to establish procedures to achieve the proper balance in this regard. For real estate investors it is important to recognize when public policy is not fully cognizant of the impact of its actions on the real estate market, because of the potential negative impact on property values.

In summary, the concept of tax base management is really one of asset management and is particularly important in States where municipalities derive much of their revenue from their real estate assessments. City officials in Concord, New Hampshire found that a five percent overall increase in the assessed value of existing property would have the same impact on the tax rate as the addition of 2,000,000 square feet (190,000 m) of new industrial property or 1,000,000 square feet (93,000 m) of new office/R&D development, both of which are likely to take fifteen or more years to realize.

In addition to being responsible for managing the tax base, a community should also be responsible for helping to ensure economic prosperity for its citizens. These two goals can be in conflict unless a long-term view is taken regarding public policy actions, and unless the impact of alternate development actions and programs and priorities are not carefully evaluated. Good tax base management may lead to even better economic development, because investors and businesses will want to be in a community. Instead of offering incentives to attract business, they may be willing to pay to come to a community because it's a good place to live, work, shop and play.

TAX LAW

Tax law is an area of legal study dealing with the statutory, regulatory, constitutional, and common-law rules that constitute the law applicable to taxation, which is the method by which the government levies on economic transactions.

TAX BRACKET

Tax brackets are the divisions at which tax rates change in a progressive tax system (or an explicitly regressive tax system, although this is much rarer). Essentially, they are the cutoff values for taxable income – income past a certain point will be taxed at a higher rate.

Imagine that there are three tax brackets: 10%, 20%, and 30%. The 10% rate applies to income from $1 to $10,000; the 20% rate applies to income from $10,001 to $20,000; and the 30% rate applies to all income above $20,000.

Under this system, someone earning $10,000 would be taxed at a rate of 10%, paying a total of $1,000. Someone earning $5,000 would pay $500, and so on. Meanwhile, someone earning $35,000 would face a more complicated calculation. The rate on the first $10,000 would be 10%; the rate from $10,001 to $20,000 would be 20%; and the rate above that would be 30%. Thus, he would pay $1,000 for the first $10,000 of income; $2,000 for the second $10,000 of income; and $4,500 for the last $15,000 of income; in total, he would pay $7,500, or about 21.4%.

TAX EXEMPTION

Various tax systems grant a tax exemption to certain organizations, persons, income, property or other items taxable under the system. Tax exemption may also refer to a personal allowance or specific monetary exemption which may be claimed by an individual to reduce taxable income under some systems. Tax exempt status may provide a potential taxpayer complete relief from tax, tax at a reduced rate, or tax on only a portion of the items subject to tax. Examples include exemption of charitable organizations from property taxes and income taxes, exemptions provided to veterans, and exemptions under cross-border or multi-jurisdictional principles. Tax exemption generally refers to a statutory exception to a general rule rather than the mere absence of taxation in particular circumstances (i.e., an exclusion). Tax exemption also generally refers to removal from taxation of a particular item or class rather than a reduction of taxable items by way of deduction of other items (i.e., a deduction). Tax exemptions may theoretically be granted at any governmental level that imposes taxation, though in some broader systems restraints are imposed on such exemptions by lower tier governmental units.

Moreover, international duty free shopping may be termed "tax-free shopping". In tax-free shopping, the goods are permanently taken outside the jurisdiction, thus paying taxes is not necessary. Tax-free shopping is also found in ships, airplanes and other vessels traveling between countries (or tax areas). Tax-free shopping is usually available in dedicated duty-free shops. However, any transaction may be duty-free given that the goods are presented to the customs when exiting the country (or tax area). In this case, a sum equivalent to the tax is paid, but then reimbursed on exit. Common in Europe, tax-free is uncommon in the United States, with the exception of Louisiana. However, current European Union rules prohibit most intra-EU tax-free trade, with the exception of certain special territories outside the tax area.

SPECIFIC MONETARY EXEMPTIONS

Some jurisdictions allow for a specific monetary reduction of the tax base, which may be referred to as an exemption. For example, the U.S. Federal and many state tax systems allow a deduction of a specified dollar amount for each of several categories of "personal exemptions." Similar amounts may be called "personal allowances." Some systems may provide thresholds at which such exemptions or allowances are phased out or removed.

EXEMPT ORGANIZATIONS

Some governments grant broad exclusions from all taxation for certain types of organization. The exclusions may be restricted to entities having various characteristics. The exclusions may be inherent in definitions or restrictions outside the tax law itself.

Approaches for exemption

There are several different approaches used in granting exemption to organizations. Different approaches may be used within a jurisdiction or especially within sub-jurisdictions. Some jurisdictions grant an overall exemption from taxation to organizations meeting certain definitions. The United Kingdom, for example, provides an exemption from rates (property taxes), and income taxes for entities governed by the Charities Law. This overall exemption may be somewhat limited by limited scope for taxation by the jurisdiction. Some jurisdictions may levy only a single type of tax,exemption from only a particular tax.

Some jurisdictions provide for exemption only from certain taxes. The United States exempts certain organizations from Federal income taxes, but not from various excise or most employment taxes.

Charitable and religious organizations

Many tax systems provide complete exemption from tax for recognized charitable organizations. Such organizations may include religious organizations (temples, mosques, churches, etc.), fraternal organizations (including social clubs), public charities (e.g., organizations serving homeless persons), or any of a broad variety of organizations considered to serve public purposes. The U.S. system exempts from Federal and many state income taxes the income of organizations that have qualified for such exemption. Qualification requires that the organization be created and operated for one of a long list of tax exempt purposes, which includes more than 28 types of organizations and also requires, for most types of organizations, that the organization apply for tax exempt status with the Internal Revenue Service, or be a religious or apostolic organization. Note that the U.S. system does not distinguish between various kinds of tax exempt entities (such as educational versus charitable) for purposes of granting exemption, but does make such distinctions with respect to allowing a tax deduction for contributions.

The UK generally exempts public charities from business rates, corporation tax, income tax, and certain other taxes.

Governmental entities

Most systems exempt internal governmental units from all tax. For multi-tier jurisdictions, this exemption generally extends to lower tier units and across units. For example, state and local governments are not subject to Federal, state, or local income taxes in the U.S.

Pension schemes

Most systems do not tax entities organized to conduct retirement investment and pension activities for employees of one or more employers or for the benefit of employees. In addition, many systems also provide tax exemption for personal pension schemes.

Educational institutions

Some jurisdictions provide separate total or partial tax exemptions for educational institutions. These exemptions may be limited to certain functions or income.

Other not-for-profit entities

Some jurisdictions provide tax exemption for other particular types of organizations not meeting any of the above categories.

Reciprocal exemptions

Some jurisdictions allow tax exemption for organizations exempt from tax in certain other jurisdictions. For example, most U.S. states allow tax exemption for organizations recognized for Federal tax purposes as tax exempt.

Sales tax

Most states and localities imposing sales and use taxes in the United States exempt resellers from sales taxes on goods held for sale and ultimately sold. In addition, most such states and localities exempt from sales taxes goods used directly in the production of other goods (i.e., raw materials).

EXEMPT INDIVIDUALS

Certain classes of persons may be granted a full or partial tax exemption within a system. Common exemptions are for veterans, clergymen or taxpayers with children (who can take "dependency exemption" for each qualifying dependent who has lived with the taxpayer. The dependent can be a natural child, step-child, step-sibling, half-sibling, adopted child, eligible foster child, or grandchild, and is usually under age 19, a full-time student under age 24, or have special needs). The exemption granted may depend on multiple criteria, including criteria otherwise unrelated to the particular tax. For example, a property tax exemption may be provided to certain classes of veterans earning less than a particular income level. Definitions of exempt individuals tend to be complex.

EXEMPT INCOME

Most income tax systems exclude certain classes of income from the taxable income base. Such exclusions may be referred to as exclusions or exemptions. Systems vary highly. Among the more commonly excluded items are:

- Income earned outside the taxing jurisdiction. Such exclusions may be limited in amount.
- Interest income earned from subsidiary jurisdictions.
- Income consisting of compensation for loss.
- The value of property inherited or acquired by gift.

Some tax systems specifically exclude from income items that the system is trying to encourage. Such exclusions or exemptions can be quite specific or very general. Among the types of income that may be include are classes of income earned in specific areas, such as special economic zones, enterprise zones, etc. These exemptions may be limited to specific industries. As an example, India provides SEZs where exporters of goods or providers of services to foreign customers may be exempt from income taxes and customs duties.

EXEMPT PROPERTY

Certain types of property are commonly granted exemption from property or transaction (such as sales or value added) taxes. These exemptions vary highly from jurisdiction to jurisdiction, and definitions of what property qualifies for exemption can be voluminous.

Among the more commonly granted exemptions are:

- Property used in manufacture of other goods (which goods may ultimately be taxable)

- Property used by a tax exempt or other parties for a charitable or other not for profit purpose
- Property considered a necessity of life, often exempted from sales taxes in the United States
- Personal residence of the taxpayer, often subject to specific monetary limitations

MULTI-TIER JURISDICTIONS

Many countries that impose tax have subdivisions or subsidiary jurisdictions that also impose tax. This feature is not unique to federal systems, like the U.S., Switzerland and Australia, but rather is a common feature of national systems. The top tier system may impose restrictions on both the ability of the lower tier system to levy tax as well as how certain aspects of such lower tier system work, including the granting of tax exemptions. The restrictions may be imposed directly on the lower jurisdiction's power to levy tax or indirectly by regulating tax effects of the exemption at the upper tier.

CROSS-BORDER AGREEMENTS

Jurisdictions may enter into agreements with other jurisdictions that provide for reciprocal tax exemption. Such provisions are common in an income [tax treaty]. These reciprocal tax exemptions typically call for each contracting jurisdiction to exempt certain income of a resident of the other contracting jurisdiction. Multi-jurisdictional agreements for tax exemption also exist. 20 of the U.S. states have entered into the Multistate Tax Compact that provides, among other things, that each member must grant a full credit for sales and use taxes paid to other states or subdivisions. The European Union members are all parties to the EU multi-country VAT harmonisation rules.

TAX CREDIT

A tax credit is a sum deducted from the total amount a taxpayer owes to the state. A tax credit may be granted for various types of taxes, such as an income tax, property tax, or VAT. It may be granted in recognition of taxes already paid, as a subsidy, or to encourage investment or other behaviors. In some systems tax credits are 'refundable' to the extent they exceed the relevant tax. Tax systems may grant tax credits to businesses or individuals, and such grants vary by type of credit.

CREDIT FOR PAYMENTS

Many systems refer to taxes paid indirectly, such as taxes withheld by payers of income, as credits rather than prepayments. In such cases, the tax credit is invariably refundable. The most common forms of such amounts are payroll withholding of income tax or PAYE, withholding of tax at source on payments to nonresidents, and input credits for value added tax.

INDIVIDUAL INCOME TAX CREDITS

Income tax systems often grant a variety of credits to individuals. These typically include credits available to all taxpayers as well as tax credits unique to individuals. Some credits may be offered for a single year only.

Low income subsidies

Several income tax systems provide income subsidies to lower income individuals by way of credit. These credits may be based on income, family status, work status, or other factors. Often such credits are refundable when total credits exceed tax liability.

United Kingdom

In the United Kingdom, the 'child tax credit' and 'working tax credit' are paid directly into the claimant's bank account or Post Office Card Account. In exceptional circumstances, these can be paid by giro however payments may stop if account details are not provided. A minimum level of child tax credits is payable to all individuals or couples with children, up to a certain income limit. The actual amount of child tax credits that a person may receive depends on these factors: the level of their income, the number of children they have, whether the children are receiving Disability Living Allowance and the education status of any children over 16.

Working tax credit is paid to single low earners with or without children who are aged 25 or over and are working over 30 hours per week and also to couples without children, at least one of whom is over 25, provided that at least one of them is working for 30 hours a week. If the claimant has children however, they may claim working tax credit from age 16 upward, provided that they are working at least 16 hours per week.

United States

The U.S. system grants the following low income tax credits:

Earned income credit: this refundable credit is granted for a percentage of income earned by a low income individual. The credit is calculated and capped based on the number of qualifying children, if any. This credit is indexed for inflation and phased out for incomes above a certain amount. For 2009, the maximum credit was $5,657. Credit for the elderly and disabled: A nonrefundable credit up to $1,125 Retirement savings credit: a nonrefundable credit of up to 50% of contributions to IRAs or similar plans, phased out at incomes above $16,000 ($24,000 for head of household and $32,000 for joint returns). Mortgage interest credit: a nonrefundable credit that may be limited to $2,000, granted under specific mortgage programs.

Family relief

Some systems grant tax credits for families with children. These credits may be on a per child basis or as a credit for child care expenses. The U.S. system offers the following nonrefundable family related income tax credits (in addition to a tax deduction for each dependent child):

- *Child credit:* Parents of children who are under age 17 at the end of the tax year may qualify for a credit up to $1,000 per qualifying child. The credit is a dollar-for-dollar reduction of tax liability, and may be listed on Line 51 of Form 1040. For every $1,000 of adjusted gross income above the threshold limit ($110,000 for married joint filers; $75,000 for single filers), the amount of the credit decreases by $50.
- *Child and dependent care credit:* If a taxpayer must pay for childcare for a child under age 13 in order to pursue or maintain gainful employment, he or she may claim a credit up to $3,000 of his or her eligible expenses for dependent care. If one parent stays home full-time, however, no child care costs are eligible for the credit.
- *Credit for adoption expenses:* A credit up to $10,000, phased out at higher incomes. Taxpayers who have incurred qualified adoption expenses in 2011 may claim either a $13,360 credit against tax owed or a $13,360 income exclusion if the taxpayer has received payments or reimbursements from his or her employer for adoption expenses. For 2012, the amount of the credit will decrease to $12,650, and in 2013 to $5,000.

Education, energy and other subsidies

Some systems indirectly subsidize education and similar expenses through tax credits.

The U.S. system has the following nonrefundable credits:

Two mutually exclusive credits for qualified tuition and related expenses. The American Opportunity Tax Credit is 100% of the first $2,000 and 25% of the next $4000 of qualified tuition expenses per year for up to two years. The Lifetime Learning Credit is 20% of the first $10,000 of cumulative expenses. These credits are phased out at incomes above $50,000 ($100,000 for joint returns) in 2009. Expenses for which a credit is claimed are not eligible for tax deduction. First time homebuyers credit up to $7,500 (closing date before Sept. 30, 2010). Credits for purchase of certain nonbusiness energy property and residential energy efficiency. Several credits apply with differing rules.

BUSINESS TAX CREDITS

Many systems offer various incentives for businesses to make investments in property or operate in particular areas. Credits may be offered against income or property taxes, and are generally nonrefundable to the extent they exceed taxes otherwise due. The credits may be offered to individuals as well as entities. The nature of the credits available varies highly by jurisdiction.

UNITED STATES

U.S. income tax has numerous nonrefundable business credits. In most cases, any amount of these credits in excess of current year tax may be carried forward to offset future taxes, with limitations. The credits include the following, available to individuals and businesses:

- Alternative motor vehicle credit: several credits are available for purchase of varying types of non-gasoline powered vehicles.
- Alternative fuel credits: a credit based on the amount of production of certain non-petroleum fuels.
- Disaster relief credits
- Credits for employing individuals in certain areas or those formerly on welfare or in targeted groups
- Credit for increasing research expenses
- A variety of industry specific credits

Many sub-Federal jurisdictions (states, counties, cities, etc.) within the U.S. offer income or property tax credits for particular activities or expenditures. Examples include credits similar to the Federal research and employment credits, property tax credits granted by cities (often called abatements) for building facilities within the city, etc. These items often are negotiated between a business and a governmental body, and specific to a particular business and property.

Federal nonrefundable investment tax credits

Tax credits, while they come in many forms, are authorized incentives under the Internal Revenue Code (and some state tax codes) to implement public policy. Congress, in an effort to encourage the private sector to provide a public benefit, allows a participating taxpayer a dollar for dollar reduction of their tax liability for investments in projects that probably would not occur but for the credits.

Federal Historic Rehabilitation Tax Credit

The legislative incentive program to encourage the preservation of "historical buildings". Congress instituted a two-tier Tax Credit incentive under the 1986 Tax Reform Act. A 20% credit is available for the rehabilitation of historical buildings and a 10% credit is available for non-historic buildings, which were first placed in service before 1936. Benefits are derived from tax credits in the year the property is placed in service, cash flow over 6 years and repurchase options in year six.

Renewable Energy/Investment Tax Credit (ITC)

This investment tax credit varies depending on the type of renewable energy project; solar, fuel cells ($1500/0.5 kW) and small wind (< 100 kW) are eligible for credit of 30% of the cost of development, with no maximum credit limit; there is a 10% credit for geothermal, microturbines (< 2 MW) and combined heat and power plants (< 50 MW). The ITC is generated at the time the qualifying facility is placed in service. Benefits are derived from the ITC, accelerated depreciation, and cash flow over a 6-8 year period.

Renewable Energy/Production Tax Credit (PTC)

Under present law, an income tax credit of 2.2 cents/kilowatt-hour is allowed for the production of electricity from utility-scale wind turbines, geothermal, solar, hydropower, biomass and marine and hydrokinetic renewable energy plants. This incentive, the renewable energy Production Tax Credit (PTC), was created under the Energy Policy Act of 1992 (at the value of 1.5 cents/kilowatt-hour, which has since been adjusted annually for inflation).

Low Income (Affordable) Housing Tax Credit (LIHTC)

Under this program, created in the 1986 Tax Reform Act, the U.S Treasury Department allocates tax credits to each state based on that states population. These credits are then awarded to developers who, together with an equity partner, develop and maintain apartments as affordable units. Benefits are derived primarily from the tax credits over a 10 year period.

Qualified School Construction Bond (QSCB)

QSCBs are U.S. debt instruments used to help schools borrow at nominal rates for the rehabilitation, repair and equipping of their facilities, as well as the purchase of land upon which a public school will be built. A QSCB holder receives a Federal tax credit in lieu of an interest payment. The tax credits may be stripped from QSCB bonds and sold separately. QSCBs were created by Section 1521 of the American Recovery and Reinvestment Act of 2009. Internal Revenue Code Section 54F also addresses QSCBs.

Work Opportunity Tax Credit (WOTC)

The Work Opportunity Tax Credit (WOTC) is a federal tax credit providing incentives to employers for hiring groups facing high rates of unemployment, such as veterans, youths and others. WOTC helps these targeted groups obtain employment so they are able to gain the skills and experience necessary to obtain better future job opportunities. The WOTC is based on the number of hours an employee works and benefits the employer directly.

American Opportunity Tax Credit (AOTC)

The American Opportunity Tax Credit (AOTC) was part of the American Recovery and Reinvestment Act, which was signed into law in February 2009. The AOTC replaced the Hope Scholarship credit for Tax Years 2009 and 2010, increased the benefits for nearly all Hope credit recipients and many other students by providing a maximum benefit up to $2,500 per student, 100 percent of their first $2,000 in tuition and 25 percent of the next $2,000, expanding the income range over which taxpayers can claim a credit, and making the credit partially refundable.

State tax credits

Approximately 43 states provide a variety of special incentive programs that utilize state tax credits. These include Brownfield credits, Film Production credits, Renewable energy credits, Historic Preservation credits and others. The amount of credit, the term of credit and the cost of the credit differs from state to state. These credits can be either in the form of a certificate, which can be purchased as an asset, or in a more traditional pass through entity. The tax credits can generally be used against insurance company premium tax, bank tax and income tax.

VALUE ADDED TAX

Resellers or producers of goods or providers of services (collectively, providers) must collect value added tax (VAT) in some jurisdictions upon billing or being paid by customers. Where these providers use goods or services provided by others, they may have paid VAT to other providers. Most VAT systems allow the amount of such VAT paid or considered paid to be used to offset VAT payments due, generally referred to as an input credit. Some systems allow the excess of input credits over VAT obligations to be refunded after a period of time.

FOREIGN TAX CREDIT

Income tax systems that impose tax on residents on their worldwide income tend to grant a foreign tax credit for foreign income taxes paid on the same income. The credit often is limited based on the amount of foreign income. The credit may be granted under domestic law and/or tax treaty. The credit is generally granted to individuals and entities, and is generally nonrefundable.

CREDITS FOR ALTERNATIVE TAX BASES

Several tax systems impose a regular income tax and, where higher, an alternative tax. The U.S. imposes an alternative minimum tax based on an alternative measure of taxable income. Mexico imposes an IETU based on an alternative measure of taxable income. Italy imposes an alternative tax based on assets. In each case, where the alternative tax is higher than the regular tax, a credit is allowed against future regular tax for the excess. The credit is usually limited in a manner that prevents circularity in the calculation.

TAX DEDUCTION

Tax deduction is a reduction of the income subject to tax, for various items, especially expenses incurred to produce income. Often these deductions are subject to limitations or conditions. Tax deductions generally are allowed only for expenses incurred that produce current benefits, and capitalization of items producing future benefit is required, sometimes with exceptions. Most systems allow recovery in some manner over a period of time of capitalized business and investment items, such as through allowances for depreciation, obsolescence, or decline in value.

Many systems reduce taxable income for personal allowances or provide a range of income subject to zero tax. In addition, some systems allow deductions from the tax base for items the tax levying government desires to encourage. Some systems distinguish among types of deductions (business versus non-business).

BUSINESS EXPENSES

Nearly all jurisdictions that tax business income allow tax deductions for expenses incurred in trading or carrying on the trade or business. Technical details of the allowance vary, and may be very general for all expenses, or very specific in respect of certain expenses. The amount of particular deductions may be limited based on character or amount, or deductions in aggregate may be limited or reduced. To be deducted, the expenses must be incurred in furthering a business. Generally, a business includes only those activities undertaken for profit.

Cost of goods sold

Nearly all income tax systems allow a deduction for cost of goods sold. This may be considered an expense, a reduction of gross income, or merely a component utilized in computing net profits. The manner in which cost of goods sold is determined has several inherent complexities, including various accounting methods. These include:

- Conventions for assigning costs to particular goods sold where specific identification is infeasible.
- Methods for attributing common costs, such as factory burden, to particular goods.
- Methods for determining when costs are recognized in computing cost of goods sold or to be sold.
- Methods for recognizing costs of goods that will not be sold or have declined in value.

Trading or ordinary and necessary business expenses

Many systems, including the UK, levy tax on all chargeable "profits of a trade" computed under local generally accepted accounting principles (GAAP). Under this approach, determination of whether an item is deductible depends upon accounting rules and judgments. By contrast, the U.S. allows as a deduction "all the ordinary and necessary expenses paid or incurred during the taxable year in carrying on any trade or business..." subject to qualifications, enhancements, and limitations. A similar approach is followed by Canada, but generally with fewer special rules. Such an approach poses significant definitional issues. Among the definitional issues often addressed are: What constitutes a trade or business? Generally, the business must be regular, continuous, substantial, and entered into with an expectation of profit.

What expenses are ordinary and necessary? The phrase deals with what expenses are appropriate to the nature of the business, whether the expenses are of the sort expected to help produce income and promote the business, and whether the expenses are not lavish and extravagant. Note that under this concept, the same sorts of expenses are generally deductible by business entities and individuals carrying on a trade or business. To the extent such expenses relate to the employment of an individual and are not reimbursed by the employer, the amount may be deductible by the individual.

Business deductions of flow-through entities may flow through as a component of the entity's net income in some jurisdictions. Deductions of flow-through entities may pass through to members of such entities separately from the net income of the entity in some jurisdictions or some cases. For example, charitable contributions by trusts, and all deductions of partnerships (and S corporations in the U.S.) are deductible by member beneficiaries or partners (or S corporation shareholders) in a manner appropriate to the deduction and the member, such as itemized deductions for charitable contributions or a component of net business profits for business expenses.

Accounting methods

One important aspect of determining tax deductions for business expenses is the timing of such deduction. The method used for this is commonly referred to as an accounting method. Accounting methods for tax purposes may differ from applicable GAAP. Examples include timing of recognition of cost recovery deductions (e.g., depreciation), current expensing of otherwise capitalizable costs of intangibles, and rules related to costs that should be treated as part of cost of goods not yet sold.

Further, taxpayers often have choices among multiple accounting methods permissible under GAAP and/or tax rules. Examples include conventions for determining which goods have been sold (such as first-in-first-out, average cost, etc.), whether or not to defer minor expenses producing benefit in the immediately succeeding period, etc.

Accounting methods may be defined with some precision by tax law, as in the U.S. system, or may be based on GAAP, as in the UK system.

Limits on deductions

Many systems limit particular deductions, even where the expenses directly relate to the business. Such limitations may, by way of example, include:

- Maximum deductions for use of automobiles
- Limits on deducting compensation of certain key employees
- Limits on lobbying or similar expenditures
- Nondeductibility of payments considered in violation of public policy, such as criminal fines
- Limits on deductions for business related entertainment.

In addition, deductions in excess of income in one endeavor may not be allowed to offset income from other endeavors. For example, the United States limits deductions related to passive activities to income from passive activities.

In particular expenses that are included in COGS cannot be deducted again as a business expense. COGS expenses include:

- The cost of products or raw materials, including freight or shipping charges;
- The cost of storing products the business sells;
- Direct labor costs for workers who produce the products; and
- Factory overhead expenses.

CAPITALIZED ITEMS AND COST RECOVERY (DEPRECIATION)

Many systems require that the cost of items likely to produce future benefits be capitalized. Examples include plant and equipment, fees related to acquisition of property, and costs of developing intangible assets (e.g., patentable inventions). Such systems often allow a tax deduction for cost recovery in a future period.

A common approach to such cost recovery is to allow a deduction for a portion of the cost ratably over some period of years. The U.S. system refers to such a cost recovery deduction as depreciation for costs of tangible assets and as amortization for costs of intangible assets. Depreciation in these systems is allowed over an estimated useful life, which may be assigned by the government for numerous classes of assets, based on the nature and use of the asset and the nature of the business. The annual depreciation deduction may be computed on a straight line, declining balance, or other basis, as permitted in each country's rules. Many systems allow amortization of the cost of intangible assets only on a straight line basis, generally computed monthly over the actual expected life or a government specified life.

Alternative approaches are used by some systems. Some systems allow a fixed percentage or dollar amount of cost recovery in particular years, often called "capital allowances." This may be determined by reference to the type of asset or business. Some systems allow specific charges for cost recovery for some assets upon certain identifiable events.

Capitalization may be required for some items without the potential for cost recovery until disposition or abandonment of the asset to which the capitalized costs relate. This is often the case for costs related to the formation or reorganization of a corporation, or certain expenses in corporate acquisitions. However, some systems provide for amortization of certain such costs, at the election of the taxpayer.

NON-BUSINESS EXPENSES

Some systems distinguish between an active trade or business and the holding of assets to produce income. In such systems, there may be additional limitations on the timing and nature of amounts that may be claimed as tax deductions. Many of the rules, including accounting methods and limits on deductions, that apply to business expenses also apply to income producing expenses.

Losses

Many systems allow a deduction for loss on sale, exchange, or abandonment of both business and non-business income producing assets. This deduction may be limited to gains from the same class of assets. In the U.S., a loss on non-business assets is considered a capital loss, and deduction of the loss is limited to capital gains. Also, in the U.S. a loss on the sale of the taxpayer's principal residence or other personal assets is not allowed as a deduction except to the extent due to casualty or theft.

Personal deductions

Many jurisdictions allow certain classes of taxpayers to reduce taxable income for certain inherently personal items. A common such deduction is a fixed allowance for the taxpayer and certain family members or other persons supported by the taxpayer. The U.S. allows such a deduction for "personal exemptions" for the taxpayer and certain members of the taxpayer's household. The UK grants a "personal allowance." Both U.S. and UK allowances are phased out for individuals or married couples with income in excess of specified levels.

In addition, many jurisdictions allow reduction of taxable income for certain categories of expenses not incurred in connection with a business or investments. In the U.S. system, these (as well as certain business or investment expenses) are referred to as "itemized deductions" for individuals. The UK allows a few of these as personal reliefs. These include, for example, the following for U.S. residents (and UK residents as noted):

- Medical expenses (in excess of 7.5% of adjusted gross income)
- State and local income and property taxes
- Interest expense on certain home loans
- Gifts of money or property to qualifying charitable organizations, subject to certain maximum limitations,
- Losses on non-income-producing property due to casualty or theft,

- Contribution to certain retirement or health savings plans (U.S. and UK),
- Certain educational expenses.

Many systems provide that an individual may claim a tax deduction for personal payments that, upon payment, become taxable to another person, such as alimony. Such systems generally require, at a minimum, reporting of such amounts, and may require that withholding tax be applied to the payment.

GROUPS OF TAXPAYERS

Some systems allow a deduction to a company or other entity for expenses or losses of another company or entity if the two companies or entities are commonly controlled. Such deduction may be referred to as "group relief." Generally, such deductions function in lieu of consolidated or combined computation of tax (tax consolidation) for such groups. Group relief may be available for companies in EU member countries with respect to losses of group companies in other countries.

TAX SHIFT

Tax shift or Tax swap is a change in taxation that eliminates or reduces one or several taxes and establishes or increases others while keeping the overall revenue the same. The term can refer to desired shifts, such as towards Pigovian taxes (typically sin taxes and ecotaxes) as well as (perceived or real) undesired shifts, such as a shift from multi-state corporations to small businesses and families. Tax swap can also refer to the sale of a security that has declined in price since its purchase and the simultaneous purchase of a similar but not identical security, in order to realize a loss for tax purposes while maintaining a position.

TAX CUT

A tax cut is a reduction in taxes. The immediate effects of a tax cut are a decrease in the real income of the government and an increase in the real income of those whose tax rate has been lowered. Due to the perceived benefit in growing real incomes among tax payers politicians have sought to claim their proposed tax credits as tax cuts. In the longer term, however, the loss of government income may be mitigated, depending on the response of tax-payers. The longer-term macroeconomic effects of a tax cut are not predictable in general, because they depend on how the taxpayers use their additional income and how the government adjusts to its reduced income.

Depending on the original tax rate, tax cuts may provide individuals and corporations with an incentive investments which stimulate economic activity. Politically Conservative opinion-makers have theorized that this can generate additional taxable income which could generate more revenue than was collected at the higher rate. This view is debated by economists.

ECONOMICS

In Keynesian economics, a tax cut has the effect of increasing GDP via the fiscal multiplier. Theories which incorporate Ricardian equivalence such as the real business cycle theory however have tax cuts producing no or little change in national income. In these models, agents anticipate future tax rises to pay for government spending and cut their own spending. In New Keynesian economics, tax cuts give a greater stimulus to the economy than that of increases in government spending.

TAX CUTS IN THE UNITED STATES

In recent decades, most "supply-siders" in the United States have been Republicans (though a significant individual tax cut was proposed by President John F. Kennedy from the Democratic Party and passed by a Democratic Congress under another Democratic president, Lyndon B. Johnson) with the belief that cutting the tax rate would stimulate investment and spending, with overall beneficial effects (including replenishment of some lost tax revenues).

President Ronald Reagan signed tax cuts into law, which some believe stimulated a doubling in total tax revenues (from five hundred billion to one trillion dollars) during the period from 1980 to 1990. However, during this period the deficit and national debt more than tripled (from $908 billion in 1980 to $3.2 trillion in 1990) because government spending rose even faster than increases in tax revenue. As a result, income tax receipts as a percent of GDP fell from 11.3% in 1981 to 9.3% in 1984 and did not to revert to original levels until the late 1990s, even though overall revenue skyrocketed in terms of real dollars. Some supply-siders like Don Lambro of the Washington Times credit the Reagan tax cuts with the eventual surpluses of the late 1990s. Others doubt this claim however and instead believe the surpluses were a result of a combination of a decrease in government spending, the passing of the Omnibus Budget Reconciliation Act of 1993 (which dictated several tax increases), and the use of the PAYGO (pay-as-you-go) system. The Center on Budget and Policy Priorities and President's Council of Economic Advisers argue that tax cuts do not pay for themselves stating that the "large reductions in income tax rates in 1981 were followed by abnormally slow growth in income tax receipts".

President George W. Bush signed two major tax cuts into law; one in 2001 and one in 2003. These are often collectively referred to as the "Bush Tax Cuts". The conservative think tank the Heritage Foundation has claimed that the Bush tax cuts have led to the rich shouldering more of the income tax burden and the poor shouldering less; while the Center on Budget and Policy Priorities states that the tax cuts have conferred the "largest benefits,by far on the highest income households." Bush is criticized for giving tax cuts to the rich and capital gains tax breaks, but some benefit extended to middle and lower income brackets as well. Bush has claimed that the tax cuts have paid for themselves but the Center on Budget and Policy Priorities argues that this is false. At the state level, former Democratic Governor Bill Richardson in recent years has supported tax cuts to spur economic growth.

CAPITAL GAINS TAX

Much discussion has occurred regarding the optimum capital gains tax rate, with some advocates calling for tax cuts in the belief that a lower rate (e.g., under 25%) will provide an incentive to investors to sell old stocks and invest in new stocks—which supply siders maintain encourages the creation of new jobs, reduces unemployment, and has the paradoxical effect of increasing tax revenues more or less immediately, an idea first proposed by economist Arthur Laffer while an advisor to Ronald Reagan.

TAX HOLIDAY

A tax holiday is a temporary reduction or elimination of a tax. Programs may be referred to as tax abatements, tax subsidies, tax holidays, or tax reduction programs. Governments usually create tax holidays as incentives for business investment. Tax holidays have been granted by governments at national, sub-national, and local levels, and have included income, property, sales, VAT, and other taxes. Some tax holidays are extra-statutory concessions, where governing bodies grant reduction in tax not necessarily authorized within the law. In developing countries, governments sometimes reduce or eliminate corporate taxes for the purpose of attracting Foreign Direct Investment or stimulating growth in selected industries.

Tax holidays stimulate community revitalization, retain City residents, attract homeowners to the City, and to reduce development costs for home-ownership and rental projects. The program provides a benefit for residents who improve their homes and encourages home shoppers to buy in the City. The tax abatement benefits stay with the property the entire length of the abatement and will transfer to any new property owner within that period.

A tax holiday may be given in respect of particular activities, in particular areas with a view to develop that area of business, or to particular taxpayers. Researchers found that on sales tax holidays, households increase the number of clothing and shoes bought by over 49 percent and 45 percent, respectively, relative to what they buy on average.

SALES TAX HOLIDAYS IN THE UNITED STATES

In New York, a statewide sales tax holiday was first enacted by the New York Legislature in 1996 and enabled the first tax-free week in January 1997. Local governments in New York were given the option of whether or not to participate; most declined. Since then, the initiative has been adopted by thirteen states. It commonly takes place as a form of tax-free weekend lasting Friday through Sunday, usually during a major shopping period for necessities, such as just before school starts. During that period, sales tax is not collected on selected items, such as clothing and school supplies. The items subject to the sales tax exemption may also be restricted by price (for example, clothing up to $100), but consumers are free to buy unlimited quantity of items.

TAX ADVANTAGE

Tax advantage refers to the economic bonus which applies to certain accounts or investments that are, by statute, tax-reduced, tax-deferred, or tax-free. Governments establish the tax advantages to encourage private individuals to contribute money when it is considered to be in the public interest. An example is retirement plans, which often offer tax advantages to incentivize savings for retirement. In the United States, many government bonds (such as state bonds or municipal bonds) may also be exempt from certain taxes.

In countries in which the average age of the population is increasing, tax advantages may put pressure on pension schemes. For example, where benefits are funded on a pay-as-you-go basis, the benefits paid to those receiving a pension come directly from the contributions of those of working age. If the proportion of pensioners to working-age people rises, the contributions needed from working people will also rise proportionately. In the United States, the rapid onset of Baby Boomer retirement is currently causing such a problem.

In order to reduce the burden on such schemes, many governments give privately funded retirement plans a tax advantaged status in order to encourage more people to contribute to such arrangements. Governments often exclude such contributions from an employee's taxable income, while allowing employers to receive tax deductions for contributions to plan funds. Investment earnings in pension funds are almost universally excluded from income tax while accumulating, prior to payment. Payments to retirees and their beneficiaries also sometimes receive favorable tax treatment. In return for a pension scheme's tax advantaged status, governments typically enact restrictions to discourage access to a pension fund's assets before retirement.

TAX INCENTIVE

A tax incentive is an aspect of a country's tax code designed to incentivize, or encourage a particular economic activity.

DISAMBIGUATION

Many "tax incentives" simply remove part or all the burden of the tax from whatever market transaction is taking place. This is because almost all taxes impose what economists call an excess burden or a deadweight loss Deadweight loss is the difference between the amount of economic productivity that would occur absent the tax and that which occurs with the tax imposed. This is illustrated by the following examples. If savings are taxed, people save less than they otherwise would. Tax non-essential goods and people buy less. Tax wages and people work less. And taxing activities like entertainment and travel reduces their consumption as well. Sometimes the goal is to reduce such market activity as in the case of taxing cigarettes. But reducing activity is most often not a goal because greater market activity is considered desirable. When a tax incentive is spoken of, it usually means removing the tax (or a portion thereof) and thereby lessening the burden, really removing a disincentive. To understand how removing a tax increases the level of market exchange by removing the excess burden, it is possible to make an analogy with the use of carrots and sticks.

PSEUDO TAX INCENTIVES

Regardless of the fact that an incentive spurs economic activity. Again, many use the term to refer to any relative change in taxation that changes economic behavior. Such pseudo-incentives include tax holidays, tax deductions, or tax abatement. These "Tax incentives" are targeted at both individuals and corporations.

Individual Incentives

Individual tax incentives are a prominent form of incentive, and include deductions, exemptions, and credits. Specific examples include the mortgage interest deduction, individual retirement account, and hybrid tax credit.

Corporate Tax Incentives

Corporate tax incentives can be raised at federal, state, and local government levels. For example, in the United States, the federal tax code provides a wide range of incentives for corporations, totaling $109 billion in 2011 according to a Tax Foundation Study. Tax Foundation categorizes US federal tax incentives into four main categories, listed below:

- Tax exclusions for local bonds valued at $12.4 billion.
- Preferences aimed at advancing social policy, valued at $9 billion.
- Preferences that directly benefit specific industries, valued at $17.4 billion.
- Preferences broadly available to most corporate taxpayers, valued at $68.7 billion.

Corporate tax incentives provided by state and local governments are also included in the US tax code, but are many times very often directed at individual companies involved in a corporate site selection project. Site selection consultants negotiate these incentives, which are typically specific to the corporate project the state is recruiting, rather than applicable to a broader industry. Examples include:

- Corporate income tax credit

- Property tax abatement
- Sales tax exemption
- Payroll tax refund

TAX REFORM

Tax reform is the process of changing the way taxes are collected or managed by the government. Tax reformers have different goals. Some seek to reduce the level of taxation of all people by the government. Some seek to make the tax system more progressive or less progressive. Others seek to simplify the tax system and make the system more understandable or more accountable. Numerous organizations have been set up to reform tax systems worldwide, often with the intent to reform income taxes or value added taxes into something considered more economically liberal. Other reforms propose tax systems that attempt to deal with externalities. Georgism claims that various forms of land tax can both deal with externalities and improve productivity.

UNITED STATES

There have been many movements in the United States to reform the collection and management of taxes.

During the late 19th century American economist, Henry George, started a global movement for tax reform whose aim was the abolition of all forms of taxation other than the Single Tax on land value. The effects of the movement on taxation policy, although diminished can still be seen in many parts of the world including Australia, New Zealand, Hong Kong, Taiwan and Singapore. Efforts to promote this form of tax reform in the United States continue under the aegis of organizations such as *The Henry George Foundation of America.*

In 1986, landmark tax reform was passed in the Tax Reform Act of 1986. In the 1990s, reform proposals arose over the double-taxation of corporate income, with a large report in 1992 by the IRS.

During the Bush administration, the President's Advisory Panel for Federal Tax Reform recommended the removal of the Alternative Minimum Tax. Several organizations are working for tax reform in the United States including Americans for Tax Reform, Americans For Fair Taxation and KillYourTaxes.com. Various proposals have been put forth for tax simplification in the United States, including the FairTax and various flat tax plans and bipartisan tax reform proposals.

In 2010, Fareed Zakaria proposed what he described as a "grand bargain" with tax reform for economic adversaries Paul Krugman and Niall Ferguson; an attempt to bridge their political divide with the creation of a simple and indirect Federal Sales Tax. Representative Chaka Fattah of Pennsylvania introduced a bill, H.R. 4646, called the *Debt Free America Act* that would introduce a 1% financial transaction tax and eliminate federal income tax. He has introduced bills calling for similar tax reform since 2004, but the bills have never made it out of committee. President Obama's tax reform proposals are highlighted in his administration's fiscal year 2013 federal budget proposal and in a framework for corporate and international tax reform presented by the administration. While some of these proposals have become irrelevant due to "The Fiscal Cliff" agreement at the end of calendar year 2012, these policies are important to highlight as they present a center-left approach to tax reform. In general, the proposals involve some marginal tax rate increases, some marginal tax rate decreases, and base broadening by closing, canceling, or limiting loopholes, deductions, credits, or other tax expenditures for top income earners and corporations.

The Congressional Budget Office and Congressional Research Service describe the President's tax reforms as:

- Extending and modifying the 2001 and 2003 Tax Reductions, popularly known as "The Bush Tax Cuts.":
- The FY2012 tax rates, resulting from the tax reductions of 2001 and 2003, would be made permanent on income, capital gains, and dividends for individuals with income below $200,000 and on couples who file joint tax returns with income below $250,000. Both income thresholds would be adjusted for inflation.
- The tax reductions would expire for individuals earning over $200,000 and couples who file joint tax returns with income above $250,000. For these income earners, the federal income tax rate would increase from 35%to 39.6%, personal exemptions would be phased out, and limits on itemized deductions would take effect. Taxes on capital gains and dividends would also increase from 15% to 20%, and to 23.8% when including the investment tax from "The Affordable Care Act" of 2010. Essentially, tax law for individuals and couples above this threshold would return to tax law from 2000.
- The President would maintain the Child Tax Credit at $1,000 and the reduced earnings threshold put in place for qualification to some or all of this tax credit.
- Expiration of the Social Security payroll tax reduction
- The payroll tax reduction for individuals and households signed into law by President Obama for 2011 and 2012 would expire in 2013 under this plan. The Social Security payroll tax for individuals and households would increase from 4.2% to 6.2%, which is the permanent rate last implemented in 2010. The Social Security payroll tax for business was not reduced as part of the temporary tax relief and will remain at 6.2%.
- Relief from the Alternative Minimum Tax
- The administration proposes to reduce the total number of taxpayers who are subject to the alternative minimum tax by permanently

setting the parameters of the tax at levels that were in effect in calendar year 2011, while indexing those parameters for inflation in the years ahead.

- Setting Limits on Deductions and Exclusions
- This proposal would limit the extent to which higher income tax payers, defined by the previous thresholds of $200,000 for individuals and $250,000 for couples, can reduce their tax liability through certain deductions and exclusions to 28 percent of those current deductions and exclusions.
- Modifying Estate and Gift Taxes
- The amount of an estate or gift that will be tax exempt will be set permanently at $3.5 million per individual and $7 million per couple in most cases. Any amount of an estate or gift set above the exemption threshold would be taxed at a rate of 45%.
- Corporate Tax Reform
- This proposal would lower the corporate tax rate from 35% to 28%, and broaden the corporate tax base by eliminating tax expenditures. Specifically, the administration would end favorable treatment of carried interest, remove expenditures for the depreciation of corporate jets, end subsidies to oil and gas companies, move from last-in-first-out to first-in-last-out accounting, and end expenditures for COLI, a provision related to corporations that purchase life insurance.
- *International Corporate Taxes:* For the foreign operations of U.S. corporations, the administration proposes a tax on excess intangibles, a minimum tax on foreign source income in low tax countries, disallowing a deduction for the cost of moving operations abroad, the allocation of interest for deferred income, and a 20% tax credit for the costs of moving an operation to the United States from abroad.

Evaluation of President Obama's Plan:

- *Simplicity:* President Obama's tax plan, while ending or capping some tax expenditures for upper income Americans and corporations, fails in truly simplifying the tax code. The plan's level of simplicity or lack thereof, is remarkably similar to the status quo, although it remains slightly simpler given that it will end a few complex corporate tax expenditures in exchange for reducing the federal corporate tax rate. This policy will marginally simplify corporate taxation, but leave the vast majority of tax expenditures for most corporations in place. However, the plan fails remarkably in simplifying the tax code for all other stakeholders, including individuals and households. While the President will cap most deductions at 28% of the current deduction rate for individuals and households earning $200,000 and $250,000 or more respectively; the plan keeps all existing expenditures for individuals and households in place. Therefore, there is no simplification of a vast majority of the 70,000 pages of internal revenue code and IRS rulings. While the President's plan ever so slightly simplifies the tax code, it receives a very low score of simplification precisely because the United States arguably has the most complex tax code in the World, and marginal changes will make little difference in altering this reality.

- *Economic Growth & Efficiency:* The President's tax plan, which contains some elements that are conducive to greater economic growth and efficiency, will marginally harm economic growth when weighing costs and benefits. According to economists Young Lee and Roger Gordon, in study that covered seventy countries and was published in the peer-reviewed Journal of Public Economics, a 1 percentage point reduction in the corporate tax raises annual GDP growth by 0.1-0.2%. Given that President Obama's plan would lower corporate taxes by 7 percentage points, the possibility of boosting annual GDP growth by 0.7%-1.4% exists according to this study. However, the study does not account for the elimination or reduction of corporate tax expenditures, which is akin to a tax increase for corporations. Given that the President's plan is revenue neutral regarding corporate taxation if the size of the economy was held constant, the effective tax rate on corporations is likely to remain in line with the status quo despite the fact that the tax would be collected differently. Therefore, any total cost or benefit to the U.S. economy as a result of President Obama's corporate tax policy would be minimal or non-existent when modeled after economists' Young Lee and Roger Gordon's peer-reviewed study. Income and payroll taxes will increase under the President's plan and this has negative implications for economic growth and efficiency according to several empirical and peer-reviewed economic studies. The payroll tax increase for social security is a 2 percentage point increase on all income earners up to $113,700 of income. This payroll tax increase is widely expected to decrease economic growth by 0.6 of a percentage point, and cost the average worker $700 in 2013. Moody's economist Mark Zandi expects that 400,000 jobs that would have otherwise been created, will not be created as a result of this tax increase. The marginal federal income tax rate increase would increase marginal tax rates on the top 2% of income earners, from 33% and 35%, to 36% and 39.6%. According to the Congressional Budget Office, this specific tax increase will marginally decrease economic growth by 0.25 percentage point and reduce job growth by 200,000 jobs in 2013. The CBO also found that extending the tax reductions for the top 2% of income earners would increase economic growth by 0.1 percentage point. Therefore, the negative effect of this specific tax is smaller when compared to the expiration of the payroll tax reduction, however; these increases in marginal rates for the top 2% do slightly and adversely impact economic growth. President Obama's alternative minimum tax (AMT) relief does not promote economic growth, but it does prevent what would otherwise amount to a tax increase on millions of middle class taxpayers in 2013, which would have adverse effects on economic growth. When the alternative minimum tax was created in 1969, it was meant to force wealthy elites, who paid little or no federal taxes due to tax expenditures, to pay more in federal taxes. However, in the over four decades since its passage, the tax has not been indexed for inflation, meaning it effects a higher percentage of taxpayers, and raises more than fourteen times the revenue it raised in 1969, when adjusted for inflation. President Obama's plan will prevent the AMT, which currently increases taxes for 4.3 million taxpayers, from increasing taxes on a total of 34 million tax payers in 2013 and 55 million taxpayers in 2022. Therefore, while this policy provision will not improve the status quo, it prevents substantial economic harm in the years to come. In the final analysis, President Obama's tax plan will reduce economic growth by at least 0.85 percentage points and reduce job growth by 600,000 jobs in 2013, when simply considering the effects of the aforementioned increases in income taxes and payroll taxes alone. While many economists and studies including a recent report from Ernst & Young LLP conclude that higher capital gains/dividends tax rates result in less saving, investment, and economic productivity by using historical and international comparisons; there is very little empirical evidence available to more concretely predict the effects of the President's plan of a 33% increase in the capital gains/dividends tax rate. Despite these negative outcomes on economic growth and efficiency, it is worth noting that a few of President Obama's proposals, including the permanent extension of the 2001 and 2003 tax reductions for 98% of taxpayers and the "patch" on the alternative minimum tax, prevent significant harm from befalling the United States economy in 2013 and beyond. This analysis is not claiming that the economy will contract by 0.85% and that unemployment will increase by 600,000 jobs in 2013, but that the result of this policy alternative entails lower economic growth and less employment than what would have otherwise been achieved had the income and payroll tax reductions been extended through 2013. Finally, this analysis does not include the effects of tax increases due to previously passed legislation, such as The Affordable Care Act of 2010, even though such legislation was supported by the President. This analysis merely covers the President's tax plan from 2012.

- *Equity:* The President's plan will improve income inequality in the United States. The increase in marginal income tax rates and the increase in the capital gains rate to 20% will lower the post-tax gross income of the top 2% of American income earners. Since affluent Americans receive a greater percentage of their gross income from capital gains and since the bottom 40% of income earners do not have taxable capital gains; the effect of this capital gains tax increase will lower the income of affluent Americans, thereby bringing about greater income equality. The increase in marginal income tax rates will have the same effect. While the increase in the social security payroll tax back to its normal, pre-2011 level will increase the tax for all income earners, the tax only affects income up to $113,700. Therefore, the rich are not as adversely affected by the tax increase as the poor and middle class. The average income earner in the top 1% will lose 1/10 of one percent of total income as a result of this tax increase. Meanwhile, the poor and middle class will lose 2 percentage points of total income. However, the 5% point increase in capital gains and 3-4.6% point increase in the income tax rate for the top 2% of income earners clearly reduce the income of affluent Americans by more than 2 percentage points. In addition, President Obama's tax plan would cap major deductions for this top group of income earners at 28% of current levels. Therefore, while the social security payroll tax increase moderates the effects of reducing income inequality, the wealthy will see a larger increase in their tax liability and a greater reduction in their post-tax income in comparison to the poor and middle class when all the moving parts of President Obama's plan are taken into consideration. Finally, if the increased tax revenue results in higher levels of government expenditure that directly benefit the poor and middle class more substantially than the upper-middle and upper class; income inequality can be further reduced. Many groups view tax equity as government's equal treatment of all taxpayers rather than government's support for the greater equality of economic outcomes. From this perspective of equity, President Obama's tax plan increases inequity for the top 2% of wage earners, who will pay an even higher and more "unfair" percentage of the federal tax burden as a result of higher rates and a cap on tax deductions and credits for this group. However, a small group of the wealthy, who earn most of their living from capital gains, dividends, and carried interest, will have to pay at the 20% (23.8% rate with The Affordable Care Act) tax rate rather than the

15% tax rate, thereby increasing their share of the total federal tax burden, and increasing equity. Overall, when considering equity from two different value perspectives, the President's tax plan has a positive effect on increasing equity.

TAX CHOICE

Tax choice is the theory that taxpayers should have more control with how their individual taxes are allocated. If taxpayers could choose which government organizations received their taxes, opportunity cost decisions would integrate their partial knowledge. For example, a taxpayer who allocated more of his taxes on public education would have less to allocate on public healthcare. Supporters argue that allowing taxpayers to demonstrate their preferences would help ensure that the government succeeds at efficiently producing the public goods that taxpayers truly value.

TAX HARMONIZATION

Tax harmonization refers to the process of making taxes identical or at least similar in a region. In practice, it usually means increasing tax in low-tax jurisdictions, rather than reducing tax in high-tax jurisdictions or a combination of both. The best example is the European Union where all countries must have a value added tax of at least 15%.

TAX COMPETITION

Tax competition, a form of regulatory competition, exists when governments are encouraged to lower fiscal burdens to either encourage the inflow of productive resources or discourage the exodus of those resources. Often, this means a governmental strategy of attracting foreign direct investment, foreign indirect investment (financial investment), and high value human resources by minimizing the overall taxation level and/or special tax preferences, creating a comparative advantage.

Some observers suggest that tax competition is generally a central part of a government policy for improving the lot of labour by creating well-paid jobs (often in countries or regions with very limited job prospects). Others suggest that it is beneficial mainly for investors, as workers could have been better paid (both through lower taxation on them, and through higher redistribution of wealth) if it was not for tax competition lowering taxation on corporation.

Many economists also argue that tax competition is beneficial in raising total tax intake due to low corporate tax rates stimulating economic growth.

It has also been argued that just as competition is good for businesses, competition is good for governments as it drives efficiencies and good governance of the public budget. From the mid 1900s governments had more freedom in setting their taxes as the barriers to free movement of capital and people were high. The gradual process of globalization is lowering these barriers and results in rising capital flows and greater manpower mobility.

IMPACT

With tax competition in the era of globalization politicians have to keep tax rates "reasonable" to dissuade workers and investors from moving to a lower tax environment. Most countries started to reform their tax policies to improve their competitiveness. However, the tax burden is just one part of a complex formula describing national competitiveness. The other criteria like total manpower cost, labor market flexibility, education levels, political stability, legal system stability and efficiency are also important.

Governments typically react with "carrot-and-stick" policies such as:

- Reduction of both personal and corporate income tax rates
- Tax breaks/holidays (i.e. time limited tax exemptions)
- Favorable tax policies for non-residents
- Raising the barriers to free movement of capital
- Not allowing companies domiciled in tax havens to bid for public contracts
- Political pressure on lower tax countries to "harmonize" (i.e. raise) their taxes

APPLICATION

The European Union (EU) illustrates the role of tax competition. The barriers to free movement of capital and people were reduced close to nonexistence. Some countries (e.g. Republic of Ireland) utilized their low levels of corporate tax to attract large amounts of foreign investment while paying for the necessary infrastructure (roads, telecommunication) from EU funds. The net contributors (like Germany) strongly oppose the idea of infrastructure transfers to low tax countries. Net contributors have not complained, however, about recipient nations such as Greece and Portugal, which have kept taxes high and not prospered. EU integration brings continuing pressure for consumption tax harmonization as well. EU member nations must have a value-added tax (VAT) of at least 15 percent (the main VAT band) and limits the set of products and services that can be included in the preferential tax band. Still this policy does not stop people utilizing the difference in VAT levels when purchasing certain goods (e.g. cars). The contributing factor are the single currency (Euro), growth of e-commerce and geographical proximity.

The political pressure for tax harmonization extends beyond EU borders. Some neighbouring countries with special tax régimes (e.g. Switzerland) were already forced to some concessions in this area.

CRITICISM

The Organisation for Economic Co-operation and Development organized an anti-tax competition project in the 1990s, culminating with the publication of "Harmful Tax Competition: An Emerging Global Issue" in 1998 and the creation of a blacklist of so-called tax havens in 2000. Blacklisted jurisdictions effectively resisted the OECD by noting that several of the member nations of OECD also were tax havens according to the OECD's own definition.

Left-wing economists generally argue that governments need tax revenue to cover debts and contingencies, and that paying to fund a welfare state is an obligation of social responsibility. Right-wing economists argue that tax competition means that taxpayers can vote with their feet, choosing the region with the most efficient delivery of governmental services. This makes the tax base of a state volitional, because the taxpayer can avoid tax by renouncing citizenship or emigrating and thereby changing tax residence.

DOUBLE TAXATION

Double taxation is the levying of tax by two or more jurisdictions on the same declared income (in the case of income taxes), asset (in the case of capital taxes), or financial transaction (in the case of sales taxes). This double liability is often mitigated by tax treaties between countries.

The term 'double taxation' is additionally used, particularly in the USA, to refer to the fact that corporate profits are taxed and the shareholders of the corporation are (usually) subject to personal taxation when they receive dividends or distributions of those profits.

INTERNATIONAL DOUBLE TAXATION AGREEMENTS

It is not unusual for a business or individual who is resident in one country to make a taxable gain (earnings, profits) in another. This person may find that he is obliged by domestic laws to pay tax on that gain locally *and* pay again in the country in which the gain was made. Since this is inequitable, many nations make bilateral double taxation agreements with each other. In some cases, this requires that tax be paid in the country of residence and be exempt in the country in which it arises. In the remaining cases, the country where the gain arises deducts taxation at source ("withholding tax") and the taxpayer receives a compensating foreign tax credit in the country of residence to reflect the fact that tax has already been paid. To do this, the taxpayer must declare himself (in the foreign country) to be non-resident there. So the second aspect of the agreement is that the two taxation authorities exchange information about such declarations, and so may investigate any anomalies that might indicate tax evasion.

EUROPEAN UNION SAVINGS TAXATION

In the European Union, member states have concluded a multilateral agreement on information exchange. This means that they will each report (to their counterparts in each other jurisdiction) a list of those savers who have claimed exemption from local taxation on grounds of not being a resident of the state where the income arises. These savers should have declared that foreign income in their own country of residence, so any difference suggests tax evasion. (For a transition period, some states have a separate arrangement. They may offer each non-resident account holder the choice of taxation arrangements: either (a) disclosure of information as above, or (b) deduction of local tax on savings interest at source as is the case for residents).

Cyprus double tax treaties

Cyprus has completed over 45 Double Taxation Treaties up to today and is also in negotiations with many countries for signing Treaties with them. The main purpose of these treaties is the avoidance of double taxation on income earned in any of these countries. Under these agreements, a credit is usually allowed against the tax levied by the country in which the taxpayer resides for taxes levied in the other treaty country and as a result the tax payer pays no more than the higher of the two rates. Further, some treaties provide for tax sparing credits whereby the tax credit allowed is not only with respect to tax actually paid in the other treaty country but also from tax which would have been otherwise payable had it not been for incentive measures in that other country which result in exemption or reduction of tax.

German taxation avoidance

If a foreign citizen is in Germany for less than a relevant 183-day period (approximately six months) and is tax resident (*i.e.*, and paying taxes on his or her salary and benefits) elsewhere, then it may be possible to claim tax relief under a particular Double Tax Treaty. The relevant 183 day period is either 183 days in a calendar year or in any period of 12 months, depending upon the particular treaty involved.

So, for example, the Double Tax Treaty with the UK looks at a period of 183 days in the German tax year (which is the same as the calendar year); thus, a citizen of the UK could work in Germany from 1 September through the following 31 May (9 months) and then claim to be exempt from German tax

INDIA

India has comprehensive Double Taxation Avoidance Agreements (DTAA) with 88(signed 88 DTAAs out of which 85 have entered into force) countries. This means that there are agreed rates of tax and jurisdiction on specified types of income arising in a country to a tax resident of another country. Under the Income Tax Act 1961 of India, there are two provisions, Section 90 and Section 91, which provide specific relief to taxpayers to save them from double taxation. Section 90 is for taxpayers who have paid the tax to a country with which India has signed DTAA, while Section 91 provides relief to tax payers who have paid tax to a country with which India has not signed a DTAA. Thus, India gives relief to both kind of taxpayer.

A large number of foreign institutional investors who trade on the Indian stock markets operate from Mauritius and the second being Singapore. According to the tax treaty between India and Mauritius, capital gains arising from the sale of shares are taxable in the country of residence of the shareholder and not in the country of residence of the company whose shares have been sold. Therefore, a company resident in Mauritius selling shares of an Indian company will not pay tax in India. Since there is no capital gains tax in Mauritius, the gain will escape tax altogether.

The Indian and Cypriot tax treaty is the only other such Indian treaty to provide for the same beneficial treatment of capital gains.

AUSTRALIA

The broad principle in Australia is that, if you're an Australian resident, you're taxed on all of your worldwide income. If you're a non-resident, you're taxed just on your Australian-sourced income. This presents some problems, because when other countries operate on the same principle (and most do), individuals are likely to end up getting taxed twice.

Say, for example, you're an Australian who's published a book in the US and earns royalty income in the US from the book. Australia would tax the income (it's worldwide income and you're a resident) and the US would tax it (you're a non-resident there, but it's US-sourced). Suddenly the governments between them have taken 60c or 70c in the dollar of your earnings. That makes it a pretty severe disincentive to invest and operate business globally.

The way around it in Australia, similar to other countries is to have Double Tax Agreements (DTA) 'Tax Treaties', where both countries compare tax laws to find where people would get taxed twice, and agree how it will be taxed in those cases. In the example of royalties, the US/AUS DTA says the US will tax it at the rate of 5%, and Australia will tax it at normal rates (ie, 30% for companies) but give you a credit for the 5% you've already paid. For Australian based residents, this ends up working out the same as if the money had been earned within Australia - whilst still providing a 5% credit to the US.

It's worth noting in both Australia and outside, that the DTAs are designed to eliminate double tax, rather than introduce tax

UNITED STATES

U.S. citizens and resident aliens abroad

The U.S. requires its citizens to file tax returns reporting their earnings wherever they reside. However, there are some measures designed to reduce the international double taxation that results from this requirement.

First, an individual who is a bona fide resident of a foreign country or is physically outside the United States for an extended time is entitled to an exclusion (exemption) of part or all of their earned income (i.e. personal service income, as distinguished from income from capital or investments.) That exemption is $97,600 for 2013, pro-rated.

Second, the United States allows a foreign tax credit by which income taxes paid to foreign countries can be offset against U.S. income tax liability attributable to foreign income. This can be a complex issue that often requires the services of a tax advisor. The foreign tax credit is not allowed for taxes paid on earned income that is excluded under the rules described in the preceding paragraph (i.e. no double dipping).

Double taxation within the United States

Double taxation can also happen within a single country. This typically happens when subnational jurisdictions have taxation powers, and jurisdictions have competing claims. In the United States a person may legally have only a single domicile. However, when a person dies different states may each claim that the person was domiciled in that state. Intangible personal property may then be taxed by each state making a claim. In the absence of specific laws prohibiting multiple taxation, and as long as the total of taxes does not exceed 100% of the value of the tangible personal property, the courts will allow such multiple taxation.

Also, since each state makes its own rules on who is a resident for tax purposes, someone may be subject to the claims by two states on his or her income. For example if someone's legal/permanent domicile is in state A, which considers only permanent domicile to which one returns for residency but he or she spends 7 months of the year (say April-October) in state B where anyone who is there longer than 6 months is considered a part-year resident, that person will then owe taxes to both states on money earned in state B. College or university students may also be subject to claims of more than one state, generally if they leave their original state to attend school, and the second state considers students to be residents for tax purposes. In some cases one state will give a credit for taxes paid to another state, but not always.

Taxation of corporate dividends

In the United States, the term "double taxation" is also used by critics to describe dividend taxation and capital gains taxation.

NO TAXATION WITHOUT REPRESENTATION

"No taxation without representation" is a slogan originating during the 1750s and 1760s that summarized a primary grievance of the British colonists in the Thirteen Colonies, which was one of the major causes of the American Revolution. In short, many in those colonies believed that, as they were not directly represented in the distant British Parliament, any laws it passed taxing the colonists (such as the Sugar Act and the Stamp Act) were illegal under the Bill of Rights 1689, and were a denial of their rights as Englishmen.

The phrase captures a sentiment central to the cause of the English Civil War, as articulated by John Hampden who said "what an English King has no right to demand, an English subject has a right to refuse" in the Ship money case. "No Taxation Without Representation," in the context of British American Colonial taxation, appeared for the first time in the February 1768 London Magazine's headline, on page 89, in the printing of Lord Camden's "Speech on the Declaratory Bill of the Sovereignty of Great Britain over the Colonies."

PRIOR TO THE AMERICAN REVOLUTION

The British Parliament had controlled colonial trade and taxed imports and exports since 1660. By the 1760s, the Americans were being deprived of a historic right. The English Bill of Rights 1689 had forbidden the imposition of taxes without the consent of Parliament. Since the colonists had no representation in Parliament, the taxes violated the guaranteed Rights of Englishmen. Parliament initially contended that the colonists had virtual representation, but the idea "found little support on either side of the Atlantic". The issue of American representation in the House of Commons (and by implication, the House of Lords) surfaced as early as 1640-41, when members of Parliament asked the Puritan colonists, as recalled by the eponymous Governor of Massachusetts Bay in his *Journal of John Winthrop*, to send representative delegates to Britain either as lobbyists or as members. This offer was initially refused on the grounds that "if we [New Englanders] should put ourselves under the protection of the Parliament, we must be then subject to such laws as they should make...[which] might prove very prejudicial to us." However, Winthrop and the Massachusetts Assembly eventually sent agents to lobby Parliamentarians, although this does not seem to have been as members of the Commons. The issue of colonial representation in Parliament continued to emerge from time-to-time, as evidenced in the writings of the Queen Anne-era historian John Oldmixon.

AMERICAN REVOLUTION

The phrase had been used for more than a generation in Ireland. By 1765, the term was in use in Boston, and local politician James Otis was most famously associated with the phrase, "taxation without representation is tyranny." In the course of the Revolutionary era (1750-1783), many arguments seeking to resolve the dispute surrounding Parliamentary sovereignty, self-governance, taxation, and the constitutional rights of 'commoners' to representation were pursued. These included:

- That the colonists were virtually represented via the 'estate' of the commons in Parliament.

- That the House of Commons was elected by resident British subjects regardless of domicile, which meant the theoretical right of colonials to stand for seats and elect candidates. This was another form of virtual representation.
- That the provincial agents virtually represented the colonists interests at Westminster.
- That constitutional authority was capable of being asserted in the House of Commons by incorporating a number of colonial commoners, elected in the colonies, and sent to Parliament. This was known as actual representation.
- That a policy of confining Parliamentary legislation and taxation to 'external' affairs, alongside recognised 'internal' autonomy of the colonies, would balance Parliamentary sovereignty and colonial self-governance. This was a popular argument in Whiggism and was another form of direct or actual representation.
- That imperial harmony was best secured between the colonial Assemblies and Parliament by adopting legislative parity under one common Crown. This was akin to the commonwealth status that Benjamin Franklin described in his Parliamentary examination.
- That the principles of self-governance were best served by means of republican independence.

Representative Proposals before 1776

In the course of the 1760s and 1770s, William Pitt the Elder, Sir William Pulteney, and George Grenville, amongst other prominent Britons and colonial Americans, such as Joseph Galloway, James Otis, Jr., Benjamin Franklin, John Adams, the London Quaker Thomas Crowley, Royal Governors such as Thomas Pownall M.P., William Franklin, Sir Francis Bernard, and the Attorney-General of Quebec, Francis Maseres, debated and circulated plans for the creation of colonial seats in London, imperial union with Great Britain, or a federally representative British Parliament with powers of taxation that was to consist of American, West Indian, Irish and British Members of Parliament. Despite the fact that these ideas were considered and discussed seriously on both sides of the Atlantic, it appears no Congressional or colonial Assemblage request for such constitutional developments was sent to Westminster.

Jared Ingersoll Snr., colonial agent for Connecticut, wrote to his American colleague, the Royal Governor of Connecticut Thomas Fitch, that following Isaac Barre's famous Parliamentary speech against the Stamp Act in 1764, Richard Jackson, M.P., supported Barre and other pro-American M.P.s by producing before the House copies of earlier Acts of Parliament that had admitted Durham and Chester seats upon their petitions for representation. The argument was put forward in Parliament that America ought to have representatives on these grounds too. Richard Jackson supposed that Parliament had a right to tax America, but he much doubted the expediency of the Stamp act. He said if it was necessary, as ministers claimed, to tax the colonies, the latter should be permitted to elect some part of the Parliament, "otherwise the liberties of America, I do not say will be lost, but will be in danger."

The Knox-Burke Debates

William Knox, an aide of George Grenville, pamphleteer and subsequent Irish Under-Secretary of State for the American Colonies, received an appointment in 1756 to the American provinces, and after his return to London in 1761, he recommended the creation of a colonial aristocracy and colonial representation in the British Parliament. He was shortly afterwards appointed agent for Georgia and East Florida, a post which he forfeited by writing in favour of the Stamp Act. In his Grenville-backed pamphlet of 1769, *The Controversy between Great Britain and her Colonies Reviewed*, Knox wrote that the colonial delegates to the Stamp Act Congress had been offered seats in the British Parliament, the offers of which they had refused. Knox submitted that,

- Whilst [the radical colonists] exclaim against Parliament for taxing them when they are not represented, they candidly declare they will not have representatives [in Parliament] lest they should be taxed...The truth...is that they are determined to get rid of the jurisdiction of Parliament...and they therefore refuse to send members to that assembly lest they should preclude themselves of [the] plea [that Parliament's] legislative acts...are done without their consent; which, it must be confessed, holds equally good against all laws, as against taxes...The colony advocates...tell us, that by refusing to accept our offer of representatives they...mean to avoid giving Parliament a pretence for taxing them.

Edmund Burke responded to Knox, who had drawn up *The Controversy between Great Britain and her Colonies Reviewed* as well as *The Present State of the Nation* (1768) under the supervision of George Grenville, by opining in his political tract *Observations on a Late State of the Nation* (1769),

- NOW comes [Knox's] American representation...Is not the reader a little astonished at the proposal of an American representation from that quarter [of Grenville's]? It is proposed merely as a project of speculative improvement; not from the necessity in the case, not to add any thing to the authority of parliament: but that we may afford a greater attention to the concerns of the Americans, and give them a better opportunity of stating their grievances, and of obtaining redress. I am glad to find the author has at length discovered that we have not given a sufficient attention to their concerns, or a proper

> redress to their grievances. His great friend [Grenville] would once have been exceedingly displeased with any person, who should tell him, that he did not attend sufficiently to those concerns. He thought he did so, when he regulated the colonies over and over again: he thought he did so, when he formed two general systems of revenue; one of port-duties, and the other of internal taxation. These systems supposed, or ought to suppose, the greatest attention to, and the most detailed information of, all their affairs. However, by contending for the American representation, he seems at last driven virtually to admit, that great caution ought to be used in the exercise of all our legislative rights over an object so remote from our eye, and so little connected with our immediate feelings; that in prudence we ought not to be quite so ready with our taxes, until we can secure the desired representation in parliament. Perhaps it may be some time before this hopeful scheme can be brought to perfect maturity; al|though the author seems to be no wise aware of any obstructions that lie in the way of it.

Burke later argued in Parliament (April 1774),

- AGAIN, and again, revert to your old principles—seek peace, and ensue it—leave America, if she has taxable matter in her, to tax herself...Nobody will be argued into slavery. Sir, let the gentlemen on the other side [of the House of Commons] call forth all their ability; let the best of them get up, and tell me, what one character of liberty the Americans have, and what one brand of slavery they are free from, if they are bound in their property and industry, by all the restraints you can imagine on commerce, and at the same time are made pack-horses of every tax you choose to impose, without the least share in granting them?"

While Parliament had a constitutional right to virtually represent the colonial subjects, these politicians were arguing, it ought not exercise that right unless it was done so in as actually representative a manner as possible. For some this meant Parliamentary inclusion, but for most this meant using the consent of the colonial Assemblies, involving the colonial Agents in policy, and using tax revenue of virtually represented colonies only for expenditure in those domains.

Heightening of Tensions

The Americans rejected the Stamp Act of 1765 brought in by British Prime Minister George Grenville, and violently rejected the remaining tax on tea imports, under the Tea Act passed in May 1773, at the Boston Tea Party on December 16, 1773. The Parliament considered this an illegal act because they believed it undermined the authority of the Crown-in-Parliament. When the British then used the military to enforce laws that the colonists believed

Parliament had passed illegally, the colonists responded by forming militias and seized political control of each colony, ousting the royal governors - with the exception of the American-born Royal Governor of Connecticut, John Trumbull, who was allowed to remain as the new Patriot Governor.

The complaint was never officially over the amount of taxation (the taxes were quite low, though ubiquitous), but always on the political decision-making process by which taxes were decided in London, i.e. without representation for the colonists in British Parliament.

Patrick Henry's resolution in the Virginia legislature implied that Americans possessed all the rights of Englishmen, that the principle of no taxation without representation was an essential part of the British Constitution, and that Virginia alone had the right to tax Virginians.

Efforts at Conciliation

This offer of actual imperial representation was likewise re-stated to the delegates of the colonies via the colonial agents in 1774, according to Connecticut-born Reverend Thomas Bradbury Chandler, in his publication *A Friendly Address to All Reasonable Americans*. In February 1775, Britain passed the Conciliatory Resolution which ended taxation for any colony which satisfactorily provided for the imperial defense and the upkeep of imperial officers.

Representative Proposals after 1776

James Macpherson, a colonial secretary of British West Florida, defended the North administration in an officially sponsored polemic in 1776 named *The Rights of Great Britain Asserted*. This work replied to the Continental Congress' July 6, 1775 *Declaration of the Causes and Necessity of Taking up Arms* by proposing that,

- Had the Americans, instead of flying to arms, submitted the same supposed grievance [as the taxed though unrepresented Palatine counties in England had], in a peaceable and dutiful manner, to the Legislature, I can perceive no reason why their request should be refused. Had they, like the County and City of Chester, represented, that "for lack of Knights and Burgesses to represent them in the High Court of Parliament, they had been oftentimes TOUCHED and GRIEVED with Acts and Statutes made within the said Court, derogatory to their most ancient jurisdictions, liberties and privileges, and prejudicial to their quietness, rest and peace;" this Country [of Britain] would, I am persuaded, have no objection to their being represented in her Parliament... If they are not madly bent on independence, let them propose the conditions on which they wish to continue as subjects...The Legislature of this Kingdom cannot possibly depart from any part of its supremacy over the Colonies;

but it is in the power of the Colonies to share in that supremacy. If they complain of being taxed without having the privilege of sending Members to Parliament, let them be represented. Nay, more: Let their representation increase in proportion to the Revenue they shall furnish. If they wish rather to vote their QUOTA towards the general supply, through their own General Courts and Assemblies, the resolution of Parliament on that subject is still open to their choice. But, as long as they assume the language of a Sovereign State, this Kingdom can enter into no negociation [sic], can meet no compromise."

The noted economist Adam Smith seconded this view in his famous 1776 publication *Wealth of Nations* when he recommended the Americans "to send fifty or sixty new representatives to Parliament" on the basis of the amount of taxes they would contribute to the Imperial coffers. Writing in October 1776 to Lord North in *Strictures upon the Declaration of the Congress* of the recent Declaration of Independence, and particularly of James Otis, Jr.'s pamphlet *Rights of the British Colonies* and its endorsement by the Massachusetts Assembly, Governor Thomas Hutchinson said,

- The Assembly of Massachusetts Bay, therefore, was the first that took any publick of the [Sugar] Act, and the first which ever took exception to the right of Parliament to impose Duties or Taxes on the Colonies, whilst they had no representatives in the House of Commons. This they did in a letter to their Agent in the summer of 1764, which they took care to print and publish before it was possible for him to receive it. And in this letter they recommend to him a pamphlet, wrote by one of their members, in which there are proposals for admitting representatives from the Colonies to fit in the House of Commons. I have this special reason, my Lord, for taking notice of this Act of the Massachusetts Assembly; that though an American representation is thrown out as an expedient which might obviate the objections to Taxes upon the Colonies, yet it was only intended to amuse the authority in England; and as soon as it was known to have its advocates here [in London], it was renounced by the colonies, and even by the Assembly of the Colony which first proposed it, as utterly impracticable."

Indeed, the resolves of the Continental Congresses of both 1765 and 1774 declared that imperial representation was too impractical on the footing that "local and other circumstances, cannot properly be represented in the British parliament".

It is important to note, however, that neither was such an offer of seats likewise formally made to the colonies, as far as current historiography has gathered, by Parliament until 1778. Parliament's Carlisle Peace Commission of 1778 nevertheless proposed to the Congress the rights of provincial representation, Congressional representation, pardons for the Congressional delegates, and above all, actual Parliamentary representation of Americans in London.

VIRTUAL REPRESENTATION

In Britain, representation was highly limited due to unequally distributed voting constituencies and property requirements; only 3% of the population could vote and they were often controlled by local gentry. This meant 'virtual representation' had come to be employed in Britain to explain the iniquities in its political life. Therefore the British government attempted to argue that the colonists had virtual representation in their interests. In English history, "no taxation without representation" was an old principle and meant that Parliament had to pass all taxes.

At first, the "representation" was held to be one of land, but, by 1700, this had shifted to the notion that, in Parliament, all British subjects had a "virtual representation." "We virtually and implicitly allow the institutions of any government of which we enjoy the benefit and solicit the protection," declared Samuel Johnson in his political pamphlet *Taxation No Tyranny*. He rejected the plea that the colonists, who had no vote, were unrepresented. "They are represented," he said, "by the same virtual representation as the greater part of England." However, the lack of an aristocracy in the colonies and a tradition of greater democracy amongst Americans gave impetus to the charge, voiced by Britons and colonists alike, that virtual representation was "sophistry".

The colonial insistence on direct representation as opposed to virtual representation has thus been seen by later commentators to have "usher[ed] in a profound political and social revolution, which rooted out most of the remaining traces of monarchic rule and feudalism inherited from the only partially complete English bourgeois revolution. The Americans carried through the bourgeois democratic revolution on a scale never before seen in history."

Constitutional Arguments in Favour

Professor Michael Zuckert, regarding Whateley's opinions that it "is the estate of the commons that is present in the constitution, and not merely these particular persons who happen to be electors", has written "Although the Americans greeted the theory of virtual representation with scorn, it is in fact an extremely plausible application of the underlying theory of the constitution, as contained in the Bill of Rights, to the situation of the colonists, to whom the "rights of Englishmen" had been promised."

Josiah Tucker, A Welsh Anglican cleric, argued in *Four Tracts on Political and Commercial Subjects* [London, 1774] that incorporation of American representatives on a demographically proportional basis as opposed to a virtual one, alongside such an equalisation in suffrage of Britons, would result in a House of Commons with too many members to function efficiently. He maintained that virtual representation was adequate because it did not effect the theoretical right of qualified British subjects across the Empire, including in England, to vote for representatives in Britain, even though "their Distance from the Place of Election" made this right "inconvenient".

Thomas Whateley, a member of Parliament who helped draft the Stamp Act, defended it in 1765 by declaring American rights were theoretically not infringed as British subjects, otherwise known as 'Commons', when he wrote that the Americans,

- Claim it is true the Privilege, which is common to all British Subjects, of being taxed only with their own Consent, given by their Representatives; and may they ever enjoy the Privilege in all its Extent: May this sacred Pledge of Liberty be preserved inviolate, to the utmost Verge of our Dominions, and to the latest Page of our History!..All British Subjects are really in the same; none are actually, all are virtually represented in Parliament; for every Member of Parliament sits in the House, not as Representative of his own Constituents, but as one of that august Assembly by which all the Commons of Great Britain are represented...It would be a singular Objection to a Man's Vote for a Member of Parliament that being represented in a provincial, he cannot be represented in a national Assembly;..We value the Right of being represented in the national Legislature as the dearest Privilege we enjoy; how justly would the Colonies complain, if they alone were deprived of it? They acknowledge Dependence upon their Mother Country; but that Dependence would be Slavery not Connection, if they bore no Part in the Government of the whole...to deny the Authority of [Parliament] is to surrender all Claims to a Share in its Councils...a permanent Title to a Share in national Councils, would be exchanged for a precarious Representation in a provincial Assembly...Happily for them, this is not their Condition. They are on the contrary a Part, and an important Part, of the Commons of Great Britain: they are represented in Parliament, in the same Manner as those Inhabitants of Britain are, who have not Voices in Elections; and they enjoy, with the Rest of their Fellow-subjects the inestimable Privilege of not being bound by any Laws, or subject to any Taxes, to which the Majority of the Representatives of the Commons have not consented."

Constitutional Arguments Against

The theory of virtual representation was attacked in Britain by Charles Pratt, 1st Earl Camden, and his ally William Pitt, 1st Earl of Chatham. It was wholly rejected in the colonies, who said the "virtual" was a cover for political corruption and was irreconcilable with their belief that government derives its just powers from the consent of the governed. Colonists said no man was represented if he were not allowed to vote. Moreover, even "If every inhabitant of America had the requisite freehold," said Daniel Dulany, "not one could vote, but upon the supposition of his ceasing to become an inhabitant of America, and becoming a resident of Great Britain." The colonists and like-minded Britons insisted that representation was achieved only through an assembly of men actually elected by the persons they were intended to represent.

The argument between the colonies and Parliament sought to resolve how the British 'commoners' of the various part of the Empire were represented most constitutionally - as Daniel Dulaney, an American Loyalist and lawyer, put it "[the] constitutional authority [of Parliament's rights to bind American subjects] depends upon the single question, Whether the Commons of Great-Britain are virtually the representatives of the Commons of America, or not.

Pitt and Camden

William Pitt argued in 1766 that the Commons of Britain ought not to tax the '"Commons of America" without gaining consent of their representatives in stating, "even under former arbitrary reigns, Parliaments were ashamed of taxing a people without their consent, and allowed them representatives. Why did [Grenville] confine himself to Chester and Durham? He might have taken a higher example in Wales—Wales, that never was taxed by Parliament till it was incorporated." He then said,

- I am no courtier of America. I stand up for this kingdom. I maintain that the Parliament has a right to bind, to restrain America. Our legislative power over the colonies is sovereign and supreme. When it ceases to be sovereign and supreme, I would advise every gentleman to sell his lands, if he can, and embark for that country. When two countries are connected together like England and her colonies, without being incorporated, the one must necessarily govern. The greater must rule the less. But she must so rule it as not to contradict the fundamental principles that are common to both...let the sovereign authority of this country over the colonies be asserted in as strong terms as can be devised, and be made to extend to every point of legislation whatsoever; that we may bind their trade, confine their manufactures, and exercise every power whatsoever, except that of taking their money out of their pockets without their consent."

In his first speeches in Parliament, Lord Camden vigorously attacked the declaratory act which was proposed to mollify the crown on the repeal of the Stamp Tax. After his first affirmation of "no taxation without representation"

Camden was attacked by British PM Grenville, Chief Justice James Mansfield, Robert Henley, 1st Earl of Northington, and others. He responded:

- [T]he British Parliament have no right to tax the Americans. I shall not consider the Declaratory Bill now lying on your table; for to what purpose, but loss of time, to consider the particulars of a Bill, the very existence of which is illegal, absolutely illegal, contrary to the fundamental laws of nature, contrary to the fundamental laws of this constitution? A constitution grounded on the eternal and immutable laws of nature; a constitution whose foundation and centre is liberty, which sends liberty to every individual who may happen to be within any part of its ample circumference. Nor, my Lords, is the doctrine new, it is as old as the constitution; it grew up with it; indeed it is its support; taxation and representation are inseparably united; God hath joined them, no British parliament can separate them; to endeavour to do it, is to stab our very vitals.... My position is this—I repeat it—I will maintain it to my last hour,—taxation and representation are inseparable; this position is founded on the laws of nature; it is more, it is itself an eternal law of nature; for whatever is a man's own, is absolutely his own; no man has a right to take it from him without his consent, either expressed by himself or representative; whoever attempts to do it, attempts an injury; whoever does it, commits a robbery; he throws down and destroys the distinction between liberty and slavery. Taxation and representation are coeval with and essential to the constitution.... [T]here is not a blade of grass growing in the most obscure corner of this kingdom, which is not, which was not ever, represented since the constitution began; there is not a blade of grass, which when taxed, was not taxed by the consent of the proprietor.... I can never give my assent to any bill for taxing the American colonies, while they remain unrepresented; for as to the distinction of a virtual representation, it is so absurd as not to deserve an answer; I therefore pass it over with contempt. The forefathers of the Americans did not leave their native country, and subject themselves to every danger and distress, to be reduced to a state of slavery: they did not give up their rights; they looked for protection, and not for chains, from their mother country; by her they expected to be defended in the possession of their property, and not to be deprived of it: for, should the present power continue, there is nothing which they can call their own; or, to use the words of Mr. Locke, 'What property have they in that, which another may, by right, take, when he pleases, to himself?'"

In an appearance before Parliament in January, 1766, former Prime Minister William Pitt stated:

- The idea of a virtual representation of America in this House is the

> most contemptible that ever entered into the head of a man. It does not deserve a serious refutation. The Commons of America, represented in their several assemblies, have ever been in possession of the exercise of this their constitutional right, of giving and granting their own money. They would have been slaves if they had not enjoyed it.

Grenville responded to Pitt, saying the disturbances in America "border on open rebellion; and if the doctrine I have heard this day be confirmed, nothing can tend more directly to produce a revolution." External and internal taxes are the same, argued Grenville.

MODERN USE IN THE UNITED STATES

In the United States, the phrase is used in Washington, D.C. as part of the campaign for a vote in Congress, to publicize the fact that Washington residents pay Federal taxes, but do not have representation in Congress. In November 2000, the D.C. Department of Motor Vehicles began issuing license plates bearing the slogan "Taxation without representation". In a show of support for the city, President Bill Clinton used the "Taxation Without Representation" plates on the presidential limousine; however, President George W. Bush had the tags replaced to those without the motto shortly after taking office. Barack Obama has announced his intention to use the plates with the motto beginning at his second inauguration.

In 2002, the city council authorized adding the slogan to the D.C. flag, but no new flag design has been approved. In 2007, the District of Columbia and United States Territories Quarters program was created based on the successful 50 State Quarters program. DC submitted designs containing the slogan, but they were rejected by the U.S. Mint.

On February 27, 2009, the phrase "Taxation without representation" was also used in the Tea Party protests, where protesters were upset over increased government spending and taxes, and specifically regarding a growing concern amongst the group that the U.S. government is increasingly relying upon a form of taxation without representation through increased regulatory levies and fees which are allegedly passed via unelected government employees who have no direct responsibility to voters and cannot be held accountable by the public through elections.

British Prime Minister John Major used a modified version of the quote, with the order reversed, in October 1995, when at the United Nations's 50th Anniversary celebrations he said, "It is not sustainable for states to enjoy representation without taxation," in order to criticize the billion-dollar arrears of the United States' payments to the UN, echoing a statement made the previous month at the opening session of the UN General Assembly by UK Foreign Secretary Malcolm Rifkind. To become citizens of the United States, immigrants most often must be permanent residents for a period of time (usually 5 years). Permanent residents must pay taxes on their worldwide income and, in most cases, cannot vote. However, throughout the 19th century, many states did allow immigrants to vote after they had declared their intention to become citizens. This was primarily because these new states were populated largely by immigrants who had not yet attained citizenship. Throughout U.S. history, non-citizens have been allowed to vote in 40 U.S. states and territories. Today, non-citizens are allowed to vote in seven jurisdictions in the United States.

The phrase is also used by other groups in America who pay various types of taxes (sales, income, property) but lack the ability to vote, such as felons (who are, in many states, barred from voting), people who work in one state and live in another (thus having to pay income tax to a state they don't live in), or people under 18.

MODERN USE IN CANADA

In Canada, Québec politician Gilles Duceppe, former leader of the Bloc Québécois, has repeatedly cited this phrase in defending the presence of his party in Ottawa. The Bloc is a Québec sovereigntist party solely running candidates in Canadian Federal elections in the province of Québec. Duceppe's evocation of the phrase implies that the proponents of Quebec's sovereigntist movement have the right to be represented in the body (which they are), the Canadian Parliament, which levies taxes upon them. He will usually cite the sentence in its original English.

USE IN AUSTRALIA

The first government of South Australia was by a Legislative Council, whose members were chosen by the Crown and from which office-bearers "Official Members" were selected by the Governor. John Stephens and his *South Australian Register* were among those who campaigned for democratic reform. Partial reform took place in 1851, when a majority of Members of the South Australian Legislative Council, 1851–1855 were elected.

TAXPAYER GROUPS

Taxpayer groups, also known as taxpayers unions, are formal nonprofit or informal advocacy groups that promote lower taxation, reductions in government spending, and limits to government debt. Many United States cities and counties have taxpayer groups. Members of these groups try to make their presence felt by attending government budget hearings, working with elected officials, and distributing their information on their views on taxing and spending. They can even initiate legislation at the state level to keep taxes and spending in check.

6

Types of Tax

DIRECT TAX

The term direct tax generally means a tax paid directly to the government by the persons on whom it is imposed. However, there are other definitions as well, under which taxes paid directly from individuals to the government are not legally classified as direct taxes, as described below.

GENERAL MEANING

In a general sense, a direct tax is one imposed upon an individual person (juristic or natural) or property (i.e. real and personal property, rental profits, livestock, crops, wages, etc.) as distinct from a tax imposed upon a transaction. In this sense, indirect taxes such as a sales tax or a value added tax (VAT) are imposed only if and when a taxable transaction occurs. People have the freedom to engage in or refrain from such transactions; whereas a direct tax (in the general sense) is imposed upon a person, typically in an unconditional manner, such as a poll-tax or head-tax, which is imposed on the basis of the person's very life or existence, or a property tax which is imposed upon the owner by virtue of ownership, rather than commercial use. Some commentators have argued that "a direct tax is one that cannot be shifted by the taxpayer to someone else, whereas an indirect tax can be."

The unconditional, inexorable aspect of the direct tax was a paramount concern of people in the 18th century seeking to escape tyrannical forms of government and to safeguard individual liberty. An 18th century writing about this kind of taxation explained:

- The power of direct taxation applies to every individual... it cannot be evaded like the objects of imposts or excise, and will be paid, because all that a man hath will he give for his head. This tax is so congenial to the nature of despotism, that it has ever been a favorite under such governments.... The power of direct taxation will further apply to every individual... however oppressive, the people will have but this alternative, either to pay the tax, or let their property be taken for all resistance will be vain.

U.S. CONSTITUTIONAL LAW SENSE

In the United States, the term "direct tax" has acquired specific meaning under constitutional law: a direct tax is a tax on property "by reason of its ownership" (such as an ordinary real estate property tax imposed on the person owning the property as of January 1 of each year) as well as a capitation (a "tax per head"). Income taxes on income from personal services such as wages are indirect taxes in this sense.

The United States Court of Appeals for the District of Columbia Circuit has stated: "Only three taxes are definitely known to be direct: (1) a capitation [...], (2) a tax upon real property, and (3) a tax upon personal property." In National Federation of Independent Business v. Sebelius, the Supreme Court held that a penalty directly imposed upon individuals for failure to possess health insurance, though a tax for constitutional purposes, is not a direct tax. The Court reasoned that the tax is not a capitation because not everyone will be required to pay it, nor is it a tax on property. Rather "it is triggered by specific circumstances."

In the United States, Article I, Section 2, Clause 3 of the Constitution requires that direct taxes imposed by the national government be apportioned among the states on the basis of population. After the 1895 *Pollock* ruling (essentially, that taxes on income from property should be treated as direct taxes), this provision made it difficult for Congress to impose a national income tax that applied to all forms of income until the 16th Amendment was ratified in 1913. After the Sixteenth Amendment, no Federal income taxes are required to be apportioned, regardless of whether they are direct taxes (taxes on income from property) or indirect taxes (all other income taxes).

DIRECT TAXATION IN OTHER COUNTRIES

Tax policy in the European Union (EU) consists of two components: direct taxation, which remains the sole responsibility of Member States, and indirect taxation, which affects free movement of goods and the freedom to provide services. With regard to European Union direct taxes, Member States have taken measures to prevent tax avoidance and double taxation. EU direct taxation covers, regarding companies, the following policies: common Consolidated Corporate Tax Base, common system of taxation applicable in the case of parent companies and subsidiaries of different Member States (to avoid withholding tax when the dividend qualifies for application of the EC Parent-Subsidiary Directive, Financial transaction tax, interest and royalty payments made between associated companies and elimination of double taxation if the payment qualifies for application of the EC Interest and Royalties Directive.

Regarding direct taxation for individuals, the policies cover taxation of savings income, dividend taxation of individuals and tackling tax obstacles to the cross-border provision of occupational pensions.

INDIRECT TAX

The term indirect tax has more than one meaning. In the colloquial sense, an indirect tax (such as sales tax, a specific tax, value added tax (VAT), or goods and services tax (GST)) is a tax collected by an intermediary (such as a retail store) from the person who bears the ultimate economic burden of the tax (such as the consumer). The intermediary later files a tax return and forwards the tax proceeds to government with the return. In this sense, the term indirect tax is contrasted with a direct tax which is collected directly by government from the persons (legal or natural) on which it is imposed. Some commentators have argued that "a direct tax is one that cannot be shifted by the taxpayer to someone else, whereas an indirect tax can be."

An indirect tax may increase the price of a good so that consumers are actually paying the tax by paying more for the products. Examples would be fuel, liquor, and cigarette taxes. An excise duty on motor cars is paid in the first instance by the manufacturer of the cars; ultimately the manufacturer transfers the burden of this duty to the buyer of the car in form of a higher price. Thus, an indirect tax is such which can be shifted or passed on. The degree to which the burden of a tax is shifted determines whether a tax is primarily direct or primarily indirect. This is a function of the relative elasticity of the supply and demand of the goods or services being taxed. Under this definition, even income taxes may be indirect.

FEATURES

1. Indirect taxation is policy often used to generate tax revenue. Indirect tax is so called as it is paid indirectly by the final consumer of goods and services while paying for purchase of goods or for enjoying services.
2. Indirect tax is broadly based since it is applied to everyone in the society whether rich or poor.
3. The tax payer who pays the tax does not bear the burden of tax; the burden is shifted to the ultimate consumers.
4. In the case of a direct tax, the taxpayer has to bear the burden of tax personally; in case of indirect tax the taxpayer and the taxbearer are not the same person.

EXCISE DUTY

Excise duty is a governmental tax meant for producers and manufacturers on certain goods.

Manufacturers are considered to be:

1. Entities who manufacture goods themselves
2. Entities who pay a fixed salary for other to manufacture these goods
3. Entities who outsource manufacturing, but manufacturing takes place from their name

To cover these costs, manufacturer adds them to COGS (costs of goods sold), where the buyer ends up paying for these costs. Thus, it is considered to be an indirect tax.

PER UNIT TAX

A per unit tax, or specific tax, is a tax that is defined as a fixed amount for each unit of a good or service sold, such as cents per kilogram. It is thus proportional to the particular quantity of a product sold, regardless of its price. Excise taxes, for instance, fall into this tax category. By contrast, an ad valorem tax is a charge based on a fixed percentage of the product value. Per unit taxes have administrative advantages when it is easy to measure quantities of the product or service being sold.

AD VALOREM TAX

An *ad valorem* tax (Latin for "according to value") is a tax based on the value of real estate or personal property. It is more common than a specific tax, a tax based on the quantity of an item, such as cents per kilogram, regardless of price.

An *ad valorem* tax is typically imposed at the time of a transaction(s) (a sales tax or value-added tax (VAT)), but it may be imposed on an annual basis (real or personal property tax) or in connection with another significant event (inheritance tax, surrendering citizenship (also known as an expatriation tax), or tariffs). In some countries stamp duty is imposed as an *ad valorem* tax.

SALES TAX

A sales tax is a consumption tax charged at the point of purchase for certain goods and services. The tax is usually set as a percentage by the government charging the tax. There is usually a list of exemptions. The tax can be included in the price (tax-inclusive) or added at the point of sale (tax-exclusive).

Ideally, a sales tax is fair, has a high compliance rate, is difficult to avoid, is charged every time an item is sold retail, and is simple to calculate and simple to collect. A conventional or retail sales tax attempts to achieve this by charging the tax only on the final end user, unlike a gross receipts tax levied on the intermediate business who purchases materials for production or ordinary operating expenses prior to delivering a service or product to the marketplace. This prevents so-called tax "cascading" or "pyramiding," in which an item is taxed more than once as it makes its way from production to final retail sale. There are several types of sales taxes: seller or vendor taxes, consumer excise taxes, retail transaction taxes, or value-added taxes.

VALUE-ADDED TAX

A value-added tax (VAT), or goods and services tax (GST), is tax on exchanges. It is levied on the added value that results from each exchange. It differs from a sales tax because a sales tax is levied on the total value of the exchange. For this reason, a VAT is neutral with respect to the number of passages that there are between the producer and the final consumer. A VAT is an indirect tax, in that the tax is collected from someone other than the person who actually bears the cost of the tax (namely the seller rather than the consumer). To avoid double taxation on final consumption, exports (which by definition are consumed abroad) are usually not subject to VAT and VAT charged under such circumstances is usually refundable.

The VAT was invented by a French economist in 1954. Maurice Lauré, joint director of the French tax authority, the *Direction générale des impôts,* as *taxe sur la valeur ajoutée* (TVA in French) was first to introduce VAT with effect from 10 April 1954 for large businesses, and extended over time to all business sectors. In France, it is the most important source of state finance, accounting for approximately 45% of state revenues.

PROPERTY TAX

A property tax, millage tax is an *ad valorem* tax that an owner of real estate or other property pays on the value of the property being taxed. There are three species or types of property: Land, Improvements to Land (immovable man made things), and Personal (movable man made things). Real estate, real property or realty are all terms for the combination of land and improvements. The taxing authority requires and/or performs an appraisal of the monetary value of the property, and tax is assessed in proportion to that value. Forms of property tax used vary between countries and jurisdictions.

APPLICATION OF A SALES OR PROPERTY TAX

United States

Ad valorem duties are important to those importing goods into the United States because the amount of duty owed is often based on the value of the imported commodity. *Ad valorem* taxes (mainly real property tax and sales taxes) are a major source of revenues for state and municipal governments, especially in jurisdictions that do not employ a personal income tax.

"*Ad valorem*" is used frequently to refer to property values by county tax assessors. In many states, the central appraisal district sends values to the county tax assessor, who determines the final tax rate to be imposed on the property. Other states use a state tax commission, which notifies the appropriate taxing authorities of the assessed value of property within their billing jurisdiction.

Ad valorem tax relates to a tax with a rate given as a proportion of the price. Virtually all state and local sales taxes in the United States are *ad valorem.* The common expression *county tax assessor* is a misnomer. Assessors do not tax nor do they assess a tax; the assessor's job is to value property (real estate, personal property, etc.), so that officials described as *tax assessors* would more accurately be called *property assessors.* After a property's value is determined by the assessor, a tax rate is determined by the appropriate taxing authority, which in turn calculates the tax due by the property owner. The tax is then collected by the tax collector.

APPLICATION OF A VALUE-ADDED TAX

United Kingdom

The third largest source of government revenues is value-added tax (VAT), charged at the standard rate of 20% on supplies of goods and services. It is therefore a tax on consumer expenditure. Certain goods and services are exempt from VAT, and others are subject to VAT at a lower rate of 5% (the reduced rate) or 0% ("zero-rated").

Canada

The Canadian Goods and Services Tax (GST) (French: Taxe sur les produits et services, TPS) is a multi-level value-added tax introduced in Canada on January 1, 1991, by Prime Minister Brian Mulroney and finance minister Michael Wilson. The GST replaced a hidden 13.5% Manufacturers' Sales Tax (MST) because it hurt the manufacturing sector's ability to export. The introduction of the GST was very controversial. As of January 1, 2012, the GST stood at 5%.

As of July 1, 2010, the federal GST and the regional Provincial Sales Tax (PST) were combined into a single value-added sales tax, called the Harmonized Sales Tax (HST). The HST is in effect in five of the ten Canadian provinces: British Columbia, Ontario, New Brunswick, Newfoundland and Labrador, and Nova Scotia. Effective April 1, 2013, the Government of British Columbia eliminated the HST and reinstated PST and GST on taxable services provided in British Columbia.

Australia

The Goods and Services Tax is a value-added tax of 10% on most goods and services sold in Australia.

It was introduced by the Howard Government on 1 July 2000, replacing the previous federal wholesale sales tax system and designed to phase out the various state and territory taxes such as banking taxes, stamp duty and land value tax. While this was the stated intent at the time, the States still charge duty on a various transactions, including but not limited to vehicle transfers and land transfers, insurance contracts and agreements for the sale of land. Many States, such as Western Australia, have made recent amendments to duties laws to phase out particular duties and clarify existing ones. The *Duties Act 2008* (WA) is available online at the Western Australian State Law Publisher

New Zealand

The Goods and Services Tax is a value-added tax of 15% on most goods and services sold in New Zealand. It was introduced by the Fourth Labour Government on 1 October 1986 at a rate of 10%. This was increased to 12.5% on 1 July 1989 and 15% on 1 October 2010.

Europe

A common VAT system is compulsory for the member states of the European Union. The EU VAT system is imposed by a series of European Union directives, the most important of which is the Sixth VAT Directive (Directive 77/388/EC). Nevertheless, some member states have negotiated variable rates (Madeira in Portugal) or VAT exemption for regions or territories. The regions below fall out of the scope of EU VAT:

- Åland Islands (Finland)
- Heligoland island, Büsingen territory (Germany)
- Guadeloupe, Martinique, French Guiana, Réunion (France)
- Mount Athos (Greece)
- Ceuta, Melilla, The Canary Islands (Spain)
- Livigno, Campione d'Italia, Lake Lugano (Italy)
- Gibraltar, The Channel Islands (United Kingdom)

Under the EU system of VAT, where a person carrying on an economic activity supplies goods and services to another person, and the value of the supplies passes financial limits, the supplier is required to register with the local taxation authorities and charge its customers, and account to the local taxation authority for VAT (although the price may be *inclusive* of VAT, so VAT is included as part of the agreed price, or *exclusive* of VAT, so VAT is payable in addition to the agreed price).

VAT that is charged by a business and paid by its customers is known as *output* VAT (that is, VAT on its output supplies). VAT that is paid by a business to other businesses on the supplies that it receives is known as *input* VAT (that is, VAT on its input supplies). A business is generally able to recover input VAT to the extent that the input VAT is attributable to (that is, used to make) its taxable outputs. Input VAT is recovered by setting it against the output VAT for which the business is required to account to the government, or, if there is an excess, by claiming a repayment from the government.

Different rates of VAT apply in different EU member states. The minimum standard rate of VAT throughout the EU is 15%, although reduced rates of VAT, as low as 5%, are applied in various states on various sorts of supply (for example, domestic fuel and power in the UK). The maximum rate in the EU is 25%.

The Sixth VAT Directive requires certain goods and services to be exempt from VAT (for example, postal services, medical care, lending, insurance, betting), and certain other goods and services to be exempt from VAT but subject to the ability of an EU member state to opt to charge VAT on those supplies (such as land and certain financial services). Input VAT that is attributable to exempt supplies is not recoverable, although a business can increase its prices so the customer effectively bears the cost of the 'sticking' VAT (the effective rate will be lower than the headline rate and depend on the balance between previously taxed input and labour at the exempt stage).

Finally, some goods and services are "zero-rated". The zero-rate is a positive rate of tax calculated at 0%. Supplies subject to the zero-rate are still "taxable supplies", i.e. they have VAT charged on them. In the UK, examples include most food, books, drugs, and certain kinds of transport. The zero-rate is not featured in the EU Sixth Directive as it was intended that the minimum VAT rate throughout Europe would be 5%. However, zero-rating remains in some Member States, most notably the UK, as a legacy of pre-EU legislation. These Member States have been granted a derogation to continue existing zero-rating but cannot add new goods or services. The UK also exempts or lowers the rate on some products depending on situation; for example milk products are exempt from VAT, but if you go into a restaurant and drink a milk drink it is VAT-able. Some products such as feminine hygiene products and baby products (nappies etc.) are charged at 5% VAT along with domestic fuel.

When goods are imported into the EU from other states, VAT is generally charged at the border, at the same time as customs duty. "Acquisition" VAT is payable when goods are acquired in one EU member state from another EU member state (this is done not at the border but through an accounting mechanism). EU businesses are often required to charge themselves VAT under the *reverse charge* mechanism where services are received from another member state or from outside of the EU.

Businesses can be required to register for VAT in EU member states, other than the one in which they are based, if they supply goods via mail order to those states, over a certain threshold. Businesses that are established in one member state but which receive supplies in another member state may be able to reclaim VAT charged in the second state under the provisions of the Eighth VAT Directive (Directive 79/1072/EC). To do so, businesses have a value added tax identification number. A similar directive, the Thirteenth VAT Directive (Directive 86/560/EC), also allows businesses established outside the EU to recover VAT in certain circumstances.

Following changes introduced on July 1, 2003, (under Directive 2002/38/EC), non-EU businesses providing digital electronic commerce and entertainment products and services to EU countries are also required to register with the tax authorities in the relevant EU member state, and to collect

VAT on their sales at the appropriate rate, according to the location of the purchaser. Alternatively, under a special scheme, non-EU businesses may register and account for VAT on only one EU member state. This produces distortions as the rate of VAT is that of the member state of registration, not where the customer is located, and an alternative approach is therefore under negotiation, whereby VAT is charged at the rate of the member state where the purchaser is located.

The differences between different rates of VAT was often originally justified by certain products being "luxuries" and thus bearing high rates of VAT, whereas other items were deemed to be "essentials" and thus bearing lower rates of VAT. However, often high rates persisted long after the argument was no longer valid. For instance, France taxed cars as a luxury product (33%) up into the 1980s, when most of the French households owned one or more cars. Similarly, in the UK, clothing for children is "zero rated" whereas clothing for adults is subject to VAT at the standard rate of 20%.

IMPACT

The theory of the firm shows that taxes on transfers can encourage firms to internalise costs and grow, whereas the absence of such transactions may result in a larger number of individually smaller firms. For example, a sales tax – unlike a VAT – would realign the incentives of a steel mill in favor of operating its own coal mine, as opposed to simply buying coal in a transaction subject to taxation; the theory of the firm's model suggests that this would be less economically efficient as it results in a decline in specialization.

FLAT TAX

A flat tax (short for flat tax rate) is a tax system with a constant marginal rate, usually applied to individual or corporate income. A flat tax falls under proportional tax as they allow certain deductions. There are various tax systems that are labeled "flat tax" even though they are significantly different.

MAJOR CATEGORIES

Flat tax proposals differ in how they define what is subject to tax.

"True" flat rate income tax

A *true* flat rate tax is a system of taxation where one tax rate is applied to all income with no deductions or exemptions.

Marginal flat tax

When deductions are allowed a 'flat tax' is a progressive tax with the special characteristic that above the maximum deduction, the rate on all further income is constant. Thus it is said to be marginally flat above that point. The conceptual difference between a true flat tax and a marginally flat tax, can be unified by recognizing that the latter simply excludes certain kinds of funds from being defined as income. Then they are both flat on "taxable" income. There are many proposed marginal flat taxes systems. Specific flat tax systems enumerated at the bottom of this article primarily intermix aspects of three high level approaches:

Flat tax with limited deductions

Modified flat taxes have been proposed which would allow deductions for a very few items, while still eliminating the vast majority of existing deductions. Charitable deductions and home mortgage interest are the most discussed exceptions, as these are popular with voters and often used. Another common theme is a single, large, fixed deduction; the concept here is that this blanket deduction rolls up a myriad of ubiquitous, fixed, living costs and has the simplifying side-effect that many (low income) people will not even have to file tax returns.

Hall–Rabushka flat tax

Designed by economists at the Hoover Institution, Hall–Rabushka is flat tax on consumption. Principally, Hall–Rabushka accomplishes a consumption tax effect by taxing income and then excluding investment. Robert Hall and Alvin Rabushka have consulted extensively in designing the flat tax systems in Eastern Europe.

Negative income tax

The negative income tax (NIT), which Milton Friedman proposed in his 1962 book *Capitalism and Freedom,* is a type of flat tax. The basic idea is the same as a flat tax with personal deductions, except that when deductions exceed income, the taxable income is allowed to become negative rather than being set to zero. The flat tax rate is then applied to the resulting "negative income," resulting in a "negative income tax" the government owes the household, unlike the usual "positive" income tax, which the household owes the government.

For example, let the flat rate be 20%, and let the deductions be $20,000 per adult and $7,000 per dependent. Under such a system, a family of four making $54,000 a year would owe no tax. A family of four making $74,000 a year would owe tax amounting to 0.20 × (74,000 " 54,000) = $4,000, as under a flat tax with deductions. But families of four earning less than $54,000 per year would owe a "negative" amount of tax (that is, it would receive money from the government). For example, if it earned $34,000 a year, it would receive a check for $4,000. The NIT is intended to replace not just the USA's income tax, but also many benefits low income American households receive, such as food stamps and Medicaid. The NIT is designed to avoid the welfare trap—effective high marginal tax rates arising from the rules reducing benefits as market income rises. An objection to the NIT is that it is welfare without a work requirement. Those who would owe negative tax would be receiving a form of welfare without having to make an effort to obtain employment. Another objection is that the NIT subsidizes industries employing low cost labor, but this objection can also be made against current systems of benefits for the working poor.

Capped flat tax

A capped flat tax is one in which income is taxed at a flat rate until a specified cap is reached. For example, in 2010, the United States Social Security and Medicare payroll tax assessed a flat rate of 7.65% on all income under $106,800 and only 1.45% above that level. Thus, someone earning $100,000 paid $7,650 (a rate of 7.65%) while someone earning $1,000,000 paid $21,122 (an effective rate of 2.11%). This cap has the effect of turning a nominally flat tax into a regressive tax.

REQUIREMENTS FOR A FULLY DEFINED SCHEMA

In devising a flat tax system, several recurring issues must be enumerated, principally with deductions and the identification of when money is earned.

Defining when income occurs

Since a central tenet of the flat tax is to minimize the compartmentalization of incomes into myriad special or sheltered cases, a vexing problem is deciding when income occurs. This is demonstrated by the taxation of interest income and stock dividends. The shareholders own the company and so the company's profits belong to them. If a company is taxed on its profits, then the funds paid out as dividends have already been taxed. It's a debatable question if they should subsequently be treated as income to the shareholders and thus subject to further tax. A similar issue arises in deciding if interest paid on loans should be deductible from the taxable income since that interest is in-turn taxed as income to the loan provider. There is no universally agreed answer to what is fair. For example, in the United States, dividends are not deductible but mortgage interest is deductible. *Thus a Flat Tax proposal is not fully defined until it differentiates* new *untaxed income from a pass-through of already taxed income.*

Policy administration

Taxes, in addition to providing revenue, can be potent instruments of policy. For example, it is common for governments to encourage social policy such as home insulation or low income housing with tax credits rather than constituting a ministry to implement these policies. In a flat tax system with limited deductions such policy administration mechanisms are curtailed. In addition to social policy, flat taxes can remove tools for adjusting economic policy as well. For example, in the United States, short-term capital gains are taxed at a higher rate than long-term gains as means to promote long-term investment horizons and damp speculative fluctuation. *Thus claims that flat taxes are cheaper/simpler to administer than others are incomplete until they factor in costs for alternative policy administration.*

Avoiding deductions

In general, the question of how to eliminate deductions is fundamental to the flat tax design: deductions dramatically affect the effective "flatness" in the tax rate. Perhaps the single biggest necessary deduction is for business expenses. If businesses were not allowed to deduct expenses, businesses with a profit margin below the flat tax rate could never earn any money since the tax on revenues would always exceed the earnings. For example, grocery stores typically earn pennies on every dollar of revenue; they could not pay a tax rate of 25% on revenues unless their markup exceeded 25%. Thus, corporations must be able to deduct operating expenses even if individual citizens cannot. A practical difficulty now arises as to identifying what is an expense for a business. For example, if peanut butter makers purchase a jar manufacturer, is that an expense (since they have to purchase jars somehow) or a sheltering of their income through investment? Flat tax systems can differ greatly in how they accommodate such gray areas. For example, the "9-9-9" flat tax proposal would allow businesses to deduct purchases but not labor costs. (This effectively taxes labor-intensive industrial revenue at a higher rate.) How deductions are implemented will dramatically change the effective total tax and thus the flatness of the tax. Thus, a flat tax proposal is not fully defined until it differentiates deductible and non-deductible expenses.

TAX EFFECTS

Equity of distribution

Introduction of flat tax may remove preexisting tax deductions. This may lead to unequal distribution for various income brackets that other tax methods also do.

Diminishing Marginal Utility

Flat tax benefits higher income brackets progressively due to decline in marginal value. For example, if a flat tax system has a large per-citizen deductible (such as the "Armey" scheme below), then it is a progressive tax. As a result, sometimes the term Flat Tax is actually a shorthand for the more proper marginally flat tax.

Administration and enforcement

One type of flat tax taxes all income once at its source. Hall and Rabushka

(1995) includes a proposed amendment to the US Revenue Code implementing the variant of the flat tax they advocate. This amendment, only a few pages long, would replace hundreds of pages of statutory language (although it is important to note that much statutory language in taxation statutes is *not* directed at specifying graduated tax rates). As it now stands, the USA Revenue Code is over 9 million words long and contains many loopholes, deductions, and exemptions which, advocates of flat taxes claim, render the collection of taxes and the enforcement of tax law complicated and inefficient. It is further argued that current tax law retards economic growth by distorting economic incentives, and by allowing, even encouraging, tax avoidance. With a flat tax, there are fewer incentives than in the current system to create tax shelters and to engage in other forms of tax avoidance. Flat tax critics contend that a flat tax system could be created with many loopholes, or a progressive tax system without loopholes, and that a progressive tax system could be as simple, or simpler, than a flat tax system. A simple progressive tax would also discourage tax avoidance.

Under a pure flat tax without deductions, every tax period a company would make a single payment to the government covering the taxes on the employees and the taxes on the company profit. For example, suppose that in a given year, ACME earns a profit of 3 million, spends 2 million in wages, and spends 1 million on other expenses the IRS deems to be taxable income, such as stock options, bonuses, and certain executive privileges. Given a flat rate of 15%, ACME would then owe the IRS (3M + 2M + 1M) × 0.15 = 900,000. This payment would, in one fell swoop, settle the tax liabilities of ACME's employees as well as the corporate taxes owed by ACME. Most employees throughout the economy would never need to interact with the IRS, as all tax owed on wages, interest, dividends, royalties, etc. would be withheld at the source. The main exceptions would be employees with incomes from personal ventures. The *Economist* claims that such a system would reduce the number of entities required to file returns from about 130 million individuals, households, and businesses, as at present, to a mere 8 million businesses and self-employed.

However this simplicity relies on there being no deductions of any kind allowed (or at least no variability in the deductions of different people). Furthermore, if income of differing types are segregated (e.g., pass-thru, long term cap gains, regular income, etc.) then complications ensue. For example, if realized capital gains were subject to the flat tax, the law would require brokers and mutual funds to calculate the realized capital gain on all sales and redemption. If there were a gain, 15% of the gain would be withheld and sent to the IRS. If there were a loss, the amount would be reported to the IRS, which would offset gains with losses and settle up with taxpayers at the end of the period. Lacking deductions this scheme cannot be used to implement economic and social policy indirectly by tax credits, and thus, as noted above, the simplifications to the government's revenue collection apparatus may be offset by new government ministries required to administer those policies.

Revenues

The Russian Federation is a considered a prime case of the success of a flat tax; the real revenues from its Personal Income Tax rose by 25.2% in the first year after the Federation introduced a flat tax, followed by a 24.6% increase in the second year, and a 15.2% increase in the third year. The Laffer curve predicts such an outcome, attributing the primary reason for the greater revenue to higher levels of economic growth stemming from the introduction of the flat tax.

The Russian example is often used as proof of the validity of this analysis, despite an International Monetary Fund study in 2006 which found that there was no sign "of Laffer-type behavioral responses generating revenue increases from the tax cut elements of these reforms" in Russia or in other countries.

Overall structure

Taxes other than the income tax (for example, taxes on sales and payrolls) tend to be regressive. Hence, making the income tax flat could result in a regressive overall tax structure. Under such a structure, those with lower incomes tend to pay a *higher* proportion of their income in total taxes than the affluent do. The fraction of household income that is a return to capital (dividends, interest, royalties, profits of unincorporated businesses) is positively correlated with total household income. Hence a flat tax limited to wages would seem to leave the wealthy better off. Modifying the tax base can change the effects. A flat tax could be targeted at income (rather than wages), which could place the tax burden equally on all earners, including those who earn income primarily from returns on investment. Tax systems could utilize a flat sales tax to target all consumption, which can be modified with rebates or exemptions to remove regressive effects (such as the proposed FairTax in the U.S.).

Border adjustable

A flat tax system and income taxes overall are not inherently border-adjustable; meaning the tax component embedded into products via taxes imposed on companies (including corporate taxes and payroll taxes) are not removed when exported to a foreign country. Taxation systems such as a sales tax or value added tax can remove the tax component when goods are exported and apply the tax component on imports. The domestic products could be at a disadvantage to foreign products (at home and abroad) that are border-adjustable, which would impact the global competitiveness of a country. However, it's possible that a flat tax system could be combined with tariffs and credits to act as border adjustments (the proposed *Border Tax Equity*

Act in the U.S. attempts this). Implementing an income tax with a border adjustment tax credit is a violation of the World Trade Organization agreement. Tax exemptions (allowances) on low income wages, a component of most income tax systems could mitigate this issue for high labour content industries like textiles that compete Globally.

In a subsequent section, various proposals for flat tax-like schemes are discussed, these differ mainly on how they approach with the following issues of deductions, defining income, and policy implementation.

RECENT AND CURRENT PROPOSALS

Flat tax proposals have made something of a "comeback" in recent years. In the United States, former House Majority Leader Dick Armey and FreedomWorks have sought support for the flat tax (Taxpayer Choice Act). In other countries, flat tax systems have also been proposed, largely as a result of flat tax systems being introduced in several countries of the former Eastern Bloc, where it is generally thought to have been successful, although this assessment has been disputed.

The countries that have recently reintroduced flat taxes have done so largely in the hope of boosting economic growth. The Baltic countries of Estonia, Latvia and Lithuania have had flat taxes of 24%, 25% and 33% respectively with a tax exempt amount, since the mid-1990s. On 1 January 2001, a 13% flat tax on personal income took effect in Russia. Ukraine followed Russia with a 13% flat tax in 2003, which later increased to 15% in 2007. Slovakia introduced a 19% flat tax on most taxes (that is, on corporate and personal income, for VAT, etc., almost without exceptions) in 2004. Romania introduced a 16% flat tax on personal income and corporate profit on 1 January 2005. Macedonia introduced a 12% flat tax on personal income and corporate profit on 1 January 2007 and promised to cut it to 10% in 2008. Albania has implemented a 10% flat tax from 2008. Bulgaria applies flat tax rate of 10% for corporate profits and personal income tax since 2008.

In the United States, while the Federal income tax is progressive, seven states — Colorado, Illinois, Indiana, Massachusetts, Michigan, Pennsylvania, and Utah — tax household incomes at a single rate, ranging from 3.07% (Pennsylvania) to 5.3% (Massachusetts). Pennsylvania even has a *pure* flat tax with no zero-bracket amount.

Paul Kirchhof, who was suggested as the next finance minister of Germany in 2005, proposed introducing a flat tax rate of 25% in Germany as early as 2001, which sparked widespread controversy. Some claim the German tax system is the most complex one in the world.

On 27 September 2005, the Dutch Council of Economic Advisors recommended a flat rate of 40% for income tax in the Netherlands. Some deductions would be allowed, and persons over 65 years of age would be taxed at a lower rate.

In the United States, proposals for a flat tax at the federal level have emerged repeatedly in recent decades during various political debates. Jerry Brown, former and current Democratic Governor of California, made the adoption of a flat tax part of his platform when running for President of the United States in 1992. At the time, rival Democratic candidate Tom Harkin ridiculed the proposal as having originated with the "Flat Earth Society". Four years later, Republican candidate Steve Forbes proposed a similar idea as part of his core platform. Although neither captured his party's nomination, their proposals prompted widespread debate about the current U.S. income tax system.

Flat tax plans that are presently being advanced in the United States also seek to redefine "sources of income"; current progressive taxes count interest, dividends and capital gains as income, for example, while Steve Forbes's variant of the flat tax would apply to wages only.

In 2005, Senator Sam Brownback, a Republican from Kansas, stated he had a plan to implement a flat tax in Washington, D.C.. This version is one flat rate of 15% on all earned income. Unearned income (in particular capital gains) would be exempt.

His plan also calls for an exemption of $30,000 per family and $25,000 for singles. Mississippi Republican Senator Trent Lott stated he supports it and would add a $5,000 credit for first time home buyers and exemptions for out of town businesses. DC Delegate Eleanor Holmes Norton's position seems unclear, however DC mayor Anthony Williams has stated he is "open" to the idea.

Flat taxes have also been considered in the United Kingdom by the Conservative Party. In September 2005, George Osborne, then in opposition, said that while he was "fully conscious that we may not be able to introduce a pure flat tax, we may be able to move towards simpler and flatter taxes." However, it was roundly rejected by Gordon Brown, then the Labour Chancellor of the Exchequer, who said that it was "An idea that they say is sweeping the world, well sweeping Estonia, well a wing of the neo-conservatives in Estonia", and criticised it thus: "The millionaire to pay exactly the same tax rate as the young nurse, the home help, the worker on the minimum wage".

EASTERN EUROPE

Advocates of the flat tax argue that the former communist states of Eastern Europe have benefited from the adoption of a flat tax. Some of these nations have experienced strong economic growth of 6% and higher in recent years, particularly the Baltic countries, who experience exceptional GDP growth of around 10% yearly.

Some argue that other factors, primarily the advent of capitalist economic systems and rapid market expansion after Soviet (communist) domination explain the rapid growth. Some argue that economic growth in these countries would likely have occurred regardless of the chosen tax system.

- Lithuania, which levies a flat tax rate of 15% (previously 20%) on its citizens, has experienced -15.8%, +1.3%, and +5.8% change in GDP from 2009-2011. The growth in 2011 is listed as being high compared to other nations in the region and 46th globally. The unemployment rate of 15.4% is listed as higher than 151 other nations and the inflation rate of 4.1% is greater than 103 other currencies including that of the European Union
- In Estonia, which has had a flat tax since 1994 (rate is 21% since 2009, previously was 26%), studies have shown that the significant increase in tax revenue experienced was caused partly by a disproportionately rising VAT revenue. Moreover, Estonia and Slovakia have high social contributions, pegged to wage levels. Both matters raise questions regarding the justice of the flat tax system, and thus its long-term political sustainability. The Estonian economist and former chairman of his country's parliamentary budget committee Olev Raju, stated in September 2005 that "income disparities are rising and calls for a progressive system of taxation are getting louder – this could put an end to the flat tax after the next election". However, this did not happen, since after the 2007 elections a right-wing coalition was formed which has stated its will to keep the flat tax in existence. However, critics argue that the tax rates these countries have are actually more progressive than flat.
- Hungary introduced a flax tax at 16% on 1 January 2011.
- According to a 2010 study published in the Brussels newspaper L'Anglophone, the tax burden for typical workers in Central and Eastern Europe's "flat tax" countries is slightly higher (40.3% versus 40.2% of the total cost of employment) than that of the progressive systems elsewhere in the EU. "Slovakia has a "flat tax" rate of 19%," wrote the authors, "but its employers pay a 35.2% contribution to social security (higher than the 34.8% in Belgium) and, in addition to the flat income tax, employees have 13.4% deducted for social security (also higher than the 13.07% in Belgium)," adding that a typical Slovak worker's Tax Freedom Day is a day later than a Finnish worker's. Slovakia reintroduced progressive tax rates in 2013.

CAPITAL GAINS TAX

A capital gains tax (CGT) is a tax on capital gains, the profit realized on the sale of a non-inventory asset that was purchased at a cost amount that was lower than the amount realized on the sale. The most common capital gains are realized from the sale of stocks, bonds, precious metals and property. Not all countries implement a capital gains tax and most have different rates of taxation for individuals and corporations. For equities, an example of a popular and liquid asset, national and state legislation often has a large array of fiscal obligations that must be respected regarding capital gains. Taxes are charged by the state over the transactions, dividends and capital gains on the stock market. However, these fiscal obligations may vary from jurisdiction to jurisdiction.

ARGENTINA

There is no specific capital gains tax in Argentina; however, there is a 9% to 35% tax for fiscal residents on their world revenues, including capital gains.....

AUSTRALIA

Capital gains tax in Australia is only payable upon realized capital gains, except for certain provisions relating to deferred-interest debt such as zero-coupon bonds. The tax is not separate in its own right, but forms part of the income tax system. The proceeds of an asset sold less its 'cost base' (the original cost plus addition for cost price increases over time) are the capital gain. Discounts and other concessions apply to certain taxpayers in varying circumstances. From the 21st of September 1999, after a report by Alan Reynolds the 50% capital gains tax discount has been in place for individuals and some trusts that acquired the asset after that time and have held the asset for more than 12 months, however the tax is levied without any adjustment to the cost base for inflation. The amount left after applying the discount is added to the assessable income of the taxpayer for that financial year.

For individuals, the most significant exemption is the family home. The sale of personal residential property is normally exempt from Capital Gains Tax, except for gains realized during any period in which the property was not being used as an individual's personal residence (for example, being leased to other tenants) or portions attributable to business use. Capital gains or losses as a general rule can be disregarded for CGT purposes when assets were acquired before 20 September 1985 (pre CGT).

AUSTRIA

Austria taxes capital gains at 25%. There is an exception for capital gains from the sale of shares of foreign entities (with opaque taxation) if the participation exceeds 10% and shares are held for over one year (so-called "Schachtelprivileg").

CANADA

Currently 50% of realized capital gains are taxed in Canada at an individual's tax rate. Some exceptions apply, such as selling one's primary residence which may be exempt from taxation. Capital gains made by investments in a Tax-Free Savings Account (TFSA) are not taxed. For example, if your capital gains (profit) is $100, you are only taxed on $50 at your marginal tax rate. That is, if you were in the top tax bracket, you would be taxed at approximately 43%. A formula for this example using the top tax bracket would be as follows:

Capital gain x 50.00% x marginal tax rate = capital gain tax
= $100 x 50.00%
= $50 x 43%
= $21.50

In this example your capital gains tax on $100 is $21.50, leaving you with $78.50. As of the 2013 budget, interest can no longer be claimed a capital gain. The formula is the same for capital losses and these can be carried forward indefinitely to offset future years' capital gains; capital losses not used in the current year can also be carried back to the previous three tax years to offset capital gains tax paid in those years.

For corporations as for individuals, only 50% of realized capital gains are taxable. The net taxable capital gains (which can be calculated as 50% of total capital gains minus 50% of total capital losses) are subject to income tax at normal corporate tax rates. If more than 50% of a small business's income is derived from specified investment business activities (which include income from capital gains) they are not permitted to claim the small business deduction. Capital gains earned on income in a Registered Retirement Savings Plan are not taxed at the time the gain is realized (i.e. when the holder sells a stock that has appreciated inside of their RRSP) but they are taxed when the funds are withdrawn from the registered plan (usually after converting to a registered income fund.) These gains are then taxed at the individual's full marginal rate. Capital gains earned on income in a TFSA are not taxed at the time the gain is realized. Any money withdrawn from a TFSA, including capital gains, are also not taxed. Unrealized capital gains are not taxed.

CHINA

The applicable tax rate for capital gains in China depends upon the nature of the taxpayer (i.e. whether the taxpayer is a person or company) and whether the taxpayer is resident or non-resident for tax purposes. It should however be noted that, unlike common law tax systems, Chinese income tax legislation does not provide a distinction between income and capital. What commonly referred by taxpayers and practitioners as capital gain tax is actually within the income tax framework, rather than a separate regime.

Tax-resident enterprises will be taxed at 25% in accordance with the Enterprise Income Tax Law. Non-resident enterprises will be taxed at 10% on capital gains in accordance with the Implementing Regulations to the Enterprise Income Tax Law. In practice, where a resident of a treaty partner alienates assets situated in China as part of its ordinary course of business the gains so derived will likely be assessed as if it is a capital gain, rather than business profit. This is somewhat contradictory with the basic principles of double taxation treaty.

The only tax circular specifically addressing the PRC income tax treatment of income derived by QFIIs from the holding and trading of Chinese securities is Guo Shui Han (2009) No.47 ("Circular 47") issued by the State Administration of Taxation ("SAT") on 23 January 2009. The circular addresses the withholding tax treatment of dividends and interest received by QFIIs from PRC resident companies, however, circular 47 is silent on the treatment of capital gains derived by QFIIs on the trading of A-shares. It is generally accepted that Circular 47 is intentionally silent on capital gains and possible indication that SAT is considering but still undecided on whether to grant tax exemption or other concessionary treatment to capital gains derived by QFIIs. Nevertheless, it is noted that there have been cases where QFIIs withdraw capital from China after paying 10% withholding tax on gains derived through share trading over years on a transaction-by-transaction basis. This uncertainty has caused significant problems for those investment managers investing in A-Shares. Guo Shui Han (2009) No. 698 ("Circular 698") was issued on 10 December 2009 addressing the PRC corporate income tax treatment on the transfer of PRC equity interest by non-PRC tax resident enterprises directly or indirectly, however has not resolved the uncertain tax position with regards A-Shares. With respect to Circular 698 itself, there are views that it is not consistent with the Enterprise Income Tax Law as well as double taxation treaties signed by the Chinese government. The validity of the Circular is controversial, especially in light of recent developments in the international arena, such as the TPG case in Australia and Vodafone case in India.

CYPRUS

As determined by the Cyprus Capital Gains Tax Law, Capital gains tax in Cyprus arising from the sale or disposition of immovable property in Cyprus or the disposal of shares of companies which own immovable property in Cyprus and not listed in a recognised stock exchange. These gains are not added to other income but are taxed separately. Gains from the sale of shares listed on the stock exchange are excluded from capital gains tax, as specified in the Capital Gains Tax (Amendment) Law, No. N119(I) of 2002. Payment of immovable property tax is paid by both individuals and companies on property owned in Cyprus.

As of January 1, 2012: Up to €120,000 0% From €120,000 to €170,000 4% From €170,001 to €300,000 5% From €300,001 to €500,000 6% From €500,001 to €800,000 7%, and Over €800,000 8% Tax remains levied on the assessed value of the property as at 1 January 1980. Capital gains tax does not apply to profits from the sale of overseas real estate by non-residents, offshore entities, or residents who were not resident when they purchased the asset. Gains accruing from disposal of immovable property held outside Cyprus and shares in companies, the property whereof consists of immovable property held outside Cyprus, will be exempted from capital gains tax. Individuals may, subject to certain conditions, may claim certain deductions from the applicable taxable gain.

CZECH REPUBLIC

Capital gains in the Czech Republic are taxed as income for companies and individuals. The Czech income tax rate for an individual's income in 2010 is a flat 15% rate. Corporate tax in 2010 is 19%. Capital gains from the sale of shares by a company owning 10% or more is entitled to participation exemption under certain terms. For an individual, gain from the sale of a primary private dwelling, held for at least 2 years, is tax exempt. Or, when not used as a main residence, if held for more than 5 years.

DENMARK

Share dividends and realized capital gains on shares are charged 27% to individuals of gains up to DKK 48,300 (2013-level, adjusted annually), and at 42% of gains above that. Carryforward of realized losses on shares is allowed.

Individuals' interest income from bank deposits and bonds, realized gains on property and other capital gains are taxed up to 59%, however, several exemptions occur, such as on selling one's principal private residence or on gains on selling bonds. Interest paid on loans is deductible, although in case the net capital income is negative, only approx. 33% tax credit applies. Companies are taxed at 25%. Share dividends are taxed at 28%.

ESTONIA

There is no separate capital gains tax in Estonia. For residents of Estonia all capital gains are taxed the same as regular income, the rate of which currently stands at 21%. Resident natural persons that have investment account can realise capital gains on some classes of assets tax free until withdrawal of funds from the investment account. For resident legal persons (includes partnerships) no tax is payable for realising capital gain (or receiving any other type of income), but only on payment of dividends, payments from capital (exceeding contributions to capital) and payments not related to business. The income tax rate for resident legal persons is 21% (payment of 79 units of dividends triggers 21 units of tax due).

FINLAND

The capital gains tax in Finland is 30% on realized capital income and 32% if the realized capital income is over 50,000 euros. The capital gains tax in 2011 was 28% on realized capital income. Carryforward of realized losses is allowed for three years. However, capital gains from the sale of residential homes is tax-free after two years of residence, with certain limitations.

FRANCE

For residents, capital gains tax on the sale of financial instruments (shares, bonds, etc..) is a flat 34.5%, which includes 15.5% of social security taxes and 19% taxes. If shares are held in a special account (called a PEA), the gain is subject only to social security taxes provided that the PEA is held for at least five years. The maximum amount that can be deposited in the PEA is €132,000.

The gain realized on the sale of a principal residence is not taxable. A gain realized on the sale of other real estate held at least 30 years, however, is not taxable, although this will become subject to 12.1% social security taxes as of 2011. (There is a sliding scale for non principal residence property owned for between 6 and 30 years. The taxable gain is reduced for each full year that the property was held, starting at the fifth year.) Non-residents are generally taxable on capital gains realized on French real estate and on some French financial instruments, subject to any applicable double tax treaty. Social security taxes, however, are not usually payable by non-residents. A French tax representative will be mandatory if you are non-resident and you sell a property for an amount over 150.000 euros or you own the real estate for more than 15 years.

GERMANY

In January 2009, Germany introduced a very strict capital gains tax (called Abgeltungsteuer in German) for shares, funds, certificates etc. Capital gains tax only applies to financial instruments (shares, bonds etc.) that have been bought after 31 December 2008. Instruments bought before this date are exempt from capital gains tax (assuming that they have been held for at least 12 months), even if they are sold in 2009 or later, barring a change of law. Certificates are treated specially, and only qualify for tax exemption if they have been bought before 15 March 2007. Real estate continues to be exempt from capital gains tax if it has been held for more than ten years. The German capital gains tax is 25% plus Solidaritätszuschlag (add-on tax initially introduced to finance the 5 eastern states of Germany - Mecklenburg-Western Pomerania, Saxony, Saxony-Anhalt, Thuringia and Brandenburg - and the cost of the reunification, but later kept in order to finance all kind of public funded projects in whole Germany), plus Kirchensteuer (church tax), resulting in an effective tax rate of about 28%. Deductions of expenses such as custodian fees, travel to annual shareholder meetings, legal and tax advice, interest paid on loans to buy shares, etc., are no longer permitted starting in 2009.

HONG KONG

In general Hong Kong has no capital gains tax. However, employees who receive shares or options as part of their remuneration are taxed at the normal Hong Kong income tax rate on the value of the shares or options at the end of any vesting period less any amount that the individual paid for the grant.

If part of the vesting period is spent outside Hong Kong then the tax payable in Hong Kong is pro-rated based on the proportion of time spent working in Hong Kong. Hong Kong has very few double tax agreements and hence there is little relief available for double taxation. Therefore, it is possible (depending on the country of origin) for employees moving to Hong Kong to pay full income tax on vested shares in both their country of origin and in Hong Kong. Similarly, an employee leaving Hong Kong can incur double taxation on the unrealized capital gains of their vested shares.

The Hong Kong taxation of capital gains on employee shares or options that are subject to a vesting period, is at odds with the treatment of unrestricted shares or options which are free of capital gains tax.

INDIA

As of 2008, equities are considered long term capital if the holding period is one year or more. Long term capital gains from equities are not taxed if shares are sold through recognized stock exchange and Securities Transaction Tax, or STT, is paid on the sale. STT in India is currently between 0.017% and 0.125% of total amount received on sale of securities through a recognized Indian stock exchange like the NSE or BSE. However short term capital gain from equities held for less than one year, is sold through recognised stock exchange and STT paid should not be considered and it is taxable at a flat rate of 15% and other surcharges, educactional cess are imposed. 15% (w.e.f. 1 April 2009.) Many other capital investments (house, buildings, real estate, bank deposits) are considered long term if the holding period is 3 or more years.

JAPAN

In Japan, there were two options for paying tax on capital gains from the sale of listed stocks. The first, Withholding Tax, taxed all proceeds (regardless of profit or loss) at 1.05%. The second method, declaring proceeds as "taxable income", required individuals to declare 26% of proceeds on their income tax statement. Many traders in Japan used both systems, declaring profits on the Withholding Tax system and losses as taxable income, minimizing the amount of income tax paid. In 2003, Japan scrapped the system above in favor of a flat 20% tax on gains, though the rate was temporarily halved at 10% and after being postponed a few times the return to the normal rate of 20% is now set for 2014. Losses can be carried forward for 3 years. Starting in 2009, losses can alternatively be deducted from dividend income declared as "Separate Income" since the tax rate on both categories is equal (i.e., 20% temporarily halved to 10%). Aggregating profits and dividends to reach a single figure taxed at the same rate is fairly innovative.

NORWAY

The individual capital gains tax in Norway is 28%. In most cases, there is no capital gains tax on profits from sale of your principal home. This tax was introduced in 2006 through a reform that eliminated the "RISK-system", which intended to avoid the double taxation of capital. The new shareholder model, introduced in 2006, aims to reduce the difference in taxation of capital and labor by taxing dividends beyond a certain level as ordinary income. This means that focus was moved from capital to individuals and their level of income. This system also introduced a deductible allowance equal to the share's acquisition value times the average rate for Treasury bills with a 3-month period adjusted for tax. Shielding interest shall secure financial neutrality in that it returns the taxpayer what he or she alternatively would have achieved in a safe, passive capital placement exempt from additional taxation. The main purpose of the allowance is to prevent adverse shifts in investment and corporate financing structure as a result of the dividend tax. According to the papers explaining the new policy, a dividend tax without such shielding could push up the pressures on the rate of return on equity investments and lead Norwegian investors from equities to bonds, property etc.

RUSSIA

There is no separate tax on capital gains; rather, gains or gross receipt from sale of assets are absorbed into income tax base. Taxation of individual and corporate taxpayers is distinctly different:

- Capital gains of individual taxpayers are tax free if the taxpayer owned the asset for at least three years. If not, gains on sales of real estate and securities are absorbed into their personal income tax base and taxed at 13% (residents) and 30% (non-residents). A tax resident is any individual residing in the Russian Federation for more than 183 days in the past year.
- Capital gains of resident corporate taxpayers operating under *general tax framework* are taxed as ordinary business profits at the common rate of 20%, regardless of the ownership period. Small businesses operating under *simplified tax framework* pay tax not on capital gains, but on gross receipts at 6% or 15%.
- Dividends that may be included into gains on disposal of securities are taxed at source at 9% (residents) and 15% (non-residents) for either corporate or individual taxpayers.

UNITED KINGDOM

Basics

Individuals who are residents or ordinarily residents in the United

Kingdom (and trustees of various trusts) are subject to an 18% capital gains tax. For people paying more than the basic rate of income tax, this increased to 28% from midnight on June 23, 2010.

There are exceptions such as for principal private residences, holdings in ISAs or gilts. Certain other gains are allowed to be rolled over upon re-investment. Investments in some start up enterprises are also exempt from CGT. Entrepreneurs' Relief allows a lower rate of CGT (10%) to be paid by people who have been involved for a year with a trading company and have a 5% or more shareholding. Shares in companies with trading properties are eligible for Entrepreneurs' Relief, but not investment properties. Every individual has an annual capital gains tax allowance: gains below the allowance are exempt from tax, and capital losses can be set against capital gains in other holdings before taxation. All individuals are exempt from tax up to a specified amount of capital gains per year. For the 2011/12 tax year this "annual exemption" is £10,600.

Corporate notes

Companies are subject to corporation tax on their "chargeable gains" (the amounts of which are calculated along the lines of capital gains tax). Companies cannot claim taper relief, but can claim an indexation allowance to offset the effect of inflation. A corporate substantial shareholdings exemption was introduced on 1 April 2002 for holdings of 10% or more of the shares in another company (30% or more for shares held by a life assurance company's long-term insurance fund). This is effectively a form of UK participation exemption. Almost all of the corporation tax raised on chargeable gains is paid by life assurance companies taxed on the I minus E basis.

The rules governing the taxation of capital gains in the United Kingdom for individuals and companies are contained in the Taxation of Chargeable Gains Act 1992.

Background to changes to 18% rate

In the Chancellor's October 2007 Autumn Statement, draft proposals were announced that would change the applicable rates of CGT as of 6 April 2008. Under these proposals, an individual's annual exemption will continue but taper relief will cease and a single rate of capital gains tax at 18% will be applied to chargeable gains. This new single rate would replace the individual's marginal (Income Tax) rate of tax for CGT purposes. The changes were introduced, at least in part, because the UK government felt that private equity firms were making excessive profits by benefiting from overly generous taper relief on business assets. The changes were criticised by a number of groups including the Federation of Small Businesses, who claimed that the new rules would increase the CGT liability of small businesses and discourage entrepreneurship in the UK. At the time of the proposals there was concern that the changes would lead to a bulk selling of assets just before the start of the 2008-09 tax year to benefit from existing taper relief. Capital Gains Tax will rise to 28% with effect from 00:00 on 23 June 2010.

Historical (useful if looking at years prior to April 2008)

Individuals paid capital gains tax at their highest marginal rate of income tax (0%, 10%, 20% or 40% in the tax year 2007/8) but from 6 April 1998 were able to claim a *taper relief* which reduces the amount of a gain that is subject to capital gains tax (reducing the effective rate of tax), depending on whether the asset is a "business asset" or a "non-business asset" and the length of the period of ownership. Taper relief provided up to a 75% reduction (leaving 25% taxable) in taxable gains for business assets, and 40% (leaving 60% taxable), for non-business assets, for an individual. Taper relief replaces indexation allowance for individuals, which can still be claimed for assets held prior to 6 April 1998 from the date of purchase until that date, but was itself abolished on 5 April 2008.

UNITED STATES

In the United States, with certain exceptions, individuals and corporations pay income tax on the net total of all their capital gains. Short-term capital gains are taxed at a higher rate: the ordinary income tax rate. The tax rate for individuals on "long-term capital gains", which are gains on assets that have been held for over one year before being sold, is lower than the ordinary income tax rate, and in some tax brackets there is no tax due on such gains. The tax rate on long-term gains was reduced in 1997 via the Taxpayer Relief Act of 1997 from 28% to 20% and again in 2003, via the Jobs and Growth Tax Relief Reconciliation Act of 2003, from 20% to 15% (for individuals, whose highest tax bracket is 15% or more), or from 10% to 5% for individuals in the lowest two income tax brackets (whose highest tax bracket is less than 15%). The reduced 15% tax rate on eligible dividends and capital gains, previously scheduled to expire in 2008, was extended through 2010 as a result of the Tax Increase Prevention and Reconciliation Act signed into law by President Bush on May 17, 2006, which also reduced the 5% rate to 0%. Toward the end of 2010, President Obama signed a law extending the reduced rate on eligible dividends until the end of 2012.

The law allows for individuals to defer capital gains taxes with tax planning strategies such as the structured sale (ensured installment sale), charitable trust (CRT), installment sale, private annuity trust, and a 1031 exchange.

The United States, unlike many other countries, taxes its citizens (with some exceptions) on their worldwide income no matter where in the world they reside. U.S. citizens therefore find it difficult to take advantage of personal tax havens. Although there are some offshore bank accounts that advertise as tax havens, U.S. law requires reporting of income from those accounts, and willful failure to do so constitutes tax evasion.

DEFERRING OR REDUCING CAPITAL GAINS TAX

Capital gains tax can be deferred or reduced if a seller utilizes the proper sales method and/or deferral technique. There are many such sales techniques and methods, each of which has its benefits and drawbacks.

- (US Only) - Tax Loss Harvesting - Realized tax losses can carry forward forever and can be applied to offset capital gains months or years in the future. Discretionary Overlay managers have developed new trading methodologies that have evolved tax loss harvesting into a year-round strategy, as opposed to year-end, which is standard to most financial advisors, and is paramount in reducing the capital gains tax burden on affluent investors.
- Charitable trust - Defer and reduce capital gains by giving equity to a charity.
- Installment Sale - Defer capital gains by taking payments from a buyer over a period of years. No protection from buyer default.
- (US only) Deferred Sales Trust- Allows the seller of property to defer capital gains tax due at the time of sale over a period of time.
- (US only) 1031 exchange - Defer tax by exchanging for "like kind" property—however, generally available only for real estate and tangible property, both of which must be business-related. Pay capital gains when they are realized (i.e. when subsequently sold).
- (US only) Roth IRA - Transactions inside an account (including capital gains, dividends, and interest) do not incur a current tax liability.
- (US only) Structured sale annuity (aka Ensured Installment Sale) - Defer and reduce capital gains tax while gaining safety and a stream of guaranteed income.
- (US only) Self Directed Installment Sale (SDIS) Allows for the deferral of capital gains taxes while removing the risks from buyer default under a traditional installment sale.
- (US only) (historical) Private annuity trust - No longer a valid tax deferral tool.
- (Canada only) - Utilize a Tax-Free Savings Account

CARBON TAX

A carbon tax is a tax levied on the carbon content of fuels. It is a form of carbon pricing. Carbon is present in every hydrocarbon fuel (coal, petroleum, and natural gas) and is released as carbon dioxide (CO 2) when they are burnt. In contrast, non-combustion energy sources—wind, sunlight, hydropower, and nuclear—do not convert hydrocarbons to CO

2. CO_2 is a heat-trapping "greenhouse" gas. Scientists have pointed to the potential effects on the climate system of releasing greenhouse gases (GHGs) into the atmosphere. Since GHG emissions caused by the combustion of fossil fuels are closely related to the carbon content of the respective fuels, a tax on these emissions can be levied by taxing the carbon content of fossil fuels at any point in the product cycle of the fuel.

Carbon taxes offer a potentially cost-effective means of reducing greenhouse gas emissions. From an economic perspective, carbon taxes are a type of Pigovian tax. They help to address the problem of emitters of greenhouse gases not facing the full (social) costs of their actions. Carbon taxes can be a regressive tax, in that they may directly or indirectly affect low-income groups disproportionately. The regressive impact of carbon taxes could be addressed by using tax revenues to favour low-income groups. However, there are about USD $550 billion in fossil fuel subsidies annually worldwide.

A number of countries have implemented carbon taxes or energy taxes that are related to carbon content. Most environmentally related taxes with implications for greenhouse gas emissions in OECD countries are levied on energy products and motor vehicles, rather than on CO_2 emissions directly.

Opposition to increased environmental regulation such as carbon taxes often centres on concerns that firms might relocate and/or people might lose their jobs. It has been argued, however, that carbon taxes are more efficient than direct regulation and may even lead to higher employment. Many large users of carbon resources in electricity generation, such as the United States, Russia and China, are resisting carbon taxation.

BACKGROUND

CO_2 and global warming

Carbon dioxide is one of several heat-trapping greenhouse gases (GHGs) emitted by humans (anthropogenic GHGs). The scientific consensus is that human-induced greenhouse gas emissions are the primary cause of global warming, and that carbon dioxide is the most important of the anthropogenic GHGs. Worldwide, 27 billion tonnes of carbon dioxide are produced by human activity annually. The physical effect of CO_2 in the atmosphere can be measured as a change in the Earth-atmosphere system's energy balance – the radiative forcing of CO_2. Carbon taxes are one of the policies available to governments to reduce GHG emissions. In the Kyoto Protocol, CO_2 emissions are regulated along with other GHGs. Different GHGs have different physical properties: the global warming potential is an internationally accepted scale of equivalence for other greenhouse gases in units of tonnes of carbon dioxide equivalent.

Economic theory

A carbon tax is an indirect tax—a tax on a transaction—as opposed to a direct tax, which taxes income. A carbon tax is also called a price instrument, since it sets a price for carbon dioxide emissions. In economic theory, pollution is considered a negative externality, a negative effect on a party not directly involved in a transaction, which results in a market failure. To confront parties with the issue, the economist Arthur Pigou proposed taxing the goods (in this case hydrocarbon fuels), which were the source of the negative externality (carbon dioxide) so as to accurately reflect the cost of the goods' production to society, thereby internalizing the costs associated with the goods' production. A tax on a negative externality is called a Pigovian tax, and should equal the marginal damage costs.

Within Pigou's framework, the changes involved are marginal, and the size of the externality is assumed to be small enough not to distort the rest of the economy. According to the scientific consensus, the impact of climate change may result in catastrophe and non-marginal changes. "Non-marginal" means that the impact could significantly reduce the growth rate in income and welfare. The amount of resources that should be devoted to avoiding climate change impacts is controversial. Policies designed to reduce carbon emissions could also have a non-marginal impact.

Prices of hydrocarbon fuels are expected to continue increasing as more countries industrialize and add to the demand on fuel supplies. In addition to creating incentives for energy conservation, a carbon tax would put renewable energy sources such as wind, solar and geothermal on a more competitive footing, stimulating their growth.

Social cost of carbon

The social cost of carbon (SCC) is the marginal cost of emitting one extra tonne of carbon (as carbon dioxide) at any point in time. To calculate the SCC, the atmospheric residence time of carbon dioxide must be estimated, along with an estimate of the impacts of climate change. The impact of the extra tonne of carbon dioxide in the atmosphere must then be converted to the equivalent impacts when the tonne of carbon dioxide was emitted. In economics, comparing impacts over time requires a discount rate. This rate determines the weight placed on impacts occurring at different times.

According to economic theory, if SCC estimates were complete and markets perfect, a carbon tax should be set equal to the SCC. Emission permits would also have a value equal to the SCC. In reality, however, markets are not perfect, and SCC estimates are not complete (Yohe *et al..*, 2007:823).

An amount of CO_2 pollution is measured by the weight (mass) of the pollution. Sometimes this is measured directly as the weight of the carbon dioxide molecules. This is called a tonne of carbon dioxide and is abbreviated "tCO_2". Alternatively, the pollution's weight can be measured by adding up only the weight of the carbon atoms in the pollution, ignoring the oxygen atoms. This is called a tonne of carbon and is abbreviated "tC". Estimates of the dollar cost of carbon dioxide pollution is given per tonne, either carbon, \$X/tC, or carbon dioxide, \$X/tCO_2. One tC is roughly equivalent to 4 tCO_2.

Estimates of the SCC are highly uncertain. Yohe *et al.* (2007:813) summarized the literature on SCC estimates: peer-reviewed estimates of the SCC for 2005 had an average value of \$43/tC with a standard deviation of \$83/tC. The wide range of estimates is explained mostly by underlying uncertainties in the science of climate change (e.g., the climate sensitivity, which is a measure of the amount of global warming expected for a doubling in the atmospheric concentration of CO_2), different choices of discount rate, different valuations of economic and non-economic impacts, treatment of equity, and how potential catastrophic impacts are estimated. Other estimates of the SCC spanned at least three orders of magnitude, from less than \$1/tC to over \$1,500/tC. The true SCC is expected to increase over time. The rate of increase will very likely be 2 to 4% per year.

Carbon leakage

Carbon leakage is the effect that regulation of emissions in one country/ sector has on the emissions in other countries/sectors that are not subject to the same regulation. Leakage effects can be both negative (i.e., increasing the effectiveness of reducing overall emissions) and positive (reducing the effectiveness of reducing overall emissions). Negative leakages, which are desirable, are usually referred to as "spill-over".

According to Goldemberg *et al.*. (1996, p. 28), short-term leakage effects need to be judged against leakage effects in the long-term. A policy that, for example, saw a carbon taxes set only in developed countries might lead to leakage of emissions to developing countries. However, a desirable negative leakage could occur due to a lowering in demands of coal, oil, and gas from the developed countries and thus the world prices. This will lead to developing countries being able to afford more of any hydrocarbon fuel type, thus being able to substitute more oil or gas for coal, in effect lowering their national emissions. In the long-run, however, if the transfer of less polluting technologies is delayed, this substitution by income effects might have no long-term benefit.

Border adjustments, tariffs and bans

A number of policies have been suggested to address concerns over competitive losses due to one country introducing a carbon tax while another country does not. Similar policies have also been suggested in an attempt to induce countries to introduce carbon taxes. Suggested policies include border tax adjustments, trade tariffs and trade bans.

Border tax adjustments would account for emissions attributable to imports from nations without a carbon price. An alternative would be trade bans or tariffs applied to non-taxing countries. It has been argued that such approaches could be disadvantageous to a target country as a trade measure (Gupta *et al*.., 2007). To date, World Trade Organization case law has not provided specific rulings on climate-related taxes. The administrative aspects of border tax adjustments has also been discussed.

Other types of taxes

Two other types of taxes that are related to carbon taxes are emissions taxes and energy taxes. An emissions tax on GHG emissions requires individual emitters to pay a fee, charge or tax for every tonne of greenhouse gas released into the atmosphere while an energy tax is charged directly on the energy commodities.

In terms of mitigating climate change, a carbon tax, which is levied according to the carbon content of fuels, is not a perfect substitute for a tax on CO_2 emissions. For example, a carbon tax encourages reduced use of hydrocarbon fuels, but it does not provide an incentive to mitigate or improve mitigation technologies, e.g. carbon capture and storage.

Energy taxes increase the price of energy uniformly, regardless of the emissions produced by the energy source (Fisher *et al*.., 1996, p. 416). An *ad valorem* energy tax is levied according to the energy content of a fuel or the value of an energy product, which may or may not be consistent with the emitted amounts of green house gases and their respective global warming potentials. Studies indicate that to reduce emissions by a certain amount, *ad valorem* energy taxes would be more costly than carbon taxes. However, although CO_2 emissions are an externality, using energy services may result in other negative externalities, e.g., air pollution. If these other externalities are accounted for, an energy tax may be more efficient than a carbon tax alone.

Petroleum (motor gasoline, diesel, jet fuel)

Many OECD countries have taxed fuel directly for many years for some applications; for example, the UK imposes duty directly on vehicle hydrocarbon oils, including petrol and diesel fuel. The duty is adjusted to ensure that the carbon content of different fuels is handled with equivalence.

While a direct tax should send a clear signal to the consumer, its use as an efficient mechanism to influence consumers' fuel use has been challenged in some areas:

- There may be delays of a decade or more as inefficient vehicles are replaced by newer models and the older models filter through the 'fleet'.
- There may be political reasons that deter policy makers from imposing a new range of charges on their electorate.
- There is some evidence that consumers' decisions on fuel economy are not entirely aligned to the price of fuel. In turn, this can deter manufacturers from producing vehicles that they judge have lower

sales potential. Other efforts, such as imposing efficiency standards on manufacturers, or changing the income tax rules on taxable benefits, may be at least as significant.

- In many countries fuel is already taxed to influence transport behavior and to raise other public revenues. Historically, they have used these fuel taxes as a source of general revenue, as their experience has been that the price elasticity of fuel is low, thus increasing fuel taxation has only slightly impacted on their economies. However, in these circumstances the policy behind a carbon tax may be unclear.

Some also note that a suitably priced tax on vehicle fuel may also counterbalance the "rebound effect" that has been observed when vehicle fuel consumption has improved through the imposition of efficiency standards. Rather than reduce their overall consumption of fuel, consumers have been seen to make additional journeys or purchase heavier and more powerful vehicles.

IMPLEMENTATION

Both energy and carbon taxes have been implemented in responses to commitments under the United Nations Framework Convention on Climate Change. In most cases where an energy or carbon tax is implemented, the tax is implemented in combination with various forms of exemptions.

Africa

South Africa

A tax on emissions has been proposed for South Africa. Announced by Finance Minister Pravin Gordhan, the tax will be implemented starting September 1, 2010 on new motor vehicles. This tax will apply at the time of sale, and will be related to the amount of CO_2 emitted by the vehicle. 75 South African Rand will be added to the price for every gram of CO_2 per kilometer the vehicle emits over 120 g/km. The tax will apply to passenger cars first and eventually to commercial vehicles. Bakkies (pickup trucks) will be taxed because they are often used as passenger vehicles: this has caused an uproar for fear of impacts on industry.

David Powels of the National Association of Automobile Manufacturers of South Africa (NAAMSA), opposes this taxation on light commercial vehicles. The tax could increase the cost of new vehicles by 2.5% and cause a decrease in total automobile sales: in addition, Powels questions the ability to accurately predict CO_2 emissions based on engine capacity. NAAMSA acknowledges the ability of carbon taxes to change consumer behavior for the betterment of the environment, but argues that this tax is not transparent enough for consumers because the taxation occurs at the time of automobile production. Powels says the tax is discriminatory because it targets new vehicles, and that the government should focus on introducing "green fuel" to South Africa. The goal of the carbon tax is to put South Africa on a "sustainable path". South Africa has produced Long Term Mitigation Scenarios (LTMS) to address climate policy issues that consider variables such as technology, investment, and policy (including carbon taxes) and to clarify South Africa's position for potential UNFCC negotiations.

Asia

China

The Chinese Government Ministry of Finance has proposed to introduce a carbon tax from 2012 or 2013, based on carbon dioxide output from hydrocarbon fuel sources such as oil and coal.

India

On July 1, 2010 India introduced a nationwide carbon tax of 50 rupees per metric tonne ($1.07/t) of coal both produced and imported into India. In India coal is used to power more than half of the country's electricity generation.

India's total coal production is estimated to reach 571.87 million tons in the year ending March 2010 and is expected to import around 100 million tons. The carbon tax expects to raise 25 billion rupees ($535 million) for the financial year 2010–2011. According to then Finance Minister Pranab Mukherjee, the clean energy tax will help to finance a National Clean Energy Fund (NCEF). Industry bodies have not favored the levy and fear that the resultant higher price of coal could trigger inflation.

While many remain apprehensive, a carbon tax is a step towards helping India meet their voluntary target to reduce the amount of carbon dioxide released per unit of gross domestic product by 25% from 2005 levels by 2020. Environment Minister Jairam Ramesh told reporters in June 2010 that a domestic tax should come before a global carbon tax, and India has imposed one while others debate the issue.

Japan

In October 2012 Japan introduced a Carbon tax with the goal to take action on mitigating dangerous climate change. The government plans to use the revenues generated from this tax to finance clean energy and energy saving projects.

In December 2009, nine industry groupings opposed a carbon tax at the opening day of the COP-15 Copenhagen climate conference stating, "Japan should not consider a carbon tax as it would damage the economy which is already among the world's most energy efficient." The industry groupings represented the oil, cement, paper, chemical, gas, electric power, auto manufacturing and electronics, and information technology sectors. The sectors state that "the government has neither studied nor explained thoroughly enough why such a carbon tax is needed, how effective and fair it is and how the payments are to be used."

In 2005, an environmental tax proposed by Japanese authorities was also delayed due to major opposition from the Petroleum Association of Japan (PAJ), other industries and consumers. The delay was "to avoid putting too much economic burden on end-users as they were already paying heavy taxes on hydrocarbon fuels amid high oil prices." The tax that was to be implemented would be 2,400 yen ($20.85 in 2005 dollars) per tonne of carbon dioxide emitted from fuels. Tax on coal would be about 1.58 yen per kilogram and that on gasoline 1.52 yen per litre (4.3 cents per gallon in 2005 dollars). Officials estimated that the tax would generate income of 37 billion yen a year for the government and result in a payment of 2,100 yen per year for an average household.

South Korea

On August 22, 2008 The Chong Wa Dae, also known as the Blue house – the executive office and official residence of the South Korean head of state, confirmed a list of 40 new administrative strategy agenda, which included substitution of a carbon tax with the current transportation tax. Most revenues of the tax amounting to an annual $11 trillion won ($10.4 billion) will be financed toward the "Low Carbon, Green Growth" move, which was announced in President Lee Myung-bak's speech marking the nation's 63rd Liberation day the week before the announcement. A carbon tax is imposed on emissions of greenhouse gases including carbon dioxide. The direct taxation system is now applied to several European countries, such as Sweden, the Netherlands and Norway, as well as several states in North America. The temporary transportation tax, one of the major objective taxes in the country, is slated to end in 2009. About 80 percent of its yield is used in transportation-related work like road construction. Additional taxation amendment could follow with a "tax on emissions" bottom line, in possible implementations of tax discrimination according to a vehicles' size and a carbon tax on the currently tax-free thermal power plants. Taxation on emissions is inevitable in that low carbon policies take substantial budget, the government says.

In February 2010, a deputy finance minister Yoon Young-sun confirmed that South Korea is considering a carbon tax to help reduce emissions 4% from 2005 levels by 2020. This would be in conjunction with a cap-and-trade program to be implemented later this year. With a tax rate of 31,828 won (25 Euros) per ton of CO_2, the South Korean government would collect 9.1 trillion won ($7.9 billion) in tax revenue based on 2007 emissions. Income from the carbon tax would be used to reduce corporate and income taxes. On July 22,

2010 Chairman Sohn Kyung-shik of the Korea Chamber of Commerce and Industry asked for the South Korean government to delay the implementation of the carbon tax: "If the government applies much stricter guidelines over carbon emissions, then companies might be burdened."

On July 13, 2010 South Korea's government announced plans to more than double its financing for green research and development projects to 3.5 trillion won ($2.9/£1.9bn) by 2013. The finance ministry decided that the new investment will be put into a new dedicated green fund operated by the state-run Korea Finance Corporation, for distribution to private sector projects. The government said that the fund forms part of a huge low-carbon investment drive that will see it invest a total of 107.4 trillion won, or two percent of the country's annual gross domestic product, on green projects between 2009 and 2013.

However, the government signaled that in addition to setting aside state funds, it will ask private companies to contribute 2.4 trillion won to the fund. It added that spending from the fund will be directed mainly toward business involved in greenhouse gas emissions reduction and promoting energy efficiency. In addition, the government intends to expand its system of tax breaks to cover new technologies in solar, wind and thermal power, low-emission vehicles, rechargeable batteries and next generation nuclear reactors.

The government also set a voluntary target last year (2009) to reduce 2020 emissions by four percent on 2005 levels by 2020, and is expected to soon announce plans for carbon trading scheme to begin in 2012.

Australia

On the 1st of July 2012 the Australian Federal government introduced a carbon price, a Carbon Tax of $23AUD per tonne of emitted CO_2-e on selected fossil fuels consumed by major industrial emitters and government bodies such as councils. The revenue raised was used to reduce income tax (by increasing the tax-free threshold) and increase pensions and welfare payments slightly to cover expected price increases, as well as introducing compensation for some affected industries.

The Carbon Tax of $23AUD in the initial financial year of 2012–2013 is scheduled to rise by 5% (nominal) per year, until transitioning to an flexible-price ETS in 2015 when the available permits will be limited in line with a pollution cap.

New Zealand

In 2005, the Fifth Labour Government proposed a carbon tax in order to meet obligations under the Kyoto Protocol. The proposal would have set an emissions price of NZ$15 per tonne of CO_2-equivalent. The planned tax was scheduled to take effect from April 2007, and applied across most economic sectors though with an exemption for methane emissions from farming and provisions for special exemptions from carbon intensive businesses if they adopted world's-best-practice standards of emissions. After the 2005 election, some of the minor parties supporting the Fifth Labour Government (NZ First and United Future) opposed the proposed tax, and it was abandoned in December 2005. In 2008, the New Zealand Emissions Trading Scheme was enacted via the Climate Change Response (Emissions Trading) Amendment Act 2008.

Europe

In Europe, a number of countries have imposed energy taxes or energy taxes based partly on carbon content. These include Denmark, Finland, Germany, Ireland, Italy, the Netherlands, Norway, Slovenia, Sweden, Switzerland, and the UK. None of these countries has been able to introduce a uniform carbon tax for fuels in all sectors.

European Union

During the 1990s, a carbon/energy tax was proposed at the EU level but failed due to industrial lobbying. In 2010, the European Commission considered implementing a pan-European minimum tax on pollution permits purchased under the European Union Greenhouse Gas Emissions Trading Scheme (EU ETS) in which the proposed new tax would be calculated in terms of carbon content rather than volume, so that fuels with high energy concentrations, despite their subsequently high carbon content, will no longer carry the same traditionally low price. According to the European Commission, the new plan will charge firms a minimum tax per metric tonne of carbon dioxide emissions at a suggested rate of €4 to €30 per tonne of CO_2.

France

On September 10, 2009, France detailed a new carbon tax with a new levy on oil, gas and coal consumption by households and businesses that was supposed to come into effect on January 1, 2010. The new carbon tax would be 17 euros (25 US dollars) per tonne of carbon dioxide (CO_2) for households and businesses, which will raise the cost of a liter of unleaded fuel by about four cents (25 US cents per gallon). The total estimated income from the carbon tax would have been between 3 and 4.5 billion euros annually, with 55 percent of profit coming from households and 45 percent coming from businesses. The tax will not apply to electricity as mostly produced by France's network of nuclear reactors.

On December 30, the bill was blocked by the French Constitutional Council. It considered the bill included too many exceptions and said they were unconstitutional. It condemned the exemptions for industries as being unequal and inefficient, pointing out that less than half the whole emissions would have been taxed and saying it was unfair to apply the tax only to fuels and heating, which accounted for a limited part of carbon emissions. Discounts and exceptions would have applied to many aspects of industry and agriculture, including fishing, trucking, and farming. French President Nicolas Sarkozy, despite his vow to "lead the fight to save the human race from global warming", did not support the bill, saying that France needed support from the rest of the European Union before it would try and proceed with a carbon tax.

In 2013 Carbon tax was again announced for France. Prime Minister Jean-Marc Ayrault launched the new Climate Energy Contribution (CEC) on September 21st, 2013. The tax will apply at a rate of €7/tonne CO2 in 2014, €14.50 in 2015 and rising to €22 in 2016.

Netherlands

The Netherlands initiated a carbon tax in 1990. However, in 1992 it was replaced with a 50/50 carbon/energy tax called the Environmental Tax on Fuels, the taxes are assessed partly on carbon content and partly on energy content. The charge was transformed into a tax and became part of general tax revenues. As such, it fell under the administration of the Ministry of Finance. The general fuel tax is collected on all hydrocarbon fuels. Fuels used as raw materials are not subject to the tax. Tax rates are based 50/50 on the energy and carbon contents of fuels. In 1996 The Regulatory Tax on Energy, another 50/50 carbon/energy tax, was also implemented. The Environmental tax and the regulatory tax are 5.16 Dutch guilder, or NLG, (~$3.13) or per metric ton of CO_2 and 27.00 NLG (~16.40) per metric ton CO_2 respectively. Under the general fuel tax, electricity is not taxed, though fuels used to produce electricity are taxable. Energy-intensive industries used to benefit from preferential rates under this tax but the benefit was cancelled in January 1997. Also, since 1997 nuclear power has been taxed under the general fuel tax at the rate of NLG 31.95 per gram of uranium-235.38 The European Environment Agency put out an Executive Summary stating "Although the 5th Environmental Action Programme of the EU in 1992 recommended the greater use of economic instruments such as environmental taxes, there has been little progress in their use since then at the EU level." However, "at Member State level, there has been a continuing increase in the use of environmental taxes over the last decade, which has accelerated in the last 5–6 year...Countries including the Netherlands and the United Kingdom."

More recently, in 2007, The Netherlands introduced a Waste Fund that is funded by a carbon-based packaging tax. This tax encourages producers to create packaging that is recyclable and was implemented to help reach the goals of recycling 65% of used packaging by 2012. The company Nedvang (Nederland van afval naar grondstof or The Netherlands from waste to value), which was set up in 2005, is the largest organization supporting producers and importers of packaged goods reaching individual company goals under the Dutch packaging decree. This decree was signed in 2005 and states that producers and importers of packaged goods are responsible for the collection and recycling of that waste, and that at least 65% of that wast has to be recycled. Producers and importers can choose to reach the goals on an individual basis or by joining an organization like Nedvang.

The Carbon-Based Tax on Packaging consists of taxing:

- Glass: € 71,80/ tonne (~$ 91.99/ tonne)
- Aluminum (including Alloys): € 950,60/ tonne (~$ 1,219.00/ tonne)
- Ferrous metals: € 158,50/ tonne (~$ 203.09/ tonne)
- Plastics: € 470,50/ tonne (~$ 602.75/ tonne)
- Paper/Cardboard: € 79,50/ tonne (~$ 101.86/ tonne)
- Wood: € 21,00/ tonne (~$ 26.90/ tonne)

Sweden

In January 1991, Sweden enacted a CO_2 tax of 0.25 SEK/kg ($100 or EUR 72 per ton) on the use of oil, coal, natural gas, liquefied petroleum gas, petrol, and aviation fuel used in domestic travel. Industrial users paid half the rate (between 1993 and 1997, 25% of the rate), and certain high-energy industries such as commercial horticulture, mining, manufacturing and the pulp and paper industry were fully exempted from these new taxes.

In 1997 the rate was raised to 0.365 SEK/kg ($150 per ton) of CO_2. In 2007, the tax was SEK 930 (EUR 101) per ton of CO_2. The full tax is paid in transport, space heating, and non-combined heat and power generation. Owing to the many exemptions, oil accounts for 96% of the revenues from the tax, although it produces less than three-quarters of CO_2 from fuel combustion. The tax is credited with spurring a significant move from hydrocarbon fuels to biomass. As Swedish Society for Nature Conservation climate change expert Emma Lindberg said, "It was the one major reason that steered society towards climate-friendly solutions. It made polluting more expensive and focused people on finding energy-efficient solutions."

"It increased the use of bioenergy", said University of Lund Professor Thomas Johansson, former director of energy and climate at the UN Development Programme. "It had a major impact in particular on heating. Every city in Sweden uses district heating. Before, coal or oil were used for district heating. Now biomass is used, usually waste from forests and forest industries."

Economic growth appears to be unaffected. Between 1990 and 2006, Sweden's economy grew by 44-46 percent (approx 2,8% annually), depending on source.,

United Kingdom

In 1993, the UK government introduced the fuel duty escalator (FDE), an environmental tax on retail petroleum products. The tax was explicitly designed to reduce carbon dioxide emissions in the transport sector. Since carbon is in fixed ratio to the quantity of fuel, the FDE roughly approximated a carbon tax. The transport lobby in the UK was extremely critical of the FDE. The FDE, which was the UK's only "real" carbon tax, failed because of the political criticism it provoked, and the automatic increase of the FDE was cancelled in 1999. Increases in fuel tax have since been discretionary.

The politically damaging fuel protests in 2000 contributed to the government decision to reduce the real rates of fuel tax. At the time, tax and duty represented more than 75% of the total pump price. In money terms, the past increments of the FDE remain in force, but in real terms, increments have been reduced by the rate of inflation. In 2006, tax represented about T! of the pump price. In addition, the UK's Climate Change Levy was introduced in 2001.

North America

Canada

In the 2008 Canadian federal election a carbon tax proposed by Liberal Party leader Stéphane Dion, known as the Green Shift, became a central issue in the campaign. It would have been revenue-neutral, with increased taxation on carbon being balanced by tax cuts for individual citizens. However, it proved to be unpopular and contributed to the defeat of Liberal Party with its worst share of the popular vote since Confederation.

Although there is no federal carbon tax, some Canadian provinces do have carbon taxes:

- Quebec: The Canadian province of Quebec became the first in Canada to introduce a carbon tax. The tax was to be imposed on energy producers starting October 1, 2007, with revenue collected used for energy-efficiency programs including public transit. The tax rate for gasoline is $CDN0.008 per liter, or about $3.50 per tonne of CO_2 equivalent.

Main article: British Columbia carbon tax

- British Columbia: On February 19, 2008, the province of British Columbia announced its intention to implement a carbon tax of $10 per tonne of Carbon dioxide equivalent (CO_2e) emissions (2.41 cents per litre on gasoline) beginning July 1, 2008, making BC the first North American jurisdiction to implement such a tax. The tax will increase each year after until 2012, reaching a final price of $30 per tonne (7.2 cents per litre at the pumps). Unlike previous proposals, legislation will keep the pending carbon tax revenue neutral by reducing corporate and income taxes at an equivalent rate. Also, the government will also reduce taxes above and beyond the carbon tax offset by $481 million over three years. In January 2010, the carbon tax was applied to biodiesel. Before the tax actually went into effect, the government of British Columbia sent out "rebate cheques" from expected revenues to all residents of British Columbia as of December 31, 2007. In January 2013, the carbon tax was collecting about $1 billion each year which was used to lower other taxes in British Columbia. Terry Lake, the minister of the environment of British Columbia, said *"It makes sense, it's simple, it's well accepted,"*

- Alberta: In July 2007 the Alberta government became the first state or province in North America to put a price on carbon when it imposed a carbon tax forcing companies that emit more than 100,000 tonnes of greenhouse gas annually to either reduce their CO_2 emissions per barrel by 12 percent, pay $15 per tonne into a technology fund, or buy an offset in Alberta to apply against their total emissions. The tax will fall most heavily on oil companies and coal-fired electricity plants. The carbon tax intends to give companies a real incentive to lower emissions while fostering technology that makes the job easier. The plan only covers the largest companies that produce 70% of Alberta's emissions. There are concerns that this is a serious omission because the smallest energy producers are often the most casual about emissions and pollution. Because Alberta has the highest greenhouse gas emissions in Canada the majority of Albertans are strongly opposed to a nationwide carbon tax. There is a fear that a nationwide carbon tax would cause Alberta's economy to suffer significantly more in proportion to other provinces. Alberta is also opposed to a Cap and Trade system it fears the trades will pull revenue out of the province, a fear not to be dismissed. Alberta's local carbon tax allows the money to stay within Alberta.

United States

There is no nationwide carbon tax levelled in the United States, although a few states and localities have introduced the tax.

Colorado

In November 2006, voters in Boulder, Colorado passed what is said to be the first municipal carbon tax. It is a tax on electricity consumption (utility bills) with deductions for using electricity from renewable sources (primarily Xcel's WindSource program). The goal is to reduce carbon emissions to those outlined in the Kyoto Protocol; specifically to reduce their emissions by 7% below 1990 levels by 2012. Tax revenues are collected by Xcel Energy and are directed to the city's Office of Environmental Affairs to fund programs to reduce community-wide greenhouse gas emissions. Boulder's Climate Action Plan (CAP) tax is expected to raise $1.6 million in 2010. The tax was increased to a maximum allowable rate by voters in 2009 to meet CAP goals. Currently the tax is set at $0.0049/kWh for residential users (ave. $21 per year), $0.0009/kWh for commercial (ave. $94 per year), and $0.0003/kWh for industrial (ave. $9,600 per year). The revenues from the tax are expected to decrease over time as businesses and residents reduce their energy use and begin to use more solar and wind power. The tax will expire on March 31, 2013.

California

In May 2008, the Bay Area Air Quality Management District, which covers nine counties in the San Francisco Bay Area, passed a carbon tax on businesses of 4.4 cents per ton of CO_2.

In 2006, the state of California, passed AB-32 (Global Warming Solutions Act of 2006), which requires California to reduce greenhouse gas emissions. To implement AB-32, the California Air Resources Board proposed a carbon tax, but has yet to reach agreement with the Western States Petroleum Association which represents the refineries in the state. The WSPA holds that AB-32 only allows a carbon tax to cover administrative costs.

HARMONIZED CARBON TAXES

Cooper (1998, 2001) has been a leading proponent of a harmonized carbon tax (a tax where the country setting the tax keeps all the revenues). Under his proposals, all participating nations would be subject to a tax at a common rate, thus achieving cost-effectiveness. A number of problems have been suggested with Cooper's proposals:

- One criticism is of the fairness of having developing countries being subject to the same tax rates as developed countries, given their relative level of welfare and responsibility for the climate problem.
- It has been asked what incentive developed countries would have to adopt a tax.
- It is possible that governments would attempt to neutralize the effects of the tax on certain economic sectors.
- Given the presence of existing tax distortions, it might not be politically feasible to implement a uniform tax rate.

SUPPORT

Former US Vice President Al Gore, although not a scientist, strongly backed a carbon tax in his book, *Earth in the Balance*, but this became a political liability after the Republicans attacked him as a "dangerous fanatic". In 2000, when Gore ran for president, one commentator labeled Gore's carbon tax proposal a "central planning solution" harking back to "the New Deal politics of his father."

In 2001, environmental scientist Lester Brown, founder of the Worldwatch Institute and founder and president of the Earth Policy Institute, outlined a detailed "tax shifting" structure which would not lead to an overall higher tax level:

- It means reducing income taxes and offsetting them with taxes on environmentally destructive activities such as carbon emissions, the generation of toxic waste, the use of virgin raw materials, the use of non-refillable beverage containers, mercury emissions, the generation of garbage, the use of pesticides, and the use of throwaway products.... activities that should be discouraged by taxing.

Brown subsequently added that such a tax shift would amount to an "honest market," explaining, "The key to restructuring the economy is the creation of an honest market, one that tells the ecological truth." In 2011 he estimated the cost of such a tax shift, including the effects of better technology, the use of renewables and "updating the concept of national security."

Former US Federal Reserve chairman Paul Volcker suggested (February 6, 2007) that "it would be wiser to impose a tax on oil, for example, than to wait for the market to drive up oil prices."

NASA climatologist James E. Hansen has argued in support of a carbon tax. In North America, the nonprofit Citizens Climate Lobby has been advocating for carbon tax legislation (specifically a progressive fee and dividend model with revenue returned to citizens in the form of a check or rebate). The organization has about 75 chapters around the United States and Canada. Former United States Congressional Representative Bob Inglis (R-South Carolina) heads the Energy and Enterprise Initiative at George Mason University which is making the conservative case for climate legislation through support for a carbon tax.

A number of businesses and business leaders also support a carbon tax. These include:

- FedEx CEO Fred Smith;
- James Owens, CEO of Caterpillar;
- and Paul Anderson, CEO and Chairman of Duke Energy.

Monica Prasad, a Northwestern University sociologist, wrote about Denmark's carbon tax in the *New York Times* in 2008. In her view, the Danish carbon tax served as an example of how to reduce emissions in the US. Prasad argued, however, that a critical component for Denmark's success in reducing carbon emissions from 1990–2005 was that the tax revenues from the carbon tax were dedicated to subsidies for firms to use for alternative, environmentally cleaner sources of energy.

Economist Laura D'Andrea Tyson wrote in June 2013: "The beauty of a carbon tax is its market-based simplicity. Economists since Adam Smith have insisted that prices are by far the most efficient way to guide the decisions of producers and consumers. Carbon emissions have an "unpriced" societal cost in terms of their deleterious effects on the earth's climate. A tax on carbon would reflect these costs and send a powerful price signal that would discourage carbon emissions." She listed several prominent economists and political figures that have supported carbon taxes.

CARBON TAXES COMPARED TO CAP-AND-TRADE

An alternative government policy to a carbon tax is a cap on greenhouse gas (GHG) emissions. Emission levels of GHGs are capped and permits to pollute are freely allocated (called "grandfathering") or auctioned to polluters. Auctioning permits has significant economic advantages over grandfathering. In particular, auctioning raises revenues that can be used to reduce distortionary taxes and improve overall efficiency. A market may be allowed for these emission permits so that polluters can trade some or all of their permits with others (cap-and-trade). A hybrid instrument of a cap and carbon tax can be made by creating a price-floor and price-ceiling for emission permits. A carbon tax can also be implemented concurrently with a cap.

Unlike a cap system with grandfathered permits, a carbon tax raise revenues. If the revenues are used to reduce other distortionary taxes, this can improve the efficiency of the tax. On the other hand, a cap with grandfathered permits can have an efficiency advantage of being applied to all industries. This provides an equal incentive at the margin for all polluters to reduce their emissions. This is an advantage over a tax that exempts or has reduced rates for certain sectors.

Views

Both cap-and-trade and carbon taxes give polluters a financial incentive to reduce their GHG emissions. Carbon taxes provide certainty regarding emission prices, while a cap provides certainty regarding emissions quantity. In a literature assessment, Fisher *et al.*. (1996:430) concluded that the choice between an international quota (cap) system, or an international carbon tax, remained ambiguous. Lu *et al.* (2012) compared a carbon tax, an emission trading, and command-and-control regulation at the industrial level. Their abstract concludes that market-based mechanisms would perform better than emission standards in achieving emission targets without affecting industrial production.

Supporters of taxes over caps

- James E. Hansen has argued in his book (*Storms of My Grandchildren*) and in an open letter to President Obama, that policies to cap carbon emissions and trade permits for them will only make money for banks and hedge funds and allow 'business-as-usual' for the chief carbon-emitting industries. He advocates phasing out and protesting against coal-fired power stations that do not have onsite carbon sequestration and imposing a progressive carbon tax.
- Carl Pope, executive director of the Sierra Club, supports a carbon

tax over cap-and-trade because employers will know exactly what they paid for the carbon dioxide they produced, and because a cap-and-trade system (with grandfathered permits) rewards those who have the highest emissions now and have done the least to reduce them previously.

- Gary Becker, a follower of the Chicago School of Economics, expressed his support for carbon taxes over cap-and-trade. Becker won the Nobel Prize in economics in 1992.
- On December 11, 2008, Rex Tillerson, the CEO of Exxonmobil, said a carbon tax is "a more direct, more transparent and more effective approach" than a cap and trade program, which he said, "inevitably introduces unnecessary cost and complexity." He also said that he hoped that the revenues from a carbon tax would be used to lower other taxes so as to be revenue neutral.
- The American Enterprise Institute, Environmental economist Jack Pezzey, economist Jeffrey Sachs (director of the Earth Institute of Columbia University), Yale economist William Nordhaus, The Earth Policy Institute, The Australia Institute, the Centre for Independent Studies, and Harvard professor, Gregory Mankiw also prefer carbon taxes to cap-and-trade.

Difficulties with taxes

According to the Carbon Trust (2009), a carbon tax suffers from combining a set price for carbon along with a transfer of revenue from industry to government. This, it is argued, guarantees that the tax will not be set at the appropriate level, but will instead be determined by the politics of large-scale revenue transfers. With a cap, however, the revenues from emission allowances can be separately negotiated with industry. Another issue with taxes is whether the emissions reductions they bring about actually exist – that is, the "additionality" of emissions reductions attributable solely to the taxes (Carbon Trust, 2009). Additionality usually requires a comparison of observed emission reductions against an estimate of the emission reductions that would have taken place without the presence of the tax (the emissions "baseline"). The additionality of a carbon tax, in this sense, is difficult to establish because other policies usually will also have impacts on levels of emissions, e.g., subsidies and regulations. (As a case in point, greenhouse gas emissions from British Columbia had fallen 4.5% between 2007 and 2010 following imposition of its carbon tax. However, it is estimated by the government that most of this decrease is, in fact, attributable to an economic recession.) There are about USD $550 billion in fossil fuel subsidies annually worldwide.

DISTRIBUTIONAL IMPACTS

In most instances, firms pass the costs of a carbon price onto consumers.

Studies typically find that poor consumers spend a greater proportion of their income on energy-intensive goods and fuel. Therefore cost increases in energy tend to impact the poor worse than the rich.

Studies by Metcalf *et al.* (2008) and Metcalf (2009) consider the possible distributional impacts of carbon taxes in the United States. The 2008 study considers three recent tax bills introduced to the US Congress. The taxes themselves are highly regressive, but when revenues from the tax are returned lump-sum, the taxes become progressive. The 2009 study looks at a carbon tax combined with a reduction in payroll taxes. It is found that this combination can be distributionally neutral. With an adjustment in Social Security payments for the lowest-income households, the carbon tax policy can be made progressive. A study by Ekins and Dresner (2004) considers the distributional impact in the UK of introducing a carbon tax and increasing fuel duty. It is found that a carbon tax can be made progressive, but that the tax would make those currently worst affected by fuel poverty more badly off. Of the policy options looked at for transport, the most effective in compensating low-income motorists is found to be an increase in fuel duties and the abolishment of vehicle excise duty.

CONSUMPTION TAX

A consumption tax is a tax on spending on goods and services. The tax base of such a tax is the money spent on consumption. Consumption taxes are usually indirect, such as a sales tax or a value added tax. However, a consumption tax can also be structured as a form of direct, personal taxation, such as the Hall–Rabushka flat tax.

TYPES

Value-added tax

A value added tax (VAT) applies to the market value added to a product or material at each stage of its manufacture or distribution. For example, if a retailer buys a shirt for $20 and sells it for $30, this tax would apply to the $10 difference between the two amounts. A simple VAT would be proportional on consumption but also be regressive on income at higher income levels (as consumption falls as a percentage of income). Savings and investment are tax-deferred until they become consumption. A VAT may exclude certain goods, intent being creating progressive effects. The tax is used in countries within the European Union. In Australia, Canada, New Zealand, and Singapore this form of national tax is called a Goods and Services Tax (GST). In Canada it is also called Harmonized Sales Tax (HST) when combined with a provincial sales tax.

Sales tax

A sales tax typically applies to the sale of goods, less often to the sales of services. The tax is applied at the point of sale.

Excise tax

An excise tax is a sales tax that applies to a specific class of goods, typically alcohol, gasoline (petrol), or tourism. The tax rate varies according to the type of good and quantity purchased and is typically unaffected by the person who purchases it.

Expenditure tax

A direct, personal consumption tax may take the form of an expenditure tax or an income tax that deducts savings and investments, such as the Hall–Rabushka flat tax. A direct consumption tax may be called an expenditure tax, a cash-flow tax, or a consumed-income tax and can be flat or progressive. Expenditure taxes have been briefly implemented in the past in India and Sri Lanka.

This form of tax applies to the difference between an individual's income and increase/decrease savings. Like the other consumption taxes, simple personal consumption taxes are regressive with respect to income. However, because this tax applies on an individual basis, it can be made as progressive as a progressive personal income tax. Just as income tax rates increase with personal income, consumption tax rates increase with personal consumption.

SAVINGS EFFECT

Consumption taxes do not tax savings, which allows invested assets to grow more quickly. If, in the absence of taxes, $1 of savings is put aside for retirement at 9% compound interest, savings will grow to $7.86 after 24 years. Alternatively, by assuming a 33% tax rate, the same $1 is reduced to about $0.67 after taxes when earned. The effective interest rate, thereafter, is reduced to 6%, since the rest of the yield is paid in taxes.

After 24 years, the balance increases only to $2.64. The cumulative taxes in the latter case are $0.96. The missing $4.26 is not lost by the economy in any sense, as the $4.26 is what the government would make in interest, if they invested their tax revenue. If the initial investment amount is not taxed when earned, but the earnings are taxed thereafter, the cumulative taxes paid are about the same, but are spread more evenly across the period and the asset grows to more than $4. These results are primarily sensitive to the rate of return. With a 3% return, most of the tax receipts come from the tax on the initial $1.00.

To the extent that taxing something results in less of it (whether income or consumption), taxing consumption instead of income should encourage both work and capital formation, which will increase economic growth, while discouraging consumption. Secondly, the tax base will be larger because *all* consumption will be taxed.

Some critics argue that sales and consumption taxes can shift the tax burden to the less well-off. The ratio of tax obligation shrinks as wealth grows because the wealthy spend proportionally less of their income on consumables. An individual unable to save will pay taxes on 100%, but individuals who save or invest a portion of their income will be taxed only on the remaining income.

PRACTICAL CONSIDERATIONS

Many proposed consumption taxes share some features with the current income tax systems. Under these proposals, taxpayers would be given exemptions and a standard deduction in order to ensure that the poor do not pay any tax. In a pure consumption tax, other deductions would not be permitted, because all savings would be deductible.

A withholding system might also be put into place in order to estimate the total tax liability. It would be difficult for many taxpayers to pay no tax all year, only to be faced with a large tax bill at the end of the year.

A consumption tax could also eliminate the concept of basis when computing the value of investments. All income that is put in investments (such as property, stocks, savings accounts) is tax-free. As the asset grows in value, it is not taxed. Only when the proceeds from the asset are spent is any tax imposed. This is in contrast with the current system where if one buys land for $10,000 and sells it for $15,000, one has a taxable gain of $5,000. A consumption tax taxes only consumption, so if one sells an investment to buy another investment, no tax is imposed.

Andrews notes the inherent problem with housing. Renters necessarily "consume" housing, so they will be taxed on the expenditure of rent. However, homeowners also consume housing in the same way, but as they pay down a mortgage, the payments are classified as savings, not consumption (because equity is being built in an asset).

The disparity is explained by what is known as the imputed rental value of a home. A homeowner could choose to rent the home to others in exchange for money but instead chooses to live in the home to the exclusion of all possible renters. Therefore, the homeowner is also consuming housing by not permitting renters to pay for and occupy the home. The amount of money that the homeowner could receive in rent is the imputed rental value of the home.

A true consumption tax would tax the imputed rental value of the home (which could be determined in the same way that valuation occurs for property tax purposes) and would not tax the increase in the value of the asset (the home). Andrews proposes to ignore this method of taxing imputed rental values because of its complexity. In the United States, home ownership is subsidized by the federal government by permitting a deduction for mortgage interest expense and exempting a significant increase in value from the capital gains tax. Therefore, treating renters and homeowners identically under a consumption tax may not be feasible in there.

Also, a consumption tax could utilize progressive rates in order to maintain "fairness." The more that someone spends on consumption, the more that the person will be taxed. The rate structure could look like the current bracket system, or a new bracket system could be implemented.

ECONOMIC IMPACT

Former senior editor of Fortune Magazine Al Ehrbar notes that proponents of a consumption tax argue its superiority to the income tax based on an economic principle called "temporal neutrality". He observes that a tax is "neutral" if it does not "alter spending habits or behavior patterns and thus does not distort the allocation of resources." In other words, taxing apples but not oranges will cause apple consumption to decrease and orange consumption to increase.

The temporal neutrality of a consumption tax, however, is that consumption itself is taxed, so it is irrelevant what good or service is being consumed in terms of allocation of resources. The only possible effect on neutrality is between consumption and savings. Taxing only consumption should, in theory, cause an increase in savings. William Gale, Co-director of the Urban-Brookings Tax Policy Center, offers a simplified way to understand a consumption tax: Assume that our current tax system remains the same but remove limitations to contributing to and removing funds from a traditional Individual Retirement Account (IRA).

Thus, a person would essentially have a bank account where they could place tax-free earnings at any time, but unsaved (or consumed) withdrawals would be subject to taxation. Having an unrestricted IRA under the current system would approximate a consumption tax at the federal level.

Many economists and tax experts favor consumption taxes over income taxes for economic growth. Consumption taxes are neutral with respect to investment. Depending on implementation (such as treatment of depreciation) and circumstances, income taxes either favor or disfavor investment.(On the whole, the US system is thought to disfavor investment.) By not disfavoring investment, a consumption tax *might* increase the capital stock, productivity, and therefore increase the size of the economy. Consumption more closely tracks long run average income. An individual or a family's income often varies dramatically from year to year. The sale of a home, a one-time job bonus, and various other events can lead to temporary high income that will push a low or middle income person into a high tax bracket. On the other hand, a wealthy individual may be temporarily unemployed and will pay no taxes.

ECOTAX

Ecotax (short for Ecological taxation) refers to taxes intended to promote ecologically sustainable activities via economic incentives. Such a policy can complement or avert the need for regulatory (command and control) approaches. Often, an ecotax policy proposal may attempt to maintain overall tax revenue by proportionately reducing other taxes (e.g. taxes on human labor and renewable resources); such proposals are known as a green tax shift towards ecological taxation.

Ecotaxes are examples of Pigouvian taxes, which are *taxes that attempt to make the private parties involved feel the social burden of their actions*. An example might be philosopher Thomas Pogge's proposed Global Resources Dividend.

TAXES AFFECTED

Examples of taxes which could be lowered or eliminated by a green tax shift are:

- Payroll, income, and, to a lesser extent, sales taxes.
- Corporate taxes (taxes on investment and entrepreneurship).
- Property taxes on buildings and other infrastructure.

Examples of ecotaxes which could be implemented or increased are:

- Carbon taxes on the use of fossil fuels by greenhouse gases produced. Old hydrocarbon taxes don't penalize green house gas (GHG) production.
- Duties on imported goods containing significant non-ecological energy input (to a level necessary to treat fairly local manufacturers)
- Severance taxes on the extraction of mineral, energy, and forestry products.
- License fees for camping, hiking, fishing and hunting and associated equipment.
- Specific taxes on technologies and products which are associated with substantial negative externalities.
- Waste disposal taxes and refundable fees.
- Steering taxes on effluents, pollution and other hazardous wastes.
- Site value taxes on the unimproved value of land.

ECONOMIC FRAMEWORKS AND STRATEGIES EMPLOYING TAX SHIFTING AND ECOTAXES

The object of a green tax shift is often to implement a "full cost accounting" or "true cost accounting", using fiscal policy to internalize market distorting externalities, which leads to sustainable wealth creation. The broader measures required for this are also sometimes called ecological fiscal reform, especially in Canada, where the government has generally employed this terminology. In some countries the name is eco-social market economy.

Tax shifting usually includes balancing taxation levels to be revenue-neutral for government and to maintain overall progressiveness. It also usually includes measures to protect the most vulnerable, such as raising the minimum income to file income tax at all, or an increase to pension and social assistance levels to offset increased costs of fuel consumption.

Basic economic theory recognizes the existence of externalities and their potential negative effects. To the extent that green taxes correct for externalities such as pollution, they correspond with mainstream economic theory. In practice, however, setting the correct taxation level or the tax collection system needed to do so is difficult, and may lead to further distortions or unintended consequences. Taxes on consumption may take the "feebate" approach advocated by Amory Lovins, in which additional fees on less sustainable products — such as sport utility vehicles — are pooled to fund subsidies on more sustainable alternatives, such as hybrid electric vehicles.

However, they may simply act as incentives to change habits and make capital investments in newer more efficient vehicles or appliances or to upgrade buildings. Small changes in corporate tax rates for instance can radically change return on investment of capital projects, especially if the averted costs of future fossil fuel use are taken into account.

The same logic applies to major consumer purchases. A "green mortgage" such as a Location Efficient Mortgage, for example, recognizes that persons who do not drive cars and live generally energy-efficient lifestyles pay far less per month than others and accordingly have more to pay a heftier mortgage bill with. This justifies lending them much more money to upgrade a house to use even less energy overall. The result is a bank taking more per month from a consumer's income as utilities and car insurance companies take less, and housing stock upgraded to use the minimum energy feasible with current technology.

Aside from energy, the refits will generally be those required to be maximally accommodating to telework, permaculture gardens (for example green roofs), and a lifestyle that is generally localized in the community not based on commuting. The last, especially, raises real state valuations for not only the neighborhood but the entire surrounding region. Consumers living sustainable lifestyles in upgraded housing will generally be unwilling to drive around aimlessly shopping, for instance, to save a few dollars on their purchases. Instead, they'll stay nearer to home and create jobs in grocery delivery and small organic grocers, spending substantially less money on gasoline and car operation costs even if they pay more for food.

PROGRESSIVE OR REGRESSIVE?

Some green tax shift proposals have been criticized as being fiscally regressive (a tax with an average tax rate that decreases as the taxpayer's income increases). Taxing negative externalities usually entails exerting a burden on consumption, and since the poor consume more and save or invest less as a share of their income, any shift towards consumption taxes can be regressive. In 2004, research by the Policy Studies Institute and Joseph Rowntree Foundation indicated that flat rate taxes on domestic rubbish, energy, water and transport use would have a relatively higher impact on poorer households. However, conventional regulatory approaches can affect prices in much the same way, while lacking the revenue-recycling potential of ecotaxes. Moreover, correctly assessing distributive impact of any tax shift requires an analysis of the specific instrument design features.

For example, tax revenue could be redistributed on a per capita basis as part of a basic income scheme; in this case, the poorest would gain what the average citizen pays as ecotaxes, minus their own small contribution (no car, small apartment...). This design would be highly progressive. Alternatively, an ecotax can have a "lifeline" design, in which modest consumption levels are priced relatively low (even zero, in the case of water), and higher consumption levels are priced at a higher rate. Furthermore, an ecotax policy package can include revenue recycling to reduce or eliminate any regressivity; an increase in an ecotax could be more than offset by a decrease in a (regressive) payroll or consumption tax. Some proponents claim a second benefit of increased employment or lower health care costs as the market and society adjust to the new fiscal policy (these claims, as with the claim "tax cuts create jobs," are often difficult to prove or disprove even after the fact).

Furthermore, pollution and other forms of environmental harm are often felt more acutely by the poor, who cannot "buy their way out" of being receptors of air pollution, water pollution, etc. Such losses, although externalities, have real economic welfare impacts. Thus by reducing environmental harm, such instruments have a progressive effect.

ECOTAX POLICIES ENACTED

An ecotax has been enacted in Germany by means of three laws in 1998, 1999 and 2002. The first introduced a tax on electricity and petroleum, at variable rates based on environmental considerations; renewable sources of electricity were not taxed. The second adjusted the taxes to favor efficient conventional power plants. The third increased the tax on petroleum. At the same time, income taxes were reduced proportionally so that the total tax burden remained constant.

The regional government of Balearic Islands (then held by an ecosocialist coalition) established an ecotax in 1999. The Balearic Island suffer a high human pressure from tourism, that at the same time provides the main source of income. The tax (€1.00 per person per day) would be paid by visitors staying at tourist resorts. This was criticized by the conservative opposition as contrary to business interests, and they abolished the tax in 2003 after seizing back the government. A variety of ecotaxes (often called "severance taxes") have been enacted by various states in the United States. The Supreme Court of the United States held in *Commonwealth Edison Co. v. Montana*, 453 U.S. 609 (1981), that in the absence of federal law to the contrary, states may set ecotaxes as high as they wish without violating the Commerce Clause or the Supremacy Clause of the United States Constitution.

Registration taxes

The Netherlands, Portugal, Canada, Spain and Finland have introduced differentiations into their car registration taxes to encourage car buyers to opt for the cleanest car models.

In the Netherlands, the new registration taxes, payable when a car is sold to its first buyer, can earn the owner of a hybrid a discount up to €6000. Spain reduced taxes for cars that produced less CO2 (some of which will be exempted), while the more consuming, like SPV and 4WD saw their taxes increased. Austria has had a registration tax based on fuel consumption for several years.

EXCISE

An excise or excise tax (sometimes called a duty of excise special tax) is an inland tax on the sale, or production for sale, of specific goods or a tax on a good produced for sale, or sold, within a country or licenses for specific activities. Excises are distinguished from customs duties, which are taxes on importation. Excises are *inland* taxes, whereas customs duties are *border* taxes.

An excise is considered an indirect tax, meaning that the producer or seller who pays the tax to the government is expected to try to recover or shift the tax by raising the price paid by the buyer. Excises are typically imposed in addition to another indirect tax such as a sales tax or value added tax (VAT). In common terminology (but not necessarily in law), an excise is distinguished from a sales tax or VAT in three ways: (i) an excise typically applies to a narrower range of products; (ii) an excise is typically heavier, accounting for a higher fraction of the retail price of the targeted products; and (iii) an excise is typically a per unit tax, costing a specific amount for a volume or unit of the item purchased, whereas a sales tax or VAT is an ad valorem tax and proportional to the price of the good.

Typical examples of excise duties are taxes on gasoline and other fuels, and taxes on tobacco and alcohol (sometimes referred to as sin tax).

DEFINITION

Etymology. The word *excise* is derived from the Dutch *accijns,* which is presumed to come from the Latin *accensare,* meaning simply "to tax".

Regulatory and legal definitions of 'excise' vary by country. For example:

- In India, an excise is described as an indirect tax levied and collected on the goods manufactured in India.
- In the United Kingdom, HM Revenue and Customs lists "alcohol, environmental taxes, gambling, holdings & movements, hydrocarbon oil, money laundering, refunds of duty, revenue trader's records, tobacco duty, and visiting forces" as being subject to excise. Some of the listed items are not *goods,* but rather services.
- The Australian Taxation Office describes an excise as "a tax levied

on certain types of goods produced or manufactured in Australia. These... include alcohol, tobacco and petroleum and alternative fuels".

In Australia, the meaning of "excise" is not merely academic, but has been the subject of numerous court cases. The High Court of Australia has repeatedly held that a tax can be an "excise" regardless of whether the taxed goods are of domestic or foreign origin; most recently, in *Ha v New South Wales* (1997), the majority of the Court endorsed the view that an excise is "an inland tax on a step in production, manufacture, sale or distribution of goods", and took a wide view of the kind of "step" which, if subject to a tax, would make the tax an excise.

RATIONALE

In defense of excises on strong drink, Adam Smith wrote: "It has for some time past been the policy of Great Britain to discourage the consumption of spirituous liquors, on account of their supposed tendency to ruin the health and to corrupt the morals of the common people." Samuel Johnson was less flattering in his 1755 dictionary: "EXCI'SE. *n.s*.... A hateful tax levied upon commodities, and adjudged not by the common judges of property, but wretches hired by those to whom excise is paid."

Monies raised through excise may be earmarked for redress of specific social costs commonly associated with the product or service being taxed. Tobacco tax revenues, for example, might be spent on government anti-smoking campaigns.

Excise duties or taxes often serve political as well as financial ends. Public safety and health, public morals, environmental protection, and national defense are all rationales for the imposition of an excise.

- Public safety and health
  - Deter individuals from harming their health by abusing substances such as tobacco and alcohol, thus making excise a kind of sumptuary tax, or
  - Deter them from engaging in morally objectionable activities such as gambling and prostitution (including solicitation and pimping) – thus making it a type of vice tax or sin tax
- Environmental protection
  - Deter individuals or organizations from harming the general environment, including curbing activities which contribute to pollution, or which harm the natural environment.
- Defense
  - Including taxation directly levied on other countries' militaries and/or governments, such as the UK's taxation on "visiting forces"
- Punitive

- Many US states impose taxes on illegal drugs, while the UK government imposes excise on money laundering and on "visiting forces" (which can be construed to mean occupying military forces). These taxes are not considered revenue sources, but rather exist to allow governments greater leverage for punishments and reparations/war reparations – based around the concept of tax evasion – which can be imposed in the event that the perpetrator is caught and tried.

CRITICISMS

Critics of excise tax have interpreted and described excise duty as simply a government's way of levying further and unnecessary taxation on the population. The presence of "refunds of duty" under the UK's list of excisable activities has been used to support this argument, as it results in taxation being implemented on persons even where they would normally be exempt from paying other types of taxes – hence why they are getting the refund in the first place.

Furthermore, excise is often somewhat similar to other taxes and sometimes doubles up with them, or as in the case of customs duties: since the two taxes largely apply to the same types of goods, people are forced to pay tax twice over on the same items (except in the case of duty-free) - once through excise upon purchase and a second time around through customs duties upon transportation. (A justification for this is that the country the items are being imported into is applying the customs partly for the same reasons as the original excise was charged, as it is the country of import which will suffer the ill environmental, health and social effects of, say, the cigarettes and alcohol being brought in; thus customs has many similar pros and cons as has excise.)

Taxation on medicines, pharmaceuticals and medical equipment has been an issue of contention, especially in developing countries, due to the fact that this tax can result in inflated prices of ordinary and even potentially lifesaving medication, as well as raise the cost of medical procedures, sometimes forcing healthcare providers to limit the number of operations performed.

As far as illegal drugs are concerned, it has also been argued that, by taxing banned substances, some US states are able to gain revenues, while the legislation protects the anonymity of the dealers –

- A dealer is not required to give his/her name or address when purchasing stamps and the Department is prohibited from sharing any information relating to the purchase of drug tax stamps with law enforcement or anyone else.

INCOME TAX

An income tax is a government levy (tax) imposed on individuals or entities (taxpayers) that varies with the income or profits (taxable income) of the taxpayer. Details vary widely by jurisdiction. Many jurisdictions refer to income tax on business entities as companies tax or corporation tax. Partnerships generally are not taxed; rather, the partners are taxed on their share of partnership items. Tax may be imposed by both a country and subdivisions thereof. Most jurisdictions exempt locally organized charitable organizations from tax.

Income tax generally is computed as the product of a tax rate times taxable income. The tax rate may increase as taxable income increases (referred to as graduated rates). Tax rates may vary by type or characteristics of the taxpayer. Capital gains may be taxed at different rates than other income. Credits of various sorts may be allowed that reduce tax. Some jurisdictions impose the higher of an income tax or a tax on an alternative base or measure of income.

Taxable income of taxpayers resident in the jurisdiction is generally total income less income producing expenses and other deductions. Generally, only net gain from sale of property, including goods held for sale, is included in income. Income of a corporation's shareholders usually includes distributions of profits from the corporation. Deductions typically include all income producing or business expenses including an allowance for recovery of costs of business assets. Many jurisdictions allow notional deductions for individuals, and may allow deduction of some personal expenses. Most jurisdictions either do not tax income earned outside the jurisdiction or allow a credit for taxes paid to other jurisdictions on such income. Nonresidents are taxed only on certain types of income from sources within the jurisdictions, with few exceptions.

Most jurisdictions require self-assessment of the tax and require payers of some types of income to withhold tax from those payments. Advance payments of tax by taxpayers may be required. Taxpayers not timely paying tax owed are generally subject to significant penalties, which may include jail for individuals or revocation of an entity's legal existence.

COMMON PRINCIPLES

While tax rules vary widely, there are certain basic principles common to most income tax systems. Tax systems in Canada, China, Germany, Singapore, the United Kingdom, and the United States, among others, follow most of the principles outlined below. Some tax systems, such as India, may have significant differences from the principles outlined below.

Taxpayers and rates

Individuals are often taxed at different rates than corporations. Individuals include only human beings. Tax systems in countries other than the USA treat an entity as a corporation only if it is legally organized as a corporation. Estates and trusts are usually subject to special tax provisions.

Other taxable entities are generally treated as partnerships. In the USA, many kinds of entities may elect to be treated as a corporation or a partnership. Partners of partnerships are treated as having income, deductions, and credits equal to their shares of such partnership items.

Separate taxes are assessed against each taxpayer meeting certain minimum criteria. Many systems allow married individuals to request joint assessment. Many systems allow controlled groups of locally organized corporations to be jointly assessed.

Tax rates vary widely. Some systems impose higher rates on higher amounts of income. Example: Elbonia taxes income below E.10,000 at 20% and other income at 30%. Joe has E.15,000 of income. His tax is E.3,500. Tax rates schedules may vary for individuals based on marital status.

Residents and nonresidents

Residents are generally taxed differently than nonresidents. Few jurisdictions tax nonresidents other than on specific types of income earned within the jurisdiction.

Residence is often defined for individuals as presence in the country for more than 183 days. Most countries base residence of entities on either place of organization or place of management and control. The United Kingdom has three levels of residence.

Defining income

Most systems define income subject to tax broadly for residents, but tax nonresidents only on specific types of income. What is included in income for individuals may differ from what is included for entities. The timing of recognizing income may differ by type of taxpayer or type of income.

Income generally includes most types of receipts that enrich the taxpayer, including compensation for services, gain from sale of goods or other property, interest, dividends, rents, royalties, annuities, pensions, and all manner of other items. Many systems exclude from income part or all of superannuation or other national retirement plan payments. Most tax systems exclude from income health care benefits provided by employers or under national insurance systems.

Deductions allowed

Nearly all income tax systems permit residents to reduce gross income by business and some other types of deductions. By contrast, nonresidents are generally subject to income tax on the gross amount of income.

Expenses incurred in a trading, business, rental, or other income producing activity are generally deductible, though there may be limitations on some types of expenses or activities. Business expenses include all manner of costs for the benefit of the activity. An allowance (as a capital allowance or depreciation deduction) is nearly always allowed for recovery of costs of assets used in the activity. Rules on capital allowances vary widely, and often permit recovery of costs more quickly than ratably over the life of the asset.

Most systems allow individuals some sort of notional deductions or an amount subject to zero tax. In addition, many systems allow deduction of some types of personal expenses, such as home mortgage interest or medical expenses.

Business profits

Only net income from business activities, whether conducted by individuals or entities is taxable, with few exceptions. Many countries require business enterprises to prepare financial statements which must be audited. Tax systems in those countries often define taxable income as income per those financial statements with few, if any, adjustments. A few jurisdictions compute net income as a fixed percentage of gross revenues for some types of businesses, particularly branches of nonresidents.

Credits

Nearly all systems permit residents a credit for income taxes paid to other jurisdictions of the same sort. Thus, a credit is allowed at the national level for income taxes paid to other countries. Many income tax systems permit other credits of various sorts, and such credits are often unique to the jurisdiction.

Alternative taxes

Some jurisdictions, particularly the United States and many of its states and Switzerland, impose the higher of regular income tax or an alternative tax. Switzerland and U.S. states generally impose such tax only on corporations and base it on capital or a similar measure.

Administration

Income tax is generally collected in one of two ways: through withholding of tax at source and/or through payments directly by taxpayers. Nearly all jurisdictions require those paying employees or nonresidents to withhold income tax from such payments. The amount to be withheld is a fixed percentage where the tax itself is at a fixed rate. Alternatively, the amount to be withheld may be determined by the tax administration of the country or by the payer using formulas provided by the tax administration. Payees are generally required to provide to the payer or the government the information needed to make the determinations. Withholding for employees is often referred to as "pay as you earn" (PAYE) or "pay as you go."

Nearly all systems require those whose proper tax is not fully settled through withholding to self assess tax and make payments prior to or with final determination of the tax. Self-assessment means the taxpayer must make a computation of tax and submit it to the government.

State, provincial, and local

Income taxes are separately imposed by sub-national jurisdictions in several countries with federal systems. These include Canada, Germany, Switzerland, and the United States, where provinces, cantons, or states impose separate taxes. In a few countries, cities also impose income taxes. The system may be integrated (as in Germany) with taxes collected at the federal level. In Income tax in Canada#Personal income taxesQuebec and the United States, federal and state systems are independently administered and have differences in determination of taxable income.

Wage based taxes

Income taxes of workers are often collected by employers under a withholding or Pay-as-you-earn tax system. Such collections are not necessarily final amounts of tax, as the worker may be required to aggregate wage income with other income and/or deductions to determine actual tax. Calculation of the tax to be withheld may be done by the government or by employers based on withholding allowances or formulas.

Retirement oriented taxes, such as Social Security or national insurance, also are a type of income tax, though not generally referred to as such. These taxes generally are imposed at a fixed rate on wages or self-employment earnings up to a maximum amount per year. The tax may be imposed on the employer, the employee, or both, at the same or different rates.

Some jurisdictions also impose a tax on employers to fund unemployment or similar government outlays. Such taxes are generally not considered income taxes.

ECONOMIC AND POLICY ASPECTS

Multiple conflicting theories have been proposed regarding the economic impact of income taxes. Income taxes are widely viewed as a Progressive tax, meaning the incidence of tax increases as income increases.

Criticisms

Tax avoidance strategies and loopholes tend to emerge within income tax codes. These get created when tax payers find legal methods to avoid paying taxes. Lawmakers then attempt to close the loopholes with additional legislation. This leads to a vicious cycle of ever more complex avoidance strategies and legislation. This vicious cycle tends to benefit large corporations and wealthy individuals that can afford the professional fees that come with ever more sophisticated tax planning, thus challenging the notion that even a marginal income tax system can be properly called a progressive tax.

The higher costs to labour and capital imposed by income tax causes deadweight loss in an economy, being the loss of economic activity from people deciding not to invest capital or use time productively due to the burden tax would impose on those activities. There is also a loss from individuals and professional advisors devoting time to tax avoiding behaviour instead of economically productive activities.

SALES TAX

A sales tax is a tax paid to a governing body for the sales of certain goods and services. Usually laws allow (or require) the seller to collect funds for the tax from the consumer at the point of purchase. Laws may allow sellers to itemize the tax separately from the price of the goods or services, or require it to be included in the price (tax-inclusive). The tax amount is usually calculated by applying a percentage rate to the taxable price of a sale. When a tax on goods or services is paid to a governing body directly by a consumer, it is usually called a use tax. Often laws provide for the exemption of certain goods or services from sales and use tax.

TYPES

A conventional or retail sales tax is only levied on the sale of a good to its final end user. Sales to businesses who later resell the goods are not charged the tax. A purchaser who is not an end user is usually issued a "resale certificate" by the taxing authority and required to provide the certificate (or its ID number) to a seller at the point of purchase, along with a statement that the item is for resale. The tax is otherwise charged on each item sold to purchasers who do not provide such a certificate and who are under the jurisdiction of the taxing authority.

Other types of sales taxes, or similar taxes, include:

- Manufacturers' sales tax: a tax on sales of tangible personal property by manufacturers and producers
- Wholesale sales tax: a tax on sales of wholesale of tangible personal property when in a form packaged and labeled ready for shipment or delivery to final users and consumers.
- Retail sales tax: a tax on sales of retail of tangible personal property to final consumers and industrial users
- Gross receipts taxes, levied on all sales of a business. This tax has been criticized for its "cascading" or "pyramiding" effect, in which an item is taxed more than once as it makes its way from production to final retail sale.
- Excise taxes, applied to a narrow range of products, such as gasoline or alcohol, usually imposed on the producer or wholesaler rather than the retail seller.
- Use tax, imposed directly on the consumer of goods purchased

without sales tax, generally items purchased from a vendor who is not under the jurisdiction of the taxing authority (e.g., a vendor in another state). Use taxes are commonly imposed by states with a sales tax, but are usually only enforced for large items such as automobiles and boats.

- Securities turnover excise tax, a tax on the trade of securities.
- Value added taxes, in which tax is charged on all sales, thus avoiding the need for a system of resale certificates. Tax cascading is avoided by applying the tax only to the difference ("value added") between the price paid by the first purchaser and the price paid by each subsequent purchaser of the same item.
- FairTax, a proposed federal sales tax, intended to replace the U.S. federal income tax.
- Turnover tax, similar to a sales tax, but applied to intermediate and possibly capital goods as an indirect tax.

Most countries in the world have sales taxes or value-added taxes at all or several of the national, state, county or city government levels. Countries in Western Europe, especially in Scandinavia have some of the world's highest valued-added taxes. Norway, Denmark and Sweden have higher VATs at 25%, Hungary has the highest at 27%, although reduced rates are used in some cases, as for groceries, art, books and newspapers.

In some jurisdictions of the United States, there are multiple levels of government which each impose a sales tax. For example, sales tax in Chicago (Cook County), IL is 10.25%—consisting of 6.25% state, 1.25% city, 1.75% county and 1% regional transportation authority. Chicago also has the Metropolitan Pier and Exposition Authority tax on food and beverage of 1% (which means eating out is taxed at 11.25%).

For Baton Rouge, Louisiana, the tax is 9%, consisting of 4% state and 5% local rate. In California, sales taxes are made up of various state, county and city taxes. The state tax is "imposed upon all retailers" for the "privilege of selling tangible personal property at retail." Strictly speaking, only the retailer is responsible for the payment of the tax; when a retailer adds this tax to the purchase price, the consumer is merely reimbursing the retailer by contractual agreement. When consumers purchase goods from out-of-state (in which case the seller owes no tax to California) the consumer is required to pay a "use tax" which is identical to the sales tax. Use tax is levied upon the "storage, use, or other consumption in this state of tangible personal property." Consumers are responsible for declaring these purchases in the same filing as their annual state income tax, but it is rare for them to do so. An exception is out of state purchase of automobiles, in which case use tax is collected by the state as part of registering the vehicle in California.

The trend has been for conventional sales taxes to be replaced by more broadly based value added taxes. Value added taxes provide an estimated 20 percent of worldwide tax revenue and have been adopted by more than 140 countries. The United States is now one of the few countries to retain conventional sales taxes.

EFFECTS

Economists at the Organisation for Economic Co-operation and Development studied the effects of various types of taxes on the economic growth of developed nations within the OECD and found that sales taxes are one of the least harmful taxes for growth.

Investopedia defines a regressive tax as "[a] tax that takes a larger percentage from low-income people than from high-income people. A regressive tax is generally a tax that is applied uniformly. This means that it hits lower-income individuals harder". Because the rate of a sales tax does not change based on a person's income or wealth, sales taxes are generally considered regressive. However, it has been suggested that any regressive effect of a sales tax could be mitigated, e.g., by excluding rent, or by exempting "necessary" items, such as food, clothing and medicines.

Enforcement of tax on remote sales

In the United States, every state with a sales tax law has a use tax component in that law applying to purchases from out-of-state mail order, catalog and e-commerce vendors, a category also known as "remote sales". As e-commerce sales have grown in recent years, noncompliance with use tax has had a growing impact on state revenues. The Congressional Budget Office estimated that uncollected use taxes on remote sales in 2003 could be as high as $20.4 billion. Uncollected use tax on remote sales was projected to run as high as $54.8 billion for 2011.

Enforcement of the tax on remote sales, however, is difficult. Unless the vendor has a physical location, or *nexus*, within a state, the vendor cannot be required to collect tax for that state. This limitation was defined as part of the Dormant Commerce Clause by the Supreme Court in the 1967 decision on National Bellas Hess v. Illinois. An attempt to require a Delaware e-commerce vendor to collect North Dakota tax was overturned by the court in the 1992 decision on Quill Corp. v. North Dakota.

The Internet Tax Freedom Act of 1998 established a commission to study the possibility of internet taxation, but the commission did not make any formal recommendations. In a report in 2003, the Congressional Budget Office warned of the economic burden of a "multiplicity of tax systems, particularly for smaller firms".

In an effort to reduce the burden of compliance with the tax laws of multiple jurisdictions, the Streamlined Sales Tax Project was organized in March 2000. Cooperative efforts in this project by 44 state governments and the District of Columbia eventually produced the Streamlined Sales and Use

Tax Agreement in 2010. This agreement establishes standards necessary for simplified and uniform sales tax laws. As of December 2010, 24 states had passed legislation conforming with the agreement. Whether the Streamlined Sales Tax can actually be applied to remote sales ultimately depends upon Congressional support, because the 1992 Quill v. North Dakota decision determined that only the U.S. Congress has the authority to enact interstate taxes.

SALES TAX AVOIDANCE

Businesses can reduce the impact of sales tax for themselves and their customers by planning for the tax consequences of all activities. Sales tax avoidance often includes the following:

- Designing invoices to reduce the taxable portion of a sale transaction. In Maryland, for example, a delivery charge is exempt from the tax when stated separately from handling and other taxable charges.
- New facilities. Jurisdictions with no sales tax or broad exemptions for certain types of business operations would be an obvious consideration in selecting a site for a new manufacturing plant, warehouse or administrative office.
- Delivery location. For a businesses operating in several jurisdictions, choosing the best location in which to take delivery can reduce or eliminate the sales tax liability. This is particularly important for an item to be sold or used in another jurisdiction with a lower tax rate or an exemption for that item. Businesses should consider whether a temporary storage exemption applies to merchandise initially accepted in a jurisdiction with a higher tax rate.
- Periodic review of record-keeping procedures related to sales and use tax. Proper supporting detail, including exemption and resale certificates, invoices and other records must be available to defend the company in the event of a sales and use tax audit. Without proper documentation, a seller can be held liable for tax not collected from a buyer.

In the United States, online retailers who have no physical presence in a given state can ship goods to customers there without collecting that state's sales tax, because as of 2011, there is no federal sales tax. Amazon.com has been criticized for not collecting sales tax, and has intentionally disaffiliated itself from businesses in certain states to continue doing so legally.

VALUE ADDED TAX

A value added tax (VAT) is a form of consumption tax. From the perspective of the buyer, it is a tax on the purchase price. From that of the seller, it is a tax only on the value added to a product, material, or service, from an accounting point of view, by this stage of its manufacture or distribution. The manufacturer remits to the government the difference between these two amounts, and retains the rest for themselves to offset the taxes they had previously paid on the inputs.

The purpose of VAT is to generate tax revenues to the government similar to the corporate income tax or the personal income tax. The value added to a product by or with a business is the sale price charged to its customer, minus the cost of materials and other taxable inputs. A VAT is like a sales tax in that ultimately only the end consumer is taxed. It differs from the sales tax in that, with the latter, the tax is collected and remitted to the government only once, at the point of purchase by the end consumer. With the VAT, collections, remittances to the government, and credits for taxes already paid occur each time a business in the supply chain purchases products.

Maurice Lauré, Joint Director of the France Tax Authority, the Direction Générale des Impôts, was first to introduce VAT on 10 April 1954, although German industrialist Dr. Wilhelm von Siemens proposed the concept in 1918. Initially directed at large businesses, it was extended over time to include all business sectors. In France, it is the most important source of state finance, accounting for nearly 50% of state revenues.

Personal end-consumers of products and services cannot recover VAT on purchases, but businesses are able to recover VAT (input tax) on the products and services that they buy in order to produce further goods or services that will be sold to yet another business in the supply chain or directly to a final consumer. In this way, the total tax levied at each stage in the economic chain of supply is a constant fraction of the value added by a business to its products, and most of the cost of collecting the tax is borne by business, rather than by the state.

Value added taxes were introduced in part because they create stronger incentives to collect than a sales tax does. Both types of consumption tax create an incentive by end consumers to avoid or evade the tax, but the sales tax offers the buyer a mechanism to avoid or evade the tax—persuade the seller that the buyer is not really an end consumer, and therefore the seller is not legally required to collect it. Therefore, the burden of determining whether the buyer's motivation is to consume or re-sell is on the seller, and the seller has no direct economic incentive to collect it. The VAT approach gives sellers a direct financial stake in collecting the tax and eliminates a decision needing to be made by the seller about whether the buyer is or is not an end consumer.

COMPARISON WITH SALES TAX

Value added tax avoids the cascade effect of sales tax by taxing only the *value added* at each stage of production. For this reason, throughout the world, VAT has been gaining favor over traditional sales taxes. In principle, VAT applies to all provisions of goods and services. VAT is assessed and collected on the value of goods or services that have been provided every time there is a transaction (sale/purchase). The seller charges VAT to the buyer, and the seller pays this VAT to the government. If, however, the purchaser is not an end user, but the goods or services purchased are costs to its business, the tax it has paid for such purchases can be deducted from the tax it charges to its customers. The government only receives the difference; in other words, it is paid tax on the gross margin of each transaction, by each participant in the sales chain.

In many developing countries such as India, sales tax/VAT are key revenue sources as high unemployment and low per capita income render other income sources inadequate. However, there is strong opposition to this by many sub-national governments as it leads to an overall reduction in the revenue they collect as well as of some autonomy.

In theory sales tax is normally charged on end users (consumers). The VAT mechanism means that the end-user tax is the same as it would be with a sales tax. The main difference is the extra accounting required by those in the middle of the supply chain; this disadvantage of VAT is balanced by application of the same tax to each member of the production chain regardless of its position in it and the position of its customers, reducing the effort required to check and certify their status. When the VAT system has few, if any, exemptions such as with GST in New Zealand, payment of VAT is even simpler.

A general economic idea is that if sales taxes are high enough, people start engaging in widespread tax evading activity (like buying over the Internet, pretending to be a business, buying at wholesale, buying products through an employer etc.). On the other hand, total VAT rates can rise above 10% without widespread evasion because of the novel collection mechanism. However, because of its particular mechanism of collection, VAT becomes quite easily the target of specific frauds like carousel fraud, which can be very expensive in terms of loss of tax incomes for states

IMPLEMENTATION

The standard way to implement a value added tax involves assuming a business owes some fraction on the price of the product minus all taxes previously paid on the good.

By the method of collection, VAT can be accounts-based or invoice-based. Under the invoice method of collection, each seller charges VAT rate on his output and passes the buyer a special invoice that indicates the amount of tax charged. Buyers who are subject to VAT on their own sales (output tax), consider the tax on the purchase invoices as input tax and can deduct the sum from their own VAT liability. The difference between output tax and input tax is paid to the government (or a refund is claimed, in the case of negative liability). Under the accounts based method, no such specific invoices are used. Instead, the tax is calculated on the value added, measured as a difference between revenues and allowable purchases. Most countries today use the invoice method, the only exception being Japan, which uses the accounts method. By the timing of collection, VAT (as well as accounting in general) can be either accrual or cash based. Cash basis accounting is a very simple form of accounting. When a payment is received for the sale of goods or services, a deposit is made, and the revenue is recorded as of the date of the receipt of funds—no matter when the sale had been made. Cheques are written when funds are available to pay bills, and the expense is recorded as of the cheque date—regardless of when the expense had been incurred. The primary focus is on the amount of cash in the bank, and the secondary focus is on making sure all bills are paid. Little effort is made to match revenues to the time period in which they are earned, or to match expenses to the time period in which they are incurred.

Accrual basis accounting matches revenues to the time period in which they are earned and matches expenses to the time period in which they are incurred. While it is more complex than cash basis accounting, it provides much more information about your business. The accrual basis allows you to track receivables (amounts due from customers on credit sales) and payables (amounts due to vendors on credit purchases). The accrual basis allows you to match revenues to the expenses incurred in earning them, giving you more meaningful financial reports.

REGISTERED

VAT registered means registered for VAT purposes, that is entered into an official VAT payers register of a country. Both natural persons and legal entities can be VAT registered. Countries that use VAT have established different thresholds for remuneration derived by natural persons/legal entities during a calendar year (or a different period), by exceeding which the VAT registration is compulsory. Natural persons/legal entities that are VAT registered are obliged to calculate VAT on certain goods/services that they supply and pay VAT into a particular state budget. VAT registered persons/entities are entitled to a VAT deduction under legislative regulations of a particular country. The introduction of a VAT can reduce the cash economy because businesses that wish to buy and sell with other VAT registered businesses must themselves be VAT registered.

IMPORTS AND EXPORTS

Being a consumption tax, VAT is usually used as a replacement for sales tax. Ultimately, it taxes the same people and businesses the same amounts of money, despite its internal mechanism being different. There is a significant difference between VAT and Sales Tax for goods that are imported and exported:

1. VAT is charged for a commodity that is exported while sales tax is not

2. Sales Tax is paid for the full price of the imported commodity, while VAT is expected to be charged only for value added to this commodity by the importer and the reseller

This means that, without special measures, goods that are imported from one country that does have VAT to another country that does not have VAT will be taxed twice. The exporting country will charge VAT and the importing country will charge sales tax. Vice versa, goods that are imported from a country that does not have VAT to another country that does have VAT will result in no sales tax for those goods, and only a fraction of the usual VAT. There are also significant differences in taxation for goods that are being imported/ exported between countries with different VATs. Sales tax does not have all those problems – it is charged in the same way for both imported and domestic goods, and it is never charged twice.

To fix this problem of VAT, nearly all countries that use VAT use special rules for imported and exported goods:

1. All imported goods are charged VAT tax for their full price when they are sold for the first time
2. All exported goods are exempted from any VAT payments

For these reasons VAT on imports and VAT rebates on exports form a common practice approved by the World Trade Organization.

CRITICISMS

The "value added tax" has been criticized as the burden of it falls on personal end-consumers of products. Some critics consider it to be a regressive tax, meaning that the poor pay more, as a percentage of their income, than the rich. Defenders argue that relating taxation levels to income is an arbitrary standard, and that the value added tax is in fact a proportional tax in that people with higher income pay more in that they consume more. The effective progressiveness or regressiveness of a VAT system can also be affected when different classes of goods are taxed at different rates. To maintain the progressive nature of total taxes on individuals, countries implementing VAT have reduced income tax on lower income-earners as well as instituted direct transfer payments to lower-income groups, resulting in lower tax burdens on the poor.

Revenues from a value added tax are frequently lower than expected because they are difficult and costly to administer and collect. In many countries, however, where collection of personal income taxes and corporate profit taxes has been historically weak, VAT collection has been more successful than other types of taxes. VAT has become more important in many jurisdictions as tariff levels have fallen worldwide due to trade liberalization, as VAT has essentially replaced lost tariff revenues. Whether the costs and distortions of value added taxes are lower than the economic inefficiencies and enforcement issues (e.g. smuggling) from high import tariffs is debated, but theory suggests value added taxes are far more efficient. Certain industries (small-scale services, for example) tend to have more VAT avoidance, particularly where cash transactions predominate, and VAT may be criticized for encouraging this. From the perspective of government, however, VAT may be preferable because it captures at least some of the value added. For example, a building contractor may offer to provide services *for cash* (i.e. without a receipt, and without VAT) to a homeowner, who usually cannot claim input VAT back. The homeowner will thus bear lower costs and the building contractor may be able to avoid other taxes (profit or payroll taxes).

Because exports are generally zero-rated (and VAT refunded or offset against other taxes), this is often where VAT fraud occurs. In Europe, the main source of problems is called carousel fraud. Large quantities of valuable goods (often microchips or mobile phones) are transported from one member state to another. During these transactions, some companies owe VAT, others acquire a right to reclaim VAT. The first companies, called 'missing traders', go bankrupt without paying. The second group of companies can 'pump' money straight out of the national treasuries. This kind of fraud originated in the 1970s in the Benelux countries. Today, the British treasury is a large victim. There are also similar fraud possibilities inside a country. To avoid this, in some countries like Sweden, the major owner of a limited company is personally responsible for taxes. This is circumvented by having an unemployed person without assets as the formal owner.

Under a sales tax system, only businesses selling to the end-user are required to collect tax and bear the accounting cost of collecting the tax. Under VAT, however, manufacturers and wholesale companies also have to hire accountants and incur accounting expenses to handle the additional paperwork required for collecting VAT, increasing overhead costs that in turn get incorporated into the cost of the item, possibly creating a cascading effect of higher prices throughout the chain of production. Manufacturers and wholesalers have a choice of retaining less profits overall, or passing on the additional cost to their customers in the form of increased prices.

Many politicians and economists in the United States consider VAT taxation on US goods and VAT rebates for goods from other countries to be unfair practice. E.g. the American Manufacturing Trade Action Coalition claims that any rebates or special taxes on imported goods should not be allowed by the rules of the World Trade Organisation. AMTAC claims that so-called "border tax disadvantage" is the greatest contributing factor to the $5.8 trillion US current account deficit for the decade of the 2000s, and estimated this disadvantage to US producers and service providers to be $518 billion in 2008 alone. Some US politicians, such as congressman Bill Pascrell, are advocating either changing WTO rules relating to VAT or rebating VAT charged on US exporters by passing the Border Tax Equity Act. Another avenue of criticism of implementing a VAT is that the increased tax passed to the consumer will increase the ultimate price paid by the consumer. However a study in Canada reveals that in fact when replacing a traditional sales tax with a VAT consumer prices actually fell.

CORPORATE TAX

Many countries impose corporate tax, also called *corporation tax* or *company tax*, on the income or capital of some types of legal entities. A similar tax may be imposed at state or lower levels. The taxes may also be referred to as income tax or capital tax. Entities treated as partnerships are generally not taxed at the entity level. Most countries tax all corporations doing business in the country on income from that country. Many countries tax all income of corporations organized in the country.

Company income subject to tax is often determined much like taxable income for individuals. Generally, the tax is imposed on net profits. In some jurisdictions, rules for taxing companies may differ significantly from rules for taxing individuals. Certain corporate acts, like reorganizations, may not be taxed. Some types of entities may be exempt from tax.

Many countries tax corporate entities on income and also tax the owners when the corporation pays a dividend. Where the owners are taxed, a withholding tax may be imposed. Generally, these taxes on owners are not referred to as corporate tax. Corporate tax or company tax refers to a tax imposed on entities that are taxed at the entity level in a particular jurisdiction. Such taxes may include income or other taxes. The tax systems of most countries impose an income tax at the entity level on certain type(s) of entities (company or corporation). Many systems additionally tax owners or members of those entities on dividends or other distributions by the entity to the members. The tax generally is imposed on net taxable income. Net taxable income for corporate tax is generally financial statement income with modifications, and may be defined in great detail within the system. The rate of tax varies by jurisdiction. The tax may have an alternative base, such as assets, payroll, or income computed in an alternative manner.

Most income tax systems provide that certain types of corporate events are not taxable transactions. These generally include events related to formation or reorganization of the corporation. In addition, most systems provide specific rules for taxation of the entity and/or its members upon winding up or dissolution of the entity.

In systems where financing costs are allowed as reductions of the tax base (tax deductions), rules may apply that differentiate between classes of member-provided financing. In such systems, items characterized as interest may be deductible, subject to interest limitations, while items characterized as dividends are not. Some systems limit deductions based on simple formulas, such as a debt-to-equity ratio, while other systems have more complex rules. Some systems provide a mechanism whereby groups of related corporations may obtain benefit from losses, credits, or other items of all members within the group. Mechanisms include combined or consolidated returns as well as group relief (direct benefit from items of another member).

Most systems also tax company shareholders on distribution of earnings as dividends. A few systems provide for partial integration of entity and member taxation. This is often accomplished by "imputation systems" or franking credits. In the past, mechanisms have existed for advance payment of member tax by corporations, with such payment offsetting entity level tax.

Many systems (particularly sub-country level systems) impose a tax on particular corporate attributes. Such non-income taxes may be based on capital stock issued or authorized (either by number of shares or value), total equity, net capital, or other measures unique to corporations.

Corporations, like other entities, may be subject to withholding tax obligations upon making certain varieties of payments to others. These obligations are generally not the tax of the corporation, but the system may impose penalties on the corporation or its officers or employees for failing to withhold and pay over such taxes. A company has been defined as a juristic person having an independent and separate existence from its shareholders. Income of the company is computed and assessed separately in the hands of the company. In certain cases, distributions from the company to its shareholders as dividends are taxed as income to the shareholders.

CORPORATION DEFINED

A corporation is a legal entity organized under the corporate or company laws of some jurisdiction. The jurisdiction may be a country or a subdivision of a country. For example, in Canada, a corporation may be organized under either Federal or provincial laws. Most jurisdictions recognize as corporations entities organized under the corporate or company laws of other jurisdictions. Under many tax systems, any entity providing limitations on the liability of all members for the actions of the entity is considered a corporation. Characterization as a corporation for tax purposes is based on the form of organization in most taxing jurisdictions. One notable exception applies for United States Federal and most state income taxes within the United States under which an entity may (with exceptions) elect to be treated as a corporation and taxed at the entity level or taxed only at the member level.

Governments may impose tax on corporations as separately from their owners. Most jurisdictions tax companies or corporations at the entity rather than the member level. Members of the corporate entity are generally not subject to tax on the entity's earnings until such earnings are distributed. By contrast, most jurisdictions tax partnerships at the member level and not the entity level. Members of a partnership are generally subject to tax on the partnership's earnings as they are earned rather than when they are distributed.

TAXATION OF CORPORATIONS

Corporations may be taxed on their incomes, property, or existence by various jurisdictions. Many jurisdictions impose a tax based on the existence or equity structure of the corporation. For example, Maryland imposes a tax on corporations organized in that state based on the number of shares of capital stock issued and outstanding. Many jurisdictions instead impose a tax based on stated or computed capital, often including retained profits.

Most jurisdictions tax corporations on their income. Generally, this tax is imposed at a specific rate or range of rates on taxable income as defined within the system. Some systems have a separate body of law or separate provisions relating to corporate taxation. In such cases, the law may apply only to entities and not to individuals operating a trade. Such laws may differentiate between broad types of income earned by corporations and tax such types of income differently. Generally, however, most such systems tax all income of a corporation in the same manner.

Some systems (e.g., Canada and the United States) tax corporations under the same framework of tax law as individuals. In such systems, there are normally taxation differences related to differences between the inherent natures of corporations and individuals or unincorporated entities. For example, individuals are not formed, amalgamated, or acquired, and corporations do not generally incur medical expenses except by way of compensating individuals.

Many systems allow tax credits for specific items. Such direct reductions of tax are commonly allowed for foreign taxes on the same income and for withholding tax. Often these credits are the same as those available to individuals or for members of flow through entities such as partnerships.

Most systems tax both domestic and foreign corporations. Often, domestic corporations are taxed on worldwide income while foreign corporations are taxed only on income from sources within the jurisdiction. Many jurisdictions imposing an income tax impose such tax income from a permanent establishment within the jurisdiction.

Corporations are also subject to property tax, payroll tax, withholding tax, excise tax, customs duties, value added tax, and other common taxes, generally in the same manner as other taxpayers. These, however, are rarely referred to as "corporate tax."

TAXABLE INCOME

Most systems impose income tax at a specified rate of tax times taxable income as defined in the system. Many systems define taxable income by reference to net income before income taxes per financial statements prepared under locally accepted accounting principles. Such income may be decreased for income subject to tax exemption. Other adjustments often apply. Some systems define taxable income within the system. The United States system defines taxable income for a corporation as all gross income (sales plus other income minus cost of goods sold and tax exempt income) less allowable tax deductions, without the allowance of the standard deduction applicable to individuals.

Principles for recognizing income and deductions may differ from financial accounting principles. Key areas of difference include differences in the timing of income or deduction, tax exemption for certain income, and disallowance or limitation of certain tax deductions. The United States system requires that these differences be disclosed in considerable detail for non-small corporations on Schedule M-3 to Form 1120.

Most systems tax resident corporations (generally those organized within the country) on their worldwide income, and nonresident corporations only on their income from sources within the country. A few systems, such as Hong Kong, tax resident and nonresident corporations only on income from sources within the country.

CORPORATE TAX RATES

Corporate tax rates generally are the same for differing types of income. However, many systems have graduated tax rate systems under which corporations with lower levels of income pay a lower rate of tax. Some systems impose tax at different rates for different types of corporations. Tax rates vary by jurisdiction. In addition, some countries have sub-country level jurisdictions that also impose corporate income tax. Some jurisdictions also impose tax at a different rate on an alternative tax base. Note that some entities may be eligible for tax exemption on part or all of their income in some jurisdictions.

Examples of corporate tax rates for a few English-speaking countries include:

- Australia: 30%, however some specialized entities are taxed at lower rates.
- Canada: Federal 11% or 15% plus provincial 1% to 16%. Note: the rates are additive.
- Hong Kong: 16.5%
- Ireland: 12.5% on trading (business) income, and 25% on nontrading income.
- New Zealand: 28%
- Singapore: 17% from 2010, however a partial exemption scheme may apply to new companies.
- United Kingdom: 21% to 26% for 2009–2011.
- United States: Federal 15% to 35%. States: 0% to 10%, deductible in computing Federal taxable income. Some cities: up to 9%, deductible in computing Federal taxable income. The Federal Alternative Minimum Tax of 20% is imposed on regular taxable income with adjustments.

DISTRIBUTION OF EARNINGS

Most systems that tax corporations also impose income tax on shareholders of corporations when earnings are distributed. Such distribution of earnings is generally referred to as a dividend. The tax may be at reduced rates. For example, the United States provides for reduced amounts of tax on dividends received by individuals and by corporations. By contrast, the United Kingdom provides for reduced amounts of tax only on dividends received by individuals.

The company law of some jurisdictions prevents corporations from distributing amounts to shareholders except as distribution of earnings. Such earnings may be determined under company law principles or tax principles. For example, the United Kingdom permits a company to make dividend distributions only up to the balance of earnings available for distribution according to its last audited accounts. In such jurisdictions, exceptions are usually provided with respect to distribution of shares of the company, for winding up, and in limited other situations.

Other jurisdictions treat distributions as distributions of earnings taxable to shareholders if earnings are available to be distributed, but do not prohibit distributions in excess of earnings. For example, under the United States system each corporation must maintain a calculation of its earnings and profits (a tax concept similar to retained earnings). A distribution to a shareholder is considered to be from earnings and profits to the extent thereof unless an exception applies. Note that the United States provides reduced tax on dividend income of both corporations and individuals.

Other jurisdictions provide corporations a means of designating, within limits, whether a distribution is a distribution of earnings taxable to the shareholder or a return of capital. For example, in Canada a corporation may designate a distribution to shareholders as a distribution of Paid Up Capital (PUC), and thus not taxable as a dividend, to the extent of remaining capital, or an eligible dividend.

OTHER CORPORATE EVENTS

Many systems provide that certain corporate events are not taxable to corporations or shareholders. Significant restrictions and special rules often apply. The rules related to such transactions are often quite complex.

Formation

Most systems treat the formation of a corporation by a controlling corporate shareholder as a nontaxable event. Many systems, including the United States and Canada, extend this tax free treatment to the formation of a corporation by any group of shareholders in control of the corporation. Generally, in tax free formations the tax attributes of assets and liabilities are transferred to the new corporation along with such assets and liabilities.

Example: John and Mary are United States residents who operate a business. They decide to incorporate for business reasons. They transfer the assets of the business to Newco, a newly formed Delaware corporation of which they are the sole shareholders, subject to accrued liabilities of the business in exchange solely for common shares of Newco. Under United States principles, this transfer does not cause tax to John, Mary, or Newco. If on the other hand Newco also assumes a bank loan in excess of the basis of the assets transferred less the accrued liabilities, John and Mary will recognize taxable gain for such excess.

Acquisitions

Corporations may merge or acquire other corporations in a manner a particular tax system treats as nontaxable to either of the corporations and/or to their shareholders. Generally, significant restrictions apply if tax free treatment is to be obtained. For example, Bigco acquires all of the shares of Smallco from Smallco shareholders in exchange solely for Bigco shares. This acquisition is not taxable to Smallco or its shareholders under U.S. or Canadian tax law if certain requirements are met, even if Smallco is then liquidated into or merged or amalgamated with Bigco.

Reorganizations

In addition, corporations may change key aspects of their legal identity, capitalization, or structure in a tax free manner under most systems. Examples of reorganizations that may be tax free include mergers, amalgamations, liquidations of subsidiaries, share for share exchanges, exchanges of shares for assets, changes in form or place of organization, and recapitalizations.

INTEREST DEDUCTION LIMITATIONS

Most jurisdictions allow a tax deduction for interest expense incurred by a corporation in carrying out its trading activities. Where such interest is paid to related parties, such deduction may be limited. Without such limitation, owners could structure financing of the corporation in a manner that would provide for a tax deduction for much of the profits, potentially without changing the tax on shareholders. For example, assume a corporation earns profits of 100 before interest expense and would normally distribute 50 to shareholders. If the corporation is structured so that deductible interest of 50 is payable to the shareholders, it will cut its tax to half the amount due if it merely paid a dividend.

A common form of limitation is to limit the deduction for interest paid to related parties to interest charged at arm's length rates on debt not exceeding a certain portion of the equity of the paying corporation. For example, interest paid on related party debt in excess of three times equity may not be deductible in computing taxable income.

The United States, United Kingdom, and French tax systems apply a more complex set of tests to limit deductions. Under the U.S. system, related party interest expense in excess of 50% of cash flow is generally not currently deductible, with the excess potentially deductible in future years.

The classification of instruments as debt on which interest is deductible or as equity with respect to which distributions are not deductible can be complex in some systems.

FOREIGN CORPORATION BRANCHES

Most jurisdictions tax foreign corporations differently than domestic corporations. No international laws limit the ability of a country to tax its nationals and residents (individuals and entities). However, treaties and practicality impose limits on taxation of those outside its borders, even on income from sources within the country.

Most jurisdictions tax foreign corporations on business income within the jurisdiction when earned through a branch or permanent establishment in the jurisdiction. This tax may be imposed at the same rate as the tax on business income of a resident corporation or at a different rate.

Upon payment of dividends, corporations are generally subject to withholding tax only by their country of incorporation. Many countries impose a branch profits tax on foreign corporations to prevent the advantage the absence of dividend withholding tax would otherwise provide to foreign corporations. This tax may be imposed at the time profits are earned by the branch or at the time they are remitted or deemed remitted outside the country. Branches of foreign corporations may not be entitled to all of the same deductions as domestic corporations. Some jurisdictions do not recognize inter-branch payments as actual payments, and income or deductions arising from such inter-branch payments are disregarded. Some jurisdictions impose express limits on tax deductions of branches. Commonly limited deductions include management fees and interest.

LOSSES

Most jurisdictions allow interperiod allocation or deduction of losses in some manner for corporations, even where such deduction is not allowed for individuals. A few jurisdictions allow losses (usually defined as negative taxable income) to be deducted by revising or amending prior year taxable income. Most jurisdictions allow such deductions only in subsequent periods. Some jurisdictions impose time limitations as to when loss deductions may be utilized.

GROUPS OF COMPANIES

Several jurisdictions provide a mechanism whereby losses or tax credits of one corporation may be used by another corporation where both corporations are commonly controlled (together, a group). In the United States and Netherlands, among others, this is accomplished by filing a single tax return including the income and loss of each group member. This is referred to as a consolidated return in the United States and as a fiscal unity in the Netherlands. In the United Kingdom, this is accomplished directly on a pairwise basis called group relief. Losses of one group member company may be "surrendered" to another group member company, and the latter company may deduct the loss against profits.

The United States has extensive regulations dealing with consolidated returns. One such rule requires matching of income and deductions on intercompany transactions within the group by use of "deferred intercompany transaction" rules.

In addition, a few systems provide a tax exemption for dividend income received by corporations. The Netherlands system provides a "participation exception" to taxation for corporations owning more than 25% of the dividend paying corporation.

TRANSFER PRICING

A key issue in corporate tax is the setting of prices charged by related parties for goods, services, or the use of property. Many jurisdictions have guidelines on such prices which allow tax authorities to adjust prices charged. Such adjustments may apply in both an international and a domestic context.

TAXATION OF SHAREHOLDERS

Most income tax systems levy tax on the corporation and, upon distribution of earnings (dividends), on the shareholder. This results in a dual level of tax. Most systems require that income tax be withheld on distribution of dividends to foreign shareholders, and some also require withholding of tax on distributions to domestic shareholders. The rate of such withholding tax may be reduced for a shareholder under a tax treaty.

Some systems tax some or all dividend income at lower rates than other income. The United States has historically provided a dividends received deduction to corporations with respect to dividends from other corporations in which the recipient owns more than 10% of the shares. For tax years 2004–2010, the United States also has imposed a reduced rate of taxation on dividends received by individuals.

Some systems currently attempt or in the past have attempted to integrate taxation of the corporation with taxation of shareholders to mitigate the dual level of taxation. As a current example, Australia provides for a "franking credit" as a benefit to shareholders. When an Australian company pays a dividend to a domestic shareholder, it reports the dividend as well as a notional tax credit amount. The shareholder utilizes this notional credit to offset shareholder level income tax.

A previous system was utilised in the United Kingdom, called the Advance Corporation Tax (ACT). When a company paid a dividend, it was required to pay an amount of ACT, which it then used to offset its own taxes. The ACT was included in income by the shareholder resident in the United Kingdom or certain treaty countries, and treated as a payment of tax by the shareholder. To the extent that deemed tax payment exceeded taxes otherwise due, it was refundable to the shareholder.

ALTERNATIVE TAX BASES

Many jurisdictions incorporate some sort of alternative tax computation. These computations may be based on assets, capital, wages, or some alternative measure of taxable income. Often the alternative tax functions as a minimum tax.

United States federal income tax incorporates an alternative minimum tax. This tax is computed at a lower tax rate (20% for corporations), and imposed based on a modified version of taxable income. Modifications include longer depreciation lives assets under MACRS, adjustments related to costs of developing natural resources, and an addback of certain tax exempt interest. The U. S. state of Michigan previously taxed businesses on an alternative base that did not allow compensation of employees as a tax deduction and allowed full deduction of the cost of production assets upon acquisition.

Some jurisdictions, such as Swiss cantons and certain states within the United States, impose taxes based on capital. These may be based on total equity per audited financial statements, a computed amount of assets less liabilities or quantity of shares outstanding. In some jurisdictions, capital based taxes are imposed in addition to the income tax. In other jurisdictions, the capital taxes function as alternative taxes.

Mexico imposes an alternative tax on corporations, the IETU. The tax rate is lower than the regular rate, and there are adjustments for salaries and wages, interest and royalties, and depreciable assets.

TAX RETURNS

Most systems require that corporations file an annual income tax return. Some systems (such as the Canadian and United States systems) require that taxpayers self assess tax on the tax return. Other systems provide that the government must make an assessment for tax to be due. Some systems require certification of tax returns in some manner by accountants licensed to practice in the jurisdiction, often the company's auditors.

Tax returns can be fairly simple or quite complex. The systems requiring simple returns often base taxable income on financial statement profits with few adjustments, and may require that audited financial statements be attached to the return. Returns for such systems generally require that the relevant financial statements be attached to a simple adjustment schedule.

By contrast, United States corporate tax returns require both computation of taxable income from components thereof and reconciliation of taxable income to financial statement income.

Many systems require forms or schedules supporting particular items on the main form. Some of these schedules may be incorporated into the main form. For example, the Canadian corporate return, Form T-2, an 8 page form, incorporates some detail schedules but has nearly 50 additional schedules that may be required. Some systems have different returns for different types of corporations or corporations engaged in specialized businesses. The United States has 13 variations on the basic Form 1120 for S corporations, insurance companies, Domestic international sales corporations, foreign corporations, and other entities. The structure of the forms and imbedded schedules vary by type of form.

Preparation of non-simple corporate tax returns can be time consuming. For example, the U.S. Internal Revenue Service states in the instructions for Form 1120 that the average time needed to complete form is over 56 hours, not including record keeping time and required attachments.

Tax return due dates vary by jurisdiction, fiscal or tax year, and type of entity. In self-assessment systems, payment of taxes is generally due no later than the normal due date, though advance tax payments may be required. Canadian corporations must pay estimated taxes monthly. In each case, final payment is due with the corporation tax return.

NEGATIVE INCOME TAX

In economics, a negative income tax (abbreviated NIT) is a progressive income tax system where people earning below a certain amount receive supplemental pay from the government instead of paying taxes to the government. Such a system has been discussed by economists but never fully implemented. It was developed by British politician Juliet Rhys-Williams in the 1940s and later by United States economist Milton Friedman.

Negative income taxes can implement a basic income or supplement a guaranteed minimum income system.

In a negative income tax system, people earning a certain income level would owe no taxes; those earning more than that would pay a proportion of their income above that level; and those below that level would receive a payment of a proportion of their shortfall, which is the amount their income falls below that level.

GENERAL WELFARE

A negative income tax is intended to create a single system that would not only pay for government, but would also fulfill the social goal of making sure that there was a minimum level of income for all. It is theorized that, with an NIT, the need for minimum wage, food stamps, welfare, social security programs and other government assistance programs could be eliminated, thus reducing the administrative effort and cost to a fraction of what it is under the current system, as well as eliminating the perverse incentives created by these overlapping aid programs, e.g. when a minimum wage worker who earns a little more nets out with less income because he is newly ineligible for aid. The worker is stuck in a welfare trap and has no incentive to seek higher wages. A NIT does not disrupt low-wage markets, whereas a minimum wage makes certain very low end jobs impossible (as anyone whose labour is valued at less than the minimum wage must be unemployed). A NIT would therefore increase the availability of cheap labour, which would enable businesses to do domestically some of the work which they would otherwise have to outsource to other countries.

A NIT would reduce administrative overhead, since the large bureaucracies responsible for administering taxation and welfare systems, with the multitude of rules, thresholds and different applications required, could be eliminated. The resources saved by eliminating these bureaucracies could then be spent on more productive government activities, or returned to the people via tax cuts.

A NIT is also expected to have an immediate stabilizing effect as well as a positive influence on the cycle of economic "boom and bust" (during recession, the minimum income aids individuals' confidence whilst businesses are aided by option to lower wages).

SPECIFIC MODELS

Various different models of negative income tax have been proposed. One model was proposed by Milton Friedman. In this version, a specified proportion of unused deductions or allowances would be refunded to the taxpayer. If, for a family of four the amount of allowances came out to $10,000, and the subsidy rate was 50% (the rate recommended by Friedman), and the family earned $6,000, the family would receive $2,000, because it left $4,000 of allowances unused, and therefore qualifies for $2,000, half that amount. Friedman feared that subsidy rates as high as those would lessen the incentive to obtain employment. He also warned that the negative income tax, as an addition to the "ragbag" of welfare and assistance programs, would only worsen the problem of bureaucracy and waste. Instead, he argued, the negative income tax should immediately replace all other welfare and assistance programs on the way to a completely laissez-faire society where all welfare is privately administered. The negative income tax has come up in one form or another in Congress, but Friedman eventually opposed it because it came packaged with other undesirable elements antithetical to the efficacy of the negative income tax. Friedman preferred to have no income tax at all, but said he did not think it was politically feasible at that time to eliminate it, so he suggested this as a less harmful income tax scheme.

Flat tax with negative income tax

The effort for reporting and supervision can be significantly reduced by combining basic income with flat income tax. The relationship between gross and net income for individuals can be adjusted to correspond roughly to current relationship at all income levels, implying that income tax is effectively progressive. A flat rate income taxation with tax exemption implements a negative income tax as well as maintaining an actual tax rate progression at extremely low administrative cost. This is achieved by paying a *tax on the tax exemption to all taxpayers,* e.g. in monthly payments. The tax on the tax exemption is computed by applying the nominal flat tax rate to the exemption. The tax on the income is drawn directly *from the source,* e.g. from an employer. The tax on income is computed by applying the nominal flat tax rate to the income.

This simple method results in an effective progressive rate taxation (although the tax rate for the taxes drawn at the source is flat) which is positive once the income exceeds the tax exemption. If, however, the income is less than the tax exemption, the effective progressive rate actually becomes negative without any involvement by any tax authority. As for the positive progression, only very high incomes would lead to an actual tax rate which is close to the nominal flat tax rate.

The tax on tax exemption also can be understood as a tax credit, which is paid back once an income has reached the level of the tax exemption. This level marks the point where paid taxes and the tax credit are equal. Above that point the state earns taxes from the taxpayer. Below that point the state pays taxes to the taxpayer.

Flat tax implementations *without* the provision of a negative income tax actually need an *additional* effort in order to *avoid* negative taxation. For such a tax, the exemption only can be paid after knowing the earned income. Flat tax implementations *with* negative income tax allow to pay the tax on the tax exemption independent of the amount of the actual income.

IMPLEMENTATION

While the notion has long been popular in some circles, its implementation has never been politically feasible. This is partly because of the very complex and entrenched nature of most countries' current tax laws: they would have to be rewritten under any NIT system. However, some countries have seen the introduction of refundable (or non-wastable) tax credits which can be paid even when there is no tax liability to be offset, such as the Earned Income Tax Credit in the United States and working tax credit in the UK. Under President Richard Nixon, a NIT proposal almost made it through Congress.

From 1968 to 1979, the largest negative income tax social experiments in the US were undertaken. The first experiment was the New Jersey Income Maintenance Experiment, proposed by MIT Economics graduate student

Heather Ross in 1967 in a proposal to the U.S. Office of Economic Opportunity. The four experiments were in:

1. The New Jersey Income Maintenance Experiment: Trenton, Passaic, Paterson, and Jersey City, New Jersey with Scranton, Pennsylvania added to increase the number of white families, 1968–1972 (1375 families)
2. The Rural Income Maintenance Experiment: Rural areas in Iowa and North Carolina, 1969–1973 (809 families)
3. Gary, Indiana, 1971–1974 (1800 families)
4. Seattle and Denver, 1971–1982 (4800 families)

In general they found that workers would decrease labor supply (employment) by two to four weeks per year because of the guarantee of income equal to the poverty threshold.

A negative income tax has been implemented for a certain bracket of low incomes in Israel.

ADVOCATES

- In Australia, a negative income tax is advocated by the Liberal Democratic Party as part of their tax policy.
- In Slovakia, welfare and tax system reform based on NIT is proposed by classical liberal Freedom and Solidarity party.
- In the United States, a negative income tax was advocated by the Green Party as part of their 2010 platform.

CRITICISM

A drawback is one common to any income-based tax system: it requires reporting and supervision in order to avoid fraud. The added expense of policing fraud could be offset by the benefit from reducing administration costs resulting in a net decrease in costs.

Another criticism is that the NIT might reduce the incentive to work, since recipients of the NIT would receive a guaranteed minimum wage equal to the government payment in the absence of employment. A series of studies in the United States beginning in 1968 attempted to test for effects on work incentives. Jodie Allen summarizes the key studies:

- The Stanford Research Institute (SRI), which analyzed the SIME/DIME findings, found stronger work disincentive effects, ranging from an average 9 percent work reduction for husbands to an average 18 percent reduction for wives. This was not as scary as some NIT opponents had predicted. But it was large enough to suggest that as much as 50 to 60 percent of the transfers paid to two-parent families under a NIT might go to replace lost earnings. They also found an unexpected result: instead of promoting family stability (the presumed result of extending benefits to two-parent working families on an equal basis), the NITs seemed to increase family breakup.

FLAT TAX

A flat tax (short for flat tax rate) is a tax system with a constant marginal rate, usually applied to individual or corporate income. A flat tax falls under proportional tax as they allow certain deductions. There are various tax systems that are labeled "flat tax" even though they are significantly different.

MAJOR CATEGORIES

Flat tax proposals differ in how they define what is subject to tax.

"True" flat rate income tax

A *true* flat rate tax is a system of taxation where one tax rate is applied to all income with no deductions or exemptions.

Marginal flat tax

When deductions are allowed a 'flat tax' is a progressive tax with the special characteristic that above the maximum deduction, the rate on all further income is constant. Thus it is said to be marginally flat above that point. The conceptual difference between a true flat tax and a marginally flat tax, can be unified by recognizing that the latter simply excludes certain kinds of funds from being defined as income. Then they are both flat on "taxable" income.

There are many proposed marginal flat taxes systems. Specific flat tax systems enumerated at the bottom of this article primarily intermix aspects of three high level approaches:

Flat tax with limited deductions

Modified flat taxes have been proposed which would allow deductions for a very few items, while still eliminating the vast majority of existing deductions. Charitable deductions and home mortgage interest are the most discussed exceptions, as these are popular with voters and often used. Another common theme is a single, large, fixed deduction; the concept here is that this blanket deduction rolls up a myriad of ubiquitous, fixed, living costs and has the simplifying side-effect that many (low income) people will not even have to file tax returns.

Hall–Rabushka flat tax

Designed by economists at the Hoover Institution, Hall–Rabushka is flat tax on consumption. Principally, Hall–Rabushka accomplishes a consumption tax effect by taxing income and then excluding investment. Robert Hall and Alvin Rabushka have consulted extensively in designing the flat tax systems in Eastern Europe.

Negative income tax

The negative income tax (NIT), which Milton Friedman proposed in his 1962 book *Capitalism and Freedom,* is a type of flat tax. The basic idea is the same as a flat tax with personal deductions, except that when deductions exceed income, the taxable income is allowed to become negative rather than being set to zero. The flat tax rate is then applied to the resulting "negative income," resulting in a "negative income tax" the government owes the household, unlike the usual "positive" income tax, which the household owes the government.

For example, let the flat rate be 20%, and let the deductions be $20,000 per adult and $7,000 per dependent. Under such a system, a family of four making $54,000 a year would owe no tax. A family of four making $74,000 a year would owe tax amounting to 0.20 × (74,000 " 54,000) = $4,000, as under a flat tax with deductions. But families of four earning less than $54,000 per year would owe a "negative" amount of tax (that is, it would receive money from the government). For example, if it earned $34,000 a year, it would receive a check for $4,000. The NIT is intended to replace not just the USA's income tax, but also many benefits low income American households receive, such as food stamps and Medicaid. The NIT is designed to avoid the welfare trap—effective high marginal tax rates arising from the rules reducing benefits as market income rises. An objection to the NIT is that it is welfare without a work requirement. Those who would owe negative tax would be receiving a form of welfare without having to make an effort to obtain employment. Another objection is that the NIT subsidizes industries employing low cost labor, but this objection can also be made against current systems of benefits for the working poor.

Capped flat tax

A capped flat tax is one in which income is taxed at a flat rate until a specified cap is reached. For example, in 2010, the United States Social Security and Medicare payroll tax assessed a flat rate of 7.65% on all income under $106,800 and only 1.45% above that level. Thus, someone earning $100,000 paid $7,650 (a rate of 7.65%) while someone earning $1,000,000 paid $21,122 (an effective rate of 2.11%). This cap has the effect of turning a nominally flat tax into a regressive tax.

REQUIREMENTS FOR A FULLY DEFINED SCHEMA

In devising a flat tax system, several recurring issues must be enumerated, principally with deductions and the identification of when money is earned.

Defining when income occurs

Since a central tenet of the flat tax is to minimize the compartmentalization of incomes into myriad special or sheltered cases, a vexing problem is deciding when income occurs. This is demonstrated by the taxation of interest income and stock dividends. The shareholders own the company and so the company's profits belong to them. If a company is taxed on its profits, then the funds paid out as dividends have already been taxed. It's a debatable question if they should subsequently be treated as income to the shareholders and thus subject to further tax. A similar issue arises in deciding if interest paid on loans should be deductible from the taxable income since that interest is in-turn taxed as income to the loan provider. There is no universally agreed answer to what is fair. For example, in the United States, dividends are not deductible but mortgage interest is deductible. *Thus a Flat Tax proposal is not fully defined until it differentiates* new *untaxed income from a pass-through of already taxed income.*

Policy administration

Taxes, in addition to providing revenue, can be potent instruments of policy. For example, it is common for governments to encourage social policy such as home insulation or low income housing with tax credits rather than constituting a ministry to implement these policies. In a flat tax system with limited deductions such policy administration mechanisms are curtailed. In addition to social policy, flat taxes can remove tools for adjusting economic policy as well. For example, in the United States, short-term capital gains are taxed at a higher rate than long-term gains as means to promote long-term investment horizons and damp speculative fluctuation. *Thus claims that flat taxes are cheaper/simpler to administer than others are incomplete until they factor in costs for alternative policy administration.*

Avoiding deductions

In general, the question of how to eliminate deductions is fundamental to the flat tax design: deductions dramatically affect the effective "flatness" in the tax rate. Perhaps the single biggest necessary deduction is for business expenses. If businesses were not allowed to deduct expenses, businesses with a profit margin below the flat tax rate could never earn any money since the tax on revenues would always exceed the earnings. For example, grocery stores typically earn pennies on every dollar of revenue; they could not pay a tax rate of 25% on revenues unless their markup exceeded 25%. Thus, corporations must be able to deduct operating expenses even if individual citizens cannot. A practical difficulty now arises as to identifying what is an expense for a business.

For example, if peanut butter makers purchase a jar manufacturer, is that an expense (since they have to purchase jars somehow) or a sheltering of their income through investment? Flat tax systems can differ greatly in how they accommodate such gray areas. For example, the "9-9-9" flat tax proposal would allow businesses to deduct purchases but not labor costs. (This effectively taxes labor-intensive industrial revenue at a higher rate.) How deductions are implemented will dramatically change the effective total tax and thus the flatness of the tax. Thus, a flat tax proposal is not fully defined until it differentiates deductible and non-deductible expenses.

TAX EFFECTS

Equity of distribution

Introduction of flat tax may remove preexisting tax deductions. This may lead to unequal distribution for various income brackets that other tax methods also do.

Diminishing Marginal Utility

Flat tax benefits higher income brackets progressively due to decline in marginal value. For example, if a flat tax system has a large per-citizen deductible (such as the "Armey" scheme below), then it is a progressive tax. As a result, sometimes the term Flat Tax is actually a shorthand for the more proper marginally flat tax.

Administration and enforcement

One type of flat tax taxes all income once at its source. Hall and Rabushka (1995) includes a proposed amendment to the US Revenue Code implementing the variant of the flat tax they advocate. This amendment, only a few pages long, would replace hundreds of pages of statutory language (although it is important to note that much statutory language in taxation statutes is *not* directed at specifying graduated tax rates). As it now stands, the USA Revenue Code is over 9 million words long and contains many loopholes, deductions, and exemptions which, advocates of flat taxes claim, render the collection of taxes and the enforcement of tax law complicated and inefficient. It is further argued that current tax law retards economic growth by distorting economic incentives, and by allowing, even encouraging, tax avoidance. With a flat tax, there are fewer incentives than in the current system to create tax shelters and to engage in other forms of tax avoidance. Flat tax critics contend that a flat tax system could be created with many loopholes, or a progressive tax system without loopholes, and that a progressive tax system could be as simple, or simpler, than a flat tax system. A simple progressive tax would also discourage tax avoidance.

Under a pure flat tax without deductions, every tax period a company would make a single payment to the government covering the taxes on the employees and the taxes on the company profit. For example, suppose that in a given year, ACME earns a profit of 3 million, spends 2 million in wages, and spends 1 million on other expenses the IRS deems to be taxable income, such as stock options, bonuses, and certain executive privileges. Given a flat rate of 15%, ACME would then owe the IRS (3M + 2M + 1M) × 0.15 = 900,000. This payment would, in one fell swoop, settle the tax liabilities of ACME's employees as well as the corporate taxes owed by ACME. Most employees throughout the economy would never need to interact with the IRS, as all tax owed on wages, interest, dividends, royalties, etc. would be withheld at the source. The main exceptions would be employees with incomes from personal ventures. The *Economist* claims that such a system would reduce the number of entities required to file returns from about 130 million individuals, households, and businesses, as at present, to a mere 8 million businesses and self-employed.

However this simplicity relies on there being no deductions of any kind allowed (or at least no variability in the deductions of different people). Furthermore, if income of differing types are segregated (e.g., pass-thru, long term cap gains, regular income, etc.) then complications ensue. For example, if realized capital gains were subject to the flat tax, the law would require brokers and mutual funds to calculate the realized capital gain on all sales and redemption. If there were a gain, 15% of the gain would be withheld and sent to the IRS. If there were a loss, the amount would be reported to the IRS, which would offset gains with losses and settle up with taxpayers at the end of the period. Lacking deductions this scheme cannot be used to implement economic and social policy indirectly by tax credits, and thus, as noted above, the simplifications to the government's revenue collection apparatus may be offset by new government ministries required to administer those policies.

Revenues

The Russian Federation is a considered a prime case of the success of a flat tax; the real revenues from its Personal Income Tax rose by 25.2% in the first year after the Federation introduced a flat tax, followed by a 24.6% increase in the second year, and a 15.2% increase in the third year. The Laffer curve predicts such an outcome, attributing the primary reason for the greater revenue to higher levels of economic growth stemming from the introduction of the flat tax.

The Russian example is often used as proof of the validity of this analysis, despite an International Monetary Fund study in 2006 which found that there was no sign "of Laffer-type behavioral responses generating revenue increases from the tax cut elements of these reforms" in Russia or in other countries.

Overall structure

Taxes other than the income tax (for example, taxes on sales and payrolls) tend to be regressive. Hence, making the income tax flat could result in a regressive overall tax structure. Under such a structure, those with lower incomes tend to pay a *higher* proportion of their income in total taxes than the affluent do. The fraction of household income that is a return to capital (dividends, interest, royalties, profits of unincorporated businesses) is positively correlated with total household income. Hence a flat tax limited to wages would seem to leave the wealthy better off. Modifying the tax base can change the effects. A flat tax could be targeted at income (rather than wages), which could place the tax burden equally on all earners, including those who earn income primarily from returns on investment. Tax systems could utilize a flat sales tax to target all consumption, which can be modified with rebates or exemptions to remove regressive effects (such as the proposed FairTax in the U.S.).

Border adjustable

A flat tax system and income taxes overall are not inherently border-adjustable; meaning the tax component embedded into products via taxes imposed on companies (including corporate taxes and payroll taxes) are not removed when exported to a foreign country. Taxation systems such as a sales tax or value added tax can remove the tax component when goods are exported and apply the tax component on imports. The domestic products could be at a disadvantage to foreign products (at home and abroad) that are border-adjustable, which would impact the global competitiveness of a country. However, it's possible that a flat tax system could be combined with tariffs and credits to act as border adjustments (the proposed *Border Tax Equity Act* in the U.S. attempts this). Implementing an income tax with a border adjustment tax credit is a violation of the World Trade Organization agreement. Tax exemptions (allowances) on low income wages, a component of most income tax systems could mitigate this issue for high labour content industries like textiles that compete Globally.

In a subsequent section, various proposals for flat tax-like schemes are discussed, these differ mainly on how they approach with the following issues of deductions, defining income, and policy implementation.

STAMP DUTY

Stamp duty is a tax that is levied on documents. Historically, this included the majority of legal documents such as cheques, receipts, military commissions, marriage licences and land transactions. A physical stamp (a revenue stamp) had to be attached to or impressed upon the document to denote that stamp duty had been paid before the document was legally effective. More modern versions of the tax no longer require an actual stamp.

The duty is thought to have originated in Spain, being introduced (or re-invented) in the Netherlands in the 1620s, France in 1651, Denmark in 1657, Prussia in 1682 and England in 1694.

TURNOVER TAX

A turnover tax is similar to a sales tax or a VAT, with the difference that it taxes intermediate and possibly capital goods. It is an indirect tax, typically on an ad valorem basis, applicable to a production process or stage. For example, when manufacturing activity is completed, a tax may be charged on some companies. Sales tax occurs when merchandise has been sold. In South Africa, the turnover tax is a simple tax on the gross income of small businesses. Businesses who elect to pay the turnover tax are exempt from VAT. Turnover tax is at a very low rate compared to most taxes, but it is calculated on gross income without any deductions.

PROPERTY TAX

A property tax (or millage tax) is a levy on property that the owner is required to pay. The tax is levied by the governing authority of the jurisdiction in which the property is located; it may be paid to a national government, a federated state, a county/geographical region, or a municipality. Multiple jurisdictions may tax the same property.

There are four broad types of property: land, improvements to land (immovable man-made objects, such as buildings), personal property (movable man-made objects), and intangible property. Real property (also called real estate or realty) means the combination of land and improvements. Under a property tax system, the government requires and/or performs an appraisal of the monetary value of each property, and tax is assessed in proportion to that value. Forms of property tax used vary among countries and jurisdictions.

A special assessment tax is sometimes confused with property tax. These are two distinct forms of taxation: one (ad valorem tax) relies upon the fair market value of the property being taxed for justification, and the other (special assessment) relies upon a special enhancement called a "benefit" for its justification.

The *property tax rate* is often given as a percentage. It may also be expressed as a per mil (amount of tax per thousand currency units of property value), which is also known as a *millage rate* or *mill* (which is also one-thousandth of a currency unit). To calculate the property tax, the authority will multiply the assessed value of the property by the mill rate and then divide by 1,000. For example, a property with an assessed value of $50,000 located in a municipality with a mill rate of 20 mills would have a property tax bill of $1,000 per year.

PAYROLL TAX

Payroll taxes are taxes that employers are required to pay when they pay their staff their salaries. Payroll taxes generally fall into two categories: deductions from an employee's wages and taxes paid by the employer based on the employee's wages. The first kind are taxes that employers are required to withhold from employees' wages, also known as withholding tax, pay-as-you-earn tax (PAYE), or pay-as-you-go tax (PAYG) and often covering advance payment of income tax, social security contributions, and various insurances (e.g., unemployment and disability). The second kind is a tax that is paid from the employer's own funds and that is directly related to employing a worker. These can consist of fixed charges or be proportionally linked to an employee's pay. The charges paid by the employer usually cover the employer's funding of the social security system, and other insurance programs.

LAND VALUE TAX

A land value tax (or site valuation tax) is a levy on the unimproved value of land only. It is an *ad valorem* tax on land that disregards the value of buildings, personal property and other improvements. A land value tax (LVT) is different from other property taxes, because these are taxes on the whole value of real estate: the combination of land, buildings, and improvements to the site.

Although the efficiency of a land value tax has been established knowledge since Adam Smith, it was perhaps most famously promoted by Henry George. In his best selling work *Progress and Poverty* (1879), George argued that when the site or location value of land was improved by public works, its economic rent was the most logical source of public revenue.

Land value taxation has currently been implemented throughout Denmark, Estonia, Russia, Singapore, and Taiwan. The tax has been applied in subregions of Australia (New South Wales), China (Hong Kong), Mexico (Mexicali), and the United States (Pennsylvania).

INHERITANCE TAX

An inheritance tax or estate tax is a levy paid by a person who inherits money or property or a tax on the estate (total value of the money and property) of a person who has died. In international tax law, there is a distinction between an estate tax and an inheritance tax: an estate tax is assessed on the assets of the deceased, while an inheritance tax is assessed on the legacies received by the beneficiaries of the estate. However, this distinction is not always respected in the language of tax laws. For example, the "inheritance tax" in the United Kingdom is a tax on the assets of the deceased, and is therefore, strictly speaking, an estate tax. In some jurisdictions the term used is death duty. For historical reasons that term is used colloquially (though not legally) in the United Kingdom and some Commonwealth nations.

GIFT TAX

In economics, a gift tax is the tax on money or property that one living person gives to another. Items received upon the death of another are considered separately under the inheritance tax. Many gifts are not subject to taxation because of exemptions given in tax laws. The gift tax amount varies by jurisdiction, and international comparison of rates is complex and fluid.

7

Economics and Tax

THEORY OF TAXATION

Several theories of taxation exist in public economics. Governments at all levels (national, regional and local) need to raise revenue from a variety of sources to finance public-sector expenditures. The details of taxation are guided by two principles: who will benefit, and who can pay.

PUBLIC EXPENDITURE

Public expenditure concerns the optimal provision of public goods. In public-finance literature, there are two theories: the ability theory (presented by Arthur Cecil Pigou) and the benefit theory (developed by Erik Lindahl). The benefit theory has a modern version, known as the "voluntary exchange" theory.

PRINCIPLES OF TAXATION

Most governments collect funds from various sources to provide public services or to finance transfer payments. Taxation is the most common source of revenue in mixed economies. Under the benefit theory, tax levels are automatically determined, because taxpayers pay proportionately for the government benefits they receive. In other words, the individuals who benefit the most from public services pay the most taxes. In analyzing the benefit approach, two models have been discussed: the Lindahl model and the Bowen model.

LINDAHL'S MODEL

Lindahl tries to solve three problems:

- Extent of state activity
- Allocation of the total expenditure among various goods and services
- Allocation of tax burden

In the Lindahl model, if SS is the supply curve of state services it is assumed that production of social goods is linear and homogenous. DDa is the demand curve of taxpayer A, and DDb is the demand curve of taxpayer B. The vertical summation of the two demand curves results in the community's total demand schedule for state services.

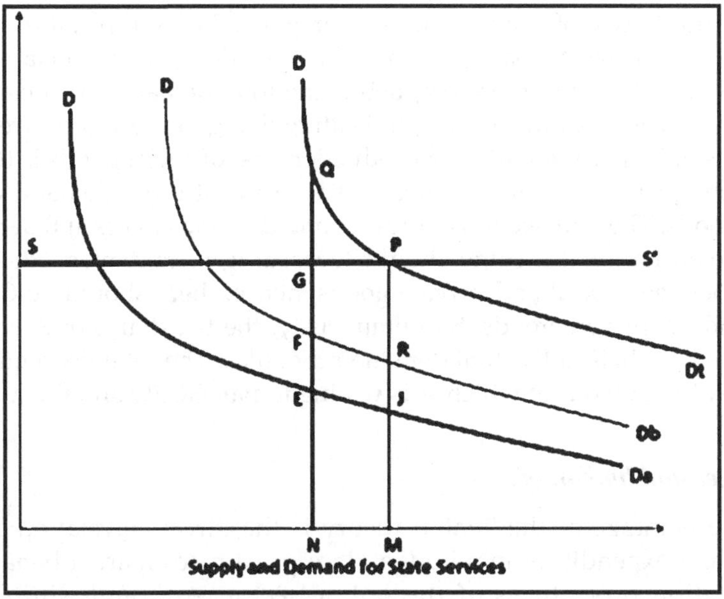

A and B pay different proportions of the cost of the services. When ON is the amount of state services produced, A contributes NE and B contributes NF; the cost of supply is NG. Since the state is non-profit, it increases its supply to OM. At this level, A contributes MJ and B contributes MR (the total cost of supply). Equilibrium is reached at point P on a voluntary-exchange basis.

Bowen's model

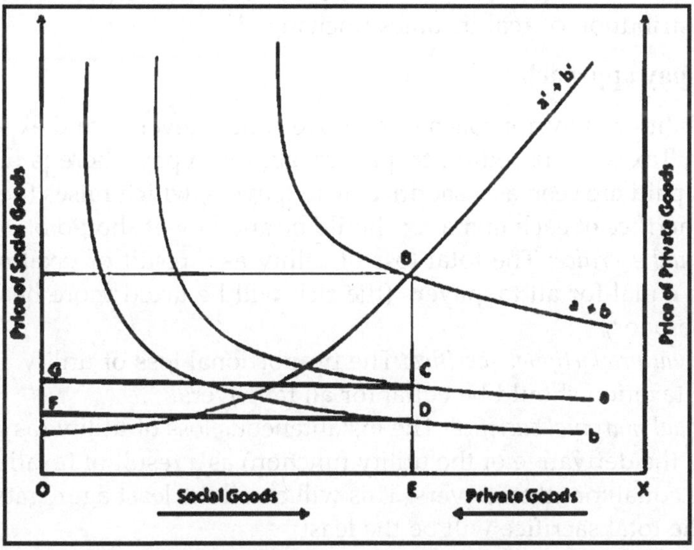

Bowen's model has more operational significance, since it demonstrates that when social goods are produced under conditions of increasing costs, the opportunity cost of private goods is foregone. For example, if there is one social good and two taxpayers (A and B), their demand for social goods is represented by a and b; therefore, a+b is the total demand for social goods. The supply curve is shown by a+b, indicating that goods are produced under conditions of increasing cost. The production cost of social goods is the value of foregone private goods; this means that a+b is also the demand curve of private goods. The intersection of the cost and demand curves at B determines how a given national income should (according to taxpayers' desires) be divided between social and private goods; hence, there should be OE social goods and EX private goods. Simultaneously, the tax shares of A and B are determined by their individual demand schedules. The total tax requirement is the area (ABEO) out of which A is willing to pay GCEO and B is willing to pay FDEO.

Advantages and limitations

The advantage of the benefit theory is the direct correlation between revenue and expenditure in a budget. It approximates market behaviour in the allocation procedures of the public sector. Although simple in its application, the benefit theory has difficulties:

- It limits the scope of government activities
- Government can neither support the poor nor take steps to stabilize the economy
- Applicable only when beneficiaries can be observed directly (impossible for most public services)
- Taxation in accord with the benefit principle would leave distribution of real incomes unchanged

Ability-to-pay approach

The ability-to-pay approach treats government revenue and expenditures separately. Taxes are based on taxpayers' ability to pay; there is no *quid pro quo*. Taxes paid are seen as a sacrifice by taxpayers, which raises the issues of what the sacrifice of each taxpayer should be and how it should be measured:

- *Equal sacrifice:* The total loss of utility as a result of taxation should be equal for all taxpayers (the rich will be taxed more heavily than the poor)
- *Equal proportional sacrifice:* The proportional loss of utility as a result of taxation should be equal for all taxpayers
- *Equal marginal sacrifice:* The instantaneous loss of utility (as measured by the derivative of the utility function) as a result of taxation should be equal for all taxpayers. This will entail the least aggregate sacrifice (the total sacrifice will be the least)

The three types of sacrifices have been demonstrated by Richard Musgrave. In the ability-to-pay model illustrated, total utility is C and marginal utility is O. CE is total utility, and CF is the marginal utility of income. When an income-yielding tax (MG) is levied, under equal absolute sacrifice, A will pay NG and B will pay TH (TH+NG=MG). Under equal proportional sacrifice, A pays RG and B pays SH (SH+RG=MG). The shares are arranged so EW÷EI=KU÷KJ. Under equal marginal sacrifice, A pays VG and B pays VH (VG+VH=MG). The aggregate sacrifice (EX+KY) is at minimum.

Mathematically, the conditions are as follows:

- Equal absolute sacrifice=U(Y)-U(Y-T), where y=income and t=tax amount
- Equal proportional sacrifice=(U(Y)-U(Y-T))/U(Y), where U(Y)=total utility from y
- Equal marginal sacrifice=(dU(Y-T))/(d(Y-T))

EFFECT OF TAXES AND SUBSIDIES ON PRICE

Taxes and subsidies change the price of goods and, as a result, the quantity consumed.

SUBSIDY IMPACT

Marginal subsidies on production will shift the supply curve to the right until the vertical distance between the two supply curves is equal to the per unit subsidy; when other things remain equal, this will decrease price paid by the consumers (which is equal to the new market price) and increase the price received by the producers. Similarly, a marginal subsidy on consumption will shift the demand curve to the right; when other things remain equal, this will decrease the price paid by consumers and increase the price received by producers by the same amount as if the subsidy had been granted to producers.

However, in this case, the new market price will be the price received by producers. The end result is that the lower price that consumers pay and the higher price that producers receive will be the same, regardless of how the subsidy is administered.

EFFECT OF ELASTICITY

Depending on the price elasticities of demand and supply, who bears more of the tax or who receives more of the subsidy may differ. Where the supply curve is more inelastic than the demand curve, producers bear more of the tax and receive more of the subsidy than consumers as the difference between the price producers receive and the initial market price is greater than the difference borne by consumers.

Where the demand curve is more inelastic than the supply curve, the consumers bear more of the tax and receive more of the subsidy as the difference between the price consumers pay and the initial market price is greater than the difference borne by producers.

AN ILLUSTRATION

The effect of this type of tax can be illustrated on a standard supply and demand diagram. Without a tax, the equilibrium price will be at *Pe* and the equilibrium quantity will be at *Qe*.

After a tax is imposed, the price consumers pay will shift to *Pc* and the price producers receive will shift to *Pp*. The consumers' price will be equal to the producers' price plus the cost of the tax. Since consumers will buy less at the higher consumer price (*Pc*) and producers will sell less at a lower producer price (*Pp*), the quantity sold will fall from *Qe* to *Qt*.

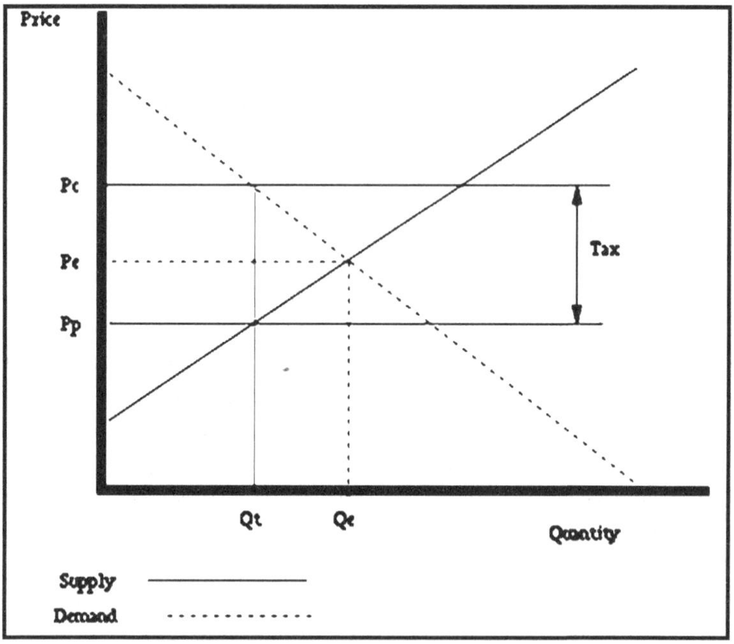

EXCESS BURDEN OF TAXATION

In economics, the excess burden of taxation, also known as the distortionary cost or deadweight loss of taxation, is one of the economic losses that society suffers as the result of a tax. Economic theory posits that distortions changes the amount and type of economic behavior from that which would occur in a free market without the tax.

Excess burdens can be measured using the average cost of funds or the marginal cost of funds (MCF). Excess burdens were first discussed by Adam Smith.

An equivalent kind of inefficiency can also be caused by subsidies (that are actually taxes with negative rates).

Economic losses due to taxes were evaluated to be as low as 2.5 cents per dollar of revenue, and as high as 30 cents per dollar of revenue (on average), and even much higher at the margins.

MEASURES OF THE EXCESS BURDEN

The cost of a distortion is usually measured as the amount that would have to be paid to the people affected by its supply, the greater the excess burden. The second is the tax rate: as a general rule, the excess burden of a tax increases with the square of the tax rate.

The average cost of funds is the total cost of distortions divided by the total revenue collected by a government. In contrast, the *marginal* cost of funds (MCF) is the size of the distortion that accompanied the last unit of revenue raised (i.e. the rate of change of distortion with respect to revenue). In most cases, the MCF increases as the amount of tax collected increases.

The standard position in economics is that the costs in a cost-benefit analysis for any tax-funded project should be increased according to the marginal cost of funds, because that is close to the deadweight loss that will be experienced if the project is added to the budget, or to the deadweight loss removed if the project is removed from the budget.

DISTORTION AND REDISTRIBUTION

In the case of progressive taxes, the distortionary effects of a tax may be accompanied by other benefits: the redistribution of dollars from wealthier people to poorer people who could possibly obtain more benefit from them.

In fact almost any tax measure will distort the economy from the path or process that would have prevailed in its absence (land value taxes are a notable exception). For example a sales tax applied to all goods will tend to discourage consumption of all the taxed items, and an income tax will tend to discourage people from earning money in the category of income that is taxed (unless they can manage to avoid being taxed). Some people may move out of the work force (to avoid income tax); some may move into the cash or black economies (where incomes are not revealed to the tax authorities).

For example, in Western nations the incomes of the relatively affluent are taxed partly to provide the money used to assist the relatively poor. As a result of the taxes (and associated subsidies to the poor), incentives are changed for both groups. The relatively rich are discouraged from declaring income and from earning marginal (extra) income, because they know that any additional money that they earn and declare will be taxed at their highest marginal tax rates. At the same time the poor have an incentive to conceal their own taxable income (and usually their assets) so as to increase the likelihood of their receiving state assistance. It can be argued that the distortion of incentives (the move away from a fiscally neutral stance that does not affect incentives) does more harm than good.

One of the main distortions sometimes said to have arisen in the USA and the UK as a result of tax policy is the creation of a permanent underclass, dependent on welfare and discouraged (by the tax system) from seeking work and betterment. In some countries the tax system can be badly designed to deal with such issues, e.g. sometimes the marginal tax rate that applies to earned income (as someone takes work attempting to escape from unemployment and welfare) is so high that the person's take-home income (post-tax and after taking account of any benefits or welfare receipts) does not increase as a result of taking work. This is known as the welfare trap.

There was an example of distortion of the economy by tax policy some years ago in the UK when cars supplied by employers to their employees were taxed at advantageous rates (e.g. encouraging the growth of company car fleets). Over several years the distortion grew to the point that the majority of cars used by working families were company cars and the dealership structures, and even the types of cars used, altered to adjust to the tax regime.

DELIBERATE DISTORTION

Not all distortions are bad; Pigovian taxes create distortions that correct for externalities and therefore have a negative MCF.

Here, the fiscal distortion is deliberate, so as to compensate for externalities. "Sin taxes" are levied on products that incur additional costs to society, such as alcohol, tobacco and pollution. Ideally, these taxes raise the price to the exact level that the market would bear if the negative externalities were included in the price. Pigovian taxes are often preferable to outright prohibition, since prohibition incites trafficking, often resulting in crime and other social costs, but no revenue.

TAX INCIDENCE

In economics, tax incidence is the analysis of the effect of a particular tax on the distribution of economic welfare. Tax incidence is said to "fall" upon the group that ultimately bears the burden of, or ultimately has to pay, the tax. The key concept is that the tax incidence or tax burden does not depend on where the revenue is collected, but on the price elasticity of demand and price elasticity of supply. The concept was brought to attention by the French Physiocrats and in particular François Quesnay who argued that the incidence of all taxation falls ultimately on landowners and is at the expense of land rent. For this reason they advocated the replacement of the multiplicity of contemporary taxes by the Single Tax, or Impôt Unique. A leading advocate of this tax was Turgot. In the first instance, however, the incidence of the tax falls elsewhere. For example, a tax on apple farmers might actually be paid by owners of agricultural land but the incidence may initially fall on consumers of apples.

Initially, the incidence of all labour related taxes such as income tax and mandatory pension contributions falls on employers. This must be so at the margin since the employee must receive more net of tax i.e. take-home than they can receive from the alternative, such as welfare benefit payments. The tax surcharge may be as high as 80%.

The theory of tax incidence has a number of practical results. For example, United States Social Security payroll taxes are paid half by the employee and half by the employer. However, some economists think that the worker is bearing almost the entire burden of the tax because the employer passes the tax on in the form of lower wages. The tax incidence is thus said to fall on the employee.

EXAMPLE OF TAX INCIDENCE

Imagine a $1 tax on every barrel of apples an apple farmer produces. If the product (apples) is price inelastic to the consumer (whereby if price rose, a small demand loss would be accounted for by the extra revenue), the farmer is able to pass the entire tax on to consumers of apples by raising the price by $1. In this example, consumers bear the entire burden of the tax; the tax incidence falls on consumers. On the other hand, if the apple farmer is unable to raise prices because the product is price elastic (if prices rose, more demand would be lost than extra revenue gained), the farmer has to bear the burden of the tax or face decreased revenues: the tax incidence falls on the farmer. If the apple farmer can raise prices by an amount less than $1, then consumers and the farmer are sharing the tax burden. When the tax incidence falls on the farmer, this burden will typically flow back to owners of the relevant factors of production, including agricultural land and employee wages.

Where the tax incidence falls depends (in the short run) on the price elasticity of demand and price elasticity of supply. Tax incidence falls mostly upon the group that responds least to price (the group that has the most inelastic price-quantity curve). If the demand curve is inelastic relative to the supply curve the tax will be disproportionately borne by the buyer rather than the seller. If the demand curve is elastic relative to the supply curve, the tax will be born disproportionately by the seller. If PED = PES the tax burden is split equally between buyer and seller. Tax incidence can be calculated using the pass-through fraction. The pass-through fraction for buyers is PES/(PES - PED). So if PED for apples is -0.4 and PES is 0.5 then the pass-through fraction to buyer would be calculated as follows: PES/PES - PED = 0.5/[0.5 - (-.0.4)] = 0.5/0.9 = 56%. 56% of any tax increase would be "paid" by the buyer; 44% would be "paid" by the seller. From the perspective of the seller, the formula is -PED/(PES - PED) = -(-0.4)/[0.5 -(-0.4)] = 0.4".9 = 44%

GRAPHICAL ANALYSIS

Inelastic supply, elastic demand

Because the producer is inelastic, he will produce the same quantity no matter what the price. Because the consumer is elastic, the consumer is very sensitive to price. A small increase in price leads to a large drop in the quantity demanded. The imposition of the tax causes the market price to increase from *P without tax* to *P with tax* and the quantity demanded to fall from *Q without tax* to *Q with tax*. Because the consumer is elastic, the quantity change is significant. Because the producer is inelastic, the price doesn't change much. The producer is unable to pass the tax onto the consumer and the tax incidence falls on the producer. In this example, the tax is collected from the producer and the producer bears the tax burden. This is known as *back shifting*.

Similarly elastic supply and demand

Most markets fall between these two extremes, and ultimately the incidence of tax is shared between producers and consumers in varying proportions. In this example, the consumers pay more than the producers, but not all of the tax. The area paid by consumers is obvious as the change in equilibrium price (between *P without tax* to*P with tax*); the remainder, being the difference between the new price and the cost of production at that quantity, is paid by the producers.

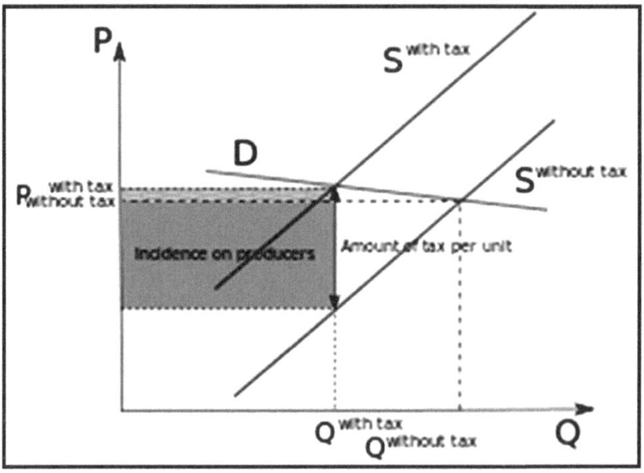

Inelastic supply, elastic demand: the burden is on producers

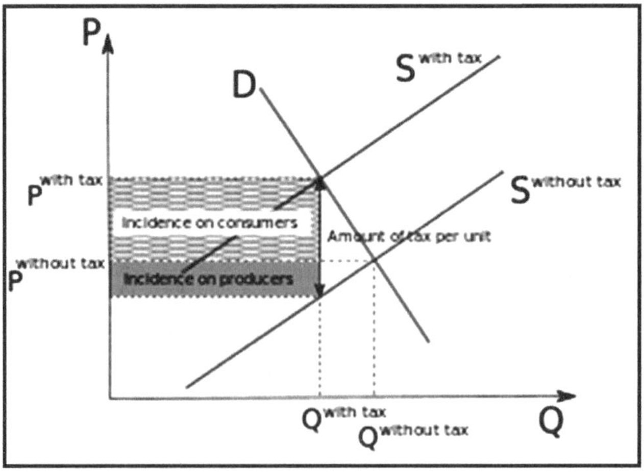

Similar elasticities: burden shared

MACROECONOMIC PERSPECTIVE

The supply and demand for a good is deeply intertwined with the markets for the factors of production and for alternate goods and services that might be produced or consumed. Although legislators might be seeking to tax the apple industry, in reality it could turn out to be truck drivers who are hardest hit, if apple companies shift toward shipping by rail in response to their new cost. Or perhaps orange manufacturers will be the group most affected, if consumers decide to forgo oranges to maintain their previous level of apples at the now higher price. Ultimately, the burden of the tax falls on people—the owners, customers, or workers.

However, the true burden of the tax cannot be properly assessed without knowing the use of the tax revenues. If the tax proceeds are employed in a manner that benefits owners more than producers and consumers then the burden of the tax will fall on producers and consumers. If the proceeds of the tax are used in a way that benefits producers and consumers, then owners suffer the tax burden. These are class distinctions concerning the distribution of costs and are not addressed in current tax incidence models. The US military offers major benefit to owners who produce offshore. Yet the tax levy to support this effort falls primarily on American producers and consumers. Corporations simply move out of the tax jurisdiction but still receive the property rights enforcement that is the mainstay of their income.

Other considerations of tax burden

Consider a 7% import tax applied equally to all imports (oil, autos, hula hoops, and brake rotors; steel, grain, everything) and a direct refund of every penny of collected revenue in the form of a direct egalitarian "Citizen's Dividend" to every person who files Income Tax returns. At the macro level (aggregate) the people as a whole will break even. But the people who consume foreign produced goods will bear more of the burden than the people who consume a mix of goods. The people who consume no foreign goods will bear none of the burden and actually receive an increase in utility. On the producer side, the tax burden distribution will depend on whether a firm produces its goods within the sovereignty or outside the sovereignty. Firms that produce goods inside the sovereignty will increase their market share and their profits when compared to firms who offshore their production. And if the current mix of firms is tilted toward offshore production then the owners of firms will be burdened more than the consumers while the workers/employees will benefit from greater employment opportunities.

Clarification

The burden from taxation is not just the quantity of tax paid (directly or indirectly), but the magnitude of the lost consumer surplus or producer surplus. The concepts are related but different. For example, imposing a $1000 per gallon of milk tax will raise no revenue (because legal milk production will stop), but this tax will cause substantial economic harm (lost consumer surplus and lost producer surplus). When examining tax incidence, it is the lost consumer and producer surplus that is important.

OTHER PRACTICAL RESULTS

The theory of tax incidence has a large number of practical results, although economists dispute the magnitude and significance of these results:

- If the government requires employers to provide employees with health care, some of the burden will fall on the employee as the employer will pass it on in the form of lower wages. Some of the burden will be borne by employer (and ultimately the customer in form of higher prices or lower quality) since both the supply of and demand for labor are highly inelastic and have few perfect substitutes. Employers need employees largely to the extent they can substitute employees for machines, and employees need employers largely to the extent they can become self-employed entrepreneurs. An uneducated population is therefore more susceptible to bearing the burden because they are more easily replaced by machines able to do unskilled work, and because they have less knowledge of how to make money on their own.
- Taxes on easily substitutable goods, such as oranges and tangerines, may be borne mostly by the producer because the demand curve for easily substitutable goods is quite elastic.
- Similarly, taxes on a business that can easily be relocated are likely be borne almost entirely by the residents of the taxing jurisdiction and not the owners of the business.
- The burden of tariffs (import taxes) on imported vehicles might fall largely on the producers of the cars because the demand curve for foreign cars might be elastic if car consumers may substitute a domestic car purchase for a foreign car purchase.
- If consumers drive the same number of miles regardless of gas prices, then a tax on gasoline will be paid for by consumers and not oil companies (this is assuming that the price elasticity of supply of oil is high, which is incorrect. In this case both the price elasticity of demand and supply are very low). Who actually bears the economic burden of the tax is not affected by whether government collects the tax at the pump or directly from oil companies.

ASSESSMENT

Assessing tax incidence is a major economics subfield within the field of public finance. Most public finance economists acknowledge that nominal tax incidence (i.e. who writes the check to pay a tax) is not necessarily identical to actual economic burden of the tax, but disagree greatly among themselves on the extent to which market forces disturb the nominal tax incidence of various types of taxes in various circumstances.

The effects of certain kinds of taxes, for example, the property tax, including their economic incidence, efficiency properties and distributional implications, have been the subject of a long and contentious debate among economists. The empirical evidence tends support different economic models under different circumstances. For example, empirical evidence on property tax incidents tends to support one economic model, known as the "benefit tax" view in suburban areas, while tending to support another economic model, known as the "capital tax" view in urban and rural areas. There is an inherent conflict in any model between considering many factors, which complicates the model and makes it hard to apply, and using a simple model, which may limit the circumstances in which its predictions are empirically useful.

LAFFER CURVE

In economics, the Laffer curve is a representation of the relationship between possible rates of taxation and the resulting levels of government revenue. It illustrates the concept of taxable income elasticity—i.e., taxable income will change in response to changes in the rate of taxation. It postulates that no tax revenue will be raised at the extreme tax rates of 0% and 100% and that there must be at least one rate where tax revenue would be a non-zero maximum. The Laffer curve is typically represented as a graph which starts at 0% tax with zero revenue, rises to a maximum rate of revenue at an intermediate rate of taxation, and then falls again to zero revenue at a 100% tax rate. The actual existence and shape of the curve is uncertain and disputed.

One potential result of the Laffer curve is that increasing tax rates beyond a certain point will be counter-productive for raising further tax revenue. A hypothetical Laffer curve for any given economy can only be estimated and such estimates are controversial. *The New Palgrave Dictionary of Economics* reports that estimates of revenue-maximizing tax rates have varied widely, with a mid-range of around 70%. Although economist Arthur Laffer does not claim to have invented the Laffer curve concept, it was popularized with policymakers following an afternoon meeting with Ford Administration officials Dick Cheney and Donald Rumsfeld in 1974 in which he reportedly sketched the curve on a napkin to illustrate his argument. The term "Laffer curve" was coined by Jude Wanniski, who was also present at the meeting. The basic concept was not new; Laffer himself notes antecedents in the writings of Ibn Khaldun and John Maynard Keynes.

THEORETICAL ISSUES

Justifications

Laffer explains the model in terms of two interacting effects of taxation:

an "arithmetic effect" and an "economic effect". The "arithmetic effect" assumes that tax revenue raised is the tax rate multiplied by the revenue available for taxation (or tax base). At a 0% tax rate, the model assumes that no tax revenue is raised. The "economic effect" assumes that the tax rate will have an impact on the tax base itself. At the extreme of a 100% tax rate, the government theoretically collects zero revenue because taxpayers change their behavior in response to the tax rate: either they have no incentive to work or they find a way to avoid paying taxes. Thus, the "economic effect" of a 100% tax rate is to decrease the tax base to zero. If this is the case, then somewhere between 0% and 100% lies a tax rate that will maximize revenue. Graphical representations of the curve sometimes appear to put the rate at around 50%, but the optimal rate could theoretically be *any* percentage greater than 0% and less than 100%. Similarly, the curve is often presented as a parabolic shape, but there is no reason that this is necessarily the case.

Jude Wanniski noted that all economic activity would be unlikely to cease at 100% taxation, but would switch from the exchange of money to barter. He also noted that there can be special circumstances where economic activity can continue for a period at a near 100% taxation rate (for example, in war time).

Various efforts have been made to quantify the relationship between tax revenue and tax rates (for example, in the United States by the Congressional Budget Office). While the interaction between tax rates and tax revenue is generally accepted, the precise nature of this interaction is debated. In practice, the shape of a hypothetical Laffer curve for a given economy can only be estimated. The relationship between tax rate and tax revenue is likely to vary from one economy to another and depends on the elasticity of supply for labor and various other factors. Even in the same economy, the characteristics of the curve could vary over time. Complexities such as progressive taxation and possible differences in the incentive to work for different income groups complicate the task of estimation. The structure of the curve may also be changed by policy decisions. For example, if tax loopholes and off-shore tax shelters are made more readily available by legislation, the point at which revenue begins to decrease with increased taxation is likely to become lower.

Laffer presented the curve as a pedagogical device to show that, in some circumstances, a reduction in tax rates will actually increase government revenue and not need to be offset by decreased government spending or increased borrowing. For a reduction in tax rates to increase revenue, the current tax rate would need to be higher than the revenue maximizing rate. In 2007, Laffer said that the curve should not be the sole basis for raising or lowering taxes.

Problems

Laffer assumes that the government would collect no income tax at a 100%

tax rate because there would be no incentive to earn income. Research has developed theoretical mathematical models in which a Laffer curve can slope continuously upwards all the way to 100%, though it is not clear whether or when the assumptions on which such mathematical models are based hold in real economies. Additionally, the Laffer curve depends on the assumption that tax revenue is used to provide a public good that is separable in utility and separate from labor supply, which may not be true in practice. The Laffer curve as presented is also simplistic in that it assumes a single tax rate and a single labor supply. Actual systems of public finance are more complex. There is serious doubt about the relevance of considering a single marginal tax rate. In addition, revenue may well be a multivalued function of tax rate - for instance, an increase in tax rate to a certain percentage may not result in the same revenue as a decrease in tax rate to the same percentage (a kind of hysteresis).

EMPIRICAL DATA

Tax rate at which revenue is maximized

The New Palgrave Dictionary of Economics reports that a comparison of academic studies yields a range of revenue maximizing rates that centers around 70%. Economist Paul Pecorino presented a model in 1995 that predicted the peak of the Laffer curve occurred at tax rates around 65%. A 1996 study by Y. Hsing of the United States economy between 1959 and 1991 placed the revenue-maximizing average federal tax rate between 32.67% and 35.21%. A 1981 paper published in the Journal of Political Economy presented a model integrating empirical data that indicated that the point of maximum tax revenue in Sweden in the 1970s would have been 70%. A paper by Trabandt and Uhlig of the NBER from 2009 presented a model that predicted that the US and most European economies were on the left of the Laffer curve (in other words, that raising taxes would raise further revenue).

Congressional Budget Office analysis

In 2005, the Congressional Budget Office (CBO) released a paper called "Analyzing the Economic and Budgetary Effects of a 10 Percent Cut in Income Tax Rates". This paper considered the impact of a stylized reduction of 10% in the then existing marginal rate of federal income tax in the US (for example, if those facing a 25% marginal federal income tax rate had it lowered to 22.5%). Unlike earlier research, the CBO paper estimates the budgetary impact of possible macroeconomic effects of tax policies, that is, it attempts to account for how reductions in individual income tax rates might affect the overall future growth of the economy, and therefore influence future government tax revenues; and ultimately, impact deficits or surpluses. In the paper's most generous estimated growth scenario, only 28% of the projected lost revenue from the lower tax rate would be recouped over a 10-year period after a 10% across-the-board reduction in all individual income tax rates. In other words, deficits would increase by nearly the same amount as the tax cut in the first five years, with limited feedback revenue thereafter. Through increased budget deficits, the tax cuts primarily benefiting the wealthy will be paid for — plus interest — by taxes borne relatively evenly by all taxpayers. The paper points out that these projected shortfalls in revenue would have to be made up by federal borrowing: the paper estimates that the federal government would pay an extra $200 billion in interest over the decade covered by the paper's analysis.

Other

Laffer has presented the examples of Russia and the Baltic states, which instituted a flat tax with rates lower than 35% and whose economies started growing soon after implementation. He has similarly referred to the economic outcome of the Kemp-Roth tax act, the Kennedy tax cuts, the 1920s tax cuts, and the changes in US capital gains tax structure in 1997. Some have also cited Hauser's Law, which postulates that US federal revenues, as a percentage of GDP, have remained stable at approximately 19.5% over the period 1950 to 2007 despite changes in marginal tax rates over the same period. Others however, have called Hauser's Law "misleading" and contend that tax changes have had large effects on tax revenues.

Optimal taxation

One of the uses of the Laffer curve is in determining the rate of taxation which will raise the maximum revenue (in other words, "optimizing" revenue collection).

However, the revenue maximizing rate should not be confused with the optimal tax rate, which economists use to describe a tax which raises a given amount of revenue with the least distortions to the economy.

RELATIONSHIP WITH SUPPLY-SIDE ECONOMICS

Supply-side economics is a school of macroeconomic thought that argues that overall economic well-being is maximized by lowering the barriers to producing goods and services (the "Supply Side" of the economy). By lowering such barriers, consumers are thought to benefit from a greater supply of goods and services at lower prices.

Typical supply-side policy would advocate generally lower income tax and capital gains tax rates (to increase the supply of labor and capital), smaller government and a lower regulatory burden on enterprises (to lower costs). Although tax policy is often mentioned in relation to supply-side economics, supply-side economists are concerned with all impediments to the supply of goods and services and not just taxation.

HISTORY

Origin

The term "Laffer curve" was reportedly coined by Jude Wanniski (a writer for *The Wall Street Journal*) after a 1974 dinner meeting at the Two Continents Restaurant in the Washington Hotel with Arthur Laffer, Wanniski, Dick Cheney, Donald Rumsfeld, and his deputy press secretary Grace-Marie Arnett. In this meeting, Laffer, arguing against President Gerald Ford's tax increase, reportedly sketched the curve on a napkin to illustrate the concept. Cheney did not accept the idea immediately, but it caught the imaginations of those present. Laffer professes no recollection of this napkin, but writes: "I used the so-called Laffer Curve all the time in my classes and with anyone else who would listen to me."

Laffer himself does not claim to have invented the concept, attributing it to 14th-century Arab scholar Ibn Khaldun and, more recently, to John Maynard Keynes.

Precedents

There are historical precedents other than those cited directly by Laffer. For example, in 1924, Secretary of Treasury Andrew Mellon wrote: "It seems difficult for some to understand that high rates of taxation do not necessarily mean large revenue to the Government, and that more revenue may often be obtained by lower rates." Exercising his understanding that "73% of nothing is nothing", he pushed for the reduction of the top income tax bracket from 73% to an eventual 24% (as well as tax breaks for lower brackets). Personal income-tax receipts rose from US$719 million in 1921 to over $1 billion in 1929, an average increase of 4.2% per year over an 8-year period, which supporters attribute to the rate cut.

Amongst others, David Hume expressed similar arguments in his essay *Of Taxes* in 1756, as did fellow Scottish economist Adam Smith, twenty years later.

The Democratic party made a similar argument in the 1880s when high revenue from import tariffs raised during the Civil War (1861–1865) led to federal budget surpluses. The Republican party, which was then based in the protectionist industrial Northeast, argued that cutting rates would lower revenues. But the Democratic party, then rooted in the agricultural South, argued tariff reductions would increase revenues by increasing the number of taxable imports. A 1997 analysis concluded that the tariff rate used was lower than the revenue maximizing rate.

An argument along similar lines has also been advocated by Ali ibn Abi Talib, the first Shia Imam and fourth Caliph of the Islamic empire; in his letter to the Governor of Egypt, Malik al-Ashtar. A careful reading of the quote below shows that he only argues for a decrease in taxes' reducing revenues, not for an optimal point where most revenues would be raised, thus missing the prototypical point of the Laffer curve. It does however imply that revenues might rise in time because of this reduction of taxes. He writes:

- If the tax-payers complain to you of the heavy incidence to taxation, of any accidental calamity, of the vagaries of the monsoons, of the recession of the means of irrigation, of floods, or destruction of their crops on account of excessive rainfall and if their complaints are true, then reduce their taxes. This reduction should be such that it provides them opportunities to improve their conditions and eases them of their troubles. Decrease in state income due to such reasons should not depress you because the best investment for a ruler is to help his subjects at the time of their difficulties. They are the real wealth of a country and any investment on them even in the form of reduction of taxes, will be returned to the State in the shape of the prosperity of its cities and improvement of the country at large. At the same time you will be in a position to command and secure their love, respect and praises along with the revenues.—Ali ibn Abi Talib, *Nahj al-Balagha, Letter 53*

IN POLITICAL DISCOURSE

Reaganomics

The Laffer curve and supply-side economics inspired Reaganomics and the Kemp-Roth Tax Cut of 1981. Supply-side advocates of tax cuts claimed that lower tax rates would generate more tax revenue because the United States government's marginal income tax rates prior to the legislation were on the *right-hand* side of the curve. As a successful actor, Reagan himself had been subject to marginal tax rates as high as 90% during World War II. During the Reagan presidency, the top marginal rate of tax in the United States fell from 70% to 31%. According to OMB historical data, federal government revenue fell from 19.0% of GDP in 1980 to 18.4% by 1989, resulting in a significant increase in federal debt-to-outlays percentages compared with both preceding and succeeding decades.

David Stockman, Ronald Reagan's budget director during his first administration and one of the early proponents of supply-side economics, was concerned that the administration did not pay enough attention to cutting government spending. He maintained that the Laffer curve was not to be taken literally — at least not in the economic environment of the 1980s United States. In *The Triumph of Politics*, he writes: "[T]he whole California gang had taken [the Laffer curve] literally (and primitively). The way they talked, they seemed to expect that once the supply-side tax cut was in effect, additional revenue would start to fall, manna-like, from the heavens. Since January, I had been explaining that there is no literal Laffer curve." Stockman also said that "Laffer wasn't wrong, he just didn't go far enough" (in paying attention to government spending). Some have criticized elements of Reaganomics on the basis of equity. For example, economist John Kenneth Galbraith believed that the Reagan administration actively used the Laffer curve "to lower taxes on the affluent". Some critics point out that tax revenues almost always rise every year, and during Reagan's two terms increases in tax revenue were more shallow than increases during presidencies where top marginal tax rates were higher. Critics also point out that since the Reagan tax cuts, income has not significantly increased for the rest of the population. This assertion is supported by studies that show the income of the top 1% nearly doubling during the Reagan years, while income for other income levels increased only marginally; income actually decreased for the bottom quintile.

Bush tax cuts

The Congressional Budget Office (CBO) has estimated that extending the Bush tax cuts of 2001–2003 beyond their 2010 expiration would increase deficits by $1.8 trillion over the following decade. Economist Paul Krugman contended that supply-side adherents did not fully believe that the United States income tax rate was on the "backwards-sloping" side of the curve and yet they still advocated lowering taxes to encourage investment of personal savings.

Outside the United States

Between 1979 and 2002, more than 40 other countries, including the United Kingdom, Belgium, Denmark, Finland, France, Germany, Norway, and Sweden cut their top rates of personal income tax. In an article about this, Alan Reynolds, a senior fellow with the libertarian think tank Cato Institute, wrote, "Why did so many other countries so dramatically reduce marginal tax rates? Perhaps they were influenced by new economic analysis and evidence from... supply-side economics. But the sheer force of example may well have been more persuasive. Political authorities saw that other national governments fared better by having tax collectors claim a medium share of a rapidly growing economy (a low marginal tax) rather than trying to extract a large share of a stagnant economy (a high average tax)."

OPTIMAL TAX

Optimal tax theory or the theory of optimal taxation is the study of designing and implementing a tax thus that a given economic criterion is optimized. Generally, this criterion consists of individuals' utility and the optimization problem involves minimizing the distortions caused by taxation. A neutral tax is a theoretical tax which avoids distortion and inefficiency completely. Other things being equal, if a tax-payer must choose between two mutually exclusive economic projects (say investments) that have the same pre-tax risk and returns, the one with the lower tax or with a tax exemption would be chosen by a rational actor. Thus economists argue that taxes generally distort behavior.

TAX REVENUE

Generating a sufficient amount of revenue to finance government is arguably the most important purpose of the tax system. Optimal taxation, which is the theory of designing and implementing taxes that reduce inefficiency and distortion in the market through Pareto optimal moves under given constraints, is constantly debated. Though inequality will always exist within even the most efficient markets, the goal of taxation is to eliminate as much inefficiency as possible and to raise revenue to fund government expenditures. With any tax, there will be an excess burden, or additional cost, to the consumer and the producer. Whenever the consumer purchases the taxed good or service, and the higher elasticity, or responsiveness, of the demanded product, the greater the excess burden is on either the consumer or producer. Those individuals or corporations who have the most inelastic demand curve pay the brunt of the excess burden curve. However, the tradeoff of placing larger taxes on inelastic goods is that the higher tax will lead to lower quantity exchanged and thus a smaller dead weight loss of reduced revenue.

Horizontal and vertical equity

When discussing what a fair and optimal tax level would be, the principle of equity, both horizontal and vertical, is important. Equity is determined by first assessing an individual's ability-to-pay. The idea of the ability-to-pay principle considers whether or not it is fair to tax someone higher just because that person has the ability and resources to pay. If it is decided that they should be required to pay more, the question of how much more arises. These questions can be analyzed through horizontal and vertical equity which are subsets of the ability-to-pay principle. Horizontal equity suggests it is fair for people of equal ability to pay the same amount in taxes. Vertical equity is the idea that people who have a higher ability to pay should pay more than those who have a lower ability to pay, as long as the increase in tax level is considered to be reasonable.

Problems with horizontal equity consist of the idea that taxing individuals with the same ability to pay implies that two individuals earning the same income should be taxed equally. However, Randall Holcombe depicts a scenario where one of these people is single while the other married with children, and that charging these people the same amount does not correctly reflect their ability to pay. Conversely, this situation can also support the opposite argument. In this same example, if one individual chooses to spend his income to support his family, and another to travel, each individual now has less money to pay taxes with. However, this raises the question on how the government should treat these choices differently if at all for taxation purposes. As Holcombe showed through his examples, it is possible to apply different tax principles to the same situation and reach a different logical solution, but as these are normative issues, it can be difficult to reach a solution. So it is up to individual societies to determine what tax structure to implement.

Vertical equity states that the government should implement higher taxes on those who have higher abilities to pay than those who have a lower ability to pay. However, problems immediately arise with vertical equity because not only do policy makers have to define what having a higher ability means, but they also have to determine what an appropriate increase in taxation is for those with a greater ability to pay. Practically, vertical equity provides no solution to these problems. Furthermore, because of the complexity of current tax policies, those who have greater incomes and greater ability to pay are able to avoid paying taxes in ways that those in the lower brackets cannot. However, the concept of vertical equity is necessary in considering how best to create and implement a fair tax code. Because it is widely agreed upon that those of higher incomes should pay more in taxes, this helps alleviate the tax burden on those whose ability to pay is lower. It is then up to policy makers to determine what this looks like and how much more higher-income earners should be required to pay.

However, as with any tax, implementing higher taxes will negatively affect incentives and alter an individual's behavior. In his article "Effects of Taxes on Economic Behavior," Martin Feldstein discusses how economic behavior determined by taxes is important for estimating revenue, calculating efficiency and understanding the negative externalities in the short-run. In his article, like much of his research on this topic, he chooses to focus primarily on how households are affected. Feldstein recognizes that high taxes deter people from actively engaging in the market, causing a lower production rate as well as a deadweight loss. Yet, because it is difficult to see tangible results of deadweight loss, policy makers largely ignore it. Feldstein expresses his frustration that policy makers have yet to grasp these concepts and therefore do not make policy that correct this wrong.

Lump-sum taxes

One type of tax that does not create a large excess burden is the lump-sum tax. A lump sum tax is a fixed tax that must be paid by everyone and the amount a person is taxed remains constant regardless of income or owned assets. It does not create excess burden because these taxes do not alter economic decisions. Because the tax remains constant, an individual's incentives and a firm's incentives will not fluctuate, as opposed to a graduated income tax that taxes people more for earning more.

Lump sum taxes can be either progressive or regressive, depending on what the lump sum is being applied to. A tax placed on car tags would be regressive because it would be the same for everyone regardless of the type of car the owner purchased and, at least in the United States, even the poor own cars. People earning lower incomes would then pay more as a percentage of their income than higher-income earners. A tax on the unimproved aspects of land tends to be a progressive tax, since the wealthier one is the more land one tends to own and the poor typically do not own any land at all.

Lump-sum taxes are not politically expedient because they sometimes require a complete overhaul of the tax system. Lump-sum taxes are also unpopular when they are assessed per capita because they are regressive and make no allowance for a citizen's ability to pay.

A one off, unexpected lump sum levy which is proportional to wealth or income is also non-distorting. In this case, although wealth or income is penalised, the unexpected nature of the tax means that there is no disincentive to asset accumulation- as by definition those accumulating such assets are unaware that a portion of those assets will be taxed in the future.

Land value taxation

Henry George most notably championed the idea of a Land value tax in *Progress and Poverty*, as a levy on the value of unimproved or natural aspects of the land, primarily location; it disregards the improvements such as buildings and irrigation. Land Value taxation has no deadweight loss because the input of production being taxed (land) is fixed in supply; it cannot hide, shrink in value, or flee to other jurisdictions when taxed.

Economic theory suggests that a pure land value tax which succeeds in avoiding taxation of improvements could actually have a negative deadweight loss (positive externality), due to productivity gains arising from efficient land use. The taxation of locational values encourages socially optimal development on land in highly valued areas, like cities, since it reduces the incentive to speculate in land prices by leaving potentially productive locations vacant or underused.

Despite its theoretical benefits, implementing land value taxes is difficult politically. However, land value tax is considered progressive, because the ownership of land values is more concentrated than other sources of revenue, such as personal income or spending. George argued that because land is the fruit of nature (not labor) and the value of location is created by the community, the revenue from land should belong to the community.

COMMODITY TAXES

Frank P. Ramsey (1927) developed a theory for optimal commodity sales taxes in his article "A Contribution to the Theory of Taxation". The problem is closely linked to the problem of socially optimal monopolistic pricing when profits are constrained to be positive, known as the Ramsey problem. He was the first to make a significant contribution to the theory of optimal taxation from an economic standpoint, and much of the literature that has followed reflects Ramsey's initial observations.

He wanted to confront the problem of how to adjust consumption tax rates, under specified constraints, so that the reduction of utility is at a minimum. In an attempt to reduce excess burden of consumption taxes, Ramsey proposed a theoretical solution that consumption taxes should be inverse to the price elasticity of demand for the good. However, practically, it is problematic to constrain social planners to one form of taxation. It is better to enable them to consider all possible tax structures.

Using Ramsey's rule as a basis for their papers, Peter Diamond and James Mirrlees propose an alternative to Ramsey's proposition by allowing the planner to consider numerous tax systems, and their model has prevailed in taxation theories. In their first paper, "Optimal Taxation and Public Production I: Production Efficiency" Diamond and Mirrlees consider the problem of imperfect information exchanged between taxpayers and the social planner. According to their argument, an individual's ability to earn income differs. Though the planner can observe income, they cannot directly observe the individual's ability or effort to earn income, so that if the planner attempts to increase taxes on those with high ability to earn an income, the individual's incentives to earn a high income decrease. They confront the government tradeoff between equality and efficiency that when higher taxes are imposed on those with the potential to earn higher wages, they are not incentivized to expend the extra effort to earn a greater income. They rely on what has been labeled the revelation principle where planners must implement a tax system that provides proper incentives for people to reveal their true wage earning abilities.

They continued this idea in the second installment of their paper "Optimal Taxation and Public Production II: Tax Rules," where they discuss marginal tax rate schedules for labor income. If the policy maker implemented a tax increase in the marginal tax rate at a lower income, it discourages the individuals at that income from working hard. However, this same increase for high-income individuals does not distort their incentives because though it raises their average tax rate, their marginal tax rate remains the same. For example, giving $100 is worth more to a low-income earner than to a high-income earner. Diamond and Mirrlees came to the conclusion that the marginal tax rate for the top earner should be equal to zero and the optimal rate must be between zero and one. This provides the correct incentives for individuals to work at their optimal level.

DEVELOPMENTS IN TAX THEORY

William J. Baumol and David F. Bradford in their article "Optimal Departures from Marginal Cost Pricing" also discuss the price distortion taxes cause. They examine the proposition that in order to reach the optimal point of allocating resources, prices that deviate from marginal cost are required. They recognize that with every tax, there is some sort of price distortion, so they state that any solution can only be the second best option and any solution proposed is under that added constraint. However, their theory differs from other literature in this topic. First, it deals with quasi-optimal pricing, looking at four options for Pareto optimality with adjusted commodity prices. Second, they express their theory in more simplified terms which incurs a loss of realistic application. Third, it combines the three discussions: the welfare theory, the contributions of the regulations and public finance. They conclude that under constraints, the best possible theory to get close to optimality, which is not "best" at all, is the systematic division between prices and marginal costs.

In his article entitled "Optimal Taxation in Theory," Gregory Mankiw reviews that current literature in theories on optimal taxation and analyzes the change in the tax theory over the past few decades. Like Diamond and Mirrlees, Mankiw recognizes the flaw in Ramsey's model that planners can raise revenue through taxes only on commodities, but also points out the weakness of Mirrlees's proposition. Mankiw argues that Diamond's and Mirrlees's theory is extremely complex because of how difficult it is to keep track of individuals producing at their maximum levels.

Mankiw provides a summary of eight lessons that represent the current thought in optimal taxation literature. They include, first the idea considering horizontal and vertical equity, that social planners should base optimal tax schedules on income rates for labor, which marks the equality and efficiency trade-off. Second, the more income an individual makes, their marginal tax schedule could actually decrease because they are discouraged from working at their optimal production level. The solution is to, after individuals reach a certain income level, ensure that the marginal tax remains steady. Third, reaching an optimal tax level could mean flat taxes. Fourth, the increase in wage inequality is directly proportionate to the extent of income redistribution as revenue is distributed to low-income earners. Fifth, taxes should not only depend on income amounts, but also on personal characteristics such as a person's wage earning capabilities. Sixth, goods produced should only be taxed as a final good and should be taxed uniformly, which leads to their seventh point that capital should also not be taxed because it is considered an input of production. Finally, policy makers should consider individuals' income histories, which require reliance on different types of taxation to derive optimal taxation.

Mankiw identifies that the tax policy has largely followed the theories laid out in tax literature because social planners believe that the flatter the tax, the better, there are declining top marginal rates in OECDcountries, and taxes on commodities are now uniform and usually only final goods are taxed. Joel Slemrod in his paper "Optimal Taxation and Optimal Tax System," argues that optimal tax theory, as it stood when Slemrod wrote this paper, was an insufficient guide to determine tax policies because policy makers had yet to find a way to implement a tax system that enticed individuals to work at their optimal level. As a solution, Slemrod proposes the theory of optimal tax systems a phrase he uses to refer to the normative theory of taxation. Slemrod advocates this theory because not only does it take into account the preferences of individuals, but also the technology involved in tax collecting. A practical application of this, for example, is implementing value-added taxes, a tax on the purchase price of a good or service, to correct tax evasion. He argues that any future tax literature in normative theory needs to focus less on consumer preferences and more on tax collecting technology and the areas of the economy that affect tax collection.

INCOME TAXES

Another aspect of optimal taxation is determining income taxes. These taxes can be regressive, flat, or progressive. In some cases, the more they earn, the more they are charged in taxes.

Individual income taxes

Emmanuel Saez in his article titled "Using Elasticities to Derive Optimal Income Tax Rates," derives a formula for optimal level of income tax using the both compensated and uncompensated elasticities. Saez writes the trade-off between equity and efficiency is a central consideration of optimal taxation, and implementing a progressive tax allows the government to reallocate their resources where they are needed most. However, this deters those of higher income levels to work at their optimal level. Saez cites Mirrlees's non-linear income tax theory1, but declares it to be limited. Instead, Saez argues that the solution to determine optimal income rates is simple—using elasticities. Obtaining an optimal tax formula for high income earners is straightforward because by determining elasticites, Saez determined that marginal tax rate for labor income needs to be between 50-80 percent in order to be at an optimal level. Saez continued that using elasticites is advantageous because it shows the different possible results and finally that numerical simulations of optimal tax formulas can be used.

James Poterba in his article called "Lifetime Incidence and the Distributional Burden of Excise Taxes," determines to show that household income measured over the long-run varies less than when analysts measure it annually. Poterba shows that excise taxes, which are taxes on consumption, may be less regressive that previous calculations indicate because they only use annual income. Furthermore, he shows that this same theory can be applied to excise taxes placed on things like gasoline, alcohol and tobacco. When the expenditure on these items is considered in correlation to the total consumption over a lifetime, it is more equally dispersed than when measured annually. Poterba argues that people need to distinguish between annual and lifetime measurements, and a failure to do this leads to overstating the degree of inequality that burdens from taxes place on the groups earning different income levels.

In the late 1970s, Arthur Laffer developed the Laffer curve, which demonstrates that changes in tax rates have an arithmetic effect, if tax rates are lowered, revenue will be decrease by the same amount, and economic effect, provides incentives for individuals to increase their work output through low tax rates, on tax revenues. The higher the taxes placed on income are, the more people lose their incentives to earn more taxable income, which causes the taxable base to shrink. This in turn, leads reduced revenue at a certain point because though taxes are higher, the tax base shrunk so there are fewer people paying taxes. Laffer constructed a graph to illustrate when this point occurs, though it does not actually determine whether a particular tax cut will raise or lower revenues. Laffer's curve is widely used because it can be applied to all taxes, not just to income taxes.

For example, since only economic actors who engage in market activity of "entering the labor market" have an income tax liability on their wages, people who are able to consume leisure or engage in household production outside the market by say providing housewife services in *lieu* of hiring a maid are taxed more lightly. With the "married filing jointly" tax unit in U.S. income tax law, the second earner's income is added to the first wage earner's taxable income and thus gets the highest marginal rate. This type of tax creates a large distortion disfavoring women from the labor force during years when the couple have great child care needs.

The requirement that married people file jointly in the United States thus is considered to run counter to optimal tax theory and Supply-side economics.

Corporate income taxes

There is an increasing amount of literature dedicated to discussing optimal taxation. Arnold Harberger is another economist who made strong headway in the area of optimal taxation and whose theory has become a commonly used one for policy makers in the area of corporation income tax. Corporation income tax is a tax imposed by the federal as well as state governments on the income a corporation receives. In the Journal of Political Economy, Harberger wrote an article called "The Incidence of the Corporation Income Tax" where he attempted to provide a theoretical framework to understand the effects that income tax on corporations has and to determine inferences of this tax in the United States. He proposed the general-equilibrium nature, in which he assumes a two-sector economy one corporate and the other not. In this model, Harberger theorizes that by redistributing the economies resources, the market will move toward a constant equilibrium in the long-run where the elasticity's of substitution are the same for both capital and labor and are then equal to the elasticity of substitution between the two goods being consumed. Furthermore, this can potentially apply to a broader range of conditions In contrast to this, Michael Feldstein contradicts Harberger's assumptions. Feldstein argues that one of Harberger's theories great shortcomings is that up until the point he was writing the article, policy makers, when determining tax changes for corporate income tax, focused solely on the effects in personal income tax. Feldstein argues that policy makers should analyze these two aspects separately and he presented a method on how to input the net effect of the changes of the efficient corporate tax rates into the individual tax returns by focusing on the vital difference between real and nominal capital income. Feldstein recognizes the shortcomings of his own model though because of the lack of insufficient data to properly compare the rates of corporate and individual taxes.

William Fox and LeAnn Luna also propose their own theory on corporate taxes in their joint article entitled "State Corporate Tax Revenue Trends: Causes and Possible Solutions" where they take on just one aspect of the debate—the role of this taxation and they purport to determine the extent of the damage done through a decrease in revenue and propose some ways they believe will reverse the trend. They determine that because the effective corporate income tax rate has fallen by one-third in two decades, the effective tax rate decline is the result of a tax base that is eroding in relation to a corporation's income and profits. This is because legislation like discretionary taxes has narrowed the taxable base.

One option to reduce the negative effect of corporate taxes on the level of private investment (and hence increase investment toward the level that would be obtained in a no-tax environment) is the provision of an Investment tax credit or Accelerated depreciation. In these cases, the rate of corporate tax payable becomes a negative function of the rate of profit reinvestment, and hence firms which increase their rate of reinvestment diminish their taxation liabilities.

In recent years, the concept of a corporate tax system incorporating deductions for 'normal' profits (where normal is defined in relation to the long-term interest rate and the risk premium) has gained some attention as a tax system which could minimise the distortionary effect of corporate taxation on the level of investment, without reducing total taxation revenue. Such a taxation system would in effect levy a higher rate of tax on projects earning 'super profits' which will likely go ahead even when taxed at a very high rate, as the post-tax rate of return on capital is designed to still be significantly higher than the threshold or 'normal' level. Conversely, the effective tax rate on marginal projects (with a return on equity closer to the 'normal' level) will be minimised. One example of such a tax system is the Australian Minerals Resource Rent Tax. When an investment tax credit or equity based deduction of profits is applied, the optimal pre-deduction and average effective rate of taxation is generally increased as the distortionary effect of a given level of taxation is diminished. If the tax rate prior to the adoption of these provisions was optimal, there is an assumption that the net marginal benefit of increased taxation is zero in the locality of the optimum rate (the marginal costs and benefits sum to zero). If the distortionary costs of capital taxation are then lowered by equity deductions or investment tax credits, then it is clear that in the region of the previous optimal rate the net marginal benefit of increases in the rate will become positive, implying the tax rate should be raised upward from this level.

Sales tax

A third consideration for optimal taxation is sales tax, which is the additional price added to the base price of a paid by the consumer at the point when they purchase a good or service. Poterba in a second article called "Retail Price Reactions To Changes in State and Local Sales Taxes," tests the premise that sales taxes on the state and local level are fully shifted to the consumers. He examines clothing prices before and after WWII. He recognizes that monetary policy is important to determine the response of nominal prices a national sales tax and points to possible differences in taxes applied at the local level as to taxes applied at a national level. Poterba finds evidence reinforcing the idea that sales taxes are fully forward shifted, which raises the consumer prices to match the tax increase.His study coincides with the original hypothesis that retail sales taxes are full shifted to retail prices.

Donald Bruce, William Fox, and M. H. Tuttle also discuss tax revenues through sales tax in their article "Tax Base Elasticities: A Multi-State Analysis of Long-Run and Short-Run Dynamics. " In this article, they look at how personal state revenues and sales tax bases elasticities change for the short and long-term in an attempt to determine the difference between them. With this information, the authors believe that states can both enhance and customize their tax structures, which can be used for careful resource planning. They found that for state personal income tax bases as compared to sales taxes, the average long-term income elasticity is more than doubled and the short-term display disproportionate results higher than the long-term elasticities. The authors contend with the conventional literature by declaring that neither the personal income tax nor the sales tax is, at least, universally, the more volatile tax. Though, the authors concede that in certain situations, the sales tax is more volatile, and in the long-term, personal income taxes are more elastic.

Furthermore, in understanding this argument, it must also be considered, as Alan Auerbach, Jagadeesh Gokhale, and Laurence Kotlikoff do in "Generational Accounting: A Meaningful Way to Evaluate Fiscal Policy," what the implications to optimal taxation are for future generations. They propose that generational accounting represents a new method for fiscal planning in the long-run, and that unlike the budget deficit, this generational accounting is not arbitrary. Instead, it is a remedy for how to approach the generation burden and effects of fiscal policy on a macroeconomic level. Ethically, it is a problem to have low taxes now, and therefore low revenue now, because it inevitably puts the burden of responsibility to pay for those expenditures on future generations. So through generational accounting, it is possible to analyze this and provide the necessary information for policy makers to change the policies needed to alter this trend. However, according to Auerbach, politicians are currently only relying on accounting and are not seeing the potential consequences that will ensue in future generations.

The incidence of sales taxes on commodities also results in distortion if say food prepared in restaurants is taxed but supermarket-bought food prepared at home is not taxed at purchase. If a taxpayer needs to buy food at fast food restaurants because he/she is not wealthy enough to purchase extra leisure time (by working less) he/she pays the tax although a more prosperous person who enjoys playing at being a home chef is taxed more lightly. This differential taxation of commodities may cause inefficiency (by discouraging work in the market in favor of work in the household).

OPTIMAL CAPITAL INCOME TAXATION

Optimal capital income taxation is a subarea of optimal tax theory which refers to the study of designing a tax on capital income thus that a given economic criterion like utility is optimized. Starting from the conceptualization of capital income as future consumption, the taxation of capital income corresponds to a differentiated consumption tax on present and future consumption. Consequently, a capital income tax results in the distortion of individuals' saving and consumption behavior as individuals substitute the more heavily-taxed future consumption with current consumption. Due to these distortions, zero taxation of capital income might be optimal, a result postulated by the Atkinson-Stiglitz theorem (1976) and the Chamley-Judd zero capital income tax result (1985/1986). Subsequent work on optimal capital income taxation has elucidated the assumptions underlying the theoretical optimality of a zero capital income tax and advanced diverse arguments for a positive (or negative) optimal capital tax.

ZERO OPTIMAL CAPITAL INCOME TAXATION

The assertion that a zero capital income tax may be optimal is based on two individual economic intuitions: (1) the Atkinson-Stiglitz theorem and (2) the result derived by Chamley (1986) and Judd (1985) based on a dynamic Ramsey model. While Mankiw, Weinzierl and Yagan (2009) invoke the Diamond-Mirrlees production efficiency theorem (DMPET) as third intuition for no capital income taxation, their arguments are refuted by Diamond and Saez (2011).

Atkinson-Stiglitz theorem (1976)

The Atkinson-Stiglitz theorem states that if non-linear taxes on earnings are available as policy tool, differential taxation of first- and second period consumption is not optimal if all consumers have preferences weakly separable between consumption and labor. Furthermore, consumers need to have homogeneous subutility functions of consumption. When applied to capital income taxation, the Atkinson-Stiglitz theorem argues that since present and future consumption are equally complementary to leisure due to weakly separable preferences (and hence there is no Corlett-Hague motive for capital income taxation), capital income taxes do not alleviate the tax distortions caused by labor income taxation while additionally distorting capital income. Thus, capital income taxation, i.e. differentiated consumption taxation, is more costly (and therefore less optimal) than pure non-linear labor income taxation.

The Chamley-Judd zero capital income tax result

The Chamley-Judd zero capital income tax result - developed in Chamley (1986) and Judd (1985) - states that in a dynamic Ramsey model featuring agents with infinite lives, an asymptotically zero tax on capital income is optimal. The result is based upon the intuition that the growth of the tax wedge between current and future consumption is related to the growth of the time horizon. So as to avoid unlimited growth in tax compounding as the horizon extends, the optimal average capital tax rate approximates zero. The result can also be interpreted in Corlett-Hague terms: As the horizon grows to infinity, both present and future consumption become equally complementary to leisure as their elasticities become constant; since, according to the Corlett-Hague rule the taxation of commodities should depend on their complementarity to leisure, present and future consumption should be taxed at equal tax rates. Although Chamley (1986) and Judd (1985) rely on steady-state properties of constant consumption and labor and, consequently, also a constant elasticity of consumption in order to argue that current and future consumption are equally complementary to leisure, Judd (1999) shows that a steady state is a sufficient but not a necessary condition for the zero capital income tax result.

The Chamley-Judd model can also be invoked when arguing that the taxation of existing wealth is superior to the taxation of future capital income due to the tax on current wealth being lump-sum as opposed to the tax on future capital income distorting intertemporal decisions. This argumentation can be found in the composition of taxation in overlapping generation models, e.g. Auerbach, Kotlikoff and Skinner (1983).

While criticisms of the Chamley-Judd model vary, a central theme attacks its critical assumption regarding infinite lives, which can also be interpreted as dynastic linkages. This assumption has been notably challenged both by general criticism leveled by behavioral economics against the standard model of intertemporal decision-making used in the Chamley-Judd model and by empirical analyses of bequests, which do not support the rigorous dynasty model required by the Chamley-Judd model.

NON-ZERO OPTIMAL CAPITAL INCOME TAXATION

A number of arguments relating to concerns for efficiency and equity may be found in the literature supporting the taxation of capital income, including (1) Corlett-Hague motives, (2) increases in consumption inequality over the life cycle, (3) heterogeneous preferences, (4) correlation between returns on savings and ability, (5) incomplete or imperfect insurance markets, (6) borrowing or liquidity constraints, (7) human capital distortions, (8) economic rents, and (9) avoidance of arbitrage between capital income and labor income taxation.

Avoidance of tax arbitrage between capital and labor incomes

For a government, distinguishing between capital and labor incomes can be difficult. This shortcoming becomes critical when individuals shift from labor income to capital income so as to take advantage of tax differentials, as evidenced in Finland by Pirttilä and Selin (2011) and in the United States by Gordon and MacKie-Mason (1995) and more recently Gordon and Slemrod (2000). The difficulty in distinguishing labor and capital income might be the most important reason for governments' reluctance to engage in the full tax exemption of capital income. Specifically, Christiansen and Tuomala (2008) find a positive optimal tax on capital income due to the presence of the ability to shift income, while Reis (2007) demonstrates that the Chamley-Judd result does not hold when tax authority cannot effectively distinguish entrepreneurial labor income and capital income.

Borrowing/liquidity constraints

Both the Atkinson-Stiglitz theorem and the Ramsay model used to derive the Chamley-Judd zero capital income tax result assume perfect capital markets. In practice, however, individuals are often borrowing-constrained, i.e. they cannot save. By taxing capital income and transferring it to the borrowing-constrained individuals, the capital market imperfection - the liquidity constraints - is alleviated at the cost of distorting saving. Equivalently, taxing saving may reduce the implicit subsidy on saving created by the borrowing constraints and thus restore efficiency in saving. Furthermore, Aiyagari (1995) and Chamley (2001) show that capital income taxation is desirable when consumption is positively correlated with savings in a model featuring borrowing-constrained agents with infinite lives and uncertainty.

Correlation between return on savings and ability

According to the second theorem of welfare economics any Pareto-efficient allocation can be achieved through the appropriate redistribution of endowments, which in the context of optimal taxation refers to the taxation of individuals' earnings ability. If - unlike the assumption in the model - the returns on saving are not equal for everyone, but are positively correlated with ability instead, capital income contains new information about an individuals' ability and should be taxed for redistributive reasons.

Human capital formation

As demonstrated by Judd (1999), a zero capital income tax is no longer neutral regarding human capital investments if these are partially consist of costs which cannot be deducted against the tax rate of future returns on saving. Then, the reduction of labor income tax distortions on investments in human capital provides a motive for capital income taxation being optimal. By increasing the relative price of future consumption and causing the substitution of financial for human savings, capital taxes act as an implicit subsidy for human capital investments at the cost of creating a distortion in fiancial serving.

Heterogeneous preferences

The zero optimal capital tax relies on the assumption of preference homogeneity. Both Mirrlees (1976) and Saez (2002) argue that high-ability might have higher saving rates due to different preferences. If this is the case, then capital income taxation is optimal for income redistribution as the individual savings level reveals information about individuals' ability, thereby facilitating the redistribution of income from high-ability to low-ability individuals. This argument is empirically borne out by research on the correlation between individuals' willingness and earnings ability.

Index